Masters and Servants

The Durham Miners' Gala, 1935.

Masters and Servants

Class and Patronage in the Making of a Labour Organisation

The Durham Miners and the English Political Tradition

Huw Beynon and Terry Austrin

Rivers Oram Press, London

First published in 1994 by
Rivers Oram Press
144 Hemingford Road, London N1 1DE

Published in the USA by
Paul and Company
Post Office Box 442, Concord, MA 01742

Set in 10/12pt Baskerville by Except*detail* Ltd, Southport
and printed in Great Britain
by T.J. Press (Padstow) Ltd, Padstow, Cornwall

Designed by Lesley Stewart

British Library Cataloguing in Publication Data
A catalogue record for this book is available from the British Library

ISBN 1-85489-001-8
1-85489-000-X pbk

To Durham Mining Families

Contents

List of Illustrations

Map

Tables

Acknowledgments

We began the research for this book in 1978. At that time we were both based in the Department of Sociology and Social Policy at the University of Durham; we now work on opposite sides of the world. In between times we have been helped by many people and institutions. We would like to record our thanks to them here.

The institutions first: to the Economic and Social Research Council who funded the initial research, and the University of Durham for its support. We visited many libraries and their staff were very helpful to us. A special thanks to: the Durham Miners' Association, Redhills Villa, Durham; the University of Durham and Southern Illinois University, USA; the Durham Record Office; the Northumberland Record Office; the Easington Past and Present Archive; Gateshead Municipal Authority.

To our friends in the Strong Words Publishing Project with whom we collaborated in some exciting ventures in the late 1970s and early 1980s; to our many friends in the Durham Miners' Association and the Durham Mining Mechanics' Association; to the many people in Durham who talked to us, listened to our questions, and patiently pointed us in the right direction.

Several people helped us in indicating historical sources, and often in following them up for us. Particular thanks are due to Frank Ennis, Keith Wilson, Pat McIntyre, Ross Forbes and Derrick Little, all of whom have written accounts of Durham and its mining legacy.

The manuscript of this book has gone through several drafts, each one involving a major revision and reconstruction. Thanks are due to those who read parts of the manuscript, offering comment and advice: Guy Boanas, Richard Brown, Anthony Harris and Helen Sampson. Special thanks to David Howell for his thorough reading of the (last but one) draft; his perceptive comments were well considered and we have taken account of most of them.

Finally, many thanks to our editor and publisher Liz Fidlon for her patience and understanding, and for her belief in this book and our work.

Prologue

Somebody ought to write a book tracing in detail the workings of an aristocratic land-owning tradition in present day English social life. Even the Durham miner would be in that book.

J.B. Priestley

IN March 1980 a society wedding took place in the City of Durham. The local paper reported:

> Two of Britain's wealthiest families were joined by marriage in Durham Cathedral yesterday. Lady Isabella Lambton, the 21-year-old youngest of five daughters of Mr and Mrs Tony Lambton of Lambton Park, Burnmoor, married banker Mr Philip Naylor-Leyland.
>
> The bridegroom, a 26-year-old former Household Cavalry Officer, will inherit £20 million from the late Earl Fitzwilliam, his mother's step-father. His inheritance includes 13,000 acres and two stately homes, one of them with 365 rooms.
>
> The dress designs were inspired by the painting of the eighteenth-century artist, Thomas Lawrence: Lady Isabella wore a dress of white, slipper satin—her silk veil was set off with a circle of yellow roses and she carried a single rose instead of a bouquet. The four bridesmaids wore silver grey, full-length dresses with white bonnets and carried posies of yellow roses.
>
> Three-hundred guests, including staff from the Lambton Estates in Northumberland and Durham went on to a champagne reception and buffet in Durham Castle's Great Hall.
>
> (*Sunderland Echo*, 19 March 1980)

The father of the bride was Anthony Lambton, son of the Fifth Earl of Durham who relinquished his title so as to continue his career in the Commons. It was he who resigned from Heath's government in 1973 after a call-girl scandal, and outfaced a rather sheepish Robin Day in his resignation interview. The family survived the scandal, and today they retain their powerful, if rather absurd, presence in the area, holding to the family motto 'The Day Will Come'.

The Lambtons are a good example of Durham's aristocracy. They had been great landowners in the county for several centuries; but in the latter half of the eighteenth century 'coal and matrimony combined to give them fame and fortune.'[1] John George, the first Earl, was born in 1792. As a young man—'radical Jack'—he sat as a Liberal MP for County Durham in the unreformed Parliament; he was made a Baron in 1828 and an Earl in 1834, and a significant political dynasty was established. This was made clear by his second marriage to the daughter of Earl Grey while his daughter married the Eighth Earl of Elgin, who served as Governor General of Canada and Viceroy of India—a position later occupied by their son Victor. Joan and Lilian, sisters of the Fifth Earl, consolidated the family's alliances. In her marriage to the Third Lord Joicey, Joan refreshed the family's links with the old coal mining aristocracy of the north. Lilian's marriage to the Thirteenth Earl of Home sealed the political links with government.

The heyday of the Lambton family was in the nineteenth century, when, under the leadership of 'radical Jack', they flourished in the northern coal trade. There, they left their mark—in pub names, street names and legend, and in the Penshaw Monument. Built on a design taken from the Greek Temple of Theseus, it stands on the top of Penshaw Hill in the centre of the county—100-feet long and 53-feet wide, on eighteen columns each measuring six-and-a-half feet in diameter. (This construction was begun in 1844, a year of intense social conflict in the coalfield.) It still dominates the skyline and the villages of the Lambton collieries beneath it.

The other significant northern coal-owning aristocratics were the Londonderrys. Londonderry (Castlereagh's half brother) moved from Ireland in the early nineteenth century, marrying into a northern coal-owning family (the Vane-Tempests), and proceeded to develop their activities in coal. Londonderry emerged as 'the acknowledged, though unloved', leader of the Conservative Party in the area.[2] Widely regarded as half mad, he was intent upon building a northern Brighton at Seaham. His concern for self-display extended to his wish for a statue depicting himself on a horse, to be set in the City of Durham. He was more successful with the statue than the resort (partly because he was not paying; partly, too, because of his threat to sink a pit in the city centre if his wishes were ignored). Both remain today as a reminder of the Londonderry heritage.

Until 1872 Durham miners were employed under an 'annual bond', a bond that tied them as servants to their masters. The struggle which led to the formation of trade unionism in the county was a struggle against this bond. Ironically, the men who met to form the Durham Miners' Association in November 1869 did so in a public house in the Market

Square in Durham, beneath the shadow of Londonderry's statue. This union, like the families of the aristocrats, developed its own traditions. Its Annual Gala (the Big Meeting) takes place in July, and goes back over a hundred years. Today the union, while formally a region within the NUM, is still referred to as 'the DMA', and these initials centre upon the union tie. The DMA's headquarters are still in Durham in a hall that was built to a grand design in 1915. Opened on 23 October as 'Redhill Villa' it survives today simply as 'Redhills', but retains, in a rundown way, its early character. Now more of a monument than a meeting place, the white marble statues of the union's earliest agents usher the visitor into an Edwardian past.

The Durham coalfield is unique. It has been involved in the commercial exploitation of coal for over five hundred years and, in the expansion of British capitalism, its coals have had a significance that is near proverbial. Yet the institutions of the labour movement were produced within the context of a deeply paternalistic society, dominated by coal-owner, church and state. The result has been a county where (in daily life, through social relationships, political parties, ceremonies and the like) the past weighs heavily upon the present. And more than this, Leister has observed how 'in no other British coalfield is there a miners' subculture so deeply ingrained.'[3] But in sharp contrast to the coalfields of Scotland and South Wales, the English coalfields for most of this century have been characterised by the dominance of a moderate Labour tradition. In this, Durham stands out as the classic case—as the centre of moderation and respectable Labour politics in Britain. Durham miners' leaders provided central figures in the Lib-Lab politics through which trade unionism developed at the turn of the century. At that time—and up until the 1930s—the area was represented by deeply reformist leaders, many of whom were Methodists. It was to a Durham constituency—Seaham, the home of the Londonderry miners—that Sidney Webb looked for a parliamentary seat in the 1920s; to be followed by Ramsay MacDonald. In the post-war period Durham provided solid support for Gaitskell in the 1950s in his struggle with the Bevanite left. This strong moderate tradition has sat oddly with the deep-rooted, popular culture of the area. This is clearly expressed in the autonomy of the local lodges and in the slogans on the banners that the villagers parade through Durham annually at their Gala. There are no union banners in the world which are the equal of those of the Durham Miners. In their numbers, their colours, their design and their complexity of motif they are an astonishing testament of a vibrant political tradition. Yet, for all the potential tension between the popular and the official culture, Durham is a place where officialdom has reigned supreme within the working class. Here, in an area densely populated by working-class people, miners became strongly organised into trade unions. Here, these trade unions also organised political life, initially within the Liberal Party and then through the Labour Party, where they gained near-total dominance in local and parliamentary elections. To understand how this political power was organised and how it related to the overall development of working-class politics in this country is a complex matter. Yet it is worth unravelling for it touches upon issues of real substance which lie at the heart of political traditions in England.

Introduction

IN 1965 Edward Thompson reflected upon the question of reformism within the British working class and the need for 'much hard research' into the ways in which the old class institutions and value systems had broken up and been replaced by new ones as the labour movement developed in the twentieth century. In this, he argued that:

> The real work of analysis remains: the sociological analysis of changing groups within the wage earning and salaried strata: the points of potential antagonism and alliance: the economic analysis, the cultural analysis, the political analysis, not only of forms of state power, but also of the bureaucracies of the labour movement.[1]

Over the last twenty years a considerable amount of progress has been made. Some of it has been directed at the changing composition of the wage and salary earning groups, with increasingly attention being paid to the rise of a middle class. So too has the state and the operation of state power been analysed, and with it a political analysis of parties, conflict and struggle. What has been neglected perhaps is the trade unions. By the turn of the century these institutions had emerged as important economic and political agents yet we know too little about how the bureaucracies of the labour movement operated: how their leaders took power and how they exercised it; how the balance between order and conflict was maintained within the organisations; how members became activists and how they related to their officials.

In understanding these organisations, the notion of 'bureaucracy' has often been used to explain the absence of a successful revolutionary politics amongst workers in Britain. As a result the problem is defined in terms of 'the bureaucrats', with a clear solution lying in 'the rank and file'. The writings of Michels have had their effect here; bureaucracies are seen as being inevitably conservative; union organisation leading inevitably toward oligarchy and *de*radicalisation. There is much in this account which is persuasive. However, this has often seemed to anaesthetise researchers producing what Gouldner identified as 'metaphysical pathos' in which 'organisation' inevitably defeats radicalism. In this way the problem is solved as it is stated, yet many important issues are left unquestioned. For example, it is clear that trade unions *do* operate differently from each other and at different times; that economic, political and cultural influences *do* affect the ways in which these organisations have operated and developed, and these factors also affect how their members have behaved and understood things. In Gouldner's view, an understanding of trade unions and radical social movements needs to go beyond the confines of the 'bureaucratization thesis' through studies which examine the variety of their organisational forms and contexts. This point has been put well, in a rather different context by Michael Burawoy:

> The industrial working class is at once the most fundamental and the most urgent link in the Marxian schema. The reconstruction of Marxism must examine how the process of production shapes the industrial working class not only objectively—that is, the type of labour it carries out—but also subjectively—that is, the struggles engendered by the specific experience or interpretation of that labour.[2]

This is the task we have set ourselves in this account of the history of the Durham miners. In this we attempt to integrate a history of mining unionism with an understanding of mining labour and of mining community and society. To many, the miners' union may seem a strange choice. This group of workers have had the histories of their trade unions better recorded than most. And so this should be. The miners numerically and politically had enormous economic and political significance within the British working class, and as such, the literature on mining (by historians, economists, sociologists, novelists) far exceeds that associated with any other occupational group in Britain. Mining unionism has been faithfully recorded by the Communist Party's historian Robin Page Arnot, and the unions in most of the mining districts have supplemented these with their own histories.[3] This is certainly true in Durham. Here the early leaders of the miners' union provided their accounts of their lives, and the building of the union.[4] More recently a historian was commissioned to provide a detailed economic account of the Durham miners between 1919 and 1960.[5] Each of these publications, in different ways, is valuable, and we have learned much from them and occasionally drew upon them quite extensively. But, these writings—individually and collectively—provide only a partial account, and do not address the central questions relating to the ways in which the character of coal mining and coal mining society related to the structure and politics of coal mining unionism.

The miners are a group of workers who have, at times, gone to the limits of the 'revolutionary framework'. Miners have been involved in battles with the state in the nineteenth and twentieth centuries which have often taken on epic proportions. The strikes of 1926 and 1984 are the best remembered occasions when the miners' union sustained national action of great duration and with enormous political potential. To these could be added the strikes of 1893, 1912, 1921, 1972 and 1974. Each of these strikes, in their different ways, threatened to 'shake the world', and served to develop an image of the miners as a strongly organised group of workers with immense industrial power. And yet there is another side of mining unionism. At the turn of the century the formal politics of mining was expressed through the election of Lib-Lab MPs, many of them union officials. Furthermore, the mining districts throughout this century have been socially stable, and essentially law abiding. Sociological writings have stressed their integrated, community form, and the deep relationship established between mine labour and family life. Often the elements identified in these accounts contrast sharply with analyses which emphasise the radical and revolutionary potential of these regions. This paradox makes a critical case for historical analysis.

We began this research in 1978, and its empirical focus has altered many times since then. Initially, our overwhelming concern was with the question of the coalfield's decline in the 1960s and the changed pattern of work and trade union relations that was established as mines were replaced by new factories. Increasingly, as we listened to people explaining the events of the post-war years in Durham, we found it hard to understand the ease with which the National Coal Board and the State was able to run down such a significant industry. In our discussion it became clear that these closures had brought about a dramatic change on the coalfield, and one that left many older people feeling disturbed. As one of them put it when we discussed the idea of progress: 'There's been some progress made, but it's been a devastating kind of progress.' Most often people illustrated their sense of change by pointing to their annual Gala; marching through the streets of the city to hear the speeches at the Race Course. ('It was a sight to behold hinny; we'll never see the likes again; not in this county; not anywhere'.) The Gala, as a phenomenon, was quite remarkable, and it was this which pushed us back historically, and into a need to provide a framework within which to understand the pattern of continuity and change within the politics of mining. This need was accelerated during the miners' strike on the coalfield in 1984–85; when images of the past, and of historical struggles, became central to the action and the discussion ('how long *were* we out in 1926?').

Throughout these changes we have maintained a reasonably clear theoretical focus; also a clear political and historical concern. In 1981 we produced a short draft version of this book as a 'working paper', and distributed two hundred and fifty copies of it—mostly locally—for discussion. Some found the historical discussion puzzling, and at odds with our other writings on changes in the 1960s. On one occasion we talked about our research with a miner in a local pub. He was taking evening classes in sociology and he wanted to know from us whether we were 'doing sociology or social history? What is the project about?'. A long discussion followed. At that time Philip Abrams was head of the Sociology Department at the University of Durham. He expressed powerfully the view that sociology and history were dominated by identical concerns. As he put it:

> In terms of their fundamental preoccupations, history and sociology are, and always have been the same....Historical sociology is not...a matter of imposing grand schemes of revolutionary development on the relationship of the past to the present. Nor is it merely a matter of recognising the historical background to the present. It is the attempt to understand the relationship of personal activity and experience on the one hand and social organisation on the other as something that is continually constructed in time....There is no necessary difference between the sociologist and the historian. Sociology which takes itself seriously must be historical sociology.[6]

We agreed, then and now, and we see this book operating in that spirit. We talked about these issues that day in the pub, and there we also touched upon ideas about 'how the social is constructed'—how the experience and understanding of being a miner or a miner's wife, or part of a miner's family, was established historically in Durham and how it changed or developed over time. Too often this is understood as 'tradition'—a term which explains, while explaining away, the question of continuity and discontinuity in social life. If anything, this has been our central concern in this study of Durham and the Durham miners. To cast light on the patterning of daily life, and its relationship with those main political institutions of the working class, the trade union and the Labour Party.

Having said this, it might be helpful for us to show how we have gone about this task. In any historical account, there is an expectation of an historical narrative which has a chronology. Indeed it can be argued that a sense of chronology and of periodisation is central to the historical craft. In this volume we have been very aware of this; aware too of the enormous detail contained in any adequate narrative. Also, of the tendency for accounts of the British Labour movements to be cast within *genres* which can be described as either *tragic* or *heroic*. In both cases (and the latter has tended to dominate), a strong teleology is evident. The British Labour movement *marches* through many of these accounts. In reflecting on the twentieth century, for example, Eric Hobsbawm has talked of the halt in 'the forward march of Labour'. Critics and supporters alike have found no difficulty with this as a formula for explaining British Labour history. While compelling, it may be that the metaphor of the march is misleading. For example, the miners have been a central group in the Labour movement in the twentieth century. No other group has attracted such *heroic* descriptions of work, community and struggle. But within many of these accounts the link between mining, solidarity, class consciousness and the Labour Party is part of an *assumed* relationship. It is seen as something which is essential to miners as proletarians. Through this framework, the early development of mining unionism is seen as the first steps upon the path which leads to the Labour Party, a national union and nationalisation in 1947. So appealing is this account that many analytic questions (some of great interest) have been either shelved or assumed away. How, for example, to explain the link between the miners and the Liberal Party? How is it, in accounts which stress the logic of class and class struggle, that 'community' emerges so frequently as a critical part of any explanation of solidarity?

Finally, a note on our sources. In this book we have used a large number of sources, and our aim has been to formulate a synthesis of much previous research, linking together an analysis of the industry and the union, and the biographical accounts of its leaders with a concern for the cultural aspects of village life and the sociological account of work and labour. In this task we have used many primary archive materials, particularly biographical accounts, newspaper reports, political diaries and lodge minute books. We developed these in the interviews we conducted with old people in the county, and through the oral history collections held at the Durham County Record Office and in the Easington Past and Present collection.[7] More generally we have spent a great deal of time sitting and listening to old miners and their wives talking—often with great dramatic force—about the past. In this we worked closely with several of our friends in the *Strong Words* collective.[8]

We have focused our researches upon places in the four quadrants of the Durham coalfield: Chopwell and Stanley in the north west, Kibblesworth and Boldon in the north and north east; Crook, Spennymoor and Bishop Auckland in the south, and west; Horden, Easington, Murton and Seaham in the south east. In this our concerns have been to provide a path, through historical analysis, between economic, political and cultural accounts; to account for the rise of mining trade unionism and a labourist bureaucracy in the context of mining life and labour; to understand the miners' unions, and their political parties both in terms of their internal operations and their wider relationship to the organisation of mining life.

These questions have required an ordering of the book which departs from a straightforwardly historical narrative. It might help the reader if we explain the course which we have taken. We begin with an account of what we have termed the Durham System and this relates to the period 1800–72. Of central importance here is the presence of an aristocratic, capitalist class employing mineworkers as bonded labourers. In this

The Durham Coalfield

context, we examine the attempts made by miners to form trade unions, focusing on the formation of the Durham Miners' Association and its relationship to national trade unionism and politics. The period covered in these chapters (2-4) is 1872-1926; special attention is given to the organisation of the union, the importance of leadership groups and the ways in which different trade union leaders have understood trade union action. These pages also chart the move of the Durham Association from its *Liberal* to its *Labour* period, and argue that there were powerful continuities as well as dislocations. Attention is directed initially to questions of class and the discussion of miners in relation to the working class in Britain at the beginning of this century. Certain 'exceptional' features are identified which distinguish miners and their organisation from other groups of workers. In this the discussion of divisions within the working class—and especially the ideas relating to a 'labour aristocracy'—are developed. This discussion of miners as a 'corporate group' is used to raise theoretical questions about the nature of the Labour Party and of British Labourism as an ideology.

We follow this with an attempt (in chapters 5-9) to locate trade union activity in the context of mining life and labour, and these chapters cover the same period as the earlier ones. Here we examine the organisation and experience of work; women and the sexual division of labour; the regulation of community life and the role of ceremony and conflict. Each of these chapters focuses upon issues of power and organisation, stressing the linkage and tension between symbolic and customary forms of life and rational forms of organisation, and the development of coal production.

From here, attention turns to formal politics—particularly the relationship between the miners' trade union and the Labour Party. The period covered here (1918-26) overlaps with earlier chapters and offers some reflection upon them. This analysis is supported by narrative accounts of political life on the coalfield: and the development of 'municipal socialism'—illustrated by an examination of the biographies of local leaders. The operation of parliamentary politics is illustrated by an analysis of three constituencies—Seaham, Bishop Auckland and Barnard Castle—each of which was represented in Parliament by 'outsiders'; Sidney Webb, and Ramsay MacDonald at Seaham and Hugh Dalton at Bishop Auckland for the Labour Party and Cuthbert Headlam at Barnard Castle for the Tories.

The final chapter—The Beginning of the End—presents an account of the 1926-39 period. Here the focus of attention returns to private enterprise and the Durham System, and considers the significance of the Labour representation for the political rule and social dominance of the employers, and the deep linkages that existed between the *economic* and the *social* manifestations of power in coalfield regions. By examining the *extent* to which the political power of the coal owners had been restricted in the 1930s, the book ends with a view of a marginalised group of employers within the capitalist class. In this way the coalfields emerge as areas ripe for social and economic reconstruction after the Second World War.

1
The Old Establishment

I conceive my colliers were really attached to my family and their old establishment.

The Third Lord Londonderry

'THE GREAT Northern Coalfield': this was how the north eastern counties of Northumberland and Durham were described in the nineteenth century. Coalmining in this area, even then, was well established. Welbourne in his account of the history of the Durham miners was clear about this. He pointed to the fact that at the turn of the nineteenth century capital had, for over 'two hundred years played a part in coal mining almost unparalleled in a County where industry was in general still poorly developed.'[1]

This peculiarity of mining was recognised by all the great early historians of capitalism. Sombart for example, described coal mining as 'one of the greatest industries at the epoch of early capitalism'.[2] He observed that it was also an industry which, in Britain, became a 'favourite undertaking' for the nobility. The 'earliness' of its development saw coal mining being established at a time when the landed classes held enormous economic and political power. Marx too understood this well, although he never dwelled upon its significance. For him, the mining industry was 'an industry distinguished from all others by the fact that in it the interests of the landowner and the capitalist coincide.'[3]

This coincidence derived from the fact that, in Britain at least, coal was owned by those who owned the land, and that coal mining as an extractive industry was readily distinguishable from manufacturing. This, together with the early development of coal mining produced an interesting paradox. Mining was an industry centrally involved in capitalist expansion. In that sense it was clearly part of the 'modern' world. However, with its expansion, so too did 'traditional' relationships of power and authority maintain themselves. In remarking on how 'many a nobleman was interested in this industry' Sombart made a significant observation on the conditions of labour. These, he said, 'in the eighteenth century, smacked of feudalism.'[4]

This paradox of continuity and change is an important one, and it is central to an understanding of the development of mining and mining politics in the north of England. Here, as Welbourne points out, 'ten generations of pitmen had been wage dependent labourers of a kind rare until the invention of the factory system'.[5] Yet this wage dependency was constructed in a world dominated by the institutions of aristocratic rule, and of rural society. In no other industry was that 'Great arch' of cultural continuity so manifestly important.[6] Yet its broader significance has rarely been noted.

Rural Society

The opening of the Alfred pit at Jarrow took place on 26 September 1803. It reveals well the Durham context.

> The fineness of the day, and the general invitation drew many thousands of people to witness the passage of the coals to the ship which lay highly decorated with colours to receive them. Early in the morning, the South Shield's bells announced the intended feast; and the ships in the South Shield's harbour immediately hoisted their colours....Several of the clergy of the Cathedral of Durham, the corporation barge of Newcastle, with several members of that body, and a great number of the most respectable gentlemen from all parts of the Country had arrived. They now proceeded to the more immediate cause of their meeting, and the wagons being loaded with coals, were taken to the ship, under the colours of the South Shield's Loyal Volunteers, which were then unfurled, and a general discharge of artillery, the music playing 'Weel may the keel row' and other appropriate tunes. It was supposed that not less than 10,000 people were assembled on this occasion. In a tent prepared for their entertainment, about 300 gentlemen sat down to dinner. The workmen, in number 500, dined at a long table without.[7]

Thirty five years later the Victoria pit was sunk inland at Sacriston; this pit was also linked to South Shields—this time by a railway. When the pit was opened a similar 'grand scheme' was planned.

> On the day, with mounting excitement, a large number of spectators gathered at the colliery, top hatted shareholders, pitmen and officials in their Sunday best, together with their wives and families.
>
> A number of the menfolk were to proceed by wagon train, down the new iron railway to the coal drops at South Shields, and see the very first coals wrought and gotten out by the Victoria

> pit, safely delivered to Tyne Dock. The band that was to accompany them on this momentous journey, played appropriate and spirit-stirring airs, as barrels of beer, meat pies, and other refreshments were loaded aboard the waiting wagons.
>
> At a given signal, amid cheering crowds, the delegation moved off, and took the slow climb up to the Daisy Hill Engine House, where a toast was made to the success of the railway. The downhill run into Waldridge, across the fell and past the Byron Pit was made without incident. On their entry into Waldridge, food and drink were handed out in liberal quantities to the villagers, and the band enlivened the festivities that followed. Upon arrival at Pelton Fell, a mile or so further on, the jolly wagoners retired to Fat Nelly's Ale House, for the purpose of further refreshments and to replenish their dwindling stocks of beer, before the final leg of the journey, along the Stanhope and Tyne Railway, to Shields. Reaching the waters of the Tyne, a further celebration was held in which the locals joined. The return journey was a riotous affair, and the owners, together with a number of respectable gentlemen were pleased to part company with their pitmen, and retire to the safety of the Lambton Arms, Chester-le-Street, where a very elegant dinner and excellent wines were provided for them.
>
> At the colliery, the merry making went on until the small hours, the men were treated to a substantial and comfortable dinner, served by their overmen, and the wives and daughters were given a grand tea followed by dancing and entertainments.[8]

Throughout the nineteenth century as pits were opened events like these were common. Sometimes 'a grand subterranean ball was held when the pit was illuminated with lamps and candles and, after each visitor had hewed a piece of coal in memory of the occasion, the pitmen and their lasses enjoyed cold punch and biscuits and the pleasure of the ballroom'.[9] Drinking, eating, dancing and pageantry (with women dressed 'to represent the genius of the mine') came together as the new industrial order was established within a framework of rural customs. On more than one occasion, Frances Anne, Marchioness of Londonderry 'entertained...upwards of 3,000 pitmen and work people, employed on her ladyship's collieries to a feast on eight bullocks, fifteen sheep, a ton of plum pudding, a ton and a half of bread, one hundred bushels of potatoes and fifty barrels of ale.'[10] Another side of this (pre-industrial) link comes across in the dress of the pitman. Up until the 1830s it was common for him to wear his hair long:

> on weekdays, tied in a queue, on Sundays spread over his shoulders. At either temple was a curl, carefully rolled in paper over a small piece of lead, so that it would dangle in fantastic

Bewicke Main Colliery. The first shaft of this colliery was sunk in 1868.

> shape down his cheeks. Over a white shirt of fine linen was drawn a pair of blue velvet breeches. Next came long stockings, of pink, purple, or blue, clocked up to the knee; next buckled shoes. The pitman's coat was of shiny blue, with an even brighter lining. His hat had several bands of yellow ribbon, into which were stuck flowers. But his greatest glory was his waist coat of brocade, his 'posy jacket', cut short to show an inch or two of shirt above the waist-band.[11]

Men like these were regularly involved in a variety of practices and events which were essentially rural in character. At Hamsterly and Byers Green, Willington and Swalwell, for example, 'there were regular "hoppings" when the smiths of the iron works or the local pitmen wrestled and ran races against each other, grinned for tobacco, and danced for ribbons with the ruddy farm girls of the neighbourhood'.[12] Throughout the county, village festivals abounded, as did gaming, cockfighting, and drinking.

There was more involved here than the survival of quaint rural customs in an industrial context. The basis of the old order was the ownership of land, and in the County of Durham this was established in the form of the County Palatine. This political institution united church and state in the person of the Prince Bishop, under whose umbrella a peculiarly powerful landowning class was established. While this altered in 1836 (when the church lands were given over to the Ecclesiastical Commissioners and the power of the Bishop modified) the nature of the coal mining industry allowed for the strengthening of the position of the landowning class within the fabric of the county. Such was their political and economic dominance that, for a generation and more, the development of an independent industrial entrepreneurial class was inhibited on the coalfield. Rural and industrial elements were held together as the old ruling class regulated the emerging capitalist economy.

As a class, its presence was always visible in its own public displays. In 1826, for example:

> Bishop Van Mildert entered his new diocese over Croft Bridge. His procession was halted on the bridge to receive the customary tribute of the Conyers Sword, and then continued on its way in the following order: Sheriff's officers on horseback bearing white wands. Three outriders, the Bishop in a carriage drawn by six horses. The Bishop's wife in a carriage drawn by four horses. The Rt Hon. and the Rev. George Viscount Barrington [Rector of Sedgefield and nephew of the late Bishop] in a carriage with four horses. Some fifty carriages of the gentry.[13]

The Bishop resided in his palace in Bishop Auckland but the centre of his diocese was the 'ancient Cathedral City of Durham'. Described by Ruskin as one of the seven wonders of the world, Durham had been a centre of feudal power. Surrounded on three sides by the steep banks of the Wear, its Cathedral and Castle shadowed the narrow medieval streets. While Newcastle emerged as the financial clearing house for the coal trade (and with this, developing as a bourgeois industrial centre) Durham remained the symbolic centre of the new economy.[14] It was at Durham in a field off Old Elvet in 1809 that the foundation stone was laid for the region's new jail by Sir Henry Vane-Tempest. He was assisted in his duty by Ralph John Lambton and the officers and brethren of the provincial Grand Lodge of Free Masons. The ceremony was carried out in the presence of the Bishop, gentry, clergy and magistrates of the county.[15] It was here too that England's third university was established by the Cathedral in 1832, with the object of continuing 'the influence of the church under a new form, adopted to meet changing circumstances'.[16]

Within the City the old style of life, linked to the Cathedral, was enhanced by the returns from capitalist expansion. Up until 1870 the Dean of the Cathedral and his twelve prebendaries offered the 'Residential Entertainment of the Cathedral Church':

> There were five or six of these given by each member of the Chapter, on a basis of two a week. The first was to the nobility and gentry, fellow-prebendaries and the more important of the county clergy; the second was to the headmaster of the Grammar School, to lesser clergy and to lawyers and doctors, the third to the Mayor and Corporation and leading citizens; the fourth to the singing men of the cathedral and the tradesmen of the town and the fifth to the King's Scholars of Durham School. The sixth was

> probably to personal friends, while once during each residence old widows were entertained at twelve o'clock in the Servants' Hall. Each of these dinners was succeeded by a little ceremony.[17]

Meals and banquets, in fact, seemed to be the order of the day, and were enjoyed in even greater splendour on the major estates of the county. This is one account by a South Durham landowner (Sir Timothy Eden) of 'Country Life' during this period:

> enormous house-parties assembled and dispersed for Stockton and Catterick races, for pheasants and partridges. Four guns at Windlestone seized the partridge record for the county with 138 brace, and a wit wrote in the Duchess's Visitors Book at Raby that he had come 'to see their Graces and to shoot their Grouses'. To the old country life were now added all the fruits and resources of industry and science, and everything here, as in commerce, was on a grand scale. Hospitality and generosity were profuse. Expense was boundless, ritual and order were elaborate. The be-ribboned cart horses and the curly woolly sheep of the Home Farm, even the pigs that were prodded with a meditative walking stick on Sundays, all were the sons and daughters of a champion This or a Champion That; and heavy prize oxen, on their way to market or an agricultural show, broke down the carts in which they were travelling. Orchids and gardenias intoxicated the hot-houses and malmaisons were fixed in the button-holes of departing guests. A thousand brace of grouse and half a thousand of pheasants were the orders of the day; and brilliant shots, crumpling tall birds in the head before a gallery of critical, softly swearing pitmen, had taken the place of the solitary pot-hunting, muzzle-loading sportsmen.[18]

If these descriptions of ceremonies and dress seem somewhat remote from Weber's account of the 'capitalist ethic' with the emphasis upon work, thrift and calculation, it is no coincidence. On the Durham coalfield capital accumulation (and profiteering) took place under the political dominance of this aristocratic class. Capitalists they were, but Durham *society* was most certainly not bourgeois. This fact was not lost upon the critical eye of the upwardly-mobile Disraeli. Commenting on the Londonderry family, he noted that 'they have a palace [Wynyard] in a vast park with forest riders and antlered deer, with all the accessories of feudal life'.[19] A life which, he noted, was based upon Seaham, and the families' collieries and blast furnaces. The same was true of the Lambton's, who then owned 17,000 acres in the north east of the county.

> The estate of the Earl of Durham [the Lambtons] was a small mining empire by the 1830s, in many respects a far cry from Trollope's Barsetshire. True there was the big house, a sham

> Gothic castle built by the first Earl, its vista from the battlements so skilfully arranged by the planting of trees that mines and miners were scarcely visible. And there were stables and horses and all the rest that went with the life of the landed gentleman. But behind the trees were the mines, burrowing so close to the house that fissures and cracks appeared in its walls not many decades after their erection. The several mines were joined by a network of private railroads that found its centre in Philadelphia, a place of machine shops and somber miners' dwellings, and Sunderland, the port from which the Lambton coals were shipped by sea in the Earl's ships to the great London market. Coal not only left its mark on the landscape of estates like the Lambtons', but it gradually came to bulk large in their revenues. And from coal it was but a short step to railroads.[20]

On the Durham coalfield therefore, county society—with its institutions of country estate, Cathedral and Church lands—remained intact as coal production increased.

Aristocrats and Coal Owners

In 1780, the mines in the north east coalfields produced 3 million tons of coal. By 1850, this had increased *five times* to 15.5 million tons. The coalfield which, in the eighteenth century provided a *third* of all British production, still produced a *quarter* of national output in the middle of the nineteenth century. This expansion was also associated with a dramatic alteration in the pattern of markets for northern coal. In 1800 only 11 percent of coal from the Durham coalfield was sold locally—the rest was shipped from the 'sea sale' collieries to the London household market. Hence 'coals to Newcastle'. By mid century, however, local rising industries had expanded and north eastern coals were used to produce gas and coke in the north. By 1870 the transformation was complete with Durham mines sending just 15 percent of their output to the London market.

In this landed society the expansion of a capitalist economy gave the landlord class access to new and huge resources of coal and a steady and expanding income. Large landowners like Londonderry and Durham employed 'viewers', managers to sink their pits and expand their wealth as coal owners. They were not exceptional in this. In Durham the established church, together with the six 'leading families' (all peers of the Realm), owned a third of the county's land.[21] As a Mining Commission report of the period put it: 'if we inquire into the general character for wealth and rank of the employers of mining labour in the Tyne and Wear, we shall find them to be the nobility and gentry and landed proprietors'.[22] In fact to list the coal owners in the nineteenth century is to produce a roll call of the area's major landed families, ranging from the Church to Dukes, Baronets and Squires.[23] When the North of England Institute of Mining Engineers was established in 1852, its patrons were the Duke of Northumberland, Lords Londonderry, Lonsdale, Grey, Durham, Warncliffe and Ravensworth, the Bishop and Dean of Durham, the Warden of Durham University and W.B. Beaumont of Bywell Hall.[24] Landlords benefited in other ways too. The church, in particular, forsook the risks involved in opening pits and employing men, by leasing the land to others and drawing a royalty payment in return. The royalty payment reflected the legal situation: the coal was *theirs*; *they* allowed others to mine it.[25]

In Durham, therefore, independent capitalist development often took a *sub-contracting* form. Speculative joint stock companies, like the Hetton Coal Company, leased the land, took the risks involved in sinking shafts to gain access to the coal, and organised the labour to extract it. It was the Hetton company in fact which, in 1821, laid out £60,000 to sink the Hetton Lyons Blossom pit—the first deep pit in the world. There were risks involved in this sinking but the potential rewards were considerable. At Hetton alone, the company estimated a profit of £360,000 in the life of the pit. Furthermore, a successful sinking at Hetton—thereby breaking into the 'concealed' coalfield—created the possibility of opening up the Durham coalfield inland, and establishing the basis for profitable expansion linked into a northern iron and steel industry. So it proved. The success of the venture at Hetton was followed by a 'great increase in [the number] of joint stock companies formed to work collieries in [the] county'.[26] New pits were sunk in the east and west of the county in a period of speculation and rapid expansion as new entrepreneurs and companies followed the aristocrats in the quest for profit in coal. Monkwearmouth, Seaham, Murton, North and South Hetton, Thornley, Haswell, Tanfield, Wingate, Esh Winning, Roddymoor, Waterhouses. All large collieries, and all sunk in the period between 1830 and 1850.

In commenting on these 'grandees of the trade', Sturgess has noted that, in the coal industry:

> the return was not unattractive to people who tied up a large part of their future in the industry and still possessed funds or credit great enough to carry them through bad times....A return on capital one or two percentage points above that to be obtained by lending at mortgage was sufficient to keep them in the trade, *especially when the control over voters which this investment brought is taken into account* [our emphasis].[27]

For these families, coal linked the eighteenth and nineteenth centuries, providing a unique bridge between the sensibilities of the old and the

'Redhills Villa'. The Durham Miners' Association's new Hall and offices: opened 23 October 1915.

practices of the new. But how could these patterns of social relations endure such rapid economic change? The truth here is that, economically and socially, these grandees proved to be remarkably adroit and flexible in pursuit of their long term interests. Something of this can be seen in the way they adapted the monopoly practice of 'the vend'.

In the eighteenth century a collection of coal owners and merchants known as the Grand Allies operated 'the vend' as a monopoly practice. Output was limited by a series of quotas, on the principle that this would limit competition, maintain prices in the London market and maximise profit. By the end of the eighteenth century however the Grand Allies had been superseded by a simple alliance between the Lords Londonderry and Durham. To quote Sturgess:

> with startling speed, the body of owner-operators was reduced to the Vane-Tempest-Stewarts [Lords Londonderry], Lambtons [Lords Durham] and Davisons....On the Tyne few coal owners operated their pits by 1800 and none could rival the scale of output of the Lambtons and the Vane-Tempest-Stewarts by 1828.[28]

In this context these aristocratic capitalists continued the mercantile practice of the vend, in collaboration with the coal traders of the Tyne. However this practice was seriously threatened by the opening of the coalfield along the Wear and the Tees and by the interests of 'the Hettonites' in unrestricted production. Fearful of the expansion of the coalfield 'under the magnesium limestone, all the way to Stockton'[29] the old coal owners, dominated by Lambton and Londonderry, sought means to extend the vend through land purchase. Collieries were held idle, others bought up to be left unused, plans to extend rail links to the pits were opposed; all in a vigorous attempt at excluding newcomers into the coal trade. The 'Hettonites' were seen as 'a rope of sand' as 'dogs [to] be brought to terms'.[30] This proved impracticable however. In the face of expanding production and developing markets the monopoly of merchant capital waned. The new owners (this time with Lambton and Londonderry in *their* numbers) broke the vend, expanded production and opened new rail links and port facilities. The monopoly of Newcastle was broken as coal from the new pits was run by rail to the new ports of Hartlepool, Sunderland and Londonderry's Seaham. Here, the commercial interests of the rural aristocracy were developed within capitalist forms as entrepreneur, church and landed family cohered across the coalfield as a class linked together in the pursuit of profit.

In this way coal emerged as the dominant economic activity in the County of Durham. In 1867 the second Earl of Durham obtained an income of £27,000 from the tenant farmers on his agricultural estates. In the same year his coal profits (excluding lessee's payments) amounted to £52,000.[31] In 1811 the population of the parish of Hetton was 322. By 1821, before the pit had opened, the figure increased to 919. Over the next ten years and following the winning of coal it had expanded to almost 6,000, placing it (in population terms at least) on a par with Durham City. As with Hetton (the product of joint-stock enterprise) so too with Londonderry's Seaham. In 1821 the population of the town stood at 198 people. Twenty years later, the numbers had increased to 2,036. After the sinking of Law Colliery in 1849 the population increased again to four and a half thousand. In 1861 over 6,000 people lived in the town which was by then a thriving coalport. Three quarters of a million tons of coal were shipped from Seaham in 1857. This tonnage had doubled by 1906.

Hetton and Seaham were not unique cases. Across the county, agriculture was replaced by coal and the company town replaced the rural village. Between 1851 and 1891 the number of people employed in mining increased from 30,000 to 85,000.[32] At this time the population increase in the County of Durham was the highest of any area in Britain. Migrants arrived from Ireland, attracted to the steel and iron works. Tin miners from Cornwall moved north, and coal miners from South Wales and Staffordshire were imported during strikes. Over decades, companies like Pease and Partners advertised for miners in Deptford and the East End of London.

The area was transformed, and a contemporary description conveys something of the impact of this transformation. It is given by a Mr Hewitt and it is based upon a journey he took on the Durham to Sunderland railway as it passed by the Broomside colliery:

> It is a mining county, and its great objects of notice on all sides are tall engine houses of its collieries and its trains of coal wagons...running up hills and down dales as if of their own accord. The sights and sounds were altogether such as must strike

> people from the south, that is those who have not been accustomed to a coal county as very strange....Here and there, you saw careering over the plain, long trains of coal wagons, without horses, or attendants, or any apparent cause of motion, but their own mad agency. They seemed, indeed, rather driven or dragged by unseen demons, for they were accompanied by the most comical whistlings and warblings, screamings and chucklings, imaginable. When you came up to one of those mad dragon trains, it was only then that you became aware of the mystery of their motion. They ran along railways and were impelled by stationary engines at a distance, which stood, often in valleys quite out of sight. A huge rope running over pulleys raised a little above the ground in the middle of the railway; and these pulleys or rollers all in busy motion on their axles, made the odd whistlings or warbles that were heard around. In truth, the sight of these rollers twirling and the great rope running without visible cause, was queer enough. Amid all these uncouth sounds and sights the voice of the cuckoo and the corn-crake came at intervals to assure me that I was on the actual earth, and in the heart of spring, and not conjured into some land of insane wheels and machinery possessed by riotous spirits.[33]

In 1850, *The Times* in a leading article, commented that the county was 'very little more than one huge colliery'.[34] It was the Durham 'coal rush'. As in California for gold, so in the north. And at the time a correspondent of the *Morning Chronicle* made clear what this involved. Drawing a contrast with his earlier descriptions of 'the cotton country' in Lancashire, he says this:

> At first the visitor will be struck by the comparative paucity of towns. The tendency of textile industry is always to the accumulation of human dwellings. The tall chimneys love to rise in clusters and every few miles along the line of rail, the train passes within gunshot of groups of huge factories strung together by closely built rows of mean cottages. But in the coal district the case is different. In traversing that undulating region the spectator will cast his eye over vast ranges of country, of particular soft and wavy outline, dotted with those buildings and scaffold apparatus which denote that beneath them a mine shaft is sunk into the earth, but totally unmarked by that luxuriant crop of towns which the power loom has called into being. The colliery population is scattered because the pits are scattered.

He explains how the economic activity of the coal mine takes place underground and how 'the coal adventurers must give each other ample elbow room', and how these activities are serviced by a 'pit row of cottages...situated near each shaft [which] affords accommodation for the population whose daily duty calls them to descend it.' The County of Durham, as a consequence:

> shows little sign of life upon its surface. The soil is cold and the trees and hedges if not stunted are not luxuriant. The visitor will not fail to observe the net of small, rude black railways, powdered with coal dust which overlay the whole country—each line stretching away in the direction of a pit heap, and dotted here and there with a convoy of coal waggons...speeding from the pit to the shipping place, at some staith' which runs into the waters of the Tyne, the Wear or the Tees.[35]

The Paternal Order

In emphasising change—the enormous economic development of the area in such a short space of time—it's important to remember the things which remained the same. The strength of the old aristocratic order lay in its flexible adaptation to the opportunities of capitalist production; however, within this, they sought to maintain critical elements of the old order, adapting those within the new system of production. In this they were assisted, by the fact that—in spite of net migration into the area—the people employed in the mines (old and new) were people of the north. For the most part, it was labourers from Durham, Yorkshire and the Scottish borders, together with lead miners from Weardale who moved into the new villages set up by the coal owners. In the 1851 census, the enumerators' return for the village of Kibblesworth revealed that only 5 percent of the 'heads of households' were born in the parish. Perhaps more important is the fact that only 10 percent hailed from beyond the north east.[36]

This pattern is confirmed across the county. What holds for Kibblesworth applies equally to Hetton-le-Hole, Murton and Seaham. Generally migration was over short rather than long distances, and it expressed a response to the established pattern of mining—where small pits were opened, rapidly worked and closed as they approached the exhaustion of their reserves. In this process mining families were created. In the 1840s one writer observed that the miners were 'made bold and savage' and that they were 'cut off from their fellow men in their interests and feelings'. The pitmen, he added, 'have an air of a primitive race'. These observations, which clearly have the air of an outsider's account, contain a further point, to the effect that:

> they marry constantly with their own people. From generation to generation family has united with family until their population has become a dark mass of relationships....They marry at about

Moving on: The internal order of the colliery village emphasised stability. However, the pattern of colliery sinking and colliery closure meant that miners and their families were regularly moving from place to place.

twenty on average and always colliery daughters; they are very clannish.[37]

The detailed researches of Lucinda Fowler into the marriage patterns of miners between 1837 and 1876 in parishes around Seaham and Easington add substance to this view. In these new expanding parts of the coalfield the miners identified tended overwhelmingly (76 percent) to be the sons of miners, who overwhelmingly (73 percent) married the daughters of miners.[38] These women, across the county, tended to have above average numbers of children. Kinship contributed strongly to the occupational culture which built up around mining. 'Dark mass of relationships' or otherwise, this stable feature of mining life was to be of critical importance as the century progressed. For as Fowler concludes, this mixture of geographical mobility and occupational immobility left 'little opportunity for outsiders'.[39]

This pattern of isolation was reinforced by the fact that the Durham coal owners operated a sophisticated system of labour regulation and control. In the north, the agricultural practice of tied cottages was well established, and it was adapted and developed in the context of the colliery village. In the 1830s and 1840s when the coalfield was opened up, villages with their colliery rows, were built quickly alongside the colliery shaft. Some (like Londonderry's Seaham) were set up as model villages, others were 'laid out with a ruthless disregard for local conditions, so important was their proximity to a successful sinking'. Again, a contemporary account is helpful. The much travelled correspondent of the *Morning Chronicle* remarked that:

> A pit row is like nothing whatever in the shape of a collection of houses that I know of in England. It is neither like a country village nor a section of the meaner part of a manufacturing town....The shops, if anything worthy of the name exists at all, are of the meanest and most miserable description. From end to end there is not a single large house, a tree, or a church spire to break the shabby uniformity of the pitmen's cottages.

He continues with a lengthy description and concludes thus:

> In a few colliery villages there is a feeble attempt at surface drainage, the liquid refuse in these channels being very frequently stagnant; but in not one pit row out of the scores I have seen, and in not one pit row I am told in Northumberland and Durham, is there a single foot of underground drainage...to carry away domestic slops. And these rows, be it observed were not built piecemeal by poor men ignorant of the importance of drainage to health and life; they were one and all constructed wholesale by the owners of the neighbouring pits, for the accommodation of their work people, and they are the only houses in which these people can possibly live.[40]

This latter point (with the strong element of moral criticism) is central to an understanding of the political structure of the Durham coalfield, at that time.

While South Wales miners living in a coalfield which developed later than Durham either bought their houses or rented from private landlords, in the north of England almost 90 percent of miners lived in company houses, which were provided as part of the wage. George Elliot, the head agent of the Londonderry Collieries, a man who started work at the age of nine as a pit boy and ended up as Tory MP for Durham, described to the Royal Commission on Trades Unions how:

> In Northumberland and Durham we find every man his house, his firing [coal] his garden and everything of that sort. A little of the paternal system is very useful because you can keep your men in times of difficulty.[41]

That this wasn't simply an 'aristocratic system', was made clear in the west of the coalfield. There, new industrial employers like Straker and Love obtained land to set up their own operations. The Pease family established the industrial company town of Darlington built upon coal, iron, rail and textiles. In Crook and through the Deerness Valley their pits produced thousands of tons of coal. Everywhere, though, the practices of the new employers bore the stamp of paternalism; a stamp that characterised labour relations and social relations generally in the Durham coalfield for a century and more.

In 1859, for example, the MP for South Durham, Henry Pease, married a Miss Lloyd in Birmingham. The *Durham Chronicle* recounted how:

> The happy event was the occasion of great rejoicing in South Durham. At Darlington, it was loudly announced by the firing of cannon and a similar mode of testifying to the joyous character of the day was adopted at Grahamsley, Roddymoor, etc. Flags floated in the breeze at the several collieries belonging to the Messrs. Pease, at the Terra Cotta works, Bankfoot Crook. The firing of cannon commenced at some of the collieries at a very early hour, and the morning stillness was broken so early as 5 o'clock by the loud boom of cannon through the air, which reverberated for miles around. A large bonfire, consisting of innumerable tar and oil barrels was lit on Billy Hill in the evening, and illuminated the country in every direction. Indeed, such is the estimation which the members of the Pease family have earned themselves among their servants, and so large an extent of the coalfield of South Durham being in their interest, that the happy event caused an almost boundless expression of joy. Gaiety and happiness held undiminished sway at the different works, and in some places music gave additional zest to the hilarity of a happy and contented set of people. The 10 schools erected by the firm had a holiday, and loud huzzas from tiny throats everywhere rent the air. A large number of viewers, connected with Bowden Close, Water Houses, Stanley, Adelaide, St. Helens, Hedley Hope, and the Terra Cotta Works sat down to a sumptuous and elegant dinner....[42]

Here we see how the new coal owners extended the 'Durham system' beyond houses and coals to include free medical attention, schooling and education. Pease and Partners even gave the system an added twist, building their colliery houses in Waterhouses and Esh Winning with the production of the company's brickworks, each brick stamped with the word 'Pease' or the initials 'F&L'. This (subliminal) presence was extended through a variety of practices, both within the village, and *underground*:

> Once a year Pease and Partners gave a 'conversazione' in the ballroom flat at Esh Colliery. This large flat at the bottom of the North Drift was made into a 'room' with wall covering and

Pit rows in South Moor near Stanley, like 'nothing whatsoever in England...neither a country village nor the section of a manufacturing town'.

> pictures, furniture, carpets and a cradle. A concert or dance was then given for the colliery families.[43]

Meanwhile, on the surface, the Pease family supplied the field, stands, labour and money for the Esh Winning flower show. The Aged Miners' home was opened by Miss Pease and within the villages no hall or school was opened without one of the family being present. The family name topped all lists of donations for colliery bands, agricultural shows, cricket competitions and the variety of cultural pursuits that made up village life.

To the extent that this provision was accompanied by the encouragement of other practices amongst the pitmen (allotments, pigeon fancying and so on) it can also be seen as fitting into a complex system of regulation and control. Within this system, the miners and their families obtained certain advantages; but these were entirely dependent upon acceptance of the defined rights and duties of the coal owners' society. In Esh Winning, for example, the Pease company employed a man called Crofton as manager. He was 'a tough old guy [who] believed in keeping miners in their place'.

> Crofton kept aloof from day to day matters in the village; he rode to Esh Winning on a horse, inspected the gardens and insisted on their being properly kept. He was the main supporter of the flower show. He was also an ardent supporter of the Church of England [St. Stephen's Mission, Esh Winning]. He is alleged to

> have known all the older pitmen by name. Parents taught their children to touch their forelocks to Mr Crofton.[44]

A feature of a paternalist order is the belief that society 'can be best managed and social evils best mitigated by men of authority, property and rank performing their respective duties toward those in their community who are bound to them by personal ties of dependency. To be a paternalist was to act toward dependents as a husband does to his wife, his children, and his servants'.[45] In this clear sense, the Durham coal owners were paternalists. They understood themselves, not simply as rational capitalists, but as men occupying a position of honour and respect within a society. This society was organised around the *public* display of rights and obligations. As such, this order required that the employers, as masters, socially regulated their own conduct. Nowhere was this more clear than in the area of welfare. At the time of the Haswell Pit Disaster in 1844 Londonderry made clear his disapproval of the Haswell Coal Company's scheme for the public subscription for the relief of the families of the victims:

> I must in the first place express my extreme regret that the Company should feel it necessary to appeal to the Public...to support and assist those whom I conceive it is the bounden duty of all proprietors of Collieries to maintain and provide for under accidents of a similar description. In proportion as the Collier or Pitman devotes his labour and runs the risk of the mines for the benefit of his Employer so is the latter in common Duty honesty and charity bound to provide for and protect those who are bereft of their protectors by any fatality that Occurs...can it be supposed by the Haswell Company that an uncertain subscription can make up to the Widows and Orphans provision and subsistence other than for a short period? The principle of levying this subscription is wrong. It is in fact subscribing for and saving the Haswell Company who ought to support the sufferers & not the Public. It is for the Benefit of the Company the lost men toil'd and fell, and it is a sacred duty on their part alone to support those they left behind.[46]

This 'sacred duty' had been accepted by Londonderry twenty-one years earlier when 56 lives were lost in the explosion at the Plane Pit. By 1845, and in the face of political organisation amongst 'his' workers, the boundaries of this duty had been expanded. While he once felt that education for the sons and daughters of miners could mean 'cramming it into the heads of those who don't feel the inclination to receive it' now he was an enthusiastic convert to the educationalist's cause. In that year he observed that schools could play an important role in 'cementing those old ties of attachment'.[47] These developments have been chronicled enthusiastically by Heesom:

> As well as free medical attention, and free housing for most of the pitmen and other employees, so long as they remained in service, Londonderry also provided free education. Originally this was limited to night schools, and to the endowment of already existing local institutions: in 1843 there were four night schools associated with the Londonderry collieries, with a total of 72 scholars, and Lord Londonderry also gave five pounds a year to a school built at Broomside in 1836. In 1844, however, Londonderry decided to improve both the condition of his pitmen's houses, and to provide them with day schools. The crowded state of some of the houses was 'productive of scenes of immorality & prejudicial to health', while the children appeared in 'a forlorn and ignorant state of wildness', which the parents seemed unwilling to do anything to correct. Londonderry therefore proposed to open three schools, one at each of his three main collieries of Pensher, Rainton, and Pillington, each to have a schoolmaster and mistress, whose salaries were to be a monthly charge on the collieries. Londonderry also promised if he thought the conduct of the pitmen deserved it, to endow the schools as well.[48]

All this was extended by his widow who argued in 1857, that 'before allowing young boys to go into the pits I shall require that they have a certain amount of education...and that a certificate to that effect shall be produced to the viewer before the boy can be employed'.[49] Furthermore she required 'a competent knowledge of the general principles of Christianity', a view shared by J.W. Pease who argued that 'a mob could never acquire any permanent ascendancy' when 'knowledge was extremely diffused throughout the population'.[50] In 1871, when opening a school in Esh Winning he echoed the sentiments of his aristocratic counterpart:

> There was nothing so bad...as when a master neglects his duty...and afterwards sees there is a feeling of discontent amongst his workmen which he feels he ought to have prevented years before.[51]

In the absence of 'neglect' Pease anticipated a 'steady, settled work-people' enjoying the 'comfort' of the relationship and contributing to 'prosperity' of their employer. As we shall soon see, where the relationship failed to work out so comfortably, violence (paternalism's dark side) ensued. For the moment though it is important to make clear the significance of paternalism as an ideology within the county. It was this ideology which gave the employers (new and old) their sense of place. It was this which—in the developing circumstances surrounding the needs of capitalist production—fashioned a series of practices which linked employer to worker.

From the eighteenth century onwards it was clear to the coal owners in Durham that the pits demanded a particular kind of labour force. The Poor Law Commission of 1834 received evidence to the effect that in Durham:

> Pitmen must be bred to their work from childhood. Their number cannot be recruited from any other class...the increase of the pit population comes solely from internal sources.[52]

In Durham society, place was finely determined by birth. The implication of this was often put by John Buddle, the most important colliery viewer in the county. Born in 1773 he organised and managed Londonderry's collieries: a man rooted in the coal trade whose 'first love always remained pit work'. He, above all others in the county was a man responsible for the management of labour, a task which he combined with strong political canvassing for Londonderry's cause in the area. In more ways than one he was the right hand man of his master. When Londonderry opened Seaham Harbour, an inscription written in brass was placed in the foundation stone. It read:

> In this undertaking, the founder has been chiefly advised by the tried experience and indefatigable industry of his valued friend and agent John Buddle Esq., of Wallsend.[53]

Buddles's views of Londonderry were equally celebratory. For:

> if the high Aristocracy of the country were more frequently to find occasion to bring themselves into personal intercourse with the working classes, and show them a little countenance and kindness, Chartism and all the other absurd causes of political excitement would evaporate like the white mist in September before the sunbeams. In this respect your Lordship has shown a brilliant and laudable example.[54]

This example was based upon reference to the miners as his Lordship's 'Little black family'. It illustrates clearly the pattern of dependency central to the paternal system. It also brings to mind slave plantation systems which operated at this time in the Southern States of the USA. That this allusion isn't entirely fanciful can be seen in a letter Buddle wrote to Lord Londonderry at the time of the Coal Commissioner's enquiries which led up to the 1842 Coal Act. He wrote that:

> what we have to guard against is any obvious legislature interference in the established customs of our particular race of pitmen. The stock can only be kept up by breeding—it never

> could be reinvented from an adult population...but if our meddling, morbid, humanity mongers get it infused into their heads that it is cruel and unnatural slavery to work in the dark and to be imprisoned twelve hours a day in the pit, a screw in the system will be let loose.[55]

Buddle's determination was to keep the various screws of the system tight. And in this he was adamant in his opposition to the freeing of labour in the coal mines. Here too the parallels with slavery are suggestive. In Alabama, for example, a mine owner remarked in 1859 that:

> it is near to impossible to prosecute my mining intents successfully with free labour...no reliance whatever can be placed upon it...I have now not a white man on my work force...I must have a negro force or give up my business.[56]

Storobin has commented on this, to the effect that throughout the slave era in the States, 'black bondsmen, both owned and hired, constituted the chief source of mine labour.'[57] In County Durham the miners weren't 'blacks', but neither were they free. They too were bonded.

2
Bonded Labour and Independent Miners

When you felt the full weight of the burden you longed to be free; you looked around but found no means of escape; you were lashed to the PLACE *by English law, and while there, constantly scorched by the employer's scorpion whip.*

William Crawford

UNTIL 1872 the miners of the north east were employed as 'bonded labourers'. The bond limited the free market for labour, tying miners to their masters for a period of a year. But it was a critical screw in the Durham system and one which was supported by all elements within the coalowning class in the north. This 'pre-capitalist practice', was underwritten by law, and was adapted to powerful effect by the coal owners—only to be broken finally by the successful organisation of the miners into a trade union.

The 'binding' ceremony was originally a yearly ritual performed simultaneously throughout the coalfield in October. A written bond, which could vary between different collieries, was read to the pitmen whose assent was given by 'stretching their hands over the shoulder of the agent and touching the top of the pen whilst he was affixing the cross to their name',[1] indicating their hiring for the year. In the Londonderry collieries this was invariably followed by a dinner at which Buddle would be prevailed upon to 'sing a vernacular song, delivering it with great verve, in the Tyneside dialect'.[2]

The history of the bond in the Durham coalfield is difficult to chart. Certainly it altered significantly throughout the period of its operation. In the early eighteenth century, for example, the bond was used much like the annual agriculture hirings. Colliery villages, viewed as typical in the nineteenth century, didn't exist, and pitmen, like migrant workers, moved annually, even seasonally:

> Many of the Durham miners were so far from being the life long, or even the year long, servants of particular masters, that there

> was a regular migration of workmen from the pits in the Wear Valley to those in South Durham every summer, and a counter migration of the same workmen every winter, when the 'land sale' pits were usually idle.[3]

In this way 'thousands of families would change districts annually and in April and May the whole mining districts were alive from side to centre with loaded vehicles from big wagons to '"cuddy" carts'. The expansion of capitalist production on the coalfield led to a general extension and tightening of the practice of the bond and a stabilisation of the labour force. The Hammonds, commenting on this development, noted that in 1765:

> A combination of masters endeavoured to turn this system of a yearly bond into a slavery nearly as gross as that which is legal in Scotland. The reason for this attempt was, strangely enough, the scarcity of pitmen due to the rapid increase in the coal trade.[4]

In that year miners struck to secure their right to move from one employer to another at the termination of their annual contract. This victory was reversed in 1793, when 'leaving certificates' were introduced into the coalfield. Under this arrangement no man could commence work 'unless [he] produced a certificate of leave from his last master'.[5] The pitmen were clear on what this would mean: where labour was scarce, no coal owner would give such a certificate, and it would be 'a binding during the will of the master'. If the men dared to move they would 'find that no other owner will hire them, but that they must be forced to work at pits which perhaps they do not like and at what wages the master pleases [or starve, or go to other parts]'.[6] However, in spite of these protests leaving certificates were reinforced legally in 1800 (under the *Act for the Security of Collieries and Mines*) subjecting miners who breached the conditions of the bond to a forty shilling fine or imprisonment. Bainbridge, writing in 1856, observed how in the Durham mines:

> if any miner shall contract with any one for a certain period, and shall absent himself from his service before the completion of the term, or be guilty of any other misdemeanour, any such Justice of the County...upon complaint made under oath by the person contracted with, or his steward or agent, may issue his warrant for apprehending the miner or Labourer, and may commit him to the house of correction for not more than three months and not less than one month.[7]

Such imprisonment was not rare; in 1867 for example, a Joseph Quinn was summonsed to appear before magistrates in Gateshead for having 'unlawfully absented himself from the Usworth Colliery, having contracted to serve the owners as hewer from the 5 April 1866 to the same date in 1867'.[8] At the same hearing John Macmillan also appeared having committed the same offence in relation to his employment at the Washington Colliery. Macmillan:

> admitted absenting himself, but complained that the atmosphere of the pit was so hot that his eyesight and head had been greatly affected, the giddiness resulting disabling him from performing his work...The atmosphere of Washington pit was warmer than that of pits generally. Defendant had not, however, complained to the owners of this, and had worked in the pit twelve months previous to entering into the present contract, which he did knowing well the temperature of the pit. Defendant was asked whether he would go back to his work, but he hesitated for a while, and insinuated that he had a wife and four children to consider. As he did not express his readiness to return to work defendant was sent to prison for one month with hard labour.[9]

The link with the law was a critical aspect of the Durham system. Here, the employer and the state were awesomely similar. In 1850 *Reynolds' Political Register* made this point clearly.

> Most of the principal coal proprietors are themselves in the commission of the peace, so it is next to impossible for a poor miner to obtain justice, or even its shadow, from any county Midas, no matter how strong the case may be in favour of the oppressed collier. Instances are constantly occurring of colliers being brought before these unpaid magistrates, and upon the sole representation of their employer, perhaps also on the commission, sentenced for the most trivial offenses to a long and tedious imprisonment.[10]

The legal backing given to the bond in the nineteenth century was accompanied by its increasing formalisation. In the eighteenth century binding money (paid by the owners to the pitmen as a form of signing-on fee) varied with the state of trade and the supply of labour. During the Napoleonic wars the extreme scarcity of labour forced up the binding money:

> 1804 was the peak year: Wallsend averaged about £8, Washington about £12, Hartley 12 guineas, the Lambton and Vane collieries about £15, Cowpen 18 guineas. In general it seems that in 1804 the Main Tyne collieries paid about £12 and the Main Wear collieries about £15. Thus several thousand collieries paid between a quarter and a third of what they could normally hope to earn in a year.[11]

The following year a high degree of organisation amongst the coal owners standardised the binding money to a payment of three and a half guineas on the Tyne and five and a half guineas on the Wear. As a consequence the total cost of binding, which had reached £200,000 in 1804 fell to £71,000 in the following year. This standardisation of the bond attacked the degrees of informal control which pitmen had been able to exercise against particular employers in particular locations. It can be seen as response by 'the masters' to the organising efforts of the miners. It was perfected in 1826 when a single printed bond replaced the individual colliery bonds.

The bond for the Hetton Coal Company Collieries for the year running from 5 April 1829 to 5 April 1830, is quite clear on what this meant for masters and servants in their respective relations to each other. The pitmen 'servants' were:

> To hew, work, fill, drive and put coals and to such other work as may be necessary for carrying on the said collieries and as they shall be directed or required to do so by the said owners.[12]

This meant that hewers could be required to work as putters or barrowmen at their 'prices'. In turn the owners could lay the pits off work as they saw fit for a period of ten days maximum. But during lay off the pitmen remained as 'servants' of the owners 'subject to their orders and liable to be employed by them in such work as they shall see fit'. The owners were also 'at liberty, if they think fit' to require miners to work on pay Saturday.

Housing was provided in the terms of the bond. The twelfth clause specified the terms:

> It also distinctly understood and agreed that the dwelling houses provided for any of the persons hereby hired or engaged are and form part of the wages of such persons.[13]

Pitmen were 'not allowed to keep a galloway, ass or dog', and they had 'to keep up the glass in the house'. Underground, the miner was required to supply his own picks and drills and to pay fines for absenteeism. This bond was marked with a cross by 588 hewers, 192 putters and 187 drivers.

In the nineteenth century the Durham coal owners operated a sophisticated system of labour and regulation and control parts of which survive to the present. It was a system which was based upon previous rural forms and relationships which in mining (in contrast to the other expanding industries) was extended and developed rather than curtailed by capitalist expansion. In this, the bond represented a detailed system for hiring and regulating labour. It was a contract which extended beyond wages, establishing (via 'free' housing and coal) economic control into the very fabric of civil society in the mining districts. So too was it used as a flexible method for disciplining labour. On the one hand miscreants could be dealt with by the law through fines and imprisonments. However, and paradoxically, in a local economy dominated by one industry, the threat of *not* being bonded was probably the deepest cut of all. That this *was* used as a threat is made clear in a letter written by a colliery viewer (George Hill) to John Buddle in 1826.

> Matthew Wigham is the name of the man whom I mentioned as the only active person here on the union but as he is not particularly objectionable, I think I'd better continue him in the employ if he wishes it tho' without him being bound, that I may have more control over him.[14]

The reference made here to 'the union' is a critical one. It points to the threat felt by the coal owners to their system of rule and to the fact that 'the Durham system' was predicated upon unfree, non-union labour. As capitalist production expanded, it adapted itself and extended its practices. In this the emergence of forms of trade union organisation amongst the miners created a critical dynamic element within the system.

Religion and Resistance

The paternal rule of the employers on the Durham coalfield in the nineteenth century was a relationship that could brook no outside interference. The strength of this is put well by Nossiter: 'more members of that trade were Whig than Tory...but when threatened by government interference or labour discontent, party differences were laid aside to resist the common enemy.'[15] Such was the case in each of the major strikes in the coalfield in the nineteenth century. In 1831 Londonderry opened negotiations with 'his' pitmen with a proclamation:

> If the pitmen of his collieries are free and independent of control from the other colliers...and can fairly enter into the usual arrangements of binding, Lord Londonderry is ready to accede to such just demands in their particular work as they require. But Lord Londonderry cannot consider these so long as his men are under the direction of others with whom he has no connection. And it would be the height of injustice for reasonable men, attached to the Soil and Property to ask Lord Londonderry to consent to their demands.[16]

Here, and repeatedly in the decades that followed, 'others' was the term which identified trade-union activists and organisers. Equally regular was the pattern of violence and victimisation which followed attempts by miners to resist the owners' terms and organise independently.

In 1832, the annual bond of service was challenged once again, and the miners of Friars' Goose Colliery in South Tyneside were threatened with eviction. They drove off the bailiffs and on 4 May faced a party of special constables armed with firearms and cutlasses. After a fracas in which five miners were shot and wounded, the soldiers arrived, arresting forty or more. Twenty men and three women were committed to Durham jail for trial at the assizes.

In 1844 the whole of the northern coalfield was affected by the strike which began on 5 April. The Durham miners had attempted to organise a national strike, through the newly-formed Miners' Association of Great Britain and Ireland, but at a meeting of delegates in Glasgow the strike call was narrowly defeated. The northern miners struck alone. In the Londonderry collieries the miners and their families were evicted from their houses. Londonderry's circular to the striking miners read:

> I have been amongst you—I have reasoned—I have pointed out to you the misery, the destruction awaiting you, by your stupid and insane unions. I gave you two weeks to consider whether you would return to your work before I proceeded to eject you from your houses. I returned to Penshaw, and I found you dogged, obstinate and determined—indifferent to my really paternal advice and kind feelings to the old families of the Vane and Tempest pitmen, who have worked for successive ages in the mines.[17]

Here, Londonderry was merely developing a pattern which the Chartist Williams had termed 'a system of extermination'. Writing in the *Northern Star* 1841 he pointed to:

> the owners of South Hetton, Hetton, Elemore and other collieries [who] have marked, all who had been guilty of doing their duty as men and as citizens...all the leading Chartists working at these collieries were informed that they might leave 'the colliery, that their services were not particularly required, and therefore the masters were not disposed to bind them.'[18]

On each of these occasions (in 1831, 1832 and again in 1844) as the Durham coalfield unfolded, Durham miners attempted to unionise. In the development of these struggles, Primitive Methodists and Chartists organised together, and as Hobsbawm has pointed out:

> Among the northern miners...Primitive Methodism was so closely identified with trade unions as to become practically a labour religion.[19]

The truth of this is made most clear in the life of Tommy Hepburn, the man generally recognised as the first union organiser on the coalfield in the nineteenth century. Born at Pelton, near Chester-le-Street in 1796, he began work as an eight-year-old boy at the Hatfield colliery. Converted to Methodism in 1822 he spent the rest of his life combining preaching with union organising. In 1831 he was the undisputed leader of the miners in Durham. In May 1839 he dominated a meeting on the Town Moor in

Newcastle. Over a hundred thousand people attended that meeting, bringing with them some two hundred banners. Hepburn made real the idea of a labour religion, and this was noted by T.J. Taylor, a government commissioner in 1844.

> A religious feeling was mixed up in a strange and striking manner with this movement. The privations which they and their families were undergoing, the difficulty of the enterprise they had embarked on, and certain misgivings as to the event appear to have laid them more than usually open to religious excitement. Frequent meetings were held in their chapels [in general those of the Primitive Methodists or 'Ranters' as they are commonly called in that part of the country] where prayers were publicly offered up for the successful result of the strike. The local preachers, the chief speakers at these prayer meetings were the men who, by a certain command of language, and by an energetic tone and manner, had acquired an influence over their fellow-workmen, and were invariably the chief promoters and abettors of the strike. They were consequently among the first, at most of the works, to be dismissed by the masters.

Taylor further noted how:

> During the strike they had regularly once a week prayer meetings at the chapels in the colliery villages, to pray to God to give them success. The men said they went 'to get their faith strengthened'. I attended one of these meetings. There were about 60 members present. Prayer was offered up for God's blessing and support during the strike, and that he would give them the victory. Everything that could be collected in the Bible about slavery and tyranny, such as Pharaoh ordering bricks to be made without straw, was urged to them.[20]

The Primitive Methodists, then, opposed the Church of the coal owners both with their reading of the Bible and their own institutions—the chapel, and the open-air public meeting. Hearn, in his suggestive account of the 'incorporation of the nineteenth century working class', reminds us that 'Methodism since the 1730s had been in continual struggle with the state-supported church; and from their start in the 1790s the Methodist sects had been in conflict with both the Church of England and the Wesleyan Methodists'.[21] He goes on to argue that:

> what facilitated the workers commitment to and participation in the Methodist sects was the basic similarity between the sect and the working-class community...Both nurtured values which were not bound to the established order.[22]

In a similar vein, Weber argued that in England: 'from their start in the

1790s, the Methodist sects have engaged in conflict with the Church of England.'[23] In Durham where Church, state and coal owner combined, this conflict was made more acute. To the Chartists, Durham was 'that priest-ridden city', and the Anglican coal owners were both 'coal mine, cottage, and slave proprietors'. As such they were vulnerable to the deepest of criticisms as the perpetrators of a system within which:

> if a man desires work and is willing to sacrifice political principle he may be a slave for twelve months and after being thus bound he cannot abstain from work a single day without a note from the colliery doctor without being subject to imprisonment.[24]

Here, the Primitive Methodists appeared as a democratic, progressive form of religion and one through which the ubiquitous power of the masters could be opposed. It resonated with a strong sense of being *within* but not *part* of society. This theme crops up repeatedly in accounts of mining life in the nineteenth century and it was made very clear in a miner's pamphlet written by W. Mitchell of Bishopwearmouth in 1844. In asking the question 'what do the miners want?' the author stresses the need for release from the tyranny of the bond and recognition of the fact that 'we no longer occupy the outer margins of civilisation'. In pressing this claim Mitchell draws attention to the fact that 'our present cessation from labour is distinguished by union, strike peacefulness and calm determination'.[25]

It was Chartism which gave voice and organisation to this sense of injustice and which combined with feelings of strength and certainty in the strikes and resistances of the 1830s and 1840s. Gammage in his classic account draws attention to the fifty to sixty thousand who made up the Chartist meeting on the Town Moor in Sunderland on Whit Monday in 1839—'the great body of the people consisted of hardy colliers who evinced the most determined spirit.'[26] As late as 1850 the Report of the Commissioner into the State of the Population in the Mining Districts drew attention to the fact that young literate miners were cutting their teeth on either 'cheap penny periodicals' or 'the newspapers and periodicals advocating Chartism and Socialism'. Hobsbawm's view of miners as 'an isolated body of men, often geographically separated from the rest of the working people and concerned less with politics than with their specialist economic struggles'[27] underestimates the significance of political and legal factors in defining the economic position of northern coal miners. His conclusion that miners took 'surprisingly little part in the radical and Chartist agitations' has been corrected nationally by Dorothy Thompson and in the north east by the careful researches of Keith Wilson. These have pointed to the ways in which the isolated solidarities of mining villages were, on occasions, mobilised into effective public agitation.

> The whole population of Coxhoe was said to have marched to Sunderland for the Whit Monday meeting of Chartists in 1839. In July the Coxhoe miners again walked the eighteen miles to Sunderland's town moor together with those from Quarrington Hill. When one of their number broke both his legs while serving as a delegate to the July meeting, the Coxhoe community supported him financially for at least seven months while he was unable to work. For the community to have helped a fellow worker in this way and for so long says much for their attitude towards the cause for which he was injured. It also says much for their powers of organising the regular round of collecting money for his support.[28]

In his account Wilson makes use of Edward Thompson's distinction between plebeian and proletarian forms of consciousness and action, seeing these 'mass meetings and demonstrations of miners' as being 'a long way from (plebeian) behaviour'. He emphasises the influence of Chartism upon miners across the coalfield 'providing a clear articulation of their grievances and the class nature of their oppression'. However this emphasis should not lead us to ignore either the plebeian continuity (the theatricality of protest via effigy burning, the spontaneity of riot and the influence of custom) nor the influence of Methodism which (through its oratory and banners) combined with Chartism in a critical manner.

Both Chartism and Primitive Methodism involved radical criticisms of the *moral* basis of the paternal order. They also provided the basis for organisation and for the establishment of principles of social regulation at variance with paternalism. As Hearn has argued:

> Through the democratic institutions of the Methodist sects, self respect was maintained in the context of collective practice, as people were encouraged to take an active and creative part in formulating decisions affecting their daily existence.[29]

In this respect, 1844 can be seen as a watershed. By that date the vend was finished. The strike which affected the coal trade in that year, and the support obtained by Hepburn and the Chartists convinced many of the employers that their future prosperity was linked to their success in handling 'the problem of labour'. What followed was a re-negotiation of the political and social space within the county and an accommodation by the owners to the political and popular cultures of the workers. Eventually this involved a recognition of the miners' trade union and removal of the bond by Act of Parliament. Equally important however was the process which saw the owners arrive at an accommodation with

Methodism which came to play a dramatically different role within the mining village.

Although they were owned by the masters, the pit villages were the homes of miners; in that sense they were 'theirs', and in times of crises, as in strikes or at the height of the Chartist organisation, the coal owners could sense their control slipping. In 1839, for example, Buddle wrote to Londonderry, expressing concern over the fact that in Shiney Row:

> it is difficult to find out their intentions as they hold private meetings every night to deliberate on the information they received from Newcastle or Sunderland.[30]

Wilson has noted how 'even in towns where there is little likelihood of violence, the residents feared what might happen if men in the nearby mining areas turned on them'.[31] Much of these fears were irrational and even prejudiced. However, to note them is to point to the potential political strength of the miners in Durham, and also to the isolation of mining villages from the rest of northern society. The separateness of this culture was something which, in times of crisis, could be turned to good effect against the coal owner. Weber has remarked on this, pointing to the ways in which 'preaching unfolds its power most strongly in periods of prophetic excitation'. However, he added that 'in the treadmill of daily living it declines sharply to an almost complete lack of influence'.[32] It was upon this treadmill (and the antagonism of the employers) that the early miners leaders were broken in the 1840s and 1850s.

The Problems of Mining Unionism

The history of mining unionism in the nineteenth century was characterised by the persistent rise and fall of local county or district organisations, set on establishing negotiating arrangements with local employers and failing. In Durham, the owners—the Masters—had persistently refused to recognise the trade unions formed in the 1820s, 1830s and 1840s, viewing them as alien forces with no constitution or place in society. The defeat of the 1844 strike—the 'long strike' as it was referred to in the county—had disastrous consequences. Trade-union membership declined rapidly and by the 1850s, while there were outbreaks of resistance and strike action, the Durham system operated with non-union labour.

These early local associations of miners also involved themselves in attempts to establish a national union of all miners, and this was, as we have seen, partly, the product of Chartism. In the 1830s and 1840s county associations had been formed in Lancashire, Yorkshire, Staffordshire and Scotland. These, together with the miners' union in Durham and Northumberland formed the Miners' Association of Great Britain and Ireland. The Association had its first meeting in Wakefield in 1841, and

THE

MARTYRDOM OF THE MINE,

OR,

A 60 YEARS' STRUGGLE FOR LIFE.

By EDWARD A. RYMER, Monk Bretton, Barnsley.

Dedicated to the Miners of England, 1898.

PRICE SIXPENCE.

Edward Rymer's account of work and labour organisation in the Durham coal mines is a rare and authentic document. It was sold widely throughout the coalfield.

Durham trade unionists were centrally involved—Martin Jude as Treasurer and David Swallow as General Secretary. In its short life this Association revealed problems which were to bedevil all attempts at mature organisation. Most difficult was the problem of building unity between miners employed by different employers who paid different wages, under different wage contracts and working conditions. Such a problem emerged clearly in 1844 when no agreement was reached on a national miners' strike. As a result the pitmen of the north struck alone and were defeated. By 1848, the Association had collapsed, and by 1853 those county unions involved in it had all but disappeared. In Durham and Northumberland trade unionists found it harder and harder to build support and many of the organisers left the county, blacklisted.

The push for trade unionism across the British coalfields reemerged in the 1860s. In 1858 the Yorkshire Miners' Association was formed, and this organisation lobbied parliament for the passage of a Bill that was to prove critical to the development of trade unionism in the mines. A persistent grievance of coal miners related to their payment, which was governed by the weight of coal they cut from the coal face and transported to the surface. Disputes over the weighing of this coal persisted across all the coalfields in the nineteenth century, and had led to a general demand by miners for a weigher of their own, to check the weights of the Master's weighman. So powerful and persistent was this claim (so morally sound were the arguments, and so disruptive were the disputes over bad weights) that in 1860 a Checkweighman Act was passed in Parliament. This Act was to be amended and developed over the next fifty years, but it was *never* repealed. In 1860 therefore coal miners received the statutory right to elect and pay a man of their choosing to check the weights. These *checkweighmen* were to emerge as figures of great significance in the coalfield, playing a critical role in mining unionism. One clear consequence of the 1860 Act, was that trade-union organisation began to develop in a significantly different way, taking root not in popular, county-wide movements, but at the local collieries around local miners' lodges. Invariably these lodges were organised by their checkweighmen.

As a consequence of these developments a meeting was called in Leeds in November 1863 to discuss the prospect of mining unionism in the coming years. The meeting lasted six days, and in the end the delegates had thrashed out an understanding upon which they would establish a national union of mineworkers. First known as the National Association of Coal, Lime and Ironstone Miners of Great Britain, it was soon shortened to the more apposite Miners' National Union. This National Union was to survive almost thirty years. Its structure and ideals clearly reflected the times, and the severe difficulties which faced trade-union development in the coalfield. In the astute assessment of Page Arnot, it depended:

> not on the constitution of any existing body, but on the strength of custom and the fellow feeling amongst all underground workers.

He added, significantly, that:

> even in the most difficult times, this national bond of association continued to exist.[33]

The leadership of the Miners' National Union was in the hands of two men whose influence over the path of mining unionism proved to be enormous. Alexander Macdonald and William Pickard. They were supported by the old Methodist Chartist—the Reverend J.R. Stephens—who served as 'union Chaplain'. Macdonald was a Scot, born in Airdrie in 1821. Like most of the men present at the meeting in Leeds, he had started work in the mines at the age of eight. Macdonald's distinctiveness rested, in part, on the fact that he had enrolled as a student at Glasgow University at the age of twenty-five. Supporting himself with savings and summer employment in the pits he studied and became known all over Scotland as a miners' leader; in his thirties he became an agitator on behalf of the miners of Great Britain. William Pickard was born in the same year, in Burnley. On the day of his marriage, he was unable to read or write. He joined the Lancashire Union in 1838, and was elected agent in 1864.

Emphasis within the Miners' National Union was placed on encouraging the stabilisation and expansion of union membership around local county Associations. The positive role of the National Union was seen to lie in organising for parliamentary reform. Page Arnot has described its aims clearly and well. They were 'concerned largely with the creation of a common policy for legislation to better conditions of life and work'. This was put firmly by Macdonald at a miners' conference in 1873, when he reflected on his past:

> it was in 1856 that I crossed the Border first to advocate a better Mines Act, true weighing, the education of the young, the restriction of the age to twelve years, the reduction of working hours to eight in every twenty four, the training of managers, the payment of wages weekly in the current coin of the realm, no truck...by 1858 we were in full action for better laws.[34]

In the 1860s, there was strong support for Macdonald's views in the north of England, most especially amongst the devout Methodist leadership of the Northumberland miners. On returning from Leeds they were determined to re-establish a county association in the north. As with all previous attempts at unionisation this involved a joint approach across the counties of Northumberland and Durham. In 1865 however the Northumberland miners, with their organisation established, broke links with the Durham men and registered themselves as a separate member of the National Union. As one commentator put it: 'Northumberland was tired of the Durham miners who had repeatedly turned order into chaos.'[35] Another expressed the Northumberland sentiment in this way: 'it was like being connected with a body of death.'

These sentiments of defeat had been conveyed at the last united meeting of the counties, held in Newcastle in 1865. The only delegate from Durham was Ned Rymer of Byers Green and Spennymoor. Rymer had spent years attempting to organise the union in the Spennymoor area of the county. In his autobiography he wrote of how:

> In my travels through the Durham coalfields I found out the chief hindrances and difficulties lying in the way of unionism. Among those were ignorance, cowardice, spies and informers, mistrust, the yearly bond, living in colliery houses or hovels, and no place in which to hold meetings except on or near colliery premises. That there are, and always were, brave men amongst the Durham miners is unquestionable; and I deeply regret that I am forced to withhold so many good men's names from this autobiography for fear of injuring them—that is if they are still living. Like myself they are getting old, and I know the con-

> ditions under which they work. There are still men mean and cowardly enough to limit or lop off the means of existence of these unionists. This, then, was my situation—no work, no means of living, the coal trade my sworn enemy. Was I to submit to bow my knee and hurry into penal servitude with slavery staring me in the face? My decision was swift and final...I plunged right into the struggle to try and arouse the Durham miners from the state of non-unionism which every sensible man saw and felt with shame.[36]

At that conference Rymer described Durham as the 'black spot in England' for mining unionism. In spite of a series of strikes—including the famous 'rocking strike' at Willington which focused on the question of weighing—trade-union organisation repeatedly foundered. Contemporary trade-union organisers put the problem down to a combination of factors amongst which were listed 'the professed recklessness and untutored nature' of the Durham pitman. Of greater significance, perhaps, was the regime of control which we have referred to as 'the Durham System'. In the 1850s, this had proven a particularly powerful weapon for 'the coal trade' in its attempts to prevent unionisation. An example of its potency had been seen in the 1844 strike and in the manifesto produced by Londonderry in defiance of his 'unreasonable pitmen'. In this manifesto he declared to the shopkeepers and tradesmen in his town of Seaham that:

> if they will give credit to pitmen who hold off work, and continue in the Union, *such men will be marked by his agents and overmen*, and will never be employed in his collieries again, and the shopkeepers may be assured that they will never have any custom or dealings with them from Londonderry's large concerns that he can in a manner prevent...it is neither fair, just or equitable that the resident trades in his own town should combine and assist the infatuated workmen or pitmen in prolonging their own miseries by continuing an insane strike, and an unjust and senseless warfare against their proprietors and masters. [our emphasis][37]

The political control which the employers exerted over the village (through the 'marking' of troublemakers) was used throughout the 1850s and 1860s to considerable effect. John Wilson wrote of the problems faced in establishing a union lodge and meeting place in Sherburn Hill. After much argument and effort a 'small lodge [was] formed'. But:

> Our difficulties did not end with the formation. The most important to us was a meetingplace, or at least a room to take the contributions. This could not be got. We tried every public house in the village, but without avail. There was a great fear, and we

> were compelled to have recourse to a field, and many a time the payments have been made and the business done in it.[38]

Eventually they obtained a room within the co-operative store, only to be turned out of this by colliery officials who decided that the room should be used as a reading room and library 'something with which to educate the workmen'. It was a need, as Wilson notes, 'never seen until then'. He remembers it in this way:

> A deputation, consisting of three of the leading officials on the colliery, were sent to meet the store committee, with an agreement ready drawn up. I was on the committee, but all the others were men in positions on the colliery. The deputation attended. They produced the agreement. I remember one clause (the vital clause). As near as I can remember it ran as follows: 'The owners of the colliery would take the room at a yearly rental for a reading room and library. The store committee could have the use of it on two nights per week for any purpose they chose, trade-union purposes excepted.' With regret I say it, in spite of the opposition myself and another could offer, the agreement was signed, and the union lodge was turned into the street; fortunately one publican had got past his fears, and we found accommodation in his house.[39]

Within the village therefore 'social space' was highly circumscribed. The Chartists had discovered this. The *Northern Star* noted in 1842 how:

> if colliers are only found talking about politics over a pot of beer, it becomes hard work for the publican to get his licence renewed.[40]

Ironically, it was to be the chapel and not the public house which provided the main physical arena for trade-union organisation in the north. And with this development came the routinisation of the evangelical sect. Opposed to drink and gambling, committed to regular work habits and the stability of family life the Methodists in their earnestness, provided an alternative cultural strand within the working class. In their support of this, employers provided land and the economic support for chapels. George Parkinson describes how this process took place under Lambton:

> Many were being saved and the colliery viewer, Tom Smith, had the good sense to see that the converted men were punctually at the pit on Monday morning instead of lounging at the public house. He offered to alter Jacob Speed's cottage at the end of the row, so that it could be used as a chapel. The colliery workmen were sent, and part of the needful timber was provided. The roof was raised several feet, partitions removed, and a gallery at each

side and at the back was put up; two large windows put in, and the doorway protected by a small porch. Thus the chapel was provided, which, with necessary alterations, has served its purpose to the present day.

Pew rent at the rate of 9d. per quarter was charged for seats in the side gallery, the money thus raised being devoted to the provision of paper, pens and ink for the writing-classes in the Sunday School. Eighteen shillings per quarter was the regular amount thus raised for some time.

The chapel thus created was the centre of almost all extra-domestic life. Its only competitor was the public-house; and gradually, all that made for good living, high character, and even the elements of education, found its home and sphere in the little sanctuary. The work was maintained at the cost of many sacrifices and much self-denial by the poorly-paid pitmen, who found in the Methodist services their consolation amidst hardships and their inspiration and hope for better things to come.[41]

The chapels, once established, provided convenient meeting halls within the villages, and even within the patronage of the employers, places through which miners and their families obtained a degree of independence within the paternal order.[42] In building their trade union however, they still faced the opposition of the employers, who would regularly use their powers to the full in the face of organised resistance. In Murton in 1865 the miners struck, and in response, the company imported 300 men and their families from Cornwall and Devon. These were followed by another 128 men, 111 of them with wives and children.

Powers such as these exerted an important obstacle to trade-union organisation in the county. In generally assessing them, it is worth considering the views of the man who had, in 1863, been responsible for organising the Durham coalfield. In a letter to the *Durham Chronicle* in October 1869, William Crawford (who was to become the first full-time General Secretary of the DMA) wrote of the obstacles that had stood in the way of establishing a trade-union organisation in the county. Here, he gave central place to the Durham phenomenon of 'yearly hirings'. In his view:

their 'beneficial effects' have been to reduce the wages of the miners from [between] 15 to 30 percent. Those yearly hirings have brought the county to the lowest possible social condition and, when brought, kept it there rendering organisation difficult. They have been the curse, the withering blighting curse of thousands of miners in that county.

The full significance of this view is perhaps illustrated by the strike that had taken place at the Monkwearmouth Colliery in Sunderland earlier that year. This strike involved the workmen in open dispute with the bond, and it was the precursor to its abolition across the county.

When hired as usual in March, the Monkwearmouth hewers were informed that due to the depressed state of coal prices their wages would be reduced from the previous year. The reduction was from 7 shillings to 5 shillings and 10 pence for a score of tubs. This price was established in the bond. By April, however the men were clear that they couldn't make a 'fair day's wage'. Receiving no concessions from the owners, they went on strike in May. During the dispute an incident took place which was seen by trade unionists as being particularly revealing of the methods adopted by the Durham employers 'to break the ranks of the workmen'. This account is by John Wilson who also became General Secretary of the DMA.

> The manager of the colliery was a man well known in the north of England coal trade, Mr R. Heckles. He, believing there was great power in a jug of beer, when the strike had continued for a fortnight sent six notes for fifty men each to get a quart of ale per man. These were placed before a meeting of 250 men 'on the offer of the beer being announced the men replied that the notes were to be sent back, as the day had gone when the men were to be bought with beer, but that beef and bread would be better, and a resolution was carried not to resume work except at last year's prices'.[43]

This strike was clearly in breach of the bond and as a result four of them were summoned to appear before the Sunderland Magistrates on 21 June 1869, where they were charged under the Masters and Servants Act. The Monkwearmouth men were represented by Mr W.P. Roberts, the Manchester solicitor who had been retained by the Durham miners in the 1840s and advised them during the 1844 Strike. During the hearing Roberts said that he had:

> been told by the most influential men amongst the workmen that they wanted to be free from the villainous and iniquitous bond, and they would undertake to leave the houses within days.

In this way, in a courtroom in the middle of a dispute, the owner's bond was for the first time cancelled by mutual consent. Wilson records how:

> The men immediately arranged for vacating the houses and handing in their lamps. In one instance this was done in a unique and striking manner. The men formed in procession, over 300 in number, each man carrying his lamp and a copy of the colliery rules. Marching to the colliery they handed in their lamps, and returned the rules of the overmen.

He adds, significantly, that by publicly attempting to enforce the bond through the Court the employers had miscalculated. The effect of the trial was to be seen in:

> the solidifying of the whole of the workmen of Wearmouth, as the deputies and others [who while passively remaining from work had never taken active part in the strike] now threw themselves into the struggle, and made common cause with the hewers...the further effect was the impetus given to the cause of unionism throughout the county.[44]

As a consequence of the strike action at Wearmouth, several of the leading trade unionists were blacklisted. Ned Cowey was one of these men. A Primitive Methodist, he was six feet three inches tall and was later described as having 'a massive and commanding presence', a 'deep voice and a gift of eloquence.' Involved in a previous strike against the bond in 1858 he was blacklisted then and spent several years as a seaman. Blacklisted again, this time he followed Matthew Rymer's earlier example and journeyed south—in his case to the coal mines of Yorkshire. There he quickly became checkweighman, and he was elected President of the Yorkshire Miners' Association in 1873, remaining in office until his death in 1903. Known as 'the iron man' he was a dedicated trade unionist who became deeply committed to the building of a national federation of coal miners.[45]

The loss of men like Cowey was significant. But the breaking of the bond at Monkwearmouth was more so. It led the way for the 1872 Act which legally removed bonded labour from all of the Durham pits. While ever mindful of Marx's reservations about the limited freedom obtained by free wage labour (a freedom to sell labour power) the political and social significance of this shift in Durham shouldn't be underestimated. The comments of another German sociologist—Georg Simmel—are perhaps appropriate, dealing as they do with the removal of bonded labour in Europe. In his view the removal of servitude had the immediate effect of 'eliminating the presence of irrevocable dependency upon a particular master'; a situation he saw as the 'real antipode to freedom'. Without the bond:

> the worker is already on his way to a personal freedom despite objective bondage. That this emergent freedom has little continuous influence upon the material situation of the worker should not prevent us from appreciating it.[46]

These observations seem particularly pertinent in the context of Durham. For here miners once described as 'reckless', 'untutored', and 'the body of death' rapidly transformed themselves into the most steadfast supporters of trade-union organisation in Britain.

This transformation was achieved thanks in no small part to the catalytic activities of men like Rymer who in the 1860s had tramped the

Tommy Ramsey 'when eggs are scarce, eggs are dear; when men are scarce, men are dear'.

county, organising meetings and linking up union activists. He describes how:

> With Byers Green as my centre I attended meetings at home, at Spennymoor, Coxhoe, Cassop, Herrington Hill, Kelloe, Trimdon, Trimdon Grange, Wingate, Thornley, Shotton, Haswell, South Hetton, Great Hetton, Dawdon, Follonsby, Houghton, Shiney Row, The Felling, Pelton Fell, West Stanley, Annfield Plain, Townlea, Crook, Evenwood, West Auckland, Willington, etc. An open-air mass meeting was held at Pittington Hill, on a pay Saturday, at which 15,000 miners were present.

That meeting was also attended by W.P. Roberts, 'the miners' Attorney General'. At Leeds, and at Pittington Hill, elements of the old Chartist organisation remained. Equally, in spite of decades of non-unionism, Rymer was able to write of sharing the platform 'with many of the best local leaders in Durham.' Mining unionism, notorious for its ebbs and flows, is also famous for its consistency—for the continuity of sets of understandings, held together by custom—which resurfaces (in some senses literally) as circumstances change. In 1865 at Pittington Hill Rymer describes how the programme for discussion:

> contained all the wrongs and iniquities suffered by the miners. On that day I declared war on the non-union monster and on the tyranny of the coal owners. After the mass meeting a delegate meeting was held on the spot, and I was authorised, at a salary of 25s. per week, to use all the means in my power to form a county union. There was no railway accommodation or trap provided, so that I was left to my own methods in reaching the several districts from home. Many of the collieries had no local union, and often I could neither get a bellman, chairman, nor refreshment—not even a place of rest. In such cases I had to call the meetings and speak without chairman in the street or on some waste ground. In order to reach home at night I had to travel perhaps six, eight or ten miles. Several times I travelled over 20 miles in a day, called a meeting, spoke in the open-air and refreshed myself from what I carried in my bag. At Spennymoor, Coxhoe, Wingate, Thornley, Hetton, Moorsley, Houghton, West Auckland, Tow Law, Stanley and one or two other places things were different. Provision was made for my comfort, and every encouragement given me.[47]

Rymer refers to this period as a 'stormy epoch'. It was one in which, as a result of agitation and organisation, the basis for trade unionism re-emerged in Durham. He records meetings regularly taking place in which trade unionists (including several of the men 'sacrificed' at Monkwearmouth), addressed miners in an attempt to build a union and to 'infuse new life into the apathetical and indifferent men of Durham.' The same names crop up. Men who were at the Leeds meeting, men who had been actively involved in the 1850s, men who were to become established as full time officials of the miners' unions. Men like Thomas Burt of Northumberland, who spoke at Sherburn Hill on 25 September 1869. For him the appeal of trade unionism clearly lay in the arena of self-interest, arguing that:

> if the miners of the County of Durham compared their condition with any of the great combined bodies of English workmen they would at once see how different their position might have been had they been counted.

There were other men too. Tommy Ramsey was one. In the north at that time people would summon attention for meetings or public announcements with a wooden rattle or crake. Ramsey travelled everywhere with his crake and through the non-union period, as a blacklisted miner, he spoke on the advantages of collectivism and trade unionism:

> when eggs are scarce, eggs are dear; when men are scarce, men are dear.

This was the simple principle of political economy which 'the crake man' delivered in the Durham villages. Often he received rough treatment and ridicule for his pains. He was a close friend of W.A. Patterson who was to become General Secretary of the Association. Patterson, a quiet man, was also blacklisted, and he chaired Burt's meeting in 1869. At that time he was the least optimistic member of this group of activists feeling that they had 'several times tried to form a union but had failed, the men appearing somehow to have no confidence in them'.

These men literally tramped the coalfield, linking together the small independent lodges and societies of unionised miners. Often sleeping, as one of them was later to note with eloquence, 'in a room whose walls were the horizon and the roof studded with the stars of heaven.' In their speeches, their first aim was to establish the moral iniquity of the System in Durham, and to offer the possibility of an alternative—built around collective support and the absence of the bond. In this way, all of these men were involved in an attack upon the moral and political basis of the old paternal order in Durham. As a group they held regular meetings, which took place after the large public meetings. They were sustained and united too by their religion—for almost all of them were Primitive Methodists, many of them lay preachers.

These Methodists, in the practice of their religion, developed skills which were easily transferable into the world of social organisation and economic bargaining. As preachers, and Sunday School teachers they became versed in public speaking; their literacy was essential as a way of life and state of mind which was easily accommodated to the routines of meeting attendance, agendas and minute taking. They created a way of life based upon respectability, responsibility and self education. But it was a way of life for a few only. Chapel-going Methodists in Chester-le-Street, Easington and Houghton, amounted to just 13 percent of the local population in 1851. Nevertheless it was through these chapels that a trade union, religious elite emerged within the working class.[48] In the 1850s these men existed as a *cadre* within coalfield society. They met regularly (often over many years), corresponded, shared information and argued over politics and legislation. As a cadre they were fuelled by their experience of exploitation and unfairness in the mine but they were formed through more general pressures within civil society of the coalfield. It was they who formed the union, established its rules and provided the first full-time officials. Once the Association was firmly established, it provided them with the basis for reproducing themselves as a leadership group within the union.

3
A County Association

We need not tell you, that there is established in Durham an Association of coal miners, whose aim is to seek by legal and moral means an improved social condition.

William Crawford

IN DURHAM, at the Market Tavern, on 20 November 1869 a meeting took place of Durham miners—all of them active trade unionists—to re-establish a trade union on the Durham coalfield. The members of that meeting formed the Durham Miners' Mutual Confident Association, a small organisation that was to grow into the established union of the Durham Miners, known universally as the DMA. In its first years the Association embraced all grades of men working in and around the collieries. Quite quickly, however, the colliery enginemen, the mechanics and the cokemen left, founding their own, separate, organisations. In 1878, these unions regrouped once again into a Federation Board, a 'federation of forces', organised to 'protect their joint interests', realising that separately 'negotiating with Owners who act as one body, we must be placed at a very serious disadvantage'. This Federation Board established a powerful basis for trade-union and political organisation across the county, and was to give rise to a distinctive form of organisation and leadership that had its roots deep in the 'Durham System'.

The Association and the Coalfield

In the nineteenth century the Durham coalfield was established as the largest, and most productive of the coalfields in Britain. In 1880, 71,000 men and boys (57,515 underground and 14,127 on the surface) were employed in the Durham mines producing 28 million tons of coal. The following forty years witnessed an enormous further expansion in coal production, with national output doubling from 133 million tons in 1875 to 264 million tons in 1910. By this time, Durham had been overtaken by

Table 3.1[1] Collieries on the Durham Coalfield c.1870

	Numbers of men employed				
					Total
Size	0–99	100–249	250–599	over 600	
Collieries	25	90	34	8	157
%	16%	57%	21%	5%	100

South Wales as the biggest of the coalfields, but it was still an enormous producer with an output of over 41 million tons, much of it for export. This increase was associated with a dramatic rise in the numbers of men employed in the Durham mines. In 1905, 88,820 men were employed underground and another 24,054 on the surface; this number had increased to 132,661, with 33,146 on the surface, by 1913.

In its scale, Durham can be contrasted with the Northumberland coalfield. In 1875, while collieries in Durham produced over 25 million tons of coal, the Northumberland output was barely one quarter of this. And although the Northumberland coalfield accelerated its output as part of the general expansion in the industry, it never produced more than a third of the Durham mines. Such was the size of the Durham coalfield that in 1869 William Crawford had considered it 'too wide and extensive for one association'. He had cited Yorkshire as an example of a single coalfield covered by more than one Association. In Durham, he argued, there was a case for three separate Associations, organised on a geographical basis. This was necessary 'to make the work not only practical but effective'. This was not the path taken, yet the warnings alert us to a further dimension of the problem faced by trade-union organisations in the county, and make clear how practical ideas of organisation, finance, and administration were centrally in the minds of these trade unionists.

In 1870, at the time of the first annual general meeting of the newly formed Association, 157 pits were working in the coalfield. Mostly they were situated in the south and west of the county, and mostly they were small. Twenty-five pits employed fewer than 25 men, and the vast majority employed between 100 and 249 men. There were thirty-four medium sized pits and just eight large collieries, with over 600 miners employed. (See Table 3.1.)

The eight large collieries were situated in the east of the county, with their deep shafts sunk through the limestone into the coal measures: they were Wearmouth (600), Houghton (600), Ryhope (900), Seaham (600), Haswell (700), Hetton (1100), Murton (800), and Tudhoe (1000). Each of these pits had elected checkweighmen, and developed a local organisation, and each had sent delegates to the early meetings of the DMA in

1869 and 1870. In the years that followed, these mines were to continue to be a powerful basis for organisation in the coalfield. At the beginning of the twentieth century they were to be joined by other, more massive, collieries as new sinkings took place and the coalfield expanded.

At its beginning, the newly-formed union had attracted just 2,500 members. Once recognised by the employers, however, and with the repeal of the bond, membership grew dramatically. By 1876 the Durham Miners' Association had 35,250 members organised in 213 active lodges. Together they returned a quarterly sum of £7,930 to the Durham Office, which in that year had moved to the new Miners' Hall at 58 North Road. This building had been commissioned after a competition involving several local architects. It cost a total of £6,000, and was indeed a grand place. It contained a council chamber large enough to seat all of its lodge delegates, which measured 52 by 34 feet. On the balcony outside stood marble statues of the union's first officials who looked out over the busy main street of the city. Above these statues was a clock tower which rose thirty feet above the main hall. The clock was illuminated at night, and in recognition of its public worth, the City Council agreed to pay the cost of its illumination. From this building the union published a weekly newspaper—the *Miners' Watchman.*

In the space of just seven years the Durham Miners' Association had established itself as an organisation of real substance. By the turn of the century its membership had passed 100,000, and the near complete unionisation of underground workers had been achieved. In Allen's assessment 'in members and solidarity Durham had become, from the shaky less than 2000 start, one of the four most powerful components within the National Miners' Union'. This growth in membership was accompanied by a:

> growth in size and scope of activity. The Durham Miners' Association had...become an institution in itself, surrounded by its own bureaucracy and with twice as many rules as it had in 1872.[2]

The speed of this development is all the more remarkable when weighed against the difficulties experienced by trade unionists in the county in the 1850s and 1860s, the more so when it is remembered that miners were formally unskilled workers and when we consider the problems encountered in the other coalfields in the Great Depression. No other group without the market advantages of skill and the control of apprenticeship achieved unionisation with such speed or with such completeness. The story of how this came about is complex, and it is one which has a bearing upon our understanding of the general process of working-class formation. It involves the development of the union as a formal organisation with increasing numbers of paid officials and funds large enough to support a wide range of activities within the coalfield.

The Miners' Hall, 58 North Road, Durham.

This process, of course, was related to forces at work in the coal mines and in the mining villages. Also it related to the ideology of the various leadership groups and their assessment of tactics, strategies and of political organisation.

From its inception, the DMA retained a solicitor. At the first meeting in Durham it was moved that 'the agitation of the proposed organisation to be directed at the yearly bond' and a resolution was sent to Macdonald, the President of the National Union, to the effect that:

> Mr MacDonald should be informed that the miners of the County of Durham considered the bond to be a great evil, and would hail with the greatest gratification any legislation enactment providing for its abolition.[3]

This preoccupation with legality is not surprising. The coal industry—most especially in the system that operated in Durham—was underpinned by law. This was made plain first in the Wearmouth strike, and again in the earliest weeks of the Association's history.

At that time the officials of the Association were employed in the mines. The secretary (a Mr A. Cairns) was checkweighman at the Thornley Colliery. This village had been a centre of radical activity in the previous two decades, and men from the Thornley mine were centrally involved in the struggle to establish the DMA. Another Thornley man—John Jackson—served on the first executive committee of the Association. On binding day in 1870, the manager of the colliery announced that he could not bind either Cairns or Jackson. As the Checkweighman Act then required that the checkweigher be employed in the mine, this refusal to bind effectively removed from the men their elected representatives. The dispute was settled in the short term through arbitration. This was the course pressed by the DMA at the time, and shows their reluctance to be involved in protracted strikes. However, a more permanent solution was clearly needed, and this was found through legislation. In 1872 the bond was abolished by Act of Parliament. During the next twenty years the Checkweighman's Act was subjected to successive amendments until, in 1894, it was established that miners were free to elect as their checkweighman any person of their choosing, the requirement that he be employed in the mine being removed.

The operation of the bond within the Durham System had been an obvious hindrance to trade-union organisation. Its abolition, and the regular and positive amendments of the Checkweighman Act in favour of an independent representation of the miners on the surface of the mine, contributed positively to the position of trade-union activists and officials in the county. It also clearly had an effect upon the confidence of the miners and their appreciation of what was possible. We have already drawn attention to the strong mood of pessimism amongst the trade-union activists in Durham in the late 1860s. Their perpetual complaint was of fecklessness and unpredictability; of a mining population which swayed from being a passive victim of the most manipulative aspects of paternalist practices to moments of aggravated fury. The desire of the activists was to regulate the behaviour of the coal miners as a *class* of workmen; to organise them in disciplined opposition to the employers, and to establish the Miners' Association as a powerful and legitimate institution within the county. The breaking of the bond was critical in this. It enabled the trade union to compete with the coal owners for the loyalty of the miner. The establishment of the trade-union, and the building up of a trade-union membership included much more than a process of rational administration and collective bargaining.

The earliest circulars written by William Crawford and distributed around the county are very revealing. Written in a powerful rhetorical style, they browbeat the miners, who boast of their status as Englishmen yet:

> as men you have lost all respect for yourselves; you have sunk beneath the dignity of men, by not resisting the aggressive policy of your employers. You have become passive slaves, by leaving your condition and interests in the hands of Durham County Coal Owners, who have moulded and fashioned your condition to suit themselves, just as easily as clay is fashioned in the hands of the potter; and who have watched your, or rather their own, interests so closely, that they have plunged you into a state of almost irretrievable ruin.

They criticise the miners for 'weakness' and liken them to murderers.

> How long do you intend pursuing this suicidal course, because suicidal it unquestionably is and I very much think that your conduct might appropriately bear the application of a much stronger term. When one person instantaneously deprives another of life, we call it murder, and the full penalty of the law is meted out to the individual. 'Serve them right', say you, and we fully endorse the sentiment. But do you ever remember that many of you, by your voluntary actions, are perpetrating a kind of prolonged heartless cruelty, by depriving, not only of comforts, but necessaries, those whom you are morally bound to protect and properly support? And I am not at all certain that such conduct should not be placed in the category of murder, seeing that, by your own acts, you continue a social condition of things, prejudicial to physical health, and are thus the means of cutting short a continuance of otherwise prolonged lives. Do not say you would, but cannot command a sufficiency of these things you ought to have. Have you ever tried—tried in that spirit of manly, not to say parental earnestness, which only makes a rebuff a spur

> to further effort, and renewed energy? Did your history present to view a class of men working in this way without being able to effect any good, you might have been pitied. But it is not so; had it been, your condition could not, would not, have been what it is today.

They held the miners open to the displeasure of God.

> On looking back, we beheld nothing but the deepest apathy, the utmost ruinous indifference, the most abject slavery, resulting as a matter of consequence, in deprivation, social misery, and shortened lives. To say that you ought to be ashamed of yourselves is language far too mild, wherewith to describe your reprehensible conduct. It is conduct which ought, and unquestionably does call forth the severe displeasure of God, and all really good men; and how any man can enter his closet, and there wrestle with God for the world's redemption, and yet stand aloof from his institution, is a query which must be left to philosophic minds to unravel. I have no hesitation in calling such conduct, the veriest cant hypocrisy, the quintessence of inconsistency. Remember that in this, there is not a neutral position; those who are not for us, are against us. You by your sloth retard, if not block, our progression. You are not only a curse to yourselves, but you are likewise a withering curse to thousands and tens of thousands of ill-clothed wives and famishing children in the County of Durham.[4]

In building the Association 'non-financial members' and 'non-unionists' were identified as a major problem. John Wilson identified them as 'the permanent disease of trade unionism, for from the origin of time there have been men who were ready to take all and give nothing.'[5] The first rule of the Association set its object as being: 'To raise funds by contributions, levies, fines and donations, for the purpose of mutual support,' and the first meetings of the Association discussed of ways of dealing with non-unionists. Wilson observes how many of the tactics discussed 'were crude' and it would be surprising if violence wasn't used, given the critical nature of the issues involved. Formally, the Association asserted the need for its members to 'keep themselves straight by the books' and for each of them to be issued with a card (referred to as a 'passcard') which would be used as proof of union membership. This 'passcard' became an important source of identity within the villages. Through its use ambiguity was removed, and villages polarised between groups of members and non-members. Men refused to share the cage with non-unionists, or to work with them. This process of polarisation (the identification of the non-unionist as 'the other') was encouraged and accelerated by the trade union. In his speeches and circulars Crawford made it clear that he favoured the total ostracism of non-unionists by DMA members and their families. In a style which became renowned, he wrote:

> You should at least be consistent. In numberless cases you refuse to descend and ascend with non-unionists. The right or wrong of such I will not now discuss; but what is the actual state of things found in many parts of the county? While you refuse to descend and ascend with these men, you walk to and from the pit, walk in and out—bye with them—nay, sometimes you work with them. You mingle with them at home over your glass of beer, in your chapels, and side by side you pray with them in your prayer meetings. The time has come when there must be plain speaking on this matter. It is no use playing at shuttlecock in this important portion of our social life. Either mingle with these men in the shaft, as you do in every other place, or let them be ostracised at all times and in every place. Regard them as unfit companions for yourselves and for your sons, and unfit husbands for your daughters. Let them be branded, as it were, with the curse of Cain, as unfit to mingle in ordinary, honest, and respectable society. Until you make up your minds to this completely and absolutely ostracise these goats of mankind, cease to complain as to any results that may arise from their action.

A theme is established here which will become a familiar one. It is of the link between the mine and the village; between 'work' and 'community'. Under the Durham system the mine and the village were spatially coterminous. Most of the men employed in the mine lived in a company house in the village. Work and life intermingled in a detailed and permanent way. The paternal system made this link clear materially (by linking employment to the house) and ideologically through a powerful and united sense of family and dependency. In this way through the method of aristocratic rule the village and the mine became united as a total system. In attempting to establish itself, the trade union needed to develop an approach which related to this reality. In Durham it wasn't feasible for the union to restrict itself to the workplace even if it had wanted to. Crawford's circular is clearly a tactical move; it is also a philosophical treatise in which trade unionism is linked not so much with *economic* bargaining as with sets of *moral* relations. To an important extent this reflected reality. In Durham the position of the worker in society (as unionist or non-unionist) was a topic which drew upon the deep range of political and philosophical antagonisms. These became a pronounced part of the affairs of the union in the 1870s, and Crawford was invariably in the forefront of the discussions. In the first years of that decade a local minister, the Rev. Blagdon of Newbottle, had announced that he 'hated and detested unions'. For this he was taken to task. His attitude was contrasted to that of Christ. The conditions of life of the working people were made clear and the parson advised that 'it is a self evident fact that nothing will render human existence so miserable and short as social destitution, bringing, as a matter of consequence, mental pressure and anxiety of mind.' Crawford continued in this vein:

> History and observation alike teach that, where a people are socially depressed, moral culture is a most difficult matter and, where moral culture is no easy task, to spiritualise is next to an utter impossibility. So that in reality, when rightly viewed, there is very near kinship, and ought to be, in making a very close connection between the Union...and the work in which this reverend gentleman is engaged. Whether or not Mr Blagdon will endorse these sentiments I cannot say; however...in future [he should]...cease to give utterance to such vehement expressions as hating and detesting that about which he seems to understand but little indeed. By pursuing such a course he will in future save himself the merited contempt of his parishioners.[6]

Church, state, and community—the early established trade union had to operate in each of these areas of life, often in adverse economic circumstances. The employers were antagonistic to mining unions (with or without the bond), and the ascendancy of the coal owners meant that much 'normal' activity was made difficult. The new union found it almost impossible to find a printer willing to take their business. In the end J.A. Veitch and Sons of Durham agreed to take the risk. This small example supports the general conclusion that in Durham the struggle for mining unionism *had* to be conducted on all fronts. Without this it would fail. But in struggling on all fronts the DMA opened up the possibility of quite dramatic successes. If it could but establish itself as an organised, legitimate force, supported by a philosophy of labour and the weight of moral sanction, it could succeed in bringing all the miners under its umbrella. And this would be a force to be reckoned with.

The Union Organised

At the first council meeting held by the Association on 21 March 1871, it was decided that it would be represented by four full-time officials (or 'agents'), who would negotiate with the employers' 'agents'. These men were required to live in Durham, were paid and housed by the Association, and were in the first years subject to annual reflection by the Council meeting. The first four fully appointed officials were immortalised in those marble statues outside the New Miners' Hall.

The president was John Foreman, known everywhere as 'Foreman of Roddymoor'. He was a checkweighman at the Roddymoor Colliery in

The First Deputation, 17 February 1872. These are the men who first represented the Durham Miners' Association in negotiations with the coal owners. They are:
Back Row—*N. Wilkinson (*Treasurer*), W.H. Patterson (*Vice-President*), M. Thompson, T. Ramsey, G. Jackson. J. Forman.*
Front Row—*W. Askew, W. Crawford (*President and Secretary*), J. Handy, T. Mitcheson.*

Crook, although he was born and brought up in the Northumberland coalfield. Incidentally, he was the only official working in the industry, and he continued to hold his position as checkweighman for four years before moving to Durham in 1874. The treasurer was Nicky Wilkinson from Trimdon Grange. He had become a tea salesman, having been sacked and blacklisted as a result of his trade-union activity. The agent was W.H. Patterson, whom we have mentioned earlier.

These men were dominated by the force and personality of the General Secretary, William Crawford. Photographs of him reveal a square set, bearded man with an intense gaze: a man not to cross lightly. Crawford as we have noted had been an organiser in Durham, but after the split in 1865 he became secretary of the Northumberland miners. He left this position (Thomas Burt succeeding him, and remaining in office for almost fifty years) to take up the secretaryship of the Cowpen co-operative store in Blyth. In 1870 he had applied for the position of agent with the newly-formed DMA, and he was selected from a number of candidates.

We have already seen something of Crawford's style. In its intensity, it had more in common with the pulpit and with the rhetoric of religious movements than with rational, bureaucratic models often associated with trade-union organisations. By his own account, Crawford attributed his position 'socially and spiritually, largely to Primitive Methodism'. In those early days what the DMA offered him was not a 'service' but a 'calling'[7]: it was the source of liberty and solution to the problem of human dignity. Strategically, it reflected Crawford's concern and determination to breathe life into that 'body of death' that had become associated with the miners of Durham. In this he also took in hand that other aspect of Durham which had offended Burt and the leaders in Northumberland; with Crawford came a 'respect for office' which was to become an enduring feature of the organisation in Durham. Metcalf has commented on this by pointing to the fact that:

> a physical type of leadership was necessary, in fact the display of a bold front was the only means of holding together the majority of miners who appreciated Crawford's manner and personality. It gained for him respect by example, in that here was one of themselves—'the pitman and the son of a pitman.' Although Crawford adopted this role, which was natural to him, men on deputations visiting the General Secretary always called him 'Mr Crawford', and took off their hats or caps before being ushered into his presence.[8]

In his evaluation Robin Page Arnot makes an interesting comparison between Crawford and Burt:

> the Durham leader, the more turbulent and fighting character, found himself following initially the same policies and methods as Thomas Burt. Crawford was perhaps not always happy in his path, partly because he retained some of the traditions of the struggles of Chartist times, whereas Burt represented the break with Chartism and Socialism.[9]

Wilson's assessment of him is also an astute one:

> Never had any man more force of character or more executive power. His individuality was very large. He had no love of platform work and the love for that sphere lessened as he grew older; but he had no superior, and few equals, in his grasp of, and power to find a solution to, the peculiar difficulties and complications which arise in an occupation like the miners'.[10]

Wilson's final summation of Crawford is also revealing. He was he said: 'a solver of difficulty and a manager of men, and in every way, fitted the part of a secretary of a trade-union organisation'.

The chairman of the Association during this period was John

Foreman. Described by Wilson as 'a most respected and gentlemanly president', he took office after the short period in which Crawford was both secretary and president. The relationship between the two men set the tone for the DMA during its lifetime. Elsewhere amongst the coal miners (e.g. Yorkshire and South Wales) the President was the dominant official. Not so in Durham. Following Crawford, it was the General Secretary whose position was most powerful. Equally important was the exceptional Durham practice of filling these two leading positions by automatic promotion rather than through direct ballot of the membership. This arrangement was referred to as 'the custom of the colliery'.

Under Crawford's leadership the Association grew in strength. It rapidly recruited members, especially from amongst the coal hewers. These were the men directly involved in cutting the coal, and in the 1850s and 1860s they had developed strong local ties and customary controls over the organisation of work in the coal mines. In one sense these controls, and the support they could generate in spontaneous action, were a source of strength. In another, they reflected the 'chaos' referred to by the Northumberland leaders. In this context the early leaders of the DMA took a series of critical decisions. In contrast to developments in other coalfields where local autonomy continued, they decided that the Durham Association would, from the outset, be a *centralised* county-wide organisation. Contrary to Crawford's early views, it was agreed that there would be no quasi-independent districts with their own agents but one *county union,* established in Durham with its own area council and area officials. In this:

> The supreme government of the Association was vested in the Council which consisted of the President, the Secretary, the Treasurer and one member elected by each financial lodge as delegate. No matter what size the lodge was, it could only have one delegate, and the elected delegate representative only had one vote.[11]

This was a critical decision, taken after much debate over the virtues of having size of membership linked to voting power. The 'one lodge, one vote' rule made for a situation where power was divided among the lodges, and where the larger districts were unable to dominate the Council meeting. Here an important balance was established in the running of the Council business. It was a balance which emphasised the *county* over the *lodge.* Increasingly it was a balance which emphasised bureaucratic rules over local custom and spontaneity.

This was well illustrated in 1870 when the Association voted to guard its funds against the unconstitutional use of strike action. A county resolution made clear that:

William Crawford MP. General Secretary, Durham Miners' Association 1872–90 'pitman and son of a pitman'.

> any colliery coming out on strike in an unconstitutional way be not allowed any support from the central fund, or have their case considered at the Central Arbitration Board.[12]

This tendency toward county regulation by powerful officials and detailed rules was pushed further by the need for the new Association to establish collective bargaining relationships with employers. Prior to 1872 the coal owners in the north were loosely linked through the North of England United Coal Trade Association. This was not a negotiating body, nor did it attempt to regulate the coal trade. Its main concern was with legal matters and issues of legislation. With a union established in Durham these things changed, and the Durham Coal Owners' Association was established. It quickly approached the DMA. In a letter to the General Secretary which began 'Mr Crawford, my dear sir' it informed the union of the existence of the Coal Owners' Association and of a resolution passed to the effect that:

> it is considered desirable that a meeting should be held between the coal owners and a deputation of the representatives of the workmen...to discuss the various questions now in agitation by the workmen with a view to their adjustment.[13]

This concern to regulate 'the various questions now in agitation' fitted well with the concern of the new DMA leadership. Uppermost in their minds was the need to establish the Association as an organisation with sufficient funds to confer upon it a permanence that had escaped earlier attempts at unionisation in the county. They were also eager to be included in a regular bargaining relationship with the coal owners, and they responded most positively to this early invitation to meet. In relation to the employers therefore 'their leading principle was amicability'. This is the assessment of John Wilson and, in support, he cites a speech made by Crawford in 1873. Here Crawford made clear the ideas which governed his behaviour as a trade-union leader—the one moral, the other strategic. As a negotiator, he argued that his concern:

> had not been to get a thing because [we] had the power, but first of all to ask the question, 'was it right that we ought to have it?'

Equally, as a leader of the DMA he was concerned that:

> true valour is not shown in reckless and heedless action, but by waiting until the foe can be met on at least equal terms.[14]

The difference between Crawford and Wilson (which will become clearer soon) is obvious here and is similar to the comparison between Crawford and Thomas Burt. While Wilson and Burt were out and out reformers, detesting confrontation, strikes and unrest, Crawford was altogether tougher and less predictable. He had to be pushed down the reformist road. In the early 1870s he was dominated by a concern to establish the union at all costs. Often (and regularly) this brought him into open conflict with his members.

The nature of these conflicts can be seen from events which took place in 1872. On 21 March the DMA leaders were involved in a conference with the coal owners. They were informed that two collieries (Haswell and Castle Eden, both in the south east of the county) were on strike. Under Crawford's direction a telegram was sent to both lodges. It read:

> We regret to hear that Haswell and Castle Eden Collieries are idle. You must know that you are wrong, and we strongly advise you to commence work tomorrow, otherwise steps will be taken

> to repudiate such reprehensible conduct, and if necessary the strongest action will be taken in the matter.[15]

Two months later another strike broke out in the south east of the coalfield, this time in Seaham. The men at the colliery stopped work in response to a change in the pattern of shift work. Again Crawford's response was both swift and direct. Again in the form of a telegram:

> Do go to work. You must know you are wrong. You will get no support. Liable to punishment. Do return.[16]

In the ensuring fracas—in which the General Secretary was roundly condemned by the Seaham men and accused of insulting them—Crawford revealed much of the nature of the county union that had become established in Durham and the style of leadership which he had developed there.

> I have been accused of both insults and incivility; and why? Because, as in the case of Seaham, my opinion has been asked, or advice sought, and where such opinion or advice has been adverse to their own preconceived ideas of right or wrong, and they have been told so decisively but courteously, then I became uncivil...
>
> I commenced my present agency amongst the miners of Durham on 16 May 1870. From then till now I have done my utmost to protect and further their interests in a fair and equitable manner. Where I have decided the doing of owners or agents to be wrong I have not been slow to condemn them, and what I have done, will do again; where I have found the workmen to be wrong, I have pursued the same course, unhesitatingly making known my views without the slightest hesitation. If any man or number of men are mean and cowardly enough to think that I shall sit and become a mere machine of repetition, I beg to clearly intimate that they are sadly mistaken.[17]

He went on to insist on his right to hold to his own views amongst 'the folly of fools and the abuse of knaves'. This became the manner with which Crawford dealt with such issues. On another occasion a complaint from the Bearpark Lodge (involving an alleged insult by Crawford to Rymer on Gala Day) was framed in a resolution to Council to the effect 'that Mr Crawford serve three months notice'. He responded forcefully, his notes in the Council Programme asserting that he 'was prepared to account for what he'd done...and after that, if the Association so minded, he was prepared to leave them, not in three months, but in three days or three hours.'

Undoubtedly the building of any organisation requires discipline, and it was this which Crawford was determined to establish from the

Association's headquarters in Durham. In relating to the employers, however, the overwhelming concern was an accommodating one, stressing conciliation and arbitration and opposing strike action. In 1873 a joint committee of coal owners and union representatives was set up. This committee would, in the words of DMA General Secretary John Wilson:

> arbitrate, appoint arbitrators, or otherwise settle all questions...relating to matters of wages, practices of working, or any other subject that might arise from time to time at any particular colliery, and which shall be referred to the consideration of the Committee by the parties concerned.[18]

This spirit of conciliation and co-operation patterned the development of the new union. It had been clearly set by Crawford who, in a phrase which is both poignant and revealing, spoke of the union being involved in establishing 'the rules in operation as between master and servant'. It was in this framework that the DMA favoured arbitration 'as a logical way of settling those differences which in trade necessarily arise between employers and employed.'[19] Arbitration was seen as having the advantage of avoiding strikes and lockouts with 'all their commercial pain and misery.' An early circular penned by Crawford addressed the question 'Arbitration or Strike?'. In it the message was clear:

> If we persistently refuse to submit the entire matter to arbitration we must be prepared to cope with the following difficulties in conducting the struggle.

The circular went on to list four problems which were to remain with the union for years to come. These were (1) strongly organised employers—'the strongest combination...the north of England ever saw'; (2) 'stacks of coal and coke laid up in every direction in the county'; (3) the likely importation of coal and coke from other districts; (4) the antagonism of the press and 'public opinion'.[20]

These conditions were not new, nor were they to end in the nineteenth century. The politics of mining union needed to ground itself in this reality. Here the tension between 'reformist tactics' and revolutionary purpose became an acute one. In Northumberland, under Burt, those conditions foretold a liberal ideology which emphasised the united interests of capital and labour. Here the reformist tactic overwhelmed all other impulses in the politics of mining. In Durham (the larger coalfield, more strongly established in the coking and gas making industries) the tensions were clearer. Undoubtedly, the legal and economic conditions of mining created tremendous difficulties for an organisation barely established. This approach to trade unionism was revealed clearly in the motif on the banner of the Monkwearmouth Colliery. It was the strike at this colliery which had finally called into question the continuation of

John Foreman, President of the DMA 1872–1900. A 'much respected and gentlemanly President...more than an agent, a friend and example' (J. Wilson).

the bond. This banner (identical to the one carried until very recently by the miners at that pit) depicted a court scene with the miners' advocate delivering his address. This is described clearly as: 'The Cancelling of the Yearly Bond by Mr Roberts in 1869'; beneath are the words : 'come let us reason together.' On the reverse side is the slogan 'in God is all our trust'.

This account—which stresses discipline and accommodation—is an incomplete one, however. It neglects both the strategic aspect of Crawford's philosophy ('waiting until the foe can be met on at least equal terms') and the fact that areas of conflict were endemic in mining. The Association (in its existence as the collective voice of free workers) needed to give expression to these conflicts. If it chose not to, it risked deep internal antagonisms. Such an occasion took place in 1879. In that year, the owners had informed the joint committee that they required a reduction of wages in the county of 20 percent for underground workers and 12.5 percent for surface workers. A series of negotiations took place in which the miners' representatives opposed the extent of the reduction but agreed to the principle of lower wages. Given the depressed condition of the coal trade, they felt that there was little option, and the committee offered the owners either a reduction of 10 and 7.5 percent, or one of 7.5 and 6 percent and a further reference to arbitration. In a circular to the lodges the committee argued that:

> You must remember that there are times when prudent men do the best and get the most they can without running all the risks which always attend a stoppage of the pits when trade is paralysed and men both suffering and disorganised.[21]

This recommendation was not accepted; in fact news of it was greeted with spontaneous dissent across the county. Wilson wrote of how 'on every hand mass meetings were held protesting against the terms'.

And added:

> as is the case in matters of this kind, orators vehement if not polished sprang up from every quarter, whose stock-in-trade consisted of epithets which they hurled at the committee.[22]

As a consequence the employers announced that on 5 April they would unilaterally reduce the wages of underground miners by 15 percent and on the surface by 10 percent. This, the Association would not accept, and a strike ensued.

The county strike of 1879, the first one organised by the Durham Miners' Association, reveals a pattern which was to become familiar. The committee was very reluctant to support a strike which would be disruptive, expensive and likely to fail. In every way the dispute seemed at odds with their desire to build the Association through prudence and careful management. In a circular they pointed out that:

> we have spent in the years over strikes amongst our members, at large and small collieries, nearly one hundred thousand pounds, and there is not a single strike either of large or small dimensions, where we have not singularly failed.[23]

These strikes had reduced the Association's funds to £22,688 (of which, Wilson reminds us, £4,861 needed to be deducted 'as money invested in the Industrial Bank and Houghton and Shotton Workmen's Hall which was not available for strike purposes'); but their defeats had a deeper significance. Unemployment was increasing in the county, and miners were laid off work.

> Look around you and what do you find? On every hand you count idle men by hundreds and thousands. Many of these men have been idle for weeks and months. All their means have long since been spent, and they are waiting for work, begging for work and cannot find it.[24]

These conditions were not propitious ones for trade unionism, and the owners were not slow to point this out. At one meeting when the employers urged the Association's representative to accept the reduction one of them reminded them that:

> there are a large number of men outside the union and these men are not with you. The logic of events will decide the issues.[25]

The response he got from an Executive Committee member however was a combative one: 'You mean the logic of circumstances, the logic of the cupboard. You have a good ally in our poverty.' The disagreement here (logic of events; logic of circumstances) goes beyond semantics and it serves to illustrate the ways in which these features of mining (let us call them circumstances of class) repeatedly established their presence upon the activities of the Miners' Association. In their attempt to operate with a logic of administration the officials were continuously brought up against the day to day circumstances of class. It was unavoidable; and the tensions came through their very personalities, as well as the administrative structure of the union.

In 1879, therefore, as a result of 'circumstances of class', the miners went on strike, and the executive committee of the Association was set up as a strike committee. That the strike had come about at all was due to the meetings and protests that were organised in villages and districts on the coalfield. These meetings continued throughout the strike. Based upon locally organised groups of miners, they organised the striking men and discussed the failings of the Association. John Wilson was scathing in his assessment of the people involved in these activities. In no small part this was influenced by the abuse he received as a member of the Executive Committee. He wrote of how, before the strike 'certain of the committee were in fear, and came into public view as little as possible' and he described a particular incident which affected him. As chairman of the Wheatley Hill lodge he was marching to a mass meeting in Durham when he was spotted as a member of the Executive Committee.

> The first words heard were 'there's one of the ****; let us put him in the river.' The crowd surged and rocked. What the consequences might have been is hard to tell, but just when the feeling ran highest and he [Wilson] was most in danger, a man was knocked back overturning a drum which stood end up; and it

> went off with a loud report, and the cry was 'they are firing guns'.[26]

In the ensuing panic Wilson ('the culprit, one of the malodorous committee') was forgotten, and he survived unscathed—physically at least, for it is clear that this incident left a deep mark upon him. During the strike and afterwards he notes how local meetings persisted which were clearly 'unconstitutional'. He notes how 'the wildest statements' were made at them, and how as a consequence, 'the minds of the members became unsettled and discussion followed'. These meetings were generally seen as being disruptive, and the Executive Committee issued a circular:

> If you determine to let these men go on, doing their endeavours to undermine your Association, then be prepared to accept with that choice all the evil consequences which must arise therefrom. These are the men who would 'rather rule in hell than serve in heaven'. They have yet to learn the most important of all attainments—viz. how to rule themselves, before presuming to guide the thousands of people in this county. If complaints are to be made let them be made regularly and right. If reformations are needed, let them be sought in keeping with the constitution.[27]

This circular was issued after the strike was settled, on terms far more favourable than the employers had attempted to impose, and in their different ways both Crawford and Wilson understood the strike as a successful event. Neither of them however approved of the practice of informal meetings of miners being organised in parallel with the formal structure of the union. In one sense they had a point. In Durham, trade-union organisation faced the problem of building a common organisation for coal miners working for different employers under different conditions. The logic of the county union was that it attempted to unite all miners and benefit them all equally. The structure of the union was developed to that end. In Durham, as we have seen, strong traditions of local autonomy and customary practice persisted, and it was this which Crawford attempted to regularise through the discipline of his office and strict adherence to the rules of the union. However, we have seen how the constitution of the union treated all lodges equally. There was a strong feeling amongst activists in the larger lodges that *they* were unfairly treated and that their aspirations and organised strength were being held back by the officials in Durham. In 1879 their 'unconstitutional' organisation served to sway opinion within the Association. The tension between the 'constitutional' and the 'unconstitutional' way would remain, however. It can be seen as an ongoing dynamic in mining unionism which was, perhaps, most pronounced in Durham.

In 1879 these methods combined to produce a successful strike. Men

The banner of the Monkwearmouth Colliery.

not members of the Association (fearful perhaps of the consequences of an even more permanent branding as 'goats of mankind') refused to start work on the new terms. Wilson, for all his opposition to the strike (he refers to it as a stoppage of work—'it is a misnomer to call it a strike; [it] shouldn't have taken place') acknowledges that:

> one beneficial effect of the stoppage was the great number of men who joined the union. When the notices terminated there were collieries where the numbers were few; but these men, as if moved by the instinct of self-preservation, ceased to work, and to a large extent became members, remaining to this day. *It was the greatest piece of missionary effort ever seen.* Instead of disunion and isolated action there was manifest loyal adhesion and solidity.[our emphasis][28]

At the outset, Crawford was also opposed to the strike; but when he saw it as unavoidable, he entered into its organisation with verve and determination and, once settled, he offered his assessment of it in his monthly circular:

> the strike which took place in the months of April and May last will ever remain an epoch in the history of the Association. A more complete success never took place. At its beginning...I was amongst those who doubted, but did not despair, and the end more than justified the expectations of the most sanguine. If we take the entire history of trade disputes, it will be found that not one ever commanded so much public sympathy. We had justice and right on our sides and we took the only wise course: viz. to let the public know it. We deplore strikes as much as anyone can do, but there are times when they become necessary and such a climax had we arrived at in April 1879....There never was a more complete stoppage of work or one which to the workmen, at least, ended more satisfactorily.[29]

This judgment on the dispute is shared by Welbourne and Metcalfe both of whom see it as a critical event, solidifying the Association's membership and establishing it as a permanent institution in the county.

The strike of 1879 is perhaps best seen as a moment when local militancy and county administration and organisation came together successfully, under circumstances which, although threatening, were not entirely dire. It was the first successful county-wide strike and, as Crawford implies, it built upon a great deal of popular support for the miners in the north. It was a clear indicator of the potential economic strength of mining unionism, and there is evidence which suggests that this fact registered most strongly with the employers. In assessing these events, it would be wrong to conclude that the obstacle to successful mining unionism lay simply in the activities of the officials, and in the bureaucratic administrative processes of the Association's structure. Certainly the officials had been opposed to the strike, but not on unreasonable grounds. In the event Crawford relished a successful confrontation with the employers. Equally, there were occasions then and subsequently when militant action could lead to defeat. The history of Durham in the 1860s had shown how local militancy could easily evaporate, and how spontaneous struggles, in isolation, carried no guarantee of building and retaining trade-union membership. What the 1879 events revealed, above all, was the importance of this tension between 'official' and 'unofficial' movements within trade unionism. Without the 'unofficial' movement there would have been no strike; yet the strike sealed the development of official unionism, and secured the future of the DMA.

County and National Trade Unionism

While mining trade unionism developed at the county level, the National Miners' Union continued through the 1870s. Burt and Crawford were its national officials, and this reflected the fact that their Associations represented the majority of all unionised miners in Britain. This same fact came to represent the growing isolation of those county organisations from the other mining organisations. This became clear in 1879, when a new national organisation—the Miners' Federation of Great Britain—was formed. Established at a conference in Newport in Monmouthshire, it was concerned to alter the pattern of trade-union organisation in the mining industry. The National Union had obtained unity between the county unions on a minimalist basis. It co-ordinated the miners' efforts in relation to statutory legislation and the activities of the parliamentary group of the TUC, but it left the day-to-day bargaining over wages and conditions of work to the county associations which operated as independent organisations. In this, the Durham and Northumberland Associations had been able to use their negotiating strength to great advantage in negotiating over wages, hours and conditions of work. They considered these issues to be a matter for local trade-union bargaining rather than the affair of parliament *or* the National Union, and they deeply resented the idea of 'outside influence'. The Miners' Federation of Great Britain marked a break with this approach. It reflected the experiences of the trade-union activists in the less well-organised coalfields and it became deeply committed to the view that the hours worked by coal miners should be limited by act of parliament. Most critically, it saw the possibility and need for strike action to be organised on a national basis. Increasingly it came to see the 'industrial' and 'legislative' wings of the union as being related. This view ran directly counter to the ideas of trade unionism being developed in Durham. Through the joint committee and its high levels of unionisation, the Durham Association had negotiated a reduction in the working week for coal hewers, and administered the level of wages through the operation of a 'sliding scale' which linked wages to the international price of coal. In its view, legislation and national bargaining would only be detrimental to the interests of miners in Durham. For them, the question of trade unionism was settled, and in this they shared the approach of many of the craft unions.

The craft unions were deeply antagonistic to the new miners' Federation, and often referred to it as another example of 'new unionism'. This was meant as a slur, linking the miners with the push for union organisation amongst the unorganised, unskilled workers and as such, it is of some interest. So too is the response given to it by the President of the MFGB, Ben Pickard. He defended the Federation in this way:

> We are twitted as being new trade unionists, I think our trade unionism will date as far back as any portion of the so-called old trade unionists. What we claim to be is simply this—that whilst we have new ideas, whilst we have desires to make progress, whilst we are in the position of wanting to have a little more of our own way than the older trade unionists seem to ask for, if that is a reason why we are to be put down as new trade unionists then we are willing to be classed in this category.

The Miners' National Union he argued 'did not go fast enough', and those affiliated to the new Federation were concerned to

> mark out a course for ourselves, for all these bodies of men, who were desirous of acting together not merely upon legislative matters but upon wage matters.[30]

The Durham miners however did not join in this endeavour. By this time the DMA's involvement in the National Union had become capricious. In November 1887 when the National Union had met in Newcastle to discuss the principles of federation Crawford, although secretary, failed to attend or to respond to telegrams asking for his views. Durham was not represented at the Newport conference and remained, with Northumberland, outside the MFGB, the two areas continuing (in a way which was to become increasingly paradoxical) as the Miners' National Union. As Page Arnot has put it:

> it was clear that neither the Durham miners nor William Crawford MP...was prepared to go along with the other counties in their movement which might lead them they know not whither.[31]

After 1879, trade unionism in Durham was secure. So too were the collective bargaining arrangements which had been established with the coal owners. Paradoxically the strike of that year had ushered in a new dawn in co-operative relationships with the employers, and John Wilson reflected:

> there is a closer spirit abroad now. The county has been in an atmosphere of amicability. May that better state take full possession and the day of strikes be gone forever.[32]

The extent to which this was successful can be seen in a publication, produced after the death of Crawford. In 455 detailed pages, this book by W.H. Patterson entitled *Durham Miners' Association—Joint Committee Decisions Agreement, Practices, Rules, etc. 1875–1892*, provided information on the range of agreements and other formalised understandings achieved in 166 pits across the coalfield. Patterson began the work when he took office as General Secretary. In his Preface, he wrote:

> The task of compiling this reference book has taken nearly three years to complete. Its scope extends over a period of seventeen years. We trust it will prove to be a plain, useful, and handy guide in cases of disputes. Hoping the decisions, agreements, practices, reports etc., may be of much assistance to our members, in coming to just conclusions at lodge meetings.[33]

The tone here is one of administrative competence and conciliation. That it ends in 1892 can be seen as ironic, as this was the year in which the Durham miners became locked in a titanic battle with the coal owners.

The period of industrial peace celebrated by Patterson was associated with a succession of 'sliding scales' which linked the wages of coal miners to the price of coal. In July 1889 the fourth (and final) sliding scale ended, and in 1892, as coal prices declined the owners announced their intention to reduce wages by ten percent. The sliding scale had survived as a simple (and seemingly just) system of wage regulation. It had been enforced by the dominance of Crawford over the executive committee and the lodges. However the mine workers had become increasingly critical of this scheme. To many it seemed that profits ought also to be regulated, and sentiments such as these had led to a succession of unofficial strikes over wages. Patterson was a quieter and more timid man than Crawford (Wilson refers to him as 'the enemy of no living man but the friend of all'); he could draw upon little of the support and respect which his predecessor had gained through years of office holding. An old man (he was to die in 1896) he came to office at a time least suited to his talents.

In 1892 the Durham employers had insisted on a reduction in wages, arguing that it needed to be a full 10 percent. The Association balloted the membership asking for full powers to settle as they could; only 12,956 followed this advice, another 40,468 voted for strike action, and on 12 March the 'Durham Lockout' began. It was to last twelve weeks, and revealed both the determination of the coal miners and the obduracy (and spite) of the employers. Throughout the strike the miners were repeatedly balloted by their officials, but they refused to settle or to give their officials freedom to negotiate. For their part the employers, once set on confrontation, made more severe their demands for settlement, turning their back on any conciliatory moves by the miners. With Crawford dead they were determined to impose a new order on the coalfield. That the strike was eventually settled on the terms demanded by the employers in March (a ten percent reduction) owed much to the intervention of the Bishop of Durham.

The 1892 strike was as influential as the strike of 1879. It was an epic industrial struggle which reverberated through the economy of the north as coal production and distribution ceased. It revealed the potential

W.H. Patterson. A founder of the Durham Miners' Association. General Secretary 1890–96. 'The enemy of no living man but the friend of all.' (J. Wilson)

power of mass trade unionism, and of the new forces which were emerging in society. Jack Lawson wrote of how the strike was 'grim, desperate and savage'.

> the men and women had fought for months. Although unconscious of it I had, even as a boy of eleven, become class conscious. A national strike is a calamity and arouses strange feelings, but a county strike is savagely bitter because its effects are more directly devastating...as the sense of defeat deepened, passions rose until the women and children were as bad as the men. Indeed, the women were the worst, as they always are on such occasions.[34]

In the aftermath of this defeat, the miners' leaders in Durham were determined not to succumb, ever again, to pressures from below in favour of militancy and strike action. They were also antagonistic to the role of the MFGB and its insistence that county unions should resist wage reductions: in their view the future of the DMA lay outside the MFGB.

However, during the 1892 strike, the coal miners of Durham had been supported by a levy organised by the national Federation. In the period which followed the return to work officials of the Federation visited the coalfield to address 'unofficial' meetings of coal miners, and lodge officials. They used these meetings to argue for the Federation and the cause of national unionism. This was deeply resented by the Durham officials: the more so when a county vote of DMA members instructed the Association to affiliate to the MFGB.

While obliged to join, the leaders of the DMA were determined not to endorse or become involved in the spirit of Federation. In part this related to their strong sense of autonomy and their reluctance to surrender power to a national organisation which they distrusted. It also related to the policy of the Federation, and the different approach which these (Liberal) trade union leaders brought the use of trade union power. This antagonism became clear in an early (and now famous) exchange of telegrams between Pickard and Patterson:

> Am sorry I cannot have a reply to a plan courteous question—Pickard
>
> Always have, always will answer a plain question if I can, but you ask me a question I cannot answer. Only let me manage my own Association and you manage yours, or will give you an exchange, you come to Durham and I'll come to Barnsley—Patterson

The situation was untenable, and it boiled over in 1893 when the MFGB faced a general assault on the wages of coal miners. John Wilson made clear that in his view the MFGB policy on wages was 'a policy of strikes and nothing else'. He carried this view forward at the MFGB conference held at the Hen and Chicken public house in Birmingham on 19-20 July. Listening to him, the delegates agreed that 'it was impossible to go forward as a single body if some unions in the Federation placed their district decisions higher than the national conference'.[35]

Offended by Wilson's morose attack the delegates were determined to bring the Durham leadership to heel. They instructed that in areas where a wage reduction had already been accepted there should be a ballot for a wage increase equivalent to the reduction. Such a policy however, was insensitive to the position of miners who had already endured a hard strike. It allowed the Durham leaders to ridicule the policies of the MFGB, to be expelled from the Federation, and separated from the major events which surrounded the national strike in 1893.

John Wilson speaking at an open-air meeting.

The strike of 1893 was the first major national miners' strike. It involved 300,000 miners and lasted sixteen weeks. It was described by Pickard as:

> one of the largest and most far-reaching of any known to have existed in the last hundred years, or indeed in the history of the world.[36]

This judgment may seem exaggerated but it is a reasonably sound one for this was the first occasion when the power of organised labour to deeply disrupt the industrial structure of the country was made clear. The strike did not involve the miners of Scotland, South Wales, Durham, Northumberland, South Staffordshire and the Forest of Dean. It was seen by many to be a 'suicidal conflict'. But it was strong enough to produce the first government intervention into a trade dispute. It also saw the mobilisation of support beyond the industry. Beatrice Webb organised a support meeting in St James's Hall which saw £255 being collected from women who were 'determined to help the starving miners and their children'. In the pages of the *Daily Chronicle,* William Morris wrote of an emerging new order 'building up from the confusion of the commercial period.' The miners, he said, were laying the foundations for something better. These ideas, and the lessons of the strike, were influential in Durham too, and they saw an increasing tension developing between the leadership and those 'unconstitutional' elements which existed in the coalfield. Increasingly this tension centred around the relation between county and national unionism. Although Durham rejoined (briefly) after Patterson's death, John Wilson's leadership ensured that the relationship was short lived. After 'six months acrimonious correspondence' the Federation Executive resolved that whatever the 'real majority' feeling may be in Durham, in that county:

> the officials, the executive committee and the council are decidedly opposed to joining the Federation. We therefore authorise the secretary to return the cheque to Mr John Wilson MP at once.[37]

Once again Page Arnot's assessment is instructive. Durham, he argued, though 'in the Federation was not of it' and the difference lay in the understanding of trade-union power itself:

> Wilson disbelieved in trade-union action of the kind contemplated [by the MFGB] and feared the effect upon class harmony of one large miners' organisation. Therefore he stood for separateness; and within each separate county for a kindly arrangement with the coal owners.[38]

The relationship between the DMA and the MFGB is illustrative of the pattern of mining unionism generally and the particular nature of the Association in Durham. It reflects upon the way in which mining trade unionism developed on a *localised* (county) basis and how the variations in local conditions produced different patterns of experience (in work and wages), different customs and often, different kinds of trade unionism. This tension between the local and the national had dominated mining unionism in the nineteenth century: it would continue (in different forms) in the twentieth.

Leadership and Ideology

The establishment of the Durham Miners' Association, and the associated repeal of the Annual Bond, marked an important break in the paternal order. Viewed in this way, 1872 can be seen as an important date, marking the moment when the coalfield finally became a part of the modern world. The date, however, is both *more* and *less* significant than this.

The bond, as we have seen, was more than a labour contract, more too than a simple 'feudal survival'. It was a central part of an extremely detailed and effective regime of labour regulation. 'The Bond' was predicated upon a society in which an established order and hierarchy was seen to reflect 'worth' and 'standing'. To a real extent the miners—the most populous group within the coalfield—were not *bona fide* members of that society. The removal of the bond suggests a change of quite dramatic proportions. Symbolically the union—the miners' own institution—can be seen as an assertion of place: its recognition by the employers as a more general social recognition of the miner within Durham society. In 1869 this association was made most clearly.

But it was clearly something less than this too, and this can be seen in the *manner* of this recognition. The union made miners formally equal members of society; this equality was based upon the union becoming an integral part of that system of power which had been established around coal. In breaking with the old order the miners' union became entrapped in it. The Webbs were acutely aware of this, arguing that the joint-committee structure and the sliding scale brought results which largely neutralised the advantages: 'the men gained their point at the cost of adopting the intellectual position of their opponents'. Others have commented on the dominance of a liberal political-economy amongst the Northern miners and linked this to the organisation of work in the mines and the importance of Durham as an exporting coalfield in the international coal market. This link was made real in the union's acceptance of (and commitment to) the 'sliding scale' and the deep effect this had upon the ways in which Durham miners thought of the market and labour. Equally, in this (albeit reformed) aristocratic society, questions of place and status took on a significance, and a 'natural' power all of their own. It was these forces which saw the Durham Miners' Association establish its headquarters in Durham (the Citadel) rather than in Newcastle, the commercial centre of the coal trade. In Durham, the initial site of the Miners' Hall was on North Road, and this building was impressive enough. In 1915 however a new Hall was opened. Redhills Villa, an almost stately building of red brick, stood impressively in its own grounds surrounded by trees and gardens. In these grounds four solid square houses were built as homes for the miners' agents. The marble statues of the first agents were moved from the balcony of North Road and placed on plinths in these gardens, to survey all those who entered the new hall. Redhills itself was enormously impressive, and its main chamber was clearly constructed to the design of men who were at home as preachers and orators. Circular in shape, the oak seats of the delegates were numbered and directed toward the central 'pulpit' area where sat the officials and the executive committee. Photographs of the men as they stood on the steps of the hall reveal a powerful sense of both respectability and ease. Through organisation and endeavour they had indeed turned the world around; they had made the world accept them as equals within it. They, the respectable leaders of the miners.

In this process, of course, these men were influenced by their chapels, and by popular ideas of life and society. One such source of ideas was *Cassell's Family Magazine*. This magazine regularly contained articles on themes such as 'How to write a good letter' and 'How I engage my servants'. It was also a source of popular fiction and in 1877 it serialised a novel by J. Berwick Harrod entitled 'Paul Knox: Pitman'. Set in the Durham mining town of Capel-le-Moors (Hetton-le-Hole), this Victorian melodrama (complete with orphans, romance, underground explosions, and class barriers) contains some interesting commentaries on the isolated nature of the mining districts, and the common views held of the mining population. Harrod described how 'there were two parties if not three amongst the miners...not by any means in active opposition to one another, but as far apart in principle and practice as light and darkness'. The 'type' which dominated public awareness as typical was based upon men who 'lived in what might be called a condition of contented barbarism.'

> Earning much and saving little, the average pitman hardly knew what to do with his loose cash and his leisure. That the husband should spend the wages as well as work for them was an axiom of Capel-le-Moors ethics, and few dreamed of any further provision for what is metaphorically styled a rainy day [or] the contribut[ion] to some friendly society more or less rotten at the core.[39]

This type of miner is presented as spending much of his leisure time drinking. There was another (diverse) group whose leisure habits became their life. Sport of all sorts was critical here—especially horse racing, dog racing and gambling. But to this could be added:

> Ratting, pugilism, sparrow-shooting from the trap, badger baiting, dog fights, and, on a small scale, cock fighting....And few were aware that a percentage of the miners were painstaking naturalists, patient florists, meek students of history and philosophy or became less lovers of music for its own sake.[40]

To this Harrod adds a *third* group. These he describes as the 'so-called religious section of the colliery community.' It is out of this group that the hero of the novel emerges as a 'gaunt, large limbed young pitman, named Paul Knox.' A paragon amongst that:

> little bank of God-fearing workmen, whose sober pious lives were a protest against the gross vanity of epicureanism that prevailed among their comrades.[41]

Knox emerges as brave, level headed, and a man forcefully opposed to iniquity in the mines; a man proud of his class, he is contrasted with a group of agitators—'trumpets to the great crusade of discontent'—led and encouraged by outsiders ('men who choose themselves') who travel the coal districts and the textile districts fermenting strife. Their leader, a man called Cowall, is described as an ex-pugilist from London, ill informed and devious. The contrast with Knox is immediate, and it is one which also finds expression in the views and writings of men like John

Wilson. It is easy to see how they, and their followers, would identify with such images of authentic miners' leaders.

All this, of course, was reinforced by the location of the Union's headquarters in Durham City. It was here, and not in the pit villages, that the leaders of the trade union came to live. A sense of what was involved in this can be gained from descriptions of the Cathedral and the social arrangements developed by the then Bishop—Bishop Westcott. Westcott was a man of liberal sensibilities who was not averse to involving himself in matters of industry. He lived in Auckland Castle, and he had insisted on visiting Auckland Park pit where had gone underground 'as an ordinary workman'. On that occasion he had been presented with an overman's leather cap which he kept in a prominent position on his sideboard at the castle. The church, of course, was also a major royalty owner with a clear material interest in affairs of the industry. In this, it is perhaps odd to recall that the Bishop played a critical role in the arbitration that took place during the 1892 strike. As John Wilson recollected:

> the good Bishop...persisted in his efforts to get the parties together. He was told that as soon as the owners were willing the [Federation] Board would meet and an arrangement was made on 1 June at Auckland Castle. A very long joint meeting took place, and then each party met in a separate room, the Bishop passing from room to room, full of solicitude for a settlement.[42]

As a consequence of this dispute and the 'general prevailing distress' it was the Bishop who prepared a new system of conciliation for the county which was accepted by the owners and the trade unions. Westcott, in fact, became known as the 'pitman's Bishop' and a close friend of John Wilson—something which the DMA leader described as an 'honour and a privilege'. He recalls how Westcott had the habit of entertaining well beyond the confines of church:

> His custom was at certain intervals to invite a number of gentlemen to his castle. It was a mixed gathering: leading employers, literary men, clergymen, economists, and trade-union leaders. As one of the last class I was always invited. His idea was to discuss social and economic questions. The mode of procedure was either to give someone connected with the two northern counties a subject which he was expected to introduce at the next meeting, or the Bishop invited some gentleman who was well known as a promoter of reform to speak on some subject within the two main ideas I have mentioned. The meetings were generally held on Thursday night and Friday. Whoever was invited was expected to be at the castle about 5 p.m. in time for tea. Between that time and dinner it was Liberty Hall. After

> dinner for an hour or two all assembled in the drawing-room, when an informal conversation took place the topic being the question of next day. Then at ten all the guests, family, and servants gathered in the chapel for prayers. On Friday morning at ten the conference opened, with the Bishop in the chair. The speaker was called upon to introduce the subject, after which the order was to speak as he called upon you, and as far as possible the different classes or representatives of various ideas were called on in turn.[43]

The miners' union, in this account, was presented as 'the last class', and its representation as a reaffirmation of an old order—albeit reformed. It was a reaffirmation endorsed by the DMA Executive Committee which, on the death of the Bishop in 1901, passed a Resolution which showed their appreciation of the Bishop as 'sympathiser, counsellor and helper'.[44]

This process of 'acceptance' was related strongly to the organisation of politics. Soon after the DMA was formed, it established a 'Franchise Association':

> although incidental to the labour organisation, and with a voluntary contribution, it was managed by the leading men in [the] Association. The names found prominently in one are found in the other.[45]

Against this background, an election fund was set up with the view to achieving parliamentary representation, and the social and political recognition of themselves as members not only of a trade union but of *society*. These men, capable, literate and administrators of new, powerful trade unions, still had no right to vote in elections. The significance of this (and the deep importance that this sense of *exclusion* had upon the politics and sensibilities of Durham miners and their leaders) is illustrated in another statement by John Wilson, made whilst introducing Joseph Chamberlain to a meeting in Newcastle in 1884. Chamberlain was a popular figure in the north amongst the miners and, on this occasion, the Percy Street Circus was packed to see Wilson prepared to present him with an illuminated address from the Durham union. Wilson describes the occasion in this way:

> 'I want you to take a good look at me'. He in surprise stared through his monocle, and the audience were silent wondering what was coming. 'Do you see anything in me that would lead you to think that I am not an Englishman?' Still the look of wonder, and still the silence, 'Because', I said, 'there are times in our history when I am not. I have never had a vote yet.' Then the idea was caught and a roar of cheers broke out which nearly raised the roof.[46]

Wilson here, of course, echoed many ideas of the Chartists which had filled the pages of the *Northern Star* three decades earlier. People didn't need medical training to choose a doctor, nor theological training to choose their religion—why special training to choose their political representative?

These ideas were given an added poignancy by the passing of the Representation of the People Act in 1867. This Act purported to extend the franchise and the benefits of citizenship to male workers in a manner which paralleled the effects of the 1832 reforms upon the middle and business classes. However, by restricting itself to boroughs (and thereby urban centres) the Act managed to exclude the majority of coal miners. While this was not a deliberate act of policy, its consequences serve to highlight once again the non-urban nature of coal mining as an industrial activity. It also added to the developing sense of social marginality within the coal-mining districts. In 1884 a further Act extended the earlier reforms to the counties and to rural districts. This was the context of Wilson's speech. Under this Act, twice as many electors were added to the rolls as was achieved in 1867. The most populous and organised of these new voters were the coal miners.

It was in this context that the miners' Federation Board had resolved that in future elections there should be 'bona fide labour candidates, selected from the workmen but run in connection with the Liberals.' 'Workmen' in this context meant, in practice, 'Agents', for the Board approved the nomination of Crawford, Wilson and Trotter for the 1885 election, with the recommended salary of £500 per year. In that election Crawford won the mid-Durham seat and Wilson was elected at Houghton-le-Spring. The Franchise Association was equally adroit in securing political representation in the newly established local authorities. In the first County Council election they won 25 percent of the seats, and their Association's nominees dominated the parish and district elections. Wilson's comments are again revealing: 'in this respect the county occupied a proud and peculiar position, for in no other county was any use made of the Act.'[47] Wilson's pride in this achievement was to be reflected in his rise to the position of Chairman of the County Council, where he served as an Alderman for New Herrington and as a magistrate. It set a pattern of relationship between the union and local politics which (in spite of important changes) would last for almost a century. It represented the operation of political clout, and for many years it was exerted through the Liberal Party.

No man more clearly demonstrates the position of the Durham Miners' Association in Durham society at the turn of the century than John Wilson. He was in many senses a remarkable trade-union leader, and we have made extensive use of his two books—*A History of the Durham Miners' Association* and *Memoirs of a Labour Leader*. Orphaned as a young boy, he worked in the Ludworth Colliery before being

Alderman John Wilson, JP, MP, General Secretary Durham Miners' Association 1896–1915.

'taken in' by a family called Stahler and moving with them to Sherburn Hill, where he was known as 'Stahler Wilson'. As a young man he experienced all the vicissitudes of a miner's life: unjustified dismissals, narrow escapes from death, and the pain of mine labour. For several years he left the industry, working as a seaman and travelling to India and the USA. He was a drinker and gambler. However 'there was a change coming'. In his autobiography he dwells on this change and his conversion to Methodism:

> the public house in port lost its attraction and the alcoholic liquors their pleasant taste. I was as fond of them as any man ought to be. The desire for gambling was shaken off in a moment—I cannot say by an act of will alone...but by some

> peculiar and unaccountable impulse, which came to me in unique and most unlikely circumstances....no-one who saw Saul set out on his way to Damascus, 'breathing out threatenings and slaughterings' would have thought he would have been stopped in the manner he was. Since that day, although differing in manner, many a man whom people looked upon as being hopeless has been pulled up, not by a great light as in his case, but still suddenly. He has seen a light they could not see, and heard a voice which was inaudible to them.[48]

Upon his conversion Wilson set about educating himself. He became a preacher and studied 'the political and social movements then before the public mind'. He joined in the struggle for trade unionism, and in the era of the bond he was elected assistant checkweighman at Haswell. The owners however refused to bind him, and he took up another position as secretary of the local Co-operative Society. He subsequently moved to Wheatley Hill where he became checkweighman and chairman of the lodge. We have noted his involvement in the 1879 strike. In 1882 he was elected as DMA agent, and for the next eight years served as Treasurer in Durham. By this time a system of tenure had been established for DMA officials, whereby they progressed from post to post in the union office. In 1890 on the death of Crawford, Wilson moved up to Financial Secretary, and then on Patterson's death in 1896 he became General Secretary. In his history of the Association, written while he was in office, he described himself as 'Alderman John Wilson J.P., Chairman of the Durham County Council and Member of Parliament for mid-Durham Division.'

Howell has commented on the 'manipulative and obfuscatory style' which Wilson developed as General Secretary of the DMA. This came across in a number of ways—most especially in the meetings of the Union's Council. This council was the key decision making body of the DMA, and in 1903 one delegate wrote to J. Ramsay MacDonald, the ILP leader, of the methods used by the General Secretary to deflect debate and criticism:

> Our friend J.W. played the game very low. It is quite a usual thing for him to do if there is any vital question to be opposed.
> *Act 1* As soon as he rises, pick a quarrel with some delegate.
> *Act 2* After which he will play the role of martyr-hero.
> *Act 3* Make a piteous appeal to the sentiment and passions of the council.
> Playing so successfully upon the feelings and passions of a large number of the delegates as to make it impossible to get a reply to his twaddle.[49]

This pattern of behaviour had become familiar to delegates who had sat with him on the MFGB committee. Before his expulsion, he and Burt co-operated in a perpetual attempt to undermine, ridicule and make inoperable the rules and resolutions of the Federation.

An example of his style was seen in the more public arena of Newcastle assizes in 1912. Wilson was bringing a libel charge against one of his own members—George Harvey, the checkweighman at the Wardley Colliery. Harvey was a syndicalist and had written a pamphlet severely critical of the DMA leader entitled: 'Does John Wilson MP, serve the working class?' The title of the pamphlet made implicit reference to the honourary Doctorate of Laws that had been conferred on Wilson by the University of Durham, and the text carried on in similar vein suggesting, among other things that Wilson, like Burt, was prepared to accept financial bribes from the employers. It was this charge which led to the court case and to Wilson's public demonstration of the style for which he had become renowned:

Harvey: Are you aware that the Board of Trade Figures prove conclusively that the condition of the working class is absolutely in decline?

Wilson: I don't know to what Board of Trade figures you refer. I should not have a clear head if I carried them all in it.

[laughter]

Harvey: Are you aware of the fact that the figures prove wages have almost been stationary for fifteen years while the cost of living has gone up by ten percent?

Harvey: Are you aware that the Board of Trade Figures prove conclusively that the condition of the working class is absolutely in decline?

Wilson: I don't know to what Board of Trade figures you refer. I should not have a clear head if I carried them all in it.

[laughter]

Harvey: Are you aware of the fact that the figures prove wages have almost been stationary for fifteen years while the cost of living has gone up by ten percent?

Wilson: I cannot confirm or dispute your figures if you get them from the Board of Trade.

Harvey: You would not dispute the fact that, as quoted by

> Lloyd George, one-third of the people of the county are almost on the verge of starvation?
>
> Wilson: If you say it is Lloyd George, then like John Bull it must be true.
>
> [more laughter][50]

Wilson won his case and was awarded £200 damages (which Harvey never paid). In Durham his power, and confidence, was supreme. He had, over four decades, established around him powerful organisation support rooted in the Methodist Chapels, and many of the Durham lodges. He maintained this dominance through detailed administrative effort, and through a ruthless bureaucratic style. This ruthless side of his personality was made clear in Durham in 1909 at the annual Miners' Gala. Earlier that year there had been an explosion in the West Stanley mine in which 168 men had been killed. The *Durham Chronicle* reported how in his address to the miners and their families:

> Alderman John Wilson stated he had received a letter from eight widows at West Stanley thanking the miners of the county of Durham for their generous support. In a kindly letter they censured the general secretary of the Durham Miners' Association, which was himself. He did not care how much men censured him for doing what he considered his duty, but when women began to censure him, then he started to look round the corner. The widows had censured him for not getting all their compensation. They had been paid compensation according to the law, and could not do more. The widows had invited him to address a meeting at West Stanley. If the miners had sent such an invitation he would have gone; but he was not going where there were 100 widows [laughter]. The best had been done for the widows. [hear, hear][51]

Such was the style of leadership, which effectively established the DMA as a Liberal trade union. It was one which was deeply rooted in Durham society and it would have its parallels in the years that followed.

4
A Labour Aristocracy?

Over attention to the possible emergence of a privileged stratum in the workforce, a labour aristocracy effectively detached from the rest of the working class, has obscured the fact that the most intractable problems in this period were political or ideological rather than economic.

Gareth Stedman Jones

THE RETENTION of political power by an aristocracy in England was, in part, a result of their landed interest in the coal mining regions. In these same regions a highly organised trade unionism emerged which encompassed broad aspects of social life. It is tempting to assert that at the turn of the century Durham possessed both an aristocracy of the land and an aristocracy of labour. Certainly, at times the term 'labour aristocrat' was used in both a common everyday sense, and by writers of all political persuasions. It was appropriated and used by Engels as well as by liberal commentators such as Hobhouse and Hobson. Later, in the first two decades of the twentieth century, it was used by Lenin to account for the nature of reformist politics, and also by Sorel to refer to the legalisation and bureaucratisation of the working class. The primary aim of all these writers was to account for the new political role of the organised working class. Their accounts can be read as attempts to understand how the working class was shaped by the peculiar combination of the aristocratic and the bourgeois in the English political tradition.

Hobsbawm has noted how the concept of the 'labour aristocracy' was:

> familiar in English socio-political debate, particularly in the 1880s. It was generally accepted that the working class in Britain at this period contained a favoured stratum; a minority but a numerically large one which was most usually identified with the artisans [i.e. the skilled employed craftsmen and workers] and

> more especially with these organised in trade union or other working-class organisations.[1]

The manner in which this 'familiar' term was incorporated into the political discourse of commentators of all persuasions is, however, more complicated than Hobsbawm suggests. For our purposes the complication concerns the ambiguity which centres on the question of the miners and their status in relation to this stratum.

Writing in 1892, Engels characterised the labour aristocracy in essentially market terms. He identified it with 'the great trade unions'.

> They are the organisation of those trades in which the labour of grown up men predominates....Here the competition neither of women and children nor of machinery has so far weakened their organised strength....They form an aristocracy among the working class; they have succeeded in enforcing for themselves a relatively comfortable position and they accept it as final.[2]

Here Engels had in mind the skilled artisans, but clearly this definition could also include the miners. However, the miners themselves were quite clear about their position. Involved in harsh, degrading labour, they did not see themselves as labour aristocrats; nor did those who had reason to investigate their general labouring and living conditions. Often living 'outside of society' in their own exclusive communities, the issue of their marginal status was of central concern to them. There was, of course, considerable variation both within and between coalfields. In Durham, the isolated south-west with its small pits and villages contrasts with the more urban locations along the Tyne and the estuary of the Wear.[3] Nevertheless, other biographies of miners are filled with references to the issue of their marginality; as a people separate from society, not central to it. John Wilson's, for example, recalls the experience of a miner who had left the coal mines for London. On one occasion he was asked who he was and where he came from. He answered: 'I am a pitman and I come from County Durham'. In Wilson's account:

> that increased the surprise of the Londoner, and he requested the Northerner to accompany him to a tavern near by, and took him into the parlour where a number of people were sitting, and made [him] walk around like a horse showing his paces at a fair, and the general cry was 'why he can walk as straight as ourselves. We thought those pitmen could only walk in a doubled-up posture owing to the cramped conditions of their work and their continual residence underground.'[4]

At the same time accounts like these contain the recognition that trade-union organisation was the potential carrier of improvement and of a new and higher status.

The miners were a group of workers who were conventionally considered as being 'unskilled' and as having low status within the working class as 'mere labourers'. In this sense they differ considerably from the skilled men referred to by Hobsbawm and Engels. However, the miners were no 'new unionists'; their trade unionism dated from early in the nineteenth century, and they were recognised to be, in G.D.H Cole's words: 'the most powerful industrial organisation in the British labour movement and perhaps in the labour movement of the whole world.'[5] This comment was made in 1923, and it reflected the organised strength of the miners which had been revealed in the largest strikes ever witnessed in Britain, first in 1893 and then again in 1912. The miners' organisations were, in fact, the first mass, national unions, and no deep understanding of this phenomenon is contained in the earlier description of labour aristocrats.

In part the power of the miners was a result of size. In 1881 the mines of Britain had employed 495,000 workers. Over the next twenty years that number almost doubled. In 1903 there were 842,000 miners and 70 percent of them were in a trade union, a proportion which was far higher than any other industry. In 1910 the mining unions, with 600,000 members, formed the largest trade union in the country; not only that, they also constituted nearly 25 percent of the total membership of *all* trade unions. The next largest union, the Amalgamated Association of Weavers, had only 122,000 members. The Engineers nationally had a membership of only 100,000—fewer even than the Durham Miners' Association. The *scale* of this is important. The miners were not only the largest group of organised workers, but they were *six* times as large as the next biggest union.[6] They were the dominant trade union in British society and they were based in an industry most uncharacteristic of British capitalist development.

To an important extent their power was functional. In a period of expansion and with a single fuel economy, coal was a critical resource fundamental to domestic production and occupying a central position in the export market. This power, both real and potential, brought the miners up against the state. In response they had developed a trade union and a parliamentary strategy to handle this situation. The miners' union, like no other, dealt on a regular basis with the committees of the state establishing a situation of negotiated corporatism from below. As such to this *organisational* dominance of the miners we must add the miners' role as the foremost representatives of *liberal* politics within the working class. From 1885 to 1915 the miners exemplified this link in a more direct manner than any other group. They were the first, and certainly the most successful occupational group to send *their own representatives* to Parliament where they sat with the Liberal Party. In this way the miners through their unions played a leading reformist role within the working class in this period. Yet this reformism seems to fit unhappily with accounts of conditions in the mines, and the industrial strength of a group which demonstrably had the capacity to unleash strike action of a crippling kind. How can this puzzle be resolved?

The Miners and the Law

Writing in 1906 the French syndicalist author Sorel observed that, in general terms, the English working class appeared to be:

> distinguished by an extraordinary lack of understanding of the class war; their ideas have remained very much dominated by medieval influences: the guild, privileged or at least protected by laws, still seems to be the ideal of working-class organisation; it is for England that the term working-class aristocracy, as a name for trade unionists, was invented, and as a matter of fact trade unionism does pursue the acquisition of legal privilege.[7]

Without accepting the link which Sorel noted between legal rights and 'medieval influences', the idea of linking trade-union development with the law is an important one. This is particularly so in the case of the miners. Indeed, Engels offered a similar interpretation when, in the 1892 edition of the *Conditions of the English Working Class,* he talked of its 'aristocracy' existing amongst its '*protected sections*'.[8] He was referring to those groups of workers whose conditions of existence were secured by an Act of Parliament which covered such areas as working conditions, hours of work and the categories of labour to be employed. In mining, the limitation placed upon the employers' use of female and child labour and the Acts which governed safety conditions and the presence of checkweighmen could be seen in this category. Used in this way, the role of law becomes a very suggestive one. It sees the development of reformist politics to be related not to simple ideas of skill or status, nor even in economic conditions (wages and the like), but rather to patterns of economic and political power and to the operation of the state. Here, support for the theories of Engels and Sorel can be drawn from the unlikely source of Sidney and Beatrice Webb.

In 1894, two years after Engels had reissued his classic text on the English working class, the Webbs published *The History of Trade Unionism.* This, their first volume on the development of the British labour movement, was followed in 1897 by *Industrial Democracy*. These two volumes were to become classic studies of British trade unionism, the original source of information for the new liberals like Hobson and Hobhouse as well as for European revolutionists like Lenin and Sorel. The attraction of the Webbs' historical analysis lay in its analytic precision. They distinguished between three methods of trade unionism—mutual insurance (supported by secret coercion), collective bargaining and legal enactment. They presented the last method—legal enactment—as the ideal form of trade-union practice, and singled out, in an approving way, the miners and the cotton operatives as the two most significant unions to adopt this method, hailed as the result of an evolutionary trend in trade unionism. And the two unions were seen as the 'most distinctively modern in their growth and pre-eminence'.[9] These unions were also, of course (and in contrast to Sorel's 'medieval influences'), the two classic unions of English industrial capitalism. As the coal and cotton industries were at the basis of English capitalist development, so too did the unions in these industries represent the 'Modern World'. They noted that these unions were distinguished by possessing 'an expert civil service exceeding in numbers and efficiency that possessed by any other trade'.[10] In referring to the conference of the MFGB, they argued:

> The Miners' Parliament, as the Conference may not improperly be called, is in many respects the most important assembly in the Trade Union world.[11]

They further characterised the MFGB as a 'predominantly political association' which campaigned for legal reform on a national basis.

This difference in method and structure of mining trade unionism had arisen from the ease with which the miners had been able to superimpose a political organisation upon an industrial one. The miners' union was able at one and the same time to organise miners both as trade unionists and as a mining electorate. Miners' agents easily doubled as their MPs, and this led to an emphasis upon legal enactment through parliamentary reform. At this point, however, the Webbs' evolutionary conceptions of trade-union institutionalisation break down. In their analysis, reformism was the ultimate end of union organisation, and there was little or no recognition that the pursuit of legislative changes would, or could, oscillate with an emphasis upon industrial power, militancy and strikes, or how in turn this would provoke a continual problem of unity within a federated union. And this indeed *was* the pattern presented by mining unionism. Rather than any evolutionary trend, mining unionism represented a new and perplexing combination of features—a national organisation whose strength rested upon a federated structure of autonomous local unions; a strong tradition of parliamentary representation, and emphasis upon statutory regulation which was on occasion supported by the militant use of strike action. The miners might appear as one of Engels's 'protected sections'. They achieved this, however, only because they were the best organised section of the working class. As such, in understanding their politics and their method of organisation, the notion of an 'aristocracy' is distinctly unhelpful; they might better be understood as constituting a critical *corporate group* within British society. This different formulation draws attention to the relationship between particular organised groups of workers and the state. By examining the degree of state regulation and statutory protection of the wage contract, it is possible to understand how the economic position of groups of workers related to questions of status and political capacity. It is particularly revealing in relation to the miners.

A Corporate Group

Throughout the nineteenth century the miners continually agitated for a Minister of Mines, and for most of the twentieth century for the state nationalisation of the industry. No groups within the British working class (with the sole exception of the cotton operatives) had secured the same degree of statutory regulation of the labour market. In 1842 the miners secured the exclusion of women from the mines; Hutchins and Harrison, the first historians of factory legislation, referred to this as 'perhaps the most high handed interference with industry enacted by the state in the nineteenth century'[12] and observed how:

> Legislative control of a very drastic nature for women in mines was demanded and granted, before even the least restriction of factory women's hours had been attempted.[13]

This observation can be applied to other aspects of mine labour and its regulation throughout the century. R. Page Arnot has commented that:

> The sixty years from 1850 to 1910 were seen in the memory of the older miners as one long history of struggle for a better Mines Act.[14]

Repeatedly the miners' officials demanded legal and official representation on all state guaranteed boards or committees concerning labour, safety and death in the mines:

> They demanded more inspectors with greater powers; that coal should be paid for by weight and not by measure; and that a Minister of Mines should be created.[15]

The Miners' National Union was formed with the specific purpose of gaining legislative changes. These included the demands that mine inspectors should be drawn from the same class as the miners' and that a proportion of the coroner's jury inquiring into fatal accidents in the mines should be working miners. In 1872 the Coal Mines Regulations Act went some way towards meeting these demands. Thomas Burt commented:

> Never before in the history of British legislation did any section

> of the working classes so thoroughly leave their impression on an Act of Parliament. All the chief principles sought for by the miners have been gained. What is the secret of this success? They have succeeded because they have looked after their own business, they have sent their own representatives and have not trusted others to look after their own affairs. No class of working men are better united than the miners, none are more publicly separated, and they have certainly brought the power of their unions to bear on this question...one voice demanding in tones clear and strong, that the life of the miner should be protected. The splendid meetings within a few weeks of each other at Stirling, Blyth, Durham, Barnsley, Leeds and other places were evidence of which no government could afford to dispense or ignore.[16]

Burt's views resonate with that twentieth century political tradition often referred to as Labourism. It was Burt who, as the leader of the Northumberland miners, sat in parliament, first as a Liberal, and at the end of his career held the title 'Father of the House'. Burt's reference to legal redress, and recognition for those groups able to 'dispense with the trust of others and manage their own affairs' is a political theme which straddles the two centuries in the history of organised labour.

The emphasis upon the law is not difficult to understand. We have seen how the particular nature of property in coal mining combined with the class structure of coalfield society in Durham in a way which saw employers having regular recourse to the Justices of the Peace and the law courts as a method of maintaining the subordination of their workers. The emphasis upon the law and upon statutory regulation however, also had a decisive impact upon the political development of the miners themselves and of the trade union which represented them. The Checkweighman Acts are a clear example. The weighing of coal had proven to be a major source of dispute and dissatisfaction in the coal industry. The 1860 Checkweighman's Act guaranteed the rights of miners to elect from their number a weigher to check the weights of the master's weighman. In 1872, 1887, 1894, and 1905 Acts were passed which further strengthened the position of the checkweighman in the colliery. As a result of this legislation, miners were guaranteed the right to elect by ballot vote their checkweighman, and to pay him themselves. The rights of the checkweighman, including his immunity from the power of the employers, were regulated by statute. In short, he was a *state guaranteed official* who could only be removed by ballot or by a Court of Summary Jurisdiction. In Durham in 1905 there were 165 working collieries, each entitled to a checkweighman guaranteed by the new Act. Across the county they made up a formidable layer of officialdom, freed from the vagaries of underground labour, resting rather upon their bargaining skills, their numeracy and literacy and their knowledge of agreements. These men, in

Durham and throughout the coal mining district, were in a critical position to guide the development of mining unionism and its political perspectives.

The Checkweighman Acts established the miners as 'a community organised by legal principles', principles which had never been extended in like manner to workers who toiled in factories or offices. In mining it was the state which provided the very basis of union organisation, coalescing as it did around the position of the checkweighman. Here the 1894 Act (which removed the need for the checkweighman to be an employee in the mine) was extremely significant. It allowed for the development of a mobile body of activists who were able to promote trade-union and political activity without the fear of losing their positions. John Wilson described the consequence of the Act. The checkweighman became:

> the mouthpiece of men when meeting the Manager, the leader in public movements and the most prominent in matters relating to the Association.[17]

The history of miners and mining has tended to pay little attention to the significance of these men in the development of trade-union politics. The development of trade unionism is related to the immediate struggles fought by the miners in the pits and in their communities. Where the checkweighman *is* mentioned, it is often in passing, and not infrequently with a pejorative tone. Foster, for example, argues that they made up a labour aristocracy on the coalfields, distinctive and separate from the men they represented. Burgess, in a similar but more detailed account, points to the separation of the official from the rank and file miner and the tendency for them to become 'employers' men':

> Although the position provided an ideal training for a trade-union official, there were aspects of it which compromised checkweighmen as miners' leaders and differentiated them from the rank and file. If they did not keep on good terms with the employer, they were refused facilities to do their jobs and the law generally sided with the employer when the case reached the courts. Since their wages were paid automatically, the conditions that determined the earnings of the rank and file did not directly affect them. Grass roots discontent arising from conditions at the workplace might well halt production and jeopardise the checkweighman's comparatively privileged position. It was not uncommon, therefore, for the checkweighman to become an employer's man; which had the effect of dividing miners from their potential leaders and was thus disruptive of community solidarity.[18]

These accounts are not without substance, even if they are seldom supported with detailed evidence of the role of checkweighmen in mining disputes. Certainly it would be wrong to identify too closely the checkweighman with trade unionism in the mines. In Durham, customary regulation of work played a central role in the development of the organised strength of the miners. However, it would be equally wrong to see in these underground conflicts and patterns of regulation the sole and authentic root of mining unionism. What gives uniqueness to trade-union organisation in the coalfields is the complex inter-relationship between *customary practices* and *legal regulation*. The checkweighman stood at the intersection of these two patterns, and the political significance of this official was, we suspect, more complex than has been generally recognised. This is especially the case if we add the fact that other acts of Parliament provided miners with the right to elect their own inspectors. Once again the contrast with factories and offices is important. Factory legislation did provide for the regulation of safety in these work places: they were subjected to surveillance by a state inspectorate. In mining, in addition to a mines inspectorate appointed by the state, the miners elected inspectors from amongst themselves. The 1887 Act made clear that:

> the persons employed in a mine may, from time to time appoint two of their number or any two persons, not being mining engineers, who are practical working miners, to inspect the mine on their own cost, and the person so appointed shall be allowed once at least in every month, accompanied if the owner, agent or manager of the mines thinks fit by himself or one or more officers of the mine, to every part of the mine, and to inspect the shafts, levels, plans, working places, return airways, ventilating apparatus, old workings and machinery.[19]

This regulation of safety was accompanied by statutory legislation under the same Act concerning the rules governing the coroners' activities with respect to deaths in the pit. All inquests were required to be carried out in the presence of an Inspector of Mines or a person appointed by the Secretary of State concerned. Courts of inquiry into such accidents were also to be appointed by the Secretary of State.

In 1908, as a result of the Hours of Work Act in which the miners' working day was set at eight hours, miners were granted the statutory right to appoint further officials to monitor the pit. The Act:

> provided for the appointment of one or more persons to direct the raising and lowering of the men at the pithead, and permits the workmen to appoint one or more of their number to be at the pithead at these times for the purpose of observing the times of lowering and raising of men.[20]

T.H. Cann JP, agent of the DMA, General Secretary 1915–24.

In 1919 the Coal Mines Act was to reduce the hours of work by statute from eight to seven.

This degree of state regulation also extended to the technical conditions of the operation of the mine. Both the Coal Mines Regulation Acts of 1872 and 1877 made provision for the certification of managers. Two documenters of the mining professions comment:

> In the absence of any Coal Mines Act, managers would not have separated out as a class. The group which they now form was *created by statute.* [Our emphasis.][21]

In the 1871 Act it had been made compulsory that any mine with thirty or more people underground had to be under the daily supervision of a state certificated manager. The managers' certificates were gained by examinations which were under the control of the Home Office. These statutes led to the formation of the National Association of Colliery Managers. The Association concerned itself with technical matters relating to mining, but was also keenly aware that: 'in this industry it is especially difficult to keep clear of politics because parliamentary regulation is always being discussed'.[22]

In the Coal Mines Act of 1911 the position of the managers was strengthened. This Act established that no owner or agent was to take part in any form of technical management unless they were certificated. The Act also brought into existence the Board for Mining Examinations. This was appointed by the Board of Trade and consisted of six representatives of the owners, six representatives of workmen employed in mining, three inspectors of miners and two persons eminent in mining knowledge. The same Act also created the category of deputy (firemen or examiner), who was also to be certificated and must be over the age of twenty-five and have at least five years' practical experience in mining.

As a result of parliamentary statute, the administrative structure of the industry also became state regulated. The technical side concerning the management and administration of the mine, the details of ventilation, lighting, shafts, haulage and rescue was supplemented by the statutory provision of workmen's officials to regulate the points of conflict over production and safety. What was created was an industry in which both the management and the miners' checkweighman were 'state guaranteed' officials. Furthermore, those regulations relevant to the practice of the mine were also extended on a national scale. In 1910 Winston Churchill, then at the Home Office, created two new posts of Labour Advisers, to be filled by Shackleton, the weavers' MP for Clitheroe, and T. Richards, a Welsh miner. A further thirty posts of sub-inspectors were created for miners and quarrymen.[23]

This process of appointment of trade-union officials into the ranks of the lower Civil Service was noted at the time by the able Guild Socialist A.P. Orage. Writing in 1914 he noted:

> it is not generally realised how successfully the present government has sterilised the socialist and labour movement by enlisting in the ranks of the bureaucracy energetic young Fabians as well as prominent socialists and labour leaders. Large posts in London, smaller posts in the provinces....The accession to the ranks of the Civil Service of a certain number of men alleged to be democrats has, of course, in no way democratised Downing Street and its purlieus. Classification still rules, appointments to the first class still being the perquisite of the universities. In this way the bureaucratic organisation is securely linked to the governing classes; they worship the same god; their tone, manners and ambition derive from the same source.[24]

Orage's account of bureaucratic officialdom and corporate inclusion of trade-union officials applied more to the miners than any other group. It was for this very reason that their officials did not view the state as a hostile force but instead as a redresser of the balance against the tyranny of the owners. This attitude imprinted itself deeply on the politics of the miners' trade unions.

The Miners and Politics

This understanding of the state and political action was clearly revealed in 1900 when most of the miners (Lancashire and Scotland excepted) chose to ignore the Labour Representation Committee and press ahead with their own 'MFGB Methods'.[25] Their view was expressed by Ben Pickard, the powerful President of the MFGB. As far as he was concerned each trade should do likewise:

> the only wise course is for each trade to select a constituency, also a candidate most suitable to the particular trade and provide the means whereby he can run as a candidate in that constituency.[26]

Further, in doing so, he advised that trade unionists should reject the assistance of middle class outsiders and small socialist sects with no financial support. In giving this advice he emphasised that the miners had successfully pursued this course of representing themselves economically and politically:

> It is a well known fact that the Federation is doing all this, and yet men have the presumption to ask you, in addition to sending members of your own, to assist in preparing schemes to send *others outside your Federation.* [our emphasis][27]

Here the corporate emphasis is clear. Also it is worth noting the similarity between Pickard's views and those of Burt quoted earlier. In spite of their differences (and here we have noted that these were many) they both express the ideas of labourism as a defensive ideology of trade. Also they can be seen to involve an ideology of trade unionism which is directly aware of its negotiations with the state. Such an ideology co-existed with both the Liberal Party and the Labour Party. It was stated with great clarity at the Annual Conference of the Miners' Federation of Great Britain which was held in Leicester in January 1897. In 1893 Keir Hardie had been actively involved in the formation of the Independent Labour Party. In the previous twenty years the agitative behaviour of Scot had not found much favour amongst the national leadership of the miners. They found his behaviour altogether too ephemeral. For Hardie trade unionism was a means to an altogether different end. For men like Alexander Macdonald and Pickard trade-union organisation was an end in itself. It was a view they shared throughout with the leadership in

Durham and Northumberland, based upon the opinion that 'ours is an exacting and worrying work'. Ned Cowey's words expressed a certain solidarity amongst men who had each entered the mines before the age of ten, and, whatever their politics, had learned things through 'the hard school'. This term was used universally and with great frequency. It was brought to bear in Leicester in 1897 as the annual conference of the MFGB discussed a resolution submitted by the Scottish Federation to the effect that:

> to secure the best conditions of industrial and social life it is absolutely necessary that the land, minerals, railways and instruments of wealth production should be owned and controlled by the state for the people.

An amendment was tabled by Yorkshire:

> that representatives to the Federal Conferences, and all Congresses act on trade-union lines as in the past, and not on socialistic lines.[28]

This amendment was passed overwhelmingly. However a Lancashire resolution to the effect that for the maintenance of British industries it was essential to nationalise the coal mines, railways and land was passed with a similar majority. Nationalisation, in the miners' union at this time was understood *not* as part of a wider *socialist* project, but rather as a way of maintaining the industry and trade unionism within it.

This early refusal of the miners' leaders in England to articulate a socialist political programme in place of their pragmatic, labourist conception of legal activity and control, has received general opprobrium from historians of the Labour movement as well as from Marxist and socialist writers. More significantly, their actions were deeply criticised by the active socialists of the period. Here, whether the argument was proposed by Sidney Webb the Fabian, or John Maclean the Scottish Marxist, or later by G.D.H. Cole the Guild Socialist, the 'villains of the piece' were the trade-union officials.

In articulating such criticism, A.P. Orage, writing in 1914, provides us with a classic account which combines the features of pragmatism with careerism and conservatism. In his view the trade-union official:

> is innocent of any theory of life. He loves authority and he loves the ordered ease of the civil servant. He has natural yearnings for a swift transition from the 'passive' conditions of waging to the 'active' influence of the bureaucratic organisation. To be a jack in office in Whitehall is to him preferable to the strenuous impotence of labour politics.[29]

This account resonates powerfully with well-established radical and revolutionary criticisms of union leadership, and it has an important degree of substance. Established in their Miners' Hall on North Road in Durham, Crawford and Wilson, these early architects of the union, fit well with the strictures of Orage. Eminently respectable men, they were concerned with protecting their position as representatives of the Durham miners, a group to which they alone could claim legitimate and official access; a group for whom they spoke in Whitehall and in the House of Commons. Given the power and prestige they obtained from the corporate nature of their organisation it is not surprising that they were reluctant to throw in their lot with 'socialists', nor that they should have a suspicion of sects and 'intellectuals'. Certainly they could claim that they were *elected* and that they were the authentic mouthpiece of the people who worked in the mines. Viewed in this way, the criticisms fall short in one vital respect. What they fail to address is the possibility that 'labourism' (as opposed to variants of socialism and Marxism) offered a perfectly comprehensible programme for organised groups of workers within the slowly developing forms of capitalist production in Britain.

In Britain, miners had pressed for legal forms of protection at work. They had pressed in similar ways for the right to organise, to publicise their views, and to have their trade unions recognised. With the extension of the vote to the working class, another arena of activity was opened up, and here too there was no necessary or compelling logic which pushed these union officials toward co-operation and involvement with 'outsiders'. The roots of a 'labourist' politics lay far deeper than the careerism or egos of these men. It can be seen in the ways in which the county unions of the miners pressed throughout the nineteenth century for their rights—i.e. the rights of miners as a group. It was these rights which were fashioned in acts of Parliament and which served to bolster a strongly corporatist (and thereby sectional) understanding in the mining areas, an understanding which went more deeply into the culture of miners and their families than may have been hitherto recognised. They were, as Jevons noted, 'to a great extent a class apart from the rest of the community.'[30] It was this which underpinned the view that the MFGB should stay independent of any political party, pressing the state for its own demands in ways which had become well established. From this perspective the shift towards affiliation to the Labour Party, and thereby union subordination to the *Party's* political programme marks a critical step. It was this view which saw the miners' representatives voting against the formation of a Labour Representation Committee at the TUC Conference in 1899. In 1900 the miners refused to engage fully with the socialist societies that founded the Labour Representation Committee. In 1906, under pressure from Scotland and South Wales the MFGB balloted its members on the issue of affiliation, but once more the vote was against. Only in 1908, after another ballot, did the miners' union finally agree to affiliate with the new Labour Party.[31] In writing on these changes, Gregory has noted how 'the politics of the coalfields underwent

Alderman William House: ILP activist, a 'friar of the new order'. President of the Durham Miners' Association 1900–17.

a change that was swifter and more far-reaching than anything before or since.' It was a change that was all the more remarkable given that the 'established and influential leaders rejected socialist thinking and fiercely rejected and resisted the concomitant idea of a new and independent Labour Party.'[32] For all that we have played down the significance of this as an ideological change, the involvement of the miners' unions in the Labour Party came to have considerable political importance as the century progressed. It is one which has all the greater interest if it is not simply assumed that the Labour Party provided the miners and their union with a *natural* home. The issues involved in this political change were raised in interesting ways in Durham.

By the first decade of the twentieth century the miners had clearly established themselves as a powerfully organised group of workers in the north of England. Their officials operated as MPs monitoring developments within the industry in the House of Commons. Locally they negotiated elaborate and detailed agreements with the employers. Miners' agents, lodge officials and checkweighmen met regularly in Durham and in the other regional centres, to discuss their policies and their problems. It is not difficult to understand why many of these men felt that they had little need of outside help. The nature and conditions of mining as a trade had produced men eminently capable of representing themselves, and leaders who were not slow to remind others of this fact. In their, reasonable, view, the miners had already achieved direct functional representation by their own members and it was by no means clear that the Labour Party with its mixture of socialist societies and trade unionists could continue to offer this. Indeed their situation almost invited the retort that as miners could, and had, achieved parliamentary representation without the Labour Party what was the advantage of them joining? It was most apparent to them that the new party needed the miners more than the miners needed it. If the party was to be a trade-union party then Wilson's programme of trade representation would seem directly relevant. If it was to be a socialist party, then the miners exclusionary practices against outsiders would be placed in jeopardy. This situation was changed through a combination of national and local factors which brought together industrial and political issues, alongside more pragmatic concerns over office-holding and career advancement.

In trade unionism change has most often been brought about by opposition groups appealing against 'betrayal' by the leaderships of their organisations. Conflict within a trade union invariably focuses around fundamental questions relating to the democratic basis of the organisation; often that takes the form of an appeal for the basic values of the organisation—solidarity, fraternity and democracy. Those pushing for change demand the ideal of an active and participatory union. In Durham at the turn of the century and in the face of Wilson's style of leadership several groups were attempting to change the DMA. The largest of these oppositional groups was made up of miners who were members of the socialist, Independent Labour Party, and they were keen to contest the political development of the DMA.

Established nationally in 1893, the ILP played an important role in Durham up to the First World War. It was the ILP with its evangelical brand of socialism which led the campaign for the DMA to rejoin the MFGB. The DMA leaders with their Liberal affiliations were contrasted with the national and rival powers of the MFGB and the Labour Party. The influence of the ILP was greatest amongst the checkweighmen, who by this time had become a powerful political force inside the union. In 1901 (with John Wilson's strong opposition to the Labour Representation Committee clearly established as union policy) this group formed an unofficial Durham 'Labour Council'. This rank and file body supported local Independent Labour candidates in elections and campaigned for the DMA to break with the Liberal Party. These checkweighmen strongly identified with the industrial policies of the MFGB which involved support for the minimum wage and the eight-hour day. This programme of course was supported by the Liberal leadership within the MFGB; in Durham these same proposals formed a *challenge* to Liberalism. This paradox related to the peculiar features of Durham. It also pointed to inconsistencies in the Liberal view of the state. These views were forcefully argued in the Durham 'Labour Council', and became more important as the coal industry entered into economic crisis.

An increasingly large group of checkweighmen supported and orchestrated these views, and linked them to the question of a new party. For them, a new party offered the additional advantage of offering ways of developing their own political ambitions. In their view the DMA had not taken fullest advantage of the 1885 Act. With a new party it could secure a dramatic increase in the numbers of miners directly represented in parliament. This view was not an unreasonable one. In the election of 1885 Wilson and Crawford had been returned as Lib-Lab MPs. Wilson chose to succeed Crawford as the representative of mid-Durham after his death in 1890, and by 1900 (after four general elections) remained the only miners' MP on the coalfield. A situation which paralleled the national picture, but one of which Wilson generally approved, arguing strongly against the political representation of miners' interests as a *class* interest. To the members of the 'Labour Council' this was merely another of Wilson's strategies for restricting their access to positions of influence and power.

While checkweighmen in Durham were attracted to the idea of a new party for tactical and pragmatic reasons, many of them also *believed* in the idea of a socialist party. The significance of the Independent Labour Party in this process was considerable. In 1905 the party had a full-time officer and 16 branches in Durham; by 1907 these had increased to 60. In its annual report of 1906 the ILP claimed Durham as being 'in the very van of the movement for Labour and Socialism'.[33] Its appeal to local Methodist activists was real and immediate. Men like Jack Lawson attempted to change and adapt their trade unionism in line with this new political vision. A mobile layer of political activists quickly moved into the newly constituted County Council and rural district councils. The ILP gave them a programme and a focus and this increased with the formation of the Labour Party. If the Liberal Party had been the Agents' Party, then the Labour Party became the arena in which the checkweighmen exerted their influence.

As the early union leaders in the 1860s had operated as a *cadre*, meeting regularly and developing arguments, so too did these men cohere as a powerful, unofficial grouping within the Durham Miners' Association. Most of them were checkweighmen, and all of them were Primitive Methodists. In the chapels and lodges of their villages they held positions of some significance and they were able to mobilise around these and gradually change the policies of the union. They campaigned on a terrain that was quite different from that of the non-union era, and this had an effect upon their mode of organisation. Their policies were ones which were directly critical of the county leadership—and of Wilson in particular. They favoured membership of the MFGB and of the Labour Representation Committee and were opposed to Wilson's Liberalism and the regional isolation which accompanied it. Their call, therefore was for a national union of miners, built around a socialist politics. By 1910 the majority of the DMA executive were socialists and W. House, one of the agents, was a member of the ILP. The new cadre was in place. Jack Lawson describes them as 'visionaries, friars of a new order, in which service was its own reward.'[34] They became the leaders of a union, which had become an established bureaucratic organisation.

The formation of this group within the officials' class was of critical importance in Durham. The leadership of the unskilled and semi-skilled unions were new to organised politics and were attracted immediately to the idea of a new Labour Party. The same was not true in the miners' unions, where established political practice exerted a powerful influence. Change required the consolidation and emergence of a new leadership group capable of pushing for change within the organisation. In Durham, a generational struggle took place within the fabric of the organisation. The checkweighmen formed a layer of activists in the union and these were 'new men' seeking a national rather than local focus. In organisational terms they were bent on ending the exclusiveness of Durham. In political terms however they carried the old traditions on into the twentieth century. The Durham Labour Party was to be a compromise between the desires of Lawson's 'friars' (a group which had been denied official recognition by the old Liberal leadership), and the routine practices of office. Moore has characterised the group as 'a small band of devoted volunteers, committed to socialism, study and debate, inviting distinguished speakers from all over the country'.[35] Moore's subsequent evaluation is important also. In his view this group was to be:

> replaced by a Party machine controlled by the Miners' Union and by 'converted' Liberals, a machine concerned with gaining and keeping power, not with political education and controversy.[36]

That many organisers of this 'machine' had received their political education in the ILP was, however, important. Equally important were the range of rules and organised behaviour that had been built up in the period of Liberal leadership. This, and the broad ideological cast created by the Methodist tradition in Victorian England exerted a powerful constraint on the radical potential of the new leadership. In opposition they had fought against Wilson's style, his undemocratic use of his position in the union and his political links with the Liberal Party. But, like him, they saw themselves as 'respectable' members of Durham Society. Like Wilson the Chapel figures powerfully in their biographies and they too would have identified with Knox, and seen in him something of their own lives. To understand them better, we need to explore more fully the nature of life in the coal mining villages of Durham in the early years of the twentieth century, at a time when the industry entered its final decade of expansion, to be followed by decades of protracted decline and conflict.[37]

5
Durham Mining Villages

All students of mining villages have stressed their extraordinary cohesion, which must be ascribed in part to their isolation and concentration upon one type of employment, in part to the common dangers of the miner's life, and in part to the absence of social change.

H. Pelling

J.M. CARMICHAEL'S painting 'Murton Colliery 1843', now hanging in the Sunderland Art Gallery, places the colliery firmly in a rural setting. The pit is located within fields where cows and horses graze and where, in the foreground, groups of men and women stroll and carouse. The smoke from the colliery stack is counterbalanced by blue skies, trees and flowers. The pit, in the background of the canvas, is neutralised by rural life. Both seem at ease in each other's company. While this painting can be criticised as idyllic, underplaying the harsher side of mining life, it demonstrates an important truth which has been handed down in popular memory. Coal mining, the central industry of capitalist expansion in Britain, took root in rural society and was held in tension within it. In Durham many of the mining villages were country villages. While they were organised in a new form around industry, and while they were covered in black coal dust they were nevertheless surrounded by fields and agriculture, and those fields played an important part in mining life.

Rural Transformations

This emphasis upon the rural is important. In the nineteenth century these villages enjoyed a rich pattern of social life based around festivals, sports and drinking. John Wilson remembered how, in the 1850s, Sherburn Hill:

> was the gathering ground at the pay weekend for gamblers, drinkers and fighters from the neighbouring collieries...ready for any and every mischief. To be like these was the goal of our youthful ambition. We used their vocabulary and followed their example. The more adept the man was, the greater our admiration for him, and the more ardent our desire to be like him. There were men in the village who were as eager for any sport or bout of fisticuffs as the visitors, and therefore the occasion was not far to seek or long to wait for.[1]

Public houses opened at 6 a.m. and stayed open throughout the day; celebrations such as the one above often lasted into Monday and Tuesday. Nor were they limited to men. Women figure centrally in the nineteenth century folk songs 'Cushie Butterfield' and 'Wor Nannie's a Maisor' which celebrate drinking and seemingly endless days of riot and abandon.[2] But, at that time, expression of this working class culture was the cause of some concern. In 1875 the editor of the *Durham Chronicle* opposed the idea of granting licenses to grocers on the grounds that it would increase female drunkenness. The Durham diocese accounted for one eighth of all drunkenness in the country and almost half of the prisoners in Durham jail were women whose 'downfall', in the view of Archdeacon Prest, 'could nearly always be traced to indulgence in intoxicating drink'.[3] In the Deerness Valley, Pease and Partners appointed missionaries and Temperance workers to their villages. The other coal owners, Londonderry and Durham included, supported an attempt to establish British Workmen's public houses which would offer 'all the advantages of drink taverns without the drink'. An attempt, it is generally agreed, which was unsuccessful.

The work of the men in the pit and women in the home also retained strong links with rural practices and customs. In people's memories too, accounts of the countryside, woodlands and rural life operate as powerful images of the past. One man recalling growing up on the Northern coalfield at the turn of the century notes:

> Now the place was nothing to write home about and certainly would get no prizes in the best-kept villages. Eight streets of houses built around the pit. A Club, Institute, two Chapels, a Church Mission and a Co-operative store. Nothing extraordinary about that. I'll try to explain the enthusiasm for my Netherton. It was the warm, down-to-earth spirit that prevailed which has always made the place special to me. As I say, the colliery village wasn't beautiful but you only had to go a few hundred yards to be right in the heart of the country. To be across those fields and woods in the spring and summertime was fantastic, with the variety of trees, plants and shrubs, bird and animal life and, on a clear day looking eastward, you could even see the sea.

Waterhouses: This colliery was one of those owned by the Pease family in the West of Durham. The houses were put up in 1862 as a 'model village'. It remained a rural industrial village throughout the twentieth century.

Similarly in the north-west of Durham in the 1920s, June Davies has written how:

> Chopwell Woods gave balance to the dirty, loveless rows of houses in the villages. The dust and fumes from the burning tip gave way to high trees and sweet-smelling flowers. The cool, clean refreshing River Derwent helped the birds to sing a better song as it rippled over stones and splashed at the edges. Kitty Shells gave us ice-cold sparkling water to drink.

Nor were these experiences simply a product of the small 'family pits' in the west of the coalfield. They remained true and central for the people who lived in the large centres. The town of Stanley, for example, situated in the north-west of the county employed over 14,000 miners in its heyday. From its main street situated on a hill, it was possible to count thirty-six sets of pulley wheels. Ted Farbidge moved to the town in April 1915. His father had been brought up on Stanley Hall Farm, and had spent time as a boy working on the screens at the Fanny Pit. On his return to Stanley, with his family and after forty years working in Medomsley, he was struck by the transformation.

> My own reaction to this urban community, after having resided in a small village in the scenic Derwent valley, was a feeling of being thrust into a land of bricks and mortar enveloped with a pungent smell of coal-fired soot and smoke, with people seemingly everywhere. Such were my first impressions when our furniture arrived at number 14 Moore Street, South Moor on a humid day, for we seemed to be eating smoke as we unloaded our furniture.

However, it was still possible to walk 'to the surrounding woods to satisfy our pleasure'. And here also:

> We quickly adjusted ourselves to this totally different environment...being helped by the people around us who were very sociable and keen to make us aware of all the amenities that were available. In this respect there was no change, for the neighbourly spirit of the mining community of South Moor was equal to that which we had experienced at Hamsterley Colliery.[4]

These experiences were shared in the north-east of the county by miners and their families who moved to Boldon. Here, however, we have an even greater sense of change. Jack Lawson has written of his move to the area in this way:

> When we came to Boldon Colliery, the sense of that closed-in-ness increased, for I had lived my life up to this time in little more than single-street communities where there was always not far off the sea and wide-stretching country, woods, and distant mountains. We now found ourselves in streets which seemed to my childish eyes miles long, an endless number of streets, every house and every street alike. They were of a very common redbrick type, instead of the stone houses to which we had been used. Barracks, barracks everywhere and noisy, bustling life. That closing-in feeling within, that sense of submergence and nothingness which I first experienced when we left the rural parts behind us and approached Newcastle, was completed on our arrival at Boldon Colliery. For, although that was forty years ago, Boldon was and still is one of the great, outstanding, up-to-date collieries. It had 2,000 workmen then, and a community of at least 10,000 men, women and children connected with the mine. It was a mass-production colliery, a rationalised concern long before the word was coined.[5]

Here we have three accounts, from Chopwell, Stanley and Boldon, of the changes which accompanied the rapid increase in coal production around the turn of the century. In the south of the county the transformation was equally dramatic. At Spennymoor and Fishburn new pits were sunk. On the coast to the south of Murton, the Horden Coal Company and the Easington Coal Company established major new collieries at Blackhall, Horden and Easington. The Horden mine grew to be the largest colliery in Europe employing close to 4,000 workers. The mine was linked to a large coke works and the whole complex became a central part of iron and steel making in the South Durham and Teesside area. These pits drew large numbers of miners from the west of the county and beyond. Bob ('Skipper') Allen remembers living in South Hetton as a small boy and travelling to the new colliery:

> I was eight years old. I would like to get a ride on the store cart. There was all carts then. I went to the back of the store and I walked in and there's the butcher hitching his galloway to the cart. I went and stood and watched him and he said 'What's thou want son?' I said 'I want a ride if I can get one.' So he said 'jump on the top.' We set away. We went up to Hawthorn down into the pump houses, did them and came to Easington Village. There were no roads. We came through the fields, and there wasn't a house. The only brickwork there was near the water works. Still we went down, all trees going down until we came to where the Diamond is now and that's where a makeshift road started. No houses anywhere mind. We went down to the Colliery. I remember clearly we came to the bottom and where the General Office is now, there was a farm—Blackburn's. I can see the pond now, with ducks swimming about. Around the gable-end there were the streets of sinkers' huts. Five houses in Front Street South were up. That was in 1905.

Easington Colliery grew quickly after this point, as part of the general expansion of coal production. In Durham this development was associated with the formation of increasingly complex corporations with industrial and financial structures extending beyond the coalfield. The Easington Coal Company, for example, was a part of the Furness Group and its board of directors brought together interests such as the Weardale Steel and Coal Company, various other coal companies (South Hetton, New Brancepeth, Trimdon, Wingate, etc.), Martins Bank and the Seaham Harbour Dock Company. This important development saw the increased concentration of economic power on the coalfield, together with the development of increasingly large coal mines with related washeries and coke-making facilities.

Nevertheless, and in spite of the expansion of this joint stock form, many aspects of the old paternal relations were retained. Housing was still owned by the company. In Easington Colliery, the rows were built

The growth of Easington Colliery 'fodder to be housed and sent down that bloody shaft'.

one after the other almost on top of the colliery shaft (see map on this page). Men reflect upon how, with all the available space, the houses were so cramped and so close to the colliery.

> It tells you how they understood the miner. We were just fodder to be housed and sent down that bloody shaft.

Rural Continuities

What is clear in these accounts (and many others could be added to them) is a picture of change as a large industrial labour force was created. However, within the context of these changes aspects of the old, rural forms were retained and developed. Rural crafts—like that of the blacksmith and joiner—expanded with coal production. In addition farming, although greatly diminished (employing just 3 percent of the population in 1900), remained a significant part of mining life. Easington Village, a mile to the west of Easington colliery, remained distinctly rural. As one woman remembers:

> It was an agricultural village. Nothing else, you see. There would be a saddler, who would repair harness's, and an old cobbler. Then there was a tailor, a butcher, a tinsmith—he used to make tins to bake your bread in, or cake tins or anything. He used to go round selling them to the different collieries. There was Murton, South Hetton and Shotton. He used to make the old-fashioned pit tin bottles. You know, they used to take a little bottle of water down the pit. The miners were that thirsty down the pit, that they used to take the clean cold water, and jam and bread as a rule.

For example, in Murton, Norman White remembers how, towards the end of the nineteenth century, his father moved from the west of the county. His family had been 'hirelings', the common term for farmworkers who:

> were picked at a Mart where the farmers sold their stock or produce. The farmer would look at the crowd seeking work and he would select the men he wanted.

At Murton, his father, Jack White:

> worked on a farm as well as working at the pit. He would take fields on to de-thistle them in his spare time. By doing this job for the farmer he would be paid in rows of potatoes when they were ready for harvest. He had a horse, cart and a garden of his own as well, where he kept pigs and hens also other fowl.

In the south and west of the coalfield in particular, mine labour retained its rural quality well into the twentieth century. It also had a family quality. One man recalled how when 'the tatties were ready for picking, the lads in the family had to go with the horse and cart to bag the potatoes after digging them up.' In Chopwell, Hilda Ashby remembers one family that lived close to her:

> there were two sons working at the pit and the father working at

the pit and two lodgers. That was five men working at the pit. The father kept pigs and hens and he took in lodgers. All these things to eke out the pay. And that house always had a pan boiling with potato peelings and we all used to take our peelings there and we'd get a sweet. And it was a regular thing to see a pig hanging in the yard because in those days you could kill them yourselves.[6]

George Alsop was born in Chopwell in 1911. His father was 'a miner all his life' but, he adds, 'that wasn't all.'

We had lodgers, pigs, and gardens. We used to come in from school after playing marbles and my father would shout 'Hey, feed the pigs.' And after you'd fed the pigs you would have to go and seek horse muck; follow the horses around!

My dad worked in the colliery and we lived in a normal sized, four-roomed colliery house. The sitting room, kitchen, two bedrooms and a small kitchenette with a tap on the wall and everywhere home-made mats on the floor. We often used to have a pig lying on the pantry floor. We used to kill our own pigs, of course, and we used to cure them. We used to go to the store and get a big block of salt and we used to rub the salt into the pig—into the various joints, cover it with salt—and it would lie six weeks. Then you turned it over and you did the same with the other side. Then it was cured and ready for eating. We used to have legs of ham, and we used to hang them from big hooks in the ceiling.[7]

In Spennymoor, where Bolckow Vaughan established a massive coal and coke complex around the Dean and Chapter Mine, the story was similar. Dick Beavis remembers:

In those days people kept their own pigs, and they often had them killed in their back yards. They would put a cabbage leaf down for it to eat and then hit it on the head with a wooden mallet, cut its throat and roll it into the tin bath where hot water was poured all over it and it was scraped clean.[8]

It was the same at Kibblesworth, in the centre of the Durham coalfield. There Mrs Stark recalls her childhood sitting on 'a grassy bank at the roadside making daisy chains' or of the local farms:

We had a farm next to the streets of houses and the farmer's wife would let me collect eggs and break up the cattle fodder with a simple machine. Her husband also had a butcher's shop and killing animals was done in a building just a few yards from the footpath. It was a common sight to see the floor covered with

> blood. Children would flock to a garden if they knew a pig was being killed.

At Kibblesworth villagers remember how:

> Everyone was a gardener. We grew most of our own food. There was just the potatoes we bought from the farmer—we picked the best ones out to eat and the small ones we'd boil for the pigs.[9]

Such accounts read somewhat oddly when placed against other, more orthodox interpretations of the miner as 'typically proletarian': these recollections resonate more with ideas of a peasant society than with a proletarian one. Clearly, however, these people were waged workers; equally clearly, their earnings were subsidised, in no small form, by extra-waged activity such as baking, poaching or keeping livestock. Of no less importance was the effect of this 'rural development' upon the strong sense of place associated with being born and brought up in one of these villages.[10] So too is the way in which images of the countryside (often as a place of escape) emerge with a powerful regularity in all accounts of mining life in Durham.

The modern mining communities of the twentieth century were established in opposition to paternalism, yet they contained within themselves some of these elements of a rural past. This combination of rural practices, mine employment and trade-union organisation produced a form of working-class experience and organisation which was at once both efficacious and distinctive. Its distinctiveness extended to many aspects of life, all of which reproduced themselves through custom. Sporting activities are a good example.

Holt has observed how at the end of the nineteenth century the coal miners in the North East remained 'happily locked into a friendly masculine and introverted sociability' based upon the pubs and 'the continuity of country sports', adding that 'whatever the sport, miners tended to play only with miners and even then rarely with miners from other coalfields'.[11] Historically, the rise of these sporting activities was related to the increasing availability of 'free time' away from the mine. The abolition of the bond and the introduction of a five-day week in 1872 encouraged a variety of sports many of them associated with gambling. These often involved the breeding and racing of animals and birds. Holt again:

> Whippets were a popular pet in pit villages....They were small enough to keep in the house and might even pay their way by catching live rabbits in the fields as well as chasing them into a trap....Dog owning was a world of its own with all sorts of ways of 'stopping' a dog or speeding it up....[However] breeding, feeding and training dogs whether for the big tracks or the small ones was not quite as popular an activity as keeping pigeons.

> Miners were the most enthusiastic pigeon fanciers...often living in identical villages close to the countryside and older sporting traditions.[12]

These traditions linked in with trade-union activity. John Wilson describes an incident which took place while he was addressing an open-air meeting of miners from the Thornley, Ludworth and Marley Hill collieries in 1884. The meeting was important and concerned the miners' loss of pay as a consequence of the coal company going into bankruptcy. The meeting also coincided with the end of a pigeon race.

> The day was fine and there was a large crowd...it was about the time when the birds were expected. Some of the men were thinking more about the match than their pay, and were watching the heavens more closely than they were listening to the speaker. Their all absorbing topic was, when would the birds arrive? Just when the orator was in the midst of one of his best sentences and highest flights of oratory, a voice was heard...'Hald thee hand 'til the slate cock comes in.' In a moment speaker and occasion were lost, and the gathering generally watched the bird, the hero of the hour, as like an arrow shot from a great bow, he came right on his 'ducket'. Then in a deliberate manner, the same voice was heard exclaiming: 'There, he's landed. Thoo can get on wi' the speech.' But rhetoric and reason were both ineffective after the slate cock had landed.[13]

In commenting on enthusiasms like these, Holt draws connection between the miners' work and their leisure pursuits. He writes of men 'cooped up for long periods in dark, damp, cramped seams', having a 'particular feeling for the natural warmth and graceful speed of dogs and birds'. Perhaps however, the historical continuity is the most important point to note, and with it the significance of fate and chance in many of these sporting activities. Equally important is the fact that these activities (and semi-professional running could be added) were not team games. In all of them, the contest was 'man against man'. As the century progressed the Durham coal miners became avid players and supporters of association football. Their involvement in the Northern League (through clubs like Crook Town and Bishop Auckland) and their support for the Newcastle and Sunderland football clubs, is well established. Nevertheless these earlier sports survived drawing upon strongly individualistic elements within mining culture. In an interesting observation, Alan Metcalfe has noted that:

> the miners were exhibiting characteristics which allowed them to survive as individuals and as members of communities within the oppressive physical conditions of work and home.[14]

In this way *heterogeneity* and individual difference were exaggerated in sport, dress and lifestyle.

> visible demonstrations of homogeneity on the other hand only occurred when they ventured out of the colliery districts, either to play sport, to shop in town or to engage in collective action.[15]

More generally, the scale and extent of the elaborately developed household economy, joined with the retained rural focus of life to provide an important and flexible base for survival and support. In 1920 for example, there were 50,000 registered allotment holders in the county. Furthermore the produce of these 'small holdings' was supplemented by poaching. The stories of poaching, the accounts of near escapes, and the details of net-knitting and ferreting filled our ears and our note books as we talked to old miners and their families, especially in the west of the county. Birds and rabbits, hares, trout and salmon, and even stag were all available, and all poached. Repeatedly we heard the view that myxomatosis was deliberately introduced to remove cheap (free) food from the miners. In Spennymoor, Dick Beavis regularly poached rabbits at night:

> I used to spend a lot of time poaching. I was the 'knitter'. I used to knit all the nets for the lads. Put them over the holes, you know, and put the ferret in. We had a long net then, about eight yards by one yard, all folded up properly, which we carried in a sack. On a pitch black night we would go out to where we would place the net: usually along some moorland stretch of burrows. Each of us knew exactly what to do: one laid the net out; the other followed with the stack pins (pointed hazel-sticks which the farmer used when he was thatching his cornstalks) to keep the net up; the other coiled the rope. I used to run around the field lashing the grass. When I got back, you could feel the net tugging and pulling with the rabbits entangled in its meshes. My mates used to run alongside it and just nip their necks.[16]

As always in Durham, the interpretation of these related activities needs to be complex. Beavis, for example, found in poaching the source of his 'political thoughts'. Here as he sought to avoid the police he asked himself 'Well whose was the land?'...I used to think 'What harm are we doing?' These thoughts quickly led to 'Who owns the pits?' and others relating to royalty payments and the like: 'They got a very good living just because they happened to own the land the coal was under, Lord Londonderry, the Bishops of Durham and people like that.' These ideas weren't uncommon ones and in the private-enterprise economy in the twentieth century, a resentment built up in the miners against the power of the coal owners and their economic and social privileges.

These practices obviously had a strategic importance, especially during industrial disputes. There is no doubt that this independent food supply affected the capacity of these workers to endure extremely long strikes. There was another side to this though; it is possible that their independent existence also enabled them to endure pressures and constrictions in work which they would otherwise have resisted. For example, it was common in Durham to refer to a practice of 'big gardens and low wages'. In 1920 Peter Lee (newly elected DMA agent and Chairman of the County Council) commented that 'gardening and poultry made for temperance and thrift',[17] virtues which were dear to his heart. Clearly, both processes operated in a way which produced in Durham a mine labour force different, in many respects, from the 'classic' proletariat identified in England by Marx and Engels. These differences, deriving from the rural nature of mining, and the operation of aspects of forced labour regimes throughout the nineteenth century, had consequences for the political culture of the coalfield, and for the ways in which understandings of class, and class conflict, were dealt with. These issues invite a further investigation of the social structure of the mining village, and the pattern of change associated with coal mining in the first half of the twentieth century.

6
Rough Cavils

The ultimate form of the 'nightmare of history' is...the fact of labour itself, and the intolerable spectacle of the back-breaking millennial toil of millions of people from the earliest moments of history.

F. Jameson

PIT WORK has always been hard. In Durham, coal as hard and as sharp as flint, lodged in thin wet seams, was for two centuries or more cut free by the sheer physical strength, skill and endurance of the miners. Generally, the expansion of mining across the county was little more than the extension of established techniques which relied upon picks and shovels, upon ponies and the endured pain and strength and accumulated experience of men.

The conditions which men worked under were looked upon with shock and disbelief by people not initiated into the practices. In 1852, one man described his visit underground in this way:

> First, then, how to descend. We see a vertical hole, or pit, pitchy dark, and surmounted by wheels to facilitate the raising of coal from the bottom of the shaft. Into one of the 'tubs', or 'buckets', used for this purpose we must now contrive to get, a matter which requires no small amount of nerve to effect. If the bottom of the bucket should give way, or the rope break, or—but it is fearful to speculate on such ifs when you are swinging over a depth of several hundred feet. Now we are descending. It is said by those who ascend in balloons that no feeling of motion is perceptible, but that the earth seems to be flying away from them while they are perfectly still and motionless. Much the same idea may be said, in reverse, in descending a coal shaft. You have no idea of the descent, but the little round hole of light seems to be flying faster and faster over your head upwards, as if it were going to the skies, and at length, in a couple of minutes, perhaps,

the orifice of the shaft has apparently turned itself in a day star, which shines far, far above you in the firmament.

Arrived at the bottom of the pit, what do we see? Nothing, or nothing but 'darkness made visible'. Every vestige of daylight is effectually shut out, and it requires some time to accustom one's eyes to the light of the candles, which appear as mere sparks or points of light in the midst of intense darkness. By degrees, however, our eyes become accustomed to the strange scene, and men are discerned moving about in galleries, or long passages, working in positions which would break the back of any ordinary workman, while boys and horses are seen to be engaged in bringing the coal to the mouth of the pit. Some of these horses go through the whole of their career without seeing the light of day—they are born in the pit, reared in the pit, and die in the pit.

The actual coal digger is called the hewer. Whether the seam be so narrow that he can hardly creep into it on his hands and knees, or whether it be lofty enough for him to stand upright in, he is the responsible workman who loosens the coal from its bed; arrangements below ground are made to suit him, he is indeed the key of the pit, the centre of the mining system.[1]

Almost a hundred years later Mark Benney described a descent into the shaft of a Durham coal mine. The bucket is replaced by a cage; and the shaft bottom is lit by electric light. What hasn't changed is the long walk to the workplace, or the nature of the work. The visitor reached the coal face with 'every muscle in his body shrieking in protest. His head aches from incessant banging of his helmet against the roof'. Resting before starting his experimental shift of work with the men, he reflects:

Lying there in the darkness, he looked back over a crowded career of social investigation and thought of all the hard work he had done. He had always considered himself a hardy man. He had worked in factories at tasks considered gruelling, and been commended for his work. He had double-trenched a garden all day and felt only pleasantly tired. He had tossed hay at harvest time and been scarcely more harassed than the labourers he had worked alongside. But this—this was different. It was like trying to do any of those other jobs while chained down by heavy manacles. He watched the other at work, and marvelled. Norman, his black muscular body glistening in the olive-coloured light of his lamp, worked easily and quickly, crawling about with the agility of a mole. There was, too, an urgency behind his work that seemed almost unnatural. His shovel drove forward and cast back not only in a steady rhythm, but a fast rhythm. When he had to hack away a bulge on the face where the shots had not broken the coal off cleanly, his pick bit into the

> mineral with a flail-like rapidity and the full weight of powerful shoulders behind it. It was full-blooded, unrelenting and unflagging effort, that would have seemed wholly admirable in a man working in the full light of day; down here, in the darkness of a two-foot seam, it was almost unbelievable. And yet it was the appropriate, probably the necessary rhythm of work here. Where bodily comfort was out of the question, there could be no half-way effort: one either worked in a sustained, tearing fury, or not at all.[2]

Hard labour then, was at the very heart of the mining industry. It was this which Ellen Wilkinson laid at the door of the coal owners ('the most short-sighted of all employers of labour') and which in her view made coal mining such a deeply conflictful industry.

> The earlier and more primitive the mine, the higher the wage cost relative to all other expenses. Hence the constant pressure of the owners to drive down wages. Despite this, it was not till after a century of coal mining that any considerable progress was made in labour-saving devices. The individual labour unit was cheap. There was always the hope of getting it cheaper. Until electricity and compressed air came into commercial use there was no source of power underground for actual coal getting except human muscle.[3]

Accident and Death

In the nineteenth century the 'risks' of capital were widely broadcast, but little publicity was given to the more fundamental risks taken by labour. The employers were not legally required to record the deaths of miners until 1815, and no adequate register of mining accidents existed before 1851. By that date there had been thirteen major mine disasters in County Durham, with the combined deaths of some 525 men. This trend continued throughout the nineteenth century with major loss of life at Burradon, Seaham, Trimdon, Tudhoe, Usworth, Elemore, Fencehouses, Hartley and Wingate. These experiences and their deep impact upon the culture of the village, found their expression in the mining ballad. In Durham Tommy Armstrong's songs were especially popular and amongst these the 'Trimdon Grange Explosion' stands out:

> Let us not think about tomorrow
> Lest we disappointed be
> All our joys may turn to sorrow
> As we all may daily see
> Today we may be strong and healthy

But how soon there comes a change
As we may learn from the explosion
That has been at Trimdon Grange.[4]

These lessons were central to the concerns of the trade union activists. Edward Rymer remembers an explosion at the Page Bank colliery, and of the continuous efforts by miners to press the need for improved ventilation:

> At this time a sad calamity happened at Page Bank Colliery. There was only one shaft, brattice being put in the middle of the whole length of the shaft for purposes of ventilation. Sparks of flames from the furnace set the brattice on fire, and several lives were lost. All hands were called out of Spennymoor pits to assist in the flooding of the mine by the use of portable water engines brought from several collieries. The River Wear being close to Page Bank we were set to work day and night until the fire was extinguished. The fields adjoining the pit were lit up, and looked like a battle-ground. This fatality and the shocking catastrophe at Hartley Colliery in 1862 brought about the agitation against single shafts, in which I took an active part from 1860 to 1871.[5]

It was through legislation and a series of Mines Acts that safety conditions improved. Yet mining remained a hazardous occupation. In 1909 an explosion in the West Stanley mine resulted in the death of 168 miners. On that occasion the *Durham Chronicle* noted that 'every single home in the town has suffered the loss of a relative or close friend'.[6]

While explosions accounted for most of the multiple deaths underground, many more men were killed in isolated accidents.[7] In 1900, 1,012 men and boys were killed in British coal mines, and by 1910 this number had increased to 1,424. Using the 1918 official statistics Frank Hodges showed that one miner was killed every six minutes, and one was severely injured every three.[8] By this time the single most significant cause of death and injury was the fall of coal and stone, often associated with inadequate roof support. This trend continued for the first half of the twentieth century. For example, in Durham, the records of the Shotton and District Mines Inspection Board reveal that in the years 1925–1946, 294 men were killed in the 19 mines that worked in the small area under its jurisdiction in the south east of the county—14 in every year; 15 in every mine. Of these fatalities 186 (64 percent) were as a result of roof falls.[9]

These accidents were remembered vividly by the men who were closely involved in them. At the Wooley Colliery in Crook in the south west of the county Jack Wilthew remembers how Norman Ayre and his 'marra' were working together. Norman waited while the other man worked along the seam.

Durham Mine Disaster: the Glebe Colliery Washington, 20 February 1908. Fourteen coal miners killed: this card commemorated their lives.

> He went through and then he was nipped. A wedge of rock, conical in shape 'like a dunce's hat' with a weight of a half-a-ton or more, fell without warning. A slight grumble in the earth, that's all. He let out a scream and that was it like. Crushed; ribcage shattered, spinal column severed, as the body was split apart. Nipped. It affected Norman; he went to work the next day, but it affected him later on. It really affected him.

In Horden, Raby Larimer remembers how men killed in the pit were pushed 'through the streets on a little handcart...two big wheels and just a coat over them, or an old blanket'. This was not an uncommon occurrence; from the time it opened until 1946, no year passed without at least one man being killed in the Horden pit. Records from the nearby Murton Colliery show that between 1887 and 1946, 218 men died underground; an average of four deaths a year. Union activists recorded these as pivotal facts of mining life. Ned Cohen, who worked at the Bewicke Main Colliery and the Ann and Betty pits of the Pelaw Main Company recalls how the Ann pit was known as the 'butchers shop'. He documented ten fatalities in thirty years at Bewicke Main and, between 1930 and 1944 another twenty five at the Ann and Betty pits at Ravensworth.[10] George Alsop provided us with a similar record for the

Chopwell mine: between 1902 and 1946, 44 men were killed there; three in 1902, another in 1907 and 1908, two more in 1909 and 1910, another four in 1912.

When old miners and their families talk of 'blood on the coals' it's to be taken literally, especially when we add to these the countless numbers of accidents, the 'bumps' and 'knocks' which at best scarred the miner's skin, at worst left him crippled. Dave Larimer had such an accident in the Horden mine.

> The stone that hit me was 7ft 6in. long and 4 ft across, I was in 3 ft and I was working by myself, I had a pneumatic pick, and it came on top of me. I had the pick like that and the stone pressing down from above was shoving the pick through my stomach. It was thrusting me; I could feel the bones breaking in my leg, all the time like that...I started pulling myself out like that, and I lay there, but my leg was smashed, and I was pulling myself out like that, you know, and I could hear the bone, the doctor said it was broken into hundreds of pieces...and I pulled myself out like that.[11]

Something of the nature of a miner's life under the Durham system can be gained from an account by Fenwick Whitfield of his time underground in the Eden Colliery, at Leadgate. Like Chopwell, the pit was owned by the Consett Iron Company and Fenwick started there as a boy of thirteen in 1907. Wounded in the war, he returned to the pit and:

> I think I must have had the record for accidents along there. I've had cuts and broken bones—all sorts. In fact I've had the same ankle that the bullet smashed broken in the pit too.
>
> I was off eleven months with that. It was the top coal that I was filling at that time...I remember I was taking the last of the coal down and the wedge was fast. So I took the pick and tried to ease it; and then the whole lot came down on top of me. The coal hit me on the top of an ankle. I just thought it was a bad strain and I didn't want to go to the hospital. I couldn't sleep and as soon as I'd get to sleep I'd wake up with these dreams—the stones chasing me. I'd been off eleven weeks and the X-ray in Newcastle showed that the ankle was badly shattered. The company doctor said I'd be no good in the pit any more. They wouldn't give me a light job. But I had to go back and I went back to my own work. I just decided that I wasn't going to be a cripple.
>
> In 1935 I had an injury to an eye. In fact two days running I got a blow in the eye from the pick-point. After the second one I got up in the morning and I couldn't see out of the eye at all; there was a great ulcer over the whole of the pupil. I went up to

> the doctor's and he said 'how sharp can you get away down to Newcastle to the Eye Infirmary?'
>
> I was in there for twelve days. I was off four months all together at that time. They gave me no hopes of the eye becoming normal again, or even improving. I had to shut the bad eye and read with just one for a bit. So I had to get glasses.
>
> Then I had a nasty gash across my knee. It was a Saturday morning shift and I'd only just started. A chap had put a prop under this miniature fault [where there had been small streams when the coal was being laid down], and it meant that I couldn't work properly. I just touched it with my pick and the damn thing fell out and down it all came. I was sitting on the cracket (you know the small stool the miners used). It was a terrible mess, there was small coals all over the top of the gash. So they sent for the ambulance and I arrived at the Consett Iron Company Infirmary at about 2 o'clock in the morning. Well, the nurse who was there tried her best, poor soul. She had to clean the damn thing and she was using swabs and she kept saying 'Am I hurting you?' I said 'You get away. You can use a scrubbing brush if you've got one to take that stuff out. It's got to come out.' Oh, it was a hell of a mess. There was this lad sitting beside me. He was looking at me, and then the wound, and back at me. The nurse looked at him and said 'You get out of here'. And she chased him out: he looked like somebody dying. Anyway, she stitched it up; but it was that dirty she couldn't clean it properly, so in two or three days time it turned septic and the stitching had to be taken out again. They had to hold the wound together with Elastoplast but that couldn't draw it together enough—it left a bad scar.
>
> Then after the last war a piece of stone fell between two planks and hit me over the kidney. The company doctor said 'I'll make you off for light work' but the National Insurance doctor reckoned I'd recovered. So I went back to hewing. This one day there was water on the face and the belt was slipping and I got my finger caught in the coupling pin. So I had to have a piece taken out of my arm and grafted on.[12]

At the end of this account he remarks, wryly, that he's 'got some dust. But not enough for compensation. Perhaps when they open me up they'll find different'.

In Crook people remember how conditions varied enormously in the collieries owned by Pease and Partners. Waterhouses was aptly named. It was a wet pit with narrow seams and men lay on their sides in water for the length of a shift, and walked home in wet clothes at the end of it. Men tell of their toe nails falling off and of their skin being permanently soggy; also of illness, of pneumonia, TB and bronchitis. The Wooley

Colliery was dryer. There the problem was dust, particularly in the Ballarat seam. Billy Simpson worked at the pit, and he'd also worked in Waterhouses. He remembers how:

> The conditions were better at Wooley but the dust was bad. Of all the fellas that worked in the Wooley Ballarat when it opened up first in 1932, 90 percent of them are dead. There's no doubt if they'd worked somewhere else they'd be alive yet. It was the dust and that hard coal. Pneumoconiosis.

Norman Ayre was one of these men and his son Dave tells of his father's illness in this way:

> I remember that there was a ritual that my father did, the phlegm and stuff used to build up, and it was jet black, and he used to spit on the fire; it was something he had to do. It was deadly: just thick black phlegm. When it was humid and warm and there wasn't any air, it was terrible to see him. In fact there's a fella next door to me exactly the same, and they say he's got bronchitis, he can only walk as far as the end of the yard. I remember with my father, eventually they come round and they said he had 25 percent pneumoconiosis, and I remember he died in hospital; he had a hernia you see, and the doctor persuaded him to go into hospital.
>
> He got over the operation, but he died of a heart attack; what with his lungs, it was just too much. There was an inquest, and they had an autopsy, and at the hospital when I went down, they showed us his lungs. The part where you breathe, well, it was just like a lump of coal really. After that we got compensation, but, you see, he was dead. That's the sort of thing that happened, and it's still happening. You can pick them all out, the old miners.

You can pick them out through the marks of the pit; the marks of pain. Even in the most casual of conversations: 'That's the year my brother was killed'; 'He was killed not long after'. Such phrases are spoken quietly, as reminders. Like in this account of pot bowling in the 1920s:

> There was often lads that could not bowl you see. They would match themselves to bowl somebody. Georgie Westmoreland lived down here, a big lad, I could bowl my cap further than he could bowl a bowl. Now he used to fancy himself as a bowler, because he was a big lad, he had bowled a time or two. Why he was a noted character, big Georgie; he got killed at the pit.

At other times the memory is closer and more disturbing. Babs Walsh of Horden remembers that on his third shift underground her grandfather,

> was in the dark with the tubs and he put his hand in this tub and it was covered in blood. The remains of a man killed in the pit. And I remember him telling us how he vomited all of his stomach up when he did that. The remains of a man in the tub.

In the same village Dave Larimer thinks of his brother who was killed underground before 'he saw his first pay. He got killed on his first pay day'. He worked at the Lumley Fencehouses pit alongside 'this' creeper, it was like a conveyor belt, and it used to come up and it gripped the axles of the little wagons, the tubs you know...and take them up this incline. The boy got his clothing caught in the creeper:

> My older brother was working with him and he was shouting 'Stop the creeper', and my brother was trying to stop it, and he was yelling. And he was trying to get him loose, and he got pulled through the creeper. He got an arm torn off...he got a leg torn off, and then he fell forty feet, and I remember as if it was yesterday when they brought him home from work...I can remember the doctor trying to push my mother out of the front door when we lived at Lumley. I can remember as if it was yesterday taking a running kick...and kicking the doctor on the shins because he pushed my mother out of the front door. Now my other brother that was working with him, he got pneumonia with shock. And he never lived very long after it.[13]

Stories (and experiences) like this; of how the boy's leg was brought to the house wrapped in brown paper by a workman who got 'a minute's notice' for his concern. So ever-present was death and injury that it became patterned into the culture of mining villages. Men stopped work when a man was killed underground: in this way death became linked to the trade union. Funerals were important occasions, often attended by the band and the lodge banner. Today people still talk of 'a chill down the spine' when they hear the Dead March played.

Death intruded in less obvious ways too. Sometimes in jokes: as in the story of the two miners, one religious the other blasphemous, who agreed while underground to compromise on their differences. Caught this day by a roof fall the Methodist immediately started to pray 'Please Jesus save us.' His marra responds: 'This is serious. Forget about the son go straight to the old man.' Then there were the myths and the miracles.

Water was always a problem in the Durham pits, and many miners met their death underground after 'an inrush of water'. John Wilson came close to such a fate, and was pointed out, for forty years and more as 'the man who came back from the dead'. Peter Graham remembers the story:

> I went to school with his granddaughter. They called her Wilson as well like. He was the man who followed his *own* coffin into

Durham Mine Disaster: West Stanley, 1909. Every family and household in the town lost a member, as 168 men and boys were killed in the underground explosion.

> the cemetery. His son died in Kelloe pit, but he came back from the dead.

John Wilson was a Deputy. On 6 May 1897 he went underground early in the morning to examine the face before the hewers began work on the foreshift. He was accompanied by the wastemen. Before the hewers could descend, a rush of water broke through the coal dividing the Kelloe pit and the Old Vale pit at Cassop. The Harvey seam was flooded out, and the water swiftly reached roof height at the shaft bottom. All hope was abandoned for Wilson and the wastemen who were trapped at the face. Four days later, after continuous pumping, the pit was cleared of water and the rescue party moved into the mine. To their amazement, they met a man walking towards them through the receding water. It was John Wilson. So convinced was the village of his death that his name had been included in the eleven coffins made for the funeral. Peter Graham again:

> They made a coffin for him, you see, but he was alive. Ten men were killed but he escaped. Then, when the pit started up again another man was killed so they used Wilson's coffin for *him*. And that's how I mean—he followed his own coffin into the cemetery. And he lived another fifty year.

Then there is chance—the accounts of men who were 'in an inch of death', or were saved from disasters and explosions by a fortuitous change of shift. Such stories make undeniable the fact that to work in the mines was to take your very life into your hand: to tempt the fates. In Easington, 'Skipper' Allen put it more straightforwardly:

> It's terrible, the dangers the miner faced. And all the time he's down there in the dark; no sunlight, breathing dust.That man, when he goes out of the house doesn't know if he's going to come back alive or not. And when he goes out of the house he's in the hands of the Lord.

The religious influence here is important and not unusual. All the same, some men will tell you that, after a particular accident or near escape they 'lost their nerve', and wouldn't go down again.

Survival

As you reflect on all accounts of death and injury, the question becomes insistent: how did these people endure such experiences? How did they manage to survive; to ride in the cage shift after shift?

At its simplest, the answer is a short one; they endured it because they had to. One of the old men we spoke to can speak for many:

> Once you're a pitman, you are a pitman and you never thought owt about it. It was your job and there was nowt else for you, so you just made the best of it. I mean it's a rough life like; it was hard work but you just had to accept it. I mean, you never thought nothing about it, about the dangers really, you just worked away. It was hard work mind.

These people lived and died within social arrangements we have referred to as 'the Durham System'; here they learned their place and what their chances were, for this system, of its very nature, filtered choice down to its finest grains. This is not to suggest that life was little more than inert acceptance. Living through such pain, people created something for themselves to help see them through—the 'culture' of the village. This 'culture' had its impact upon votes, upon strikes and upon political demands. It had its effect upon the Durham System too and upon the world of the employers. The weight of 'the system', and the struggles for independence within and beyond it raise (in microcosm) some of the broadest questions of working-class history and sociology.

In the many conversations we have had with men and women who lived in the 'Durham System' the *absence* of choice is stressed again and again. People talk of mining as 'not a job, it was a way of life'. They tell how 'you just went to the pit. It was automatic'. There is talk too of 'mining stock' and of the entry into pit work as being 'more or less instinct'. Yet some were determined to escape from the pit. Maurice Ridley lived in Stanley:

> Being a mining area there was nothing else but going into one or other of the local pits. You were destined to go into the pits through being the son of your father. It was an automatic thing, unquestioned. The girls either stayed at home and helped mother, or they went into domestic service. There was no such thing as commercial or other training for girls.
>
> The many children of real ability were as deprived of further education as anything else. We were set to be hewers of wood and drawers of water. Lads and lasses, practically all from the same backgrounds, without the opportunity of any wide reading apart from our school library and the effort of the teachers. If a teacher was absent I was scheduled to go in and take a class of nine year olds and do the hour's teaching. 'Right you are Ridley you will go in there, this is the arithmetical form you will show them'. And we just used to do this automatically at twelve and thirteen, because our basic education was finished. We had no chance of getting out of the situation we were in, none whatsoever.
>
> At fourteen, the day you finished, you went down to the local colliery. Friday night you finished, and our fathers would say 'Right, Pit Office'; and you'd be interviewed, and straight into the pit on the Monday. That was me. I had twelve months work at the local colliery prior to the 1926 lockout. Although I wasn't involved in the hard work at the coal face [working with ponies and so on] it was a bitter experience. To have to go down there and do really heavy types of work under conditions that were not really suitable for any human being. Let's face it, I'm very clear in my own mind that coal mining is one of the occupations that [if one could organise or run one's life without it], should not be on. We were expected to do things that the horses couldn't do. We were more expendable really than the ponies that we were working with. But neither of us should have been in such a situation—horses nor men.
>
> I started at the Morrison Busty, one of the new collieries within a few miles of where I lived, in 1929. At the same time I took up WEA class studies on economics and also (as this wouldn't provide me with the possibility of a job) evening classes in English, commerce shorthand, and Accounts. I was doing this simultaneously with my work in the pits. By that time I was almost nineteen years of age, and beginning to see a different attitude to many things. I became involved in the union lodge. It was quite unusual for nineteen and twenty year old miners to be

Trapper boys with their lamps, waiting to go underground.

> active trade union-wise, but the older miners gave me every help and support. So I was involved 60–70 hours a week; but it was all interesting, and the only thing that I hated about it all was the fact that I was back in the pit. I only weighed 8 stone, I wasn't strong enough and big enough to do what I had to do as a hand putter, alongside lads eleven and twelve stone. I never ever came to terms with that. I was physically exhausted and mentally almost around the bend. Nothing could change my attitude on the importance of miners or mining communities; but for me, with my physique, I decided that I had to fight out of the dreadful situation I was placed in. I just worked and worked to get out.[14]

William Bell also escaped from the pit. He was born in Tow Law and as a boy he remembers how his father was badly injured there in the Black Prince mine.

> There was no first aid, and after a long delay he was brought home, cramped up and laid on a bittern of straw in a horse-drawn coop cart which trundled along the farrowed black earth road. The occasion seemed of no more importance than the delivery of a sack of potatoes.[15]

William started underground at Hamsteels colliery in 1910, and, as he put it he had 'mixed feelings':

> I was entering a phase to merge my life with an older generation, suddenly I had become a responsible being. I felt proud of the thought of coming to help support the home and elated at the thought of a little pocket money at weekends. My ego had received a great boost. Sons of fathers in colliery tied cottages were expected to become miners upon leaving school, and at fourteen years of age I signed up—on the blackest day of my life. Was there ever a greater denial of freedom, no say or choice in the occupation I might wish to follow, no regard for capacities and aptitudes for higher forms of service? The bondage which was that of my father was inflicted upon me under conditions that were oppressive and hateful....My first working day in the mines by its very harshness is indelible in my mind. It is unthinkable that there was no initial introduction to the mine in the company of a responsible person to get the feel of underground workings with all the dangers....Each and every day at the entrance of the pit gave the build-up of resentment, to enter the mine just as the rising sun was showing on the horizon in the east and to reemerge as it was disappearing in the west gave an acute depressed feeling; it was as if I was being cheated and robbed of life itself.
>
> Seeing no hope of escape and in a spirit of resignation, I was determined to rise above the worst features by advancing my position in mining. I attended evening classes...at the Johnson Technical School, Durham City...[then] surprisingly opportunity of escape to freedom did come my way. The newly-formed Durham County Water Board advertised for staff to take charge of districts for the collection of water rates. This was the last throw of the dice; I took a chance on it and made an application when out of the blue it came my way....In the October of 1925 I started a new life and left behind me all that was loathsome in the dark underground.[16]

These accounts, while coming from unusual people, shouldn't be seen as untypical. For many boys who had seen the effect of pit work upon men's bodies, the pit became a threatening presence. Dave Ayre was brought up in Crook.

> When I was a kid I remember my father. He wasn't working at Wooley; he had a job in the Valley: that's the Deerness Valley, and they never had any transport, so he had to walk to the Valley and back, all weathers. I can remember one night in foreshift that was when they worked overnight—he hadn't come in, and there was a hell of a blizzard, a terrific storm, and he hadn't come back, and naturally my mother was really upset, and she got us up—well, I can remember I heard her stirring around, and I got up,

> and I said 'Look, like, I'd better gan out and find him'; and I wouldn't be...I'd only be six or seven year old, but I was the eldest you see. Anyway she went out, and with the other people went to look for them; anyway, he eventually came, and he was absolutely clapped out, and I can remember this as if to the day, and he was soaked to the skin and he was covered, black, you know, because there wasn't any pithead baths, and he laid, well collapsed, on the floor. He was absolutely buggered, and I bet he laid there for half an hour or three quarters of an hour before he got up. And he was a big sort, a stout fella, and then he would be in his 40s. So I mean it must have, it was really exhaustion...and he went to work the next day, and to just do that for a living....But you can imagine half a village having to do this, and you can imagine the impact it had on certain kids.[17]

George Alsop, as a child of ten or eleven, had seen the corpse of a man wheeled through the streets of Chopwell on a cart: 'they had just ordinary sacks, coal sacks, thrown over him'. At fourteen he was clear that:

> I didn't want to go down the pit, I really didn't, but I hadn't any other option. After the strike I was off work for two years and I was only getting 1s 6d. a week from the assistance. I always remember my father. With it being a big family he used to point at me and say 'he's not ganning in the pit', being the youngest, 'your not ganning in the pit'. But I had to. There wasn't any other jobs available, other than the Council. But you had to be very fortunate to fall in for a council job; because once a bloke got one of these jobs he didn't let it go.[18]

Most people, through circumstance or temperament (mostly a combination of both) remained in the jobs they were given underground. The structure of the village and the fabric of village life had a way of making the unbearable normal; even desirable. Ernie Laws, in Crook, gives an account of mining life which emphasises the closed nature of life in a mining village:

> There were no factories around here then. You worked down the pit or at the coke ovens. There was nothing else. I had five brothers and we all worked at the pit. You see the manager knew exactly when a lad was leaving school. He knew when every boy was fourteen, and he'd send for the father to take the lad up as soon as he left school. I left school on the Friday and started at the pit on the Monday.
>
> Once you were a pitman you never thought owt about it. It was your job and there was nothing else for you.

Wherever there was an option, through family contacts or chance, men

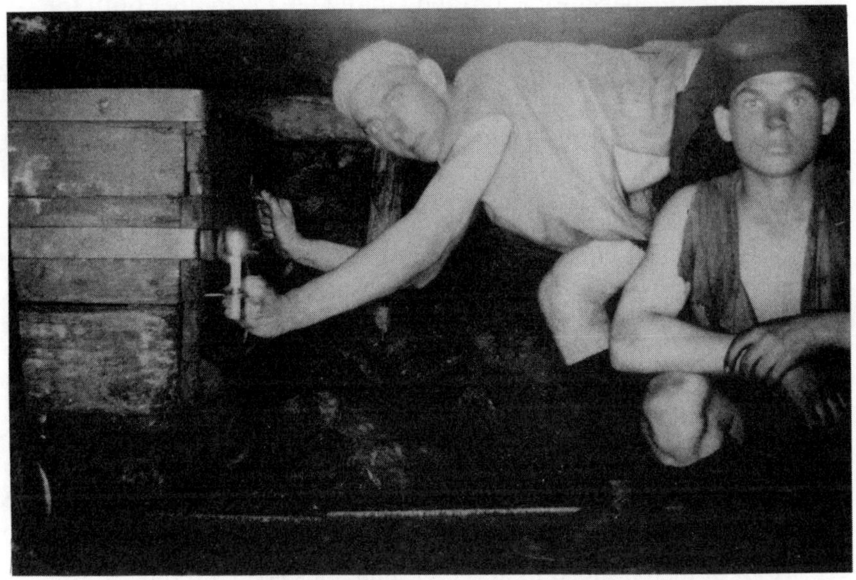

Hand putting: 'the men are the ponies'.

tell of their *mothers'* resistance to pit work. George Bestford's uncle, for example, was a saddler in Weardale: 'My mother didn't want me to go down the pit. She took me away on the Saturday to this uncle...he was going to train me to be a saddler.' However, such a course split young boys away from their friends, and often they resisted. George remembers how his uncle was 'as deaf as a stone':

> He had a big trumpet that you had to shout down, like a horn. He'd put it in his ear and I had to shout down it. Well I thought I'm not stopping here; my mother went back and I'll bet before she was home in Tursdale I was at Dawdon with my grandfather. And I was down the pit on the Monday. My mother didn't know for a while but eventually she found out I was in the pit, and she said that if I was to be a miner I had just as well go down the pit at Tursdale nearer where we lived. So that's what I did.[19]

Bob Grey lived in Crook, and he had a similar experience. His mother had a fish business:

> We had a little horse and cart and she wanted to put me into the business on my own. We owned the shop next door and I was out hawking fish and fruit and one thing and another. That went on for nearly a year, but I wasn't happy with it. All the lads that I was going around with were in the pit. All the talk was about the pit. I was outside it. So I was fifteen when I started. I went and

> asked the manager for a job, and I didn't tell my mother until the Sunday that I was starting work on the Monday at the pit. She played hell!

Mostly though there was no option. Dick Beavis was the youngest of six boys, and in spite of his mother's anguish, he too followed his brothers into the pit.

> As a kid I didn't understand it all: I just didn't understand. My mother said 'There's no work: there's either the pits or the 'Hiring''. You had to go to Bishop Auckland where the farmers examined you—to see if you were fit enough to milk a cow, you know. Well the stories that used to come back from lads who'd been to 'The Hirings'. They were living in little tiny white-washed huts miles away from anywhere. And my mother said 'You don't want to go up there!'[20]

And the 'Durham System' was designed to keep the pits manned. At its heart was the 'colliery house'. Henry Ashby:

> A lot of men decided to never let their sons go down the pit. But in those days you had to leave a record of your family with the pit manager. And on the fourteenth birthday the manager would say 'Send your son along to see me tomorrow'. 'No I'm sorry, he's not going down the pit'. 'You send him along to see me'. 'No, he's not going down the pit.' And then 'Look you have a colliery house? You work in the colliery? If you want to keep your home and your job just send him along'. That was how it was. You see, they had to produce the next generation of miners. I remember the last time that it happened. It was during the last war and the chap was able to reply: 'I don't live in a colliery house—I live in a council house'. And his son didn't go down the pit.[21]

The colliery house was seen as a benefit, all the same. George Alsop explains how his mind worked in his early twenties:

> When I got married I used to think hard about what to do. Six and sixpence a shift: and two bairns. This was my train of thinking at that time: 'if I could only get a colliery house I would get my coals'. Two big things: you got a free supply of coal, and you got a free house. Now that tied you to the colliery. The last thing that you thought about then was going somewhere else to find another job. You never thought about branching out to say 'wey I wonder if I could get a different job oot the pit'.
>
> You used to complain every day about going to the pit. You'd complain about the conditions that you were working under, and you were seeing that your family wasn't brought up properly. But it seemed as if you were shackled. You thought 'wey if I gan

and get another job I'll have to get oot the hoose; forst thing I'll have to do when I gan for a job is to be sure that I get a hoose'. So you were more or less tied.

Tied cottages, that's what they were. I had a sister put out on the streets through the tied cottage. Furniture and everything was put out on the street, because her husband wasn't working at the colliery....But that was the way things were. We had no choice in these matters. The colliery dictated our life. And this is the fallacy in what some lads say: 'wey what made me stop in the pit was the comradeship'. That's bloody nonsense to me. It was just necessity.[22]

Work, Life and Manhood

If the fabric of the village was ordered in a way which made labour in the mine a necessary evil, social relationships underground can be seen to reinforce this pattern. For it was here, through work and payment, and by way of progress through a variety of tasks, that boys became men. This is made clear in an account by a man who began work underground in 1837:

> On that level of life, I passed from childhood to manhood through the ordinary curriculum of the northern pit boy's lot. I graduated successively from the starting-point of a doorkeeper in the mine at nine years of age, through all the stages of a miner's toil and its dangers, till at twenty one years of age I took my degree as a coal hewer, this being the highest unofficial position attainable, at the cost of the hardest form of mine-labour known. Like an apprentice completing his 'time', so the 'putter', or conveyor of coal, becoming a hewer, has reached his highest level, and in the old pit phrase, 'He's now a man for hissel'.[23]

Boys who began work at the pit, would, in the bigger pits occasionally begin with a job on the surface. They'd work in the lamp cabin or on the 'screens' where the shakers sorted the coals. 'Bump, bump, bump the noise and the conditions were terrible—bump, bump, bump all the time, ten hours a day. You'd get home and you were still at work, lying in bed you couldn't get to sleep bump, bump, bump'. Most often boys started work underground. Time after time old men will say today how 'I finished school on the Friday and I was underground on the Monday'. There, more often than not, they went 'trapping'. The ventilation of the mines depends entirely upon trap doors being kept shut and on their being properly closed after the carriages conveying the coal have passed them. The boys were entrusted with this important task. They sat

Marras.

holding a string attached to the door, and pulled it the moment they heard the coal trucks approaching.

The nature of these jobs (vital yet isolated) often made the 'apprenticeship of the mine' a frightening experience, through which boys were quickly (even brutally) made aware of the discipline of work. This is Edward Rymer's account of how he experienced this in the 1840s. Working at the Buddle Pit near Pittington in the north east of the coalfield, Edward Rymer described the system as one of 'physical slavery' and explains how:

> Under such a system it was found impossible to gain either instruction or to cultivate the better part of one's nature. The Buddle Pit opened out to me a mystery in mining life, which will never be effaced from my memory. The tubs were sent through the mine drawn by horses. Changing of tubs at the 'flats' took place by lifting them on to a platform, covered over with metal flags. The rails on which the tubs ran were ledged, and the road was called the 'barrow way,' while the putter was known as the 'barrow man.' The yelling of those young fellows all day long, half naked, black, and covered by sweat and foam, made the place like a veritable pandemonium, unknown to all but pitmen. I was sent to mind two doors up an incline, and the drivers flung coal and shouted to frighten me as they went to and fro with the horses and tubs. The wagon-man, Tommy Dixon by name, visited me, and cheered me on through the gloomy night; and when I wept for my mother, he sang that nice little hymn:

> In darkest shades if Thou appear
> My dawning has begun

> He also brought me some cake, and stuck a candle beside me. Sad thoughts dyed my feeble sight with tears which I could not restrain.[24]

Almost a hundred years later Bob Porter started trapping at the Horden Colliery:

> You had to open and shut a door. The door was for ventilation and when the door was open, it pulled the ventilation the wrong way. So as soon as the putter came through (that's the lad with a 'gallower', and he has the tub behind him. The gallower is pulling it out all the time)...I had to shut the door immediately, to keep the air ventilation right. I was on there three days, for eight hours in the dark because the putters took my lamp off me. Their lamps went out so they took mine.

Along the coast at the Dawdon pit, George Bestford was introduced to the job by the overman:

> When I went there first the overman said to me 'you hear that noise [it was the air coming through the door] now that's the sea. So if you go to sleep and neglect that door the sea will come in'. And of course I was too frightened to go to sleep. I was frightened to death.

Boys were also entrusted with the task of pumping water.

> The first job I had down the pit was the job called 'hand pumping'. There used to be a big swally of water where the putters used to have to cut through, and if the water wasn't kept down to a certain level, the place wouldn't be workable. The place was no higher than the height of a table and we used to sit crouched down for seven-and-a-quarter hours every day. Seven-and-a-quarter hours sitting with a little candle burning. I used to put a chalk mark on the rail and pump for about an hour. Then I would go and see how far the water had come down and put another chalk mark on to see if I was beating the water.

At the same time, Ernie Raine started work at the east Hetton Colliery in Kelloe. Ernie's grandfather was one of the men killed at the pit when John Wilson made his miraculous escape, and it was this same Wilson who gave the young boy his instructions:

> My job was to pump water with a hand pump. The place I was to do this job was far away from anyone who happened to be working in this district and a man called John William Wilson

> had the job of taking me to my pump, showing me how to prime it, and there I had to stand on a duck board out of the water, and make the handle go as fast as I could.
>
> After about an hour or so, he told me he was going to leave me. Before he went he made a clay man. He showed me this, and it was quite a good model of a man. This he placed on the edge of the water, 'now' he said 'I shall be away for an hour or so, but when I come back I hope you have not let the little man drown'. Off he went. How long he was away I can't tell, all I can say is it was the most lonely, and frightening time I ever spent in my early life. While he was gone I thought all kinds of awful things, once or twice I was certain I heard someone shout my name. I went out to the pipe end, but no one was there. I was so frightened I remember in my plight I almost stumbled. If I had I do believe it would have set me mad.
>
> I got to my pump after those two runs out to the pipe end. I hung my lamp up on the nail provided for it, and again began to pump, then I thought of the little model. I rushed to the water's edge, it was only a few yards from the pump. I could not find the little man. So I went back, got my lamp and there in the clear water I saw the little man. I paddled in got him out and placed him about an eighteen inches this side of the water's edge; and back to the pump that all my poor strength could go.
>
> Soon after this Mr Wilson came back I was so glad to see his light in the distance that I began to sing, but not for long, Mr Wilson went past me, lifted the little idol, and brought it back to me. He said, 'Ernie, this man has been drowned while I was gone.' This I denied, so he got me by the ear, took me almost a yard into the water, to show me a hidden chalk mark. This also was like a man. He said, 'I also left the President of the United States, Mr Washington, and he tells me you let our friend drown, pulled him back, and told a big lie'.

These first shifts in the world underground were hard ones. Men talk repeatedly of the exhaustion that enveloped their bodies.

> When I got home on my first day it was around eleven forty-five am, my mother was on the step looking for me. I could see her in the distance, and the lads were chaffing me about it, saying she'll have a spotted dog ready for you when you get in. This may have been so, only I don't remember. All I know was I was so tired. After a bath I got into bed and was there until work time the next day. This I repeated many times in my first few years at the mine.

This process of discipline and surveillance was supported by a more complex and social process associated with the mining community.

There may have been some resistance to 'going down the mine', but there was also a strong attachment to the value of the 'family name'. Boys took their family names into the pit; they were identified as the son, nephew, brother and cousin of other miners. To be born into a family with a 'good name' involved with it the responsibility of living up to this name in your daily life. To step out of line in the pit, in a way which brought dishonour on the family name, ran the risk of retribution at home which was far more severe than could be delivered by any deputy or overman. As one man put it to us

> to have a 'good name' meant that you carried it with you everywhere you went and you couldn't do anything that would let your name down!

And another:

> If anything went wrong at the pit, you could be sure that my father knew about it before I got home. He would hear about it through the community. So I'd have one telling off at work and a worse one when I got home.

The experience of these early shifts, so vividly remembered after half a century and more, had a deep and lasting effect upon these people and upon their emerging character as workmen. Its harshness, and the absence of women, pressed itself upon the life of the growing boy. Exhorted to 'be a man', not to cry in the face of fear or on the experience of a 'bump', there, in the mystery and the darkness, they became hardened and disciplined into pit labour. Remembering this, some men tell of kindnesses shown to them in adversity, others of the bullying attitude of the men, especially of deputies and overmen; of being 'clouted about by the men'; as they learned to endure the all male world. Norman Collins in Easington:

> It was cruel the way the other lads treated you. The initiation into work was to be stripped by the other boys and greased all over. That grease took 3 or 4 days to get off.

William Bell, writing of a similar experience twenty years earlier, is more explicit. At his first 'bait time' he remarks how:

> the putters, with more than horse play, threw me down and held me while one of them removed my short trousers and poured oil from a midgie [lamp] over my penis and genitals and massaged with soot. Considering there were no bath amenities, it was a condition to be endured for a very long time.

It was here, underground amongst men alone, that boys learned of sex. Bell mentions another incident which occurred when he:

> went into another place where putters and drivers assembled at bait time, and in so doing found two adolescents on their backs masturbating in competition to prove which of the two could effect an orgasm first. Strange to relate, my presence was no cause for embarrassment.[25]

In the mine, men talked with the language of the workplace ('pitmatic' is the term still used to describe it). They worked, often wearing little more than their boots, for hours on end in a place without light, with no sanitary facilities and where the only 'running water' flowed out of the earth itself. Here, work, masculinity and life became inextricably entwined. George Parkinson:

> Still, I was a man, and I knew it. There was no more drudging at home. I was entitled to as much meat as I wanted, and others were cleared out to make a seat for me. Even mother slightly deferred to me, was distantly kind, and bought me ready-made clothes. No more elder brothers' reach-me-downs, or cast-off boots. I sat up to the table with my elder brothers and father, black from pit, paraded my knowledge of pit technique, and generally tried to live up to my newly acquired status. It was worth while getting up at five o'clock in the morning for that. True, I didn't like the new pit shirts of coarse blue flannel which scraped my skin so that even to this day the very memory sets my teeth on edge. Now that I was a wage-earner I could go out at night for as long as I liked and where I liked. Thus ten hours a day in the dark prison below really meant freedom for me.[26]

In that prison, boys progressed from the menial task of trapping and pumping into those directly involved with coal haulage and coal cutting. First, though, boys worked with the ponies. Dick Beavis:

> The stables were about a hundred yards from the shaft and all the men were stripping off. It was really hot and humid. And my job, with the other lads, was 'tracing' the tubs up the line from the putters who had brought them from the face, and they'd leave them for us and we'd trace up and down a thousand times in a shift! And the poor old ponies would be bumping their backs. And your lamp would go out and you'd be in the dark and have to light it again.

Here again it was up to you to find your feet. One man remembers how:

> You had to learn to yoke the pony, how to hook him on to the tubs. A lad showed you, but you had to pick it up in your spare time. You'd watch the other lads while you were trapping.

Others weren't so lucky:

> I was only fourteen, and had never coupled a tub on, or never used a pony before this, so being slow at coupling on; and the men who were pushing the tubs to me shouting to get a move on, I got my head caught in between the tubs in my panic.

Old men still remember the name of their first pony. Many will talk endlessly about the 'galloways' they worked with underground and each pit at one time or another had one pony who was remarkable in one way or another;

> A lot of the lads were very kind to the ponies. They'd get very attached to them. Particularly if one was a good worker. They'd pinch carrots and turnips from the fields on the way to work for them. You'd tell your mother, you know, about the pony how it was a good pony—and she'd say 'Oh; take an apple for the poor thing!' One for me, the other for the pony.

As always there's humour:

> There was this particular pony who worked with this fella who had a cleft palate. And it was a wonderful pony; great. He'd do anything. Well I had to work with him this day and so I said 'Get on there boy!' and he wouldn't move. And I couldn't work it out 'Get on there boy!'. Then I saw what it was: 'Net on...!' So all that shift I was speaking like that...'Net on...'

And sadness too:

> I used to think if ever I came back into this world I wouldn't want to be a pit pony. They worked them into the ground. When the ponies were lamed, there were no humane killers you know. Just the hammer or the pick. Then roll them over, saw their legs off and take them out.

Here then, away from 'normal society', underground amongst men, through bumps and headaches, through a mixture of fear and hardship, through the occasional acts of brutality as well as those of comradeship and kindness, boys learned about the mine.

Then they were ready to become real miners: and this began with 'putting'. This was the term used to describe the job of transporting the coal from the workings to the main roadways. Most often it involved the use of a pony, although in the low seams of the undercapitalised mines in the west the tubs were pushed by men; this was 'hand putting'. There was a brief induction period. Putters and hewers were paid on piece rates, but for a brief period boys would be employed as 'datal putters', on a flat rate until they got the hang of it. Pretty quickly, though, they were on their own. As Bob Porter approached his sixteenth birthday he was told to visit 'the office':

> 'How old are you now? You're sixteen aren't you?' I said, 'I'm sixteen on Friday.' He says, 'Aye, that's what I've sent you for. On Monday your datal putting is stopped, you'll be a putter from now on, so you're on your own.' So that's the way things were run in those days, and by God, it was rough work. Then our Bill started work after me. He was eleven month younger than me, and he'd been down the pit about two years and then he got away putting, as well. I've seen me and him strip off there and count each other for the most knots on our backs. My mother used to have the big pan on the hob there. She used to put the cold water in. She used to say, 'Now there's the soap and flannel, get washed and get away to bed.' We was that tired, there was many a time, she'd come down at half past seven the next morning, to get the other bairns off to school, and we were still lying there black. Then the game was on! She had to start all afresh. We got many a rollicking over that.

The 'knots' he refers to were called 'buttons' in other parts of the coalfield. These were the scabs that formed on cuts along the vertebrae of your spine as you caught your back against the roof. George Bestford explains:

> They never made the roof higher than they had to, you see. If the tub was a yard high they would have the roof about four inches above that. It saved them a lot of money! But it used to be so low that if you were stiff and couldn't get your back down low enough, you'd take the skin off your back—we used to call it 'knocking the buttons off'. If you wore a vest it would get stuck into the cuts and when you took it off—it was like pulling your back off![27]

And this was when you were fit! Many men remember going putting when they had unlanced boils on their backs ('if you banged a boil on the top it was the most infernal pain') and in other states of ill health because 'you just couldn't afford to miss work. If you didn't work you didn't eat. It was as simple as that. There was no Welfare State in those days'. Matty Hutton, at the Easington Colliery, reflects upon this, and upon how:

> It's hard to talk about really; it's hard to describe it. It's so different from today. You take young lads, sixteen or seventeen; putting. All they had on was their small hoggers, a small hessian bag tied around their waist—the 'arse flapper' it was called—and a lamp hanging down between their knees. Sat down, crouched upon the shafts—the limmers—with the roof just above the top of the tub and squashed up between the tub and the pony. His face was right up to the pony's backside and some of those ponies used to smell. He'd be there, wringing with sweat, pushed up

> against the pony's tail and that was like a wire brush rubbing against his skin. It's hard to believe really.

At the Wooley Colliery in Crook there were forty ponies—'twenty putting Galloways and twenty drawing Galloways. They had Galloways there until it closed in 1960'. Arthur Askew remembers how:

> Driving them was not so bad, but little putting Galloways were awkward little devils. They'd go any way but the right way. They'd pull tubs from the brake and off the rails. Fellas used to get angry with them. I've known fellas hit them with bricks over the top of the tub because they couldn't get by the tub.' It was wicked at one time. Really wicked. They used to stay down there all the time you know. They never got up.

At the Easington Colliery it was the same. Billy Dunn:

> We had it bad, but it was worse for the ponies. These ponies would work one shift one day and two the next. They'd get three shifts out of them while they got two out of us. But they could be hard work you know. Some of the stallions especially. They thought they'd work harder, be more frisky. But some of them were uncontrollable. Then they'd change its name and move him to another pit.

In every pit there are tales of men being 'unnecessarily cruel' to the ponies, and in equal number with those which talk of close attachment between man and beast. At the heart of both these responses lay the fact that men were dependent upon horse power. The putters carried small whips which they used to encourage ponies along the narrow tunnel ways. To the whip were added other techniques (pulling their tails, putting sacks over their heads) and folk lore aimed at encouraging recalcitrant animals.

This however was preferable to hand putting. In Tursdale men reflect on how in the Brockwell seam 'they made the men the ponies'.

> The men had to shove the tubs. They were iron tubs—eight-hundred-weight tubs—on steel plates. It was pretty tough to push them along. If you filled them too full they would catch in the top, and if you didn't fill them full enough, by the time they reached bank they weren't the weight they were supposed to be. So you had to be very, very careful.

All this energy, this strength and frustration was built around the requirement of providing empty tubs to be filled with coal and delivered to bank. The men at the centre of this system were the *coal hewers*. It was toward hewing that the line of job progression gravitated, and within this occupational hierarchy it was the hewer who called the shots. He was the

A group of coal miners at the Sherburn House Colliery c.1900.

king pin: the producer of coal. It was the coal hewers who were most centrally involved in the building of the union. It was not for nothing that the DMA was (for 80 years and more) referred to as 'the hewers' union'. It was their experience, and seniority which gave rise to ideas of power residing 'at the point of the pick'. Also to jokes: about a pick being a shaft with a pick blade at one end and a bloody fool at the other. In the mining villages of Durham these men were accorded great status. Countless tales were told to us about the achievements and the social characteristics of certain 'big hewers'. In Crook, Bob Gray told us how in the 1920s:

> It was a hewing match every day....There was a chap called Ben West and there was another chap called Addison and another called Mick Charlton and they were the three big hewers in the Colliery...they were bloody engines, man. Mick Charlton, I've heard them say, used to eat a leg of mutton when he went in for his meal after he's worked his shift.

By virtue of such strenuous labour, and astute negotiations through their union, the hewers worked considerably shorter hours than the putters or the trapper lads and the haulage workers. Sturgess (who sees the hewers as the 'aristocrats of the workforce') describes this situation as an 'indication not merely of their higher status, but also of the inability of the putters to keep up with their rate of coal getting'.[28] It was this power, resting with the hewer, coupled with the organisation of work (which saw putters progressing to hewing), which complicated the position of the DMA within the MFGB. These hewers had, in effect, established through organisation shorter hours of work than the MFGB were demanding through statute. These men dominated the DMA's organisation, numerically and through its officials at lodge and county level. In 1891, for example, the DMA recorded 48,000 members; of these 30,000 were hewers.

Writing of the hewer in the nineteenth century Rymer noted how:

> Coal hewing in the north made many capital workmen, especially where picks, wedges, hammers, and drills had to be used. And to see the real pitman stripped to his 'buff', in short breeches, low shoes, and cotton skullcap, swinging his 5lb. pick, while the sweat runs down his face, is a sight which can never be forgotten.

This account stresses the arduous nature of the hewer's work, and the enormous physical strength involved. These features, taken together with the dangers of the work, became patterned into a complex and contradictory appreciation of the miner: in one view debased (the savage, excluded from 'moral society'), and in another respected with an almost religious awe. Rymer, for example, continued by arguing that:

> If ever man deserved reward for honest labour and the love and respect of his country, that man is the miner.[29]

As we have seen, these contrasting perceptions played a part in the early conflicts between the trade union and the coal owners in Durham, and became central to an understanding of the politics of Labour in the twentieth century.

What is absent in these accounts however is a reference to the *skill* of the coal hewer. Coal mining was formally an unskilled occupation. No apprenticeship system existed whereby new recruits were trained or formally instructed in the trade. Rather, in the Durham system, the miner was 'bred' and recruited to the coal mine by way of an elaborate system of social controls and legal regulations. In this process the skills of the coal hewer were often unrecognised—both by the masters and by labour historians. While no formal system of instruction operated in the Durham mines, it is clear that the pattern of progression through jobs *did* operate as a training process of a sort. Men often referred to their 'apprenticeship' underground and it is clear that a considerable amount of knowledge and understanding was transmitted informally, both at work or in the village and the home. Will Paynter, reflecting on his time in the South Wales coal mines, has written of the 'art' of the coal miner's work, drawing upon a unity of skills and knowledge born out of underground experience which involved:

> learning how to prepare the coal, holding underneath the seam...understanding the grain of the coal, preparing and erecting roof supports, and maintaining roadways.[30]

The importance of this awareness of geology, of the 'feel' of the workplace and the ordinary and unspoken features of work in a coal mine was clearly recognised by the Chairman of the National Association of Colliery Managers in 1887. At the Annual Meeting of the Association he drew particular attention to Rule 39 which stated that:

> No person now employed as a coal getter shall be allowed to work alone...in the face of the workings until he has two years experience of such work under the supervision of skilled workmen.[31]

Equally, in 1881 when *The Royal Commission on Accidents in the Mines* asked Cuthbert Berkley, a viewer for John Bowes and Partners, for the reasons behind adopting particular patterns of working in the Durham pits, he replied:

> I think myself in one particular district long wall may be best and in another pillar and stall. It will depend upon the experience gained by the men in each of those seams and they can tell which will be best for the particular seam...It must be left to the experience of the miner.[32]

These skills developed as machines began to be introduced on coal faces. In his *Textbook on Coalmining*, published in 1907, Boulton wrote:

> The satisfactory performance of a machine depends pre-eminently on the men in charge of it, on their skill and attention, their energy and determination. They should understand its construction, so as to be able to keep it at its highest working efficiency, and they must be miners of experience in the working face, knowing something of the working of coal seams and the support of the roof.[33]

This skill was increasingly recognised by the state: most clearly in the Mines Act of 1911. This Act legally established the position of Deputy in the mine; it also required that inexperienced miners became qualified face workers, through two years of work under the supervision of 'skilled workmen'.

Custom, Work and Conflict

The organisation of face work revolved around the hewers. In Durham these men historically worked together in pairs, in a system of coal mining known as the 'bord and pillar' system. This, in essence involved working the coal seam bit by bit, via a series of small 'rooms' (the bord). This system was labour intensive and relatively cost effective for the employers. The alternative system (which became more general and mechanised) was known as the 'long wall' system. In this arrangement, the small rooms were replaced by a long coal face which would be worked cooperatively by larger groups of men. In each system the coal hewers contributed significantly to the overall organisation of the work process.[34]

Coal hewers did not work alone, but with other men who they knew as 'marras'. The basic 'marra group' involved a couple of men, but the size of the group varied with the production system. In Durham these men were paid collectively a common 'note', the wages being divided amongst the workmen in a manner of their choice. As a central part of this system, the hewers chose their own workmates. These men were often from the same family; equally often they became close (lifetime) friends.

> The word marra had a deep meaning, for it signified that they agreed to work with each other and that they would share equally their joint production on pay day. Marrering was popular amongst families and relatives and also with individuals who had common interests but in the main, choice was according to inclination. As no two men are alike in appearance, the same applies where strength and skill are concerned, and it was not unusual for some men to be as much as 30 percent more productive than their partners and remain marras throughout their coal hewing life.[35]

The 'marra system' became a central part of capitalist mining in the north of England. It was allied to another system—the system of 'cavilling'—which regulated the ways in which workplaces were allocated in the coal mine. Basically, this involved the quarterly drawing of lots to determine the places where the work groups would be employed in the coal mine. As a practice it lasted well into the twentieth century. A account of the cavilling arrangements in the nineteenth century describes how:

> As each working place was called, a set of men was drawn from the hat until every place had been filled; during the proceedings a goodly crowd was always present to hear their fate.
>
> The four cavilling days of the year were decisive and binding

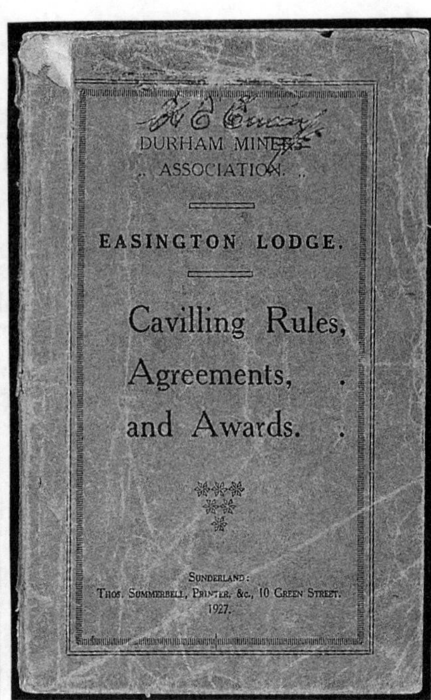

Cavilling Rule books from the Boldon and Easington Lodges. Each lodge had its own rulebook which was used to organise and settle disputes relating to the allocation of workmen to their place of work underground.

> for the next thirteen weeks and the luck of the draw for good or ill could affect the family's fortunes.[36]

Given the variety of different working conditions underground (height of seam, presence of faults, stone, gas, water, etc.) the place where a man worked was of great importance. Through the cavilling system, the hewers refused management the right to allocate men to places. Instead places were allocated to marras through the laws of chance. Cavilling (and trust in chance) was used to cover many dilemmas. While the Deaf Hill and Trimdon collieries were owned by different employers, the men cavilled together for work in both the pits until 1885.[37] It was also used in the face of lay offs and the sack. In times of unemployment miners argued that all men of the villages—both employed and unemployed—should be included in the cavil.

To be drawn to an 'easy' place could mean the difference between frugality and 'excess'. At the Chopwell pit at the turn of the century, one part of the pit was known as the 'piano flat'. To work there for three months guaranteed the wage that would supply a piano for the front room. As Fairbridge puts it:

It was not surprising that a few miners and their wives were known to have, and practise, superstitious beliefs, such as some women were known to leave their fire unlit on the day in question and then put the cat in the oven for luck. An odd man would not under any circumstances, pass a woman in the early hours of the morning without taking extreme evasive action to preserve his luck. Those of both sexes with strong Methodist traditions were known to pray in church and at home for understanding.

By and large, the larger proportion of those concerned faced the day with a certain amount of apprehension. If they were in a cavil which gave them the average or above average wage—they had a natural fear for the worst, while the minority in below average wage cavils looked hopefully to the future with full knowledge that things couldn't get much worse. In the main, with few exceptions, men awaited the outcome of the ballot in a calm and rational manner and expressed their disgust if the result meant reduced pay with the expression 'Just my Bloody Luck' if he liked his beer. His Methodist counterpart would substitute 'Blooming' for 'Bloody', in the expression.

On the other hand, if a favourable draw was their lot, many would declare that it was not before time as they were entitled to a break.[38]

But cavilling had another edge to it, one which fortified the pitman through the nineteenth century as well as the depression of the 1930s. It allowed men to regulate their relationship with their employer through daily practice. Grievances were often handled through a 'refusal to cavil' for places at the appointed time. The strength of these customary practices can be seen in the accounts of advice given to colliery managers at the turn of the century.

Colliery custom is one of the strongest pleas...and managers cannot be too careful to prevent undesirable practices becoming established. Even while such custom is opposed to county practice and agreement, it is difficult to effect an alteration and in no case can, once established, be altered except by agreement or by application to the Committee. In one such case during the year the owners asked that the practice of the colliery, which was to be idle on cavilling Monday should be brought into accordance with county practice. The application was strongly resisted by the workmens' representatives, and was referred by the Committee to the two Associations, who eventually agreed that it should not be pressed.[39]

Through cavilling then, men (and women) obtained a sort of fairness for each other within a hard and blatantly unjust world. It brought a rough sort of democracy to the village where men—no matter how big or powerful—were all equal before the laws of chance. As a practice it can be seen to have had more in sympathy with the gambling life style than with the severe morality of the Methodists. Its importance to the pit and to village life can be gauged from the extensive (and formalised) rules which regulated their operations. When the Easington pit was established in 1912 a list of thirty-two rules covering 'flats to be cavilled for the sunway round' were established for hewers and putters. At Silksworth as late as 1943 the cavilling rules included 28 for hewers working on bord and pillar or long wall faces and a further 11 for putters. These rules were published in small booklets, each carrying the name of the lodge and the copious detail of how arrangements at the mine and disputes over workplaces should be decided.

What comes through strongly in these accounts of mining work and labour is the significance of the culture of the coal miners and the colliery villages within the system of production. David Douglass, in his radical and analytic account of Durham mining life noted how the marra system, based upon the:

> principle of self-selection, maintains group standards of workmen. If a workman does not meet the standards of the group he will be informally told by his mates to improve, get some kip and plenty of grub or at the next quarter they will be getting somebody else to join them and he will have to find another set of marras perhaps not as hard-working, and earning...less money. If the demoted worker is unable to find marras then he will be placed with other men of his same standard by the management... he may even find himself on datal work.[40]

Here, it is clear, that the disciplining power (one that built up through the induction period in the mine and then in putting) is exerted most strongly by the work team. Douglass put it succinctly when he says that 'marraships were formed...according to capacity for work'. In this way the weak and idle were separated from the strong and the industrious. This pattern of segregation was reinforced in village life where the idea of being 'unable to get marras' was taken as a sign of severe social disapproval.

> It was a terrible threat that; to be excluded, not to have marras. It was like a curse, like being cast out—out of the community.

The biblical reference here is important. So too is the way in which the marra system and its components underpinned an ethic of hard work which was linked to ideas of masculinity, of strength and toughness. Miners, as we have seen, taught their sons to endure pain and fear 'like a man'. Linked to this hardening process were powerful ideas associated with social solidarity. These ideas can be seen as an important component in the life of the coal miner and help answer our earlier questions about the social survival of his form of labour. Equally important is the fact that this mining culture served as a means of resistance. Customary practices provided the coal miners in Durham with means of regulating and restricting the activities of the employers. At a deeper level however, these practices and the attachment of honour to death in a manner which has strong parallels in military life can be seen as necessary supports for the production system. In a real way private enterprise coal mining could not have survived without the coal miners whose values, principles and attitudes came to form a central part of the system itself.

7
A Labour of Love

To be born a woman has been to be born within an allotted and confined space, into the keeping of men.

J. Berger

IN DURHAM the colliery villages were organised in a way which best supplied and serviced men and boys for the pit. The family was the source of supply. Employment of women below the surface was made illegal in 1842. Yet women rarely worked underground after 1780 and it seems that the general employment of women within mining operations was severely restricted during the nineteenth century. In 1875, official reports tell us that thirteen women were employed on the Durham coalfield, and by 1886 this number was reduced to three. This again contrasts with other mining areas where women were extensively employed underground and, following the 1842 Mines Act, as surface workers. In the coal districts of Lancashire and Yorkshire where the textile industries had expanded alongside the coal mines, women worked in factories. In the urban centres of Sunderland and Tyneside, and in the west (where the Pease family employed women in its textile mills), there were limited employment prospects for women, but over most of the coalfield this wasn't the case. As a consequence, there was little source of paid employment for women in the Durham villages. It is interesting to take Seaham Urban District as an example here. Seaham was the model town planned by Londonderry to challenge Brighton in its design. In addition to coal mines, it had a thriving dock and was always an important commercial and administrative centre. At the beginning of the twentieth century the south east of the county played a central part in the expansion of industry, with new pits being sunk and workers and their families moving into the new housing provided by the coal owners. The 1921 census records how there were 6,053 females, aged twelve and over resident in Seaham Urban District. Of these, 5,224 (85 percent) were classified as 'unoccupied and retired'. Of the 829 who were employed, 125 were in various professional occupations, 182 in commercial and financial activity and the remainder in 'personal service'. We will comment on these aspects of employment later; here these statistics help illustrate the fact that the employment of women in the area was extremely limited.

In this world girls grew up to be women in the home just as the boys grew into men in the mine. Both had their own 'careers', and in their construction, ideas of sexuality and gender were of central importance. This fact was clear to all in the community. George Parkinson who, on being left underground as a trapper-boy with his brother remembers his father saying: 'I wish you'd both been lasses'.[1] What this man probably knew, however, was that the boys would not have welcomed the change. In Durham, to be a 'man' was to work in the mine; and this had value. The place of a woman was in the house and in domestic work. This work came to have much less status within the community. Yet work it was, and hard work too. Scott and Tilly have commented on this more generally in connection with the nineteenth century:

> Whether or not all work is done at home, all family members are expected to work. It is simply assumed that women will work, for their contributions are valued as necessary for the survival of the family unit.[2]

So too in Durham in the twentieth century. Here, life was about work; for boys and girls. And in this, family and kinship, those key institutions of affection, were strongly textured by pragmatism and need. It was the women whose lives dealt most deeply with these contradictions and ambivalences. To cope with them was all part of growing up—as a girl.

Work for Girls

Mrs Taylor was born in Horden in 1898. She recollects her early life in this way:

> You remember the washing days, don't you? I could wash when I was fourteen, doing possing, a big mangle, you had to go into the yard to wash. I went out to work for people in the colliery houses. I used to go for couples, I used to go washing bedrooms on a Friday and I got half a crown for doing all that work—half-a-crown and I thought I was well paid.
>
> I went into service when I was 15 down to Roker. I had to get up at 6 o'clock in the morning, and do a brass step, scour all the fronts, and if I made one wrong mark, out I had to go again, 6 o'clock in the morning, in the winter—cold winter. I was allowed no breakfast, I had to go without anything to eat or drink. I'd do my work that I had to do before 8 o'clock, then I'd have to shout the landlady up and have breakfast all ready. I was allowed two

nights off a week. For 3s 6d. a week.

I was married when I was seventeen. Ask my husband, I could do anything, paper [the walls] anything in the house.[3]

As the boys passed through a work 'career' so did the girls. Oddly and for all the associated images of manliness and toughness it was the boys who were tied most closely to their families and parents. Employment in the pit linked them to their fathers, uncles, brothers and cousins. Wages from the pit kept him at home, and home was where he stayed until he married and had a house of his own. The boys became men at work and men at home. For the girls, however, growing up, and earning money involved leaving the family and working in the homes of other people. This took place in a number of different ways. At the back of it all however was one main fact: 'in a mining village there was no paid work for girls'. Hilda Ashby explains the consequences this had in the villages of north west Durham in the 1920s:

A lot of women would have loved the extra work but there was no work. Not like the mill towns. Some women would take in washing or do papering, but in a colliery village there were no prosperous people either. Maybe a doctor or the colliery manager. My auntie used to take in washing and she would do a fortnight's washing for four people. Wash and starch and iron four people's clothes for a fortnight for 10s. One family in Chopwell had three daughters. They never married, and they used to make quilts and clippie mats. And they would work all week around this big frame and every week they would deliver either a mat or a quilt. People would pay so much a week for them. And they'd get £3. Out of that they'd have to buy the wool for at least £1 which would leave the three of them £2 for a week's work.

All the girls, when they became fourteen years old used to go down to Newcastle in service. And they used to get a half day off every fortnight and every Wednesday. In Chopwell you'd see all the girls coming home and then on every other Sunday afternoon. They used to get about ten bob a week and their keep. The two girls next door to us were in service. There were no washing machines and so they had to do all the washing. I know those two used to hate it. They were always leaving and coming home and their mother was always going mad. And she was always saying, 'You want to get yourselves a boy friend'. Someone who would marry them to take them off their hands. And this day she went on about them not having boy friends and Florrie, she says, 'Mother, there's two million surplus women in the country so somebody has to go without a man.' 'But aye,' she says, 'bonny hard lines when two out of my family have to go without.'[4]

Interestingly, this uneven distribution of boys and girls between families (especially when combined with death and a degree of occupational differentiation) produced some basis for paid work within the villages. Where a family had 'all boys' an arrangement would often be made with another where girls predominated.[5] More regularly young girls, especially in the poorest families, would do housework in other homes. In Horden, for example, Mrs Stevenson remembers how she began to earn money by looking after the baby of one of the 'head clerks at the colliery', a Mr Archer.

> She had a small baby, you know, I went really just to take her out, but I gradually got so that I used to wash up, and clean the shoes and do the front steps. If they had visitors at night, I used to go early to wash all the dishes. All the dishes used to be left, you know, wash all of them, and put the cloth on. Put the cups for the breakfast and clean the shoes. Many a time I did all of that, and he used to come down, let me in and go back to bed. I used to go about 6.45. All of the young lads were going to work then. They used to start about 7 in the morning. Oh I was there, till I was married. I left to be married, you know. And that was the only place I had liked. All for 5s a week.[6]

This woman was 'at place' in her home village. Other girls found employment in the few shops that existed. Mrs Harrison for example. She had hoped to become a nurse, but her family couldn't afford to pay for her training. Instead she worked at the fish and chip shop:

> When I left school, I got a job in a fish shop and that was 5s a week and this 5s a week was very important. And I used to work from 8 o'clock in the morning, and I used to scrub out, come here, get a drink of tea, come back in the afternoon and peel fish and potatoes, come home and get out dinner, which was a big meal and always put on about teatime you know...because this was when the men came in from work, your fathers. Then I'd go back and serve at night.[7]

Hilda Ashby also stayed in Chopwell, and she regarded herself as fortunate:

> I would have hated to go into service. I was in dread of it. And if I hadn't had to look after my father I would have had to go. As it was I got one of the very few jobs in the village for a girl. I was favoured to have that job I had. I used to clean the picture hall in the morning and take the tickets at night. But to be in service—I would have hated that.[8]

Her good fortune rested on the fact that she had to look after her father.

Other girls, those with many brothers or with a widowed father, also stayed at home to run the house. Mrs Stevenson's elder sister, for example,

> stopped at home. She was about 35 years old when she got married. Well, she never had a house, she stayed with my mother and father, because by then we were nearly all up and married, I think there was just our Norma and Lily, the youngest ones at home. Well, then my mother died, and my sister stayed on and looked after my father. She had him all her married life.[9]

Other women found themselves in this position also:

> I suppose I would have wanted to go away but my father died and I felt that responsibility towards my mother, you see.[10]

This woman, like the others, makes clear that the norm for girls in the mining villages of Durham was 'to go away', to get 'a place'. In this way they passed from being a daughter in one family, to a servant in the home of a stranger, before marrying and running their own homes. In 1851 two-thirds of all domestic servants in England were daughters of rural labourers.[11] As the coalfields expanded, however, it was these areas which emerged as the chief suppliers of servants in the late nineteenth and early twentieth century. By 1901 a million and a half people (most of them women) were employed in domestic service, and this had become the largest occupational group in the country—larger even than the miners.[12] Dorothy Marshall in her review of the history of domestic service in England concluded that in the nineteenth century, 'there was more discontent with conditions than is apparent in previous centuries', noting that 'the sense of inferiority both toward their employer and to the outside world was greater', and that 'by the twentieth century all these tendencies had become more marked...the number of men who entered its ranks declined steadily and for women it became...more and more a way of earning a living only to be adopted under economic pressure when more attractive openings were not available.'[13] In Durham, these pressures of economic necessity and restricted choice combined in a powerful way. For the one hundred years that preceded the Second World War, single women formed the largest category of people who moved out of the county.

For some young girls, in families where relationships were harsh and resources poor, the passage 'into service' was clearly established as a break with the family home. It was this way for this young woman in south west Durham:

> I started off at 12 years old scrubbing a cement floor for an old woman at New Shildon. I used to scrub out her kitchen and her back kitchen on a Friday night for 6d...that went on till I was 14, when I was sent in to farm service at Horse Junction. That was my kick off. My mother bought me two pairs of black stockings, two

> pinafores and things like that. And then, when it was time to go, said 'Alice, this is the last you'll get from home, you're going now.'[14]

For others it was something of an adventure. Mavis Collins, for example, remembers how:

> When I left school, I couldn't wait to leave Horden. I went 'to place' at Harrogate. The Labour Exchange got me the job. It was a sort of guest house for Lords and Ladies and I was a scullery maid downstairs and my friend was a maid upstairs. It was very strict we had to be in by half past eight at night.

What all girls shared was a clear awareness of the options opened to them, and the limits these placed upon their lives.

> A woman rarely went out to work but on the other hand there was also no work to get, just domestic work. I mean I was in domestic work. I was at Benfield Hall in Berwick. I was just a kitchen maid, when I first went, I went to train as a cook, but I never got to that stage. I stayed about three years, but I was very lonely there...there was a butler, a cook, me, two housemaids and a nanny.[15]

Edie Bestford was born in Happyland, a small row of terraced cottages near Annfield Plain in north west Durham. Her mother had been one of seven sisters:

> They all worked as domestic workers for farmers. She told me that she used to have to get up at 3 o'clock in the morning on a washing day and go down the garden to wring out the clothes that had been steeped in tubs overnight, ready to be washed. Often in the winter she had to break the ice.
>
> I had to go into service, more or less like the men who had to go down the mine. It was a living. My mother would have liked to put us to a trade. She wanted me to be a dressmaker but, of course, having a family she couldn't wait until a dressmaker could take me. There was a very good dressmaker in the village but she couldn't take me for about a year or a year and a half. So that was how I got into service or into a 'place' as we used to say.[16]

'Service' then was as predominant in its impact upon the lives of Durham girls, as the pit was for the boys. Less harsh perhaps in its impact upon the body but, in contrast to mining, it was a life led amongst strangers. In the pit and the village, custom, friendships and the union came together in a way which clearly established daily life as something familiar, known and regulated. At 'place' the young girl (although occasionally with her sister) worked at jobs with which she was familiar but in a world that was apart from her own. The unknown and the idea of chance, ill luck or good fortune, figure most powerfully in the recollections of these women. Mrs Harrison put it in this way:

> they were either lucky or unlucky. Some of them had terrible lives because they were worked to death from morning till night. If they were lucky and they got into a nice house with a nice mistress, it was a wonderful life for them really, because they lived in a nice place they saw nice places. For all they worked hard it was still better than being in places like this.[17]

Most women remember—nice places or not—that they worked hard:

> Well, I got up at 5.30 on a morning, there was the big old fashioned ranges [cookers] to clean out, the fires to light. But before I got in the mice used to be running left, right and centre. I used to be frightened of them, and would wait till they got away. Then I would start with the stoves, I had them all to blacklead every day because that's where all the cooking was done, in the big ovens. I had to do all those things before I got my breakfast, it was hard work as well. I used to get two hours off in the afternoon, we had a rest room which we used to go into. In fact it wasn't two hours off because we all had the linen to sew and mending sheets to do in your offtime, so there wasn't any offtime. They were terrible for holding parties, like banquets. The hard work was done at night time. All the cooking was done then, and I had all the washing-up to do. So I started at 5.30 on a morning and worked till 11 or 12 at night.[18]

The work was often in the homes of the privileged, the rulers. Edie Bestford, at the age of fifteen and a half, went to work for Lady Eden (the mother of Anthony Eden) at Windleston Hall, near Spennymoor in South Durham. Edie's father was lodge treasurer and she talked with him a lot about politics. She remembers how:

> The Edens weren't nice people! You could tell they hadn't much time for the workers. I remember I had to be in at 7 o'clock in the evenings. One day cook told us, 'Her Ladyship says that you all have to be in at seven. Because these awful miners are about and you never know what might happen to you.' I told her, 'I'm not frightened of the miners. My father and brothers are miners.'[19]

While their brothers worked underground, the 'place' for their sisters was 'below stairs'—both were 'servants' to the 'masters'. However the boys had the union and the customary relationships of fellow workers to help regulate their time at work. In contrast the girls experienced the moral supervision of the ruling class. Margaret Powell remembers it in this way:

> In fact all my life in domestic service I've found that employers

Slingsby, Robert, Thomas and Ernest Eden, sons of S.A.D. Eden, colliery owner. 'You could tell they hadn't much time for the workers.'

> were always greatly concerned with your moral welfare. They couldn't have cared less about your physical welfare; so long as you were able to do the work, it didn't matter in the least to them whether you had back-ache, or what ache, but anything to do with your morals they considered was their concern. That way they called it 'looking after the servants' taking an interest in those below. They didn't worry about the long hours you put in, the lack of freedom and the poor wages, so long as you worked hard and knew that God was in Heaven and that he'd arranged for it that you lived down below and laboured, and that they lived upstairs in comfort and luxury, that was alright with them.[20]

As in the pit, it was 'us and them'; masters and servants. These 'places' employed girls, who thereby became independent and, in some cases, able to send money home to their parents. To be sacked, and unemployed, however, created major problems. As one woman put it: 'the girls used to dread to come home to tell their mothers that they'd got the sack'.[21] This process (of having no place at home) was a critical disciplining experience for the young women. As the boys became hardened by the pit, learning to cope with their pain and fears, so too did the girls learn endurance. As one woman put it to us: 'you learned to be humble' because, for girls, the costs of rebellion were often doubly sharp.

> I hated it, it was awful. I was knocked up by the mistress at a quarter to six on a morning and I worked till 8 o'clock and then went to bed, everyday of the week barring Sundays, when I was allowed to walk the three miles to the Chapel. I had 3s 6d. a week.
>
> I stayed for eleven months and a fortnight, and then I ran away. There was the boss and mistress, 5 boys, a farm lad and myself there, and one of the boys was 14, just a year younger than I was. One day he took a running kick at me so—I don't know why I did it—but I brought my hand flat across his face. He ran away and told his mother, who came out and had me a good hiding. I went to my room and packed my little bag and waited till about 4 o'clock. I got up and crept downstairs and walked up to the junction station where I had some friends that I had made at Chapel. They lent me the train fare home. And what a greeting when I arrived back, from my mother! 'Alice', she said 'what are you doing here?' 'Mother, I've run away!' I replied. She said 'your father will kill you'. When he got home he set about me with the buckle end of his belt. Oh yes, you hadn't to run away.[22]

Occasionally, and with the support of family, some young women did affect the terms of their employment. Eleanor Charlton's account reveals how a rebellious young girl could use the dependence of the upper classes on the daughters of pitmen to her advantage. She went from Chopwell to work as a housemaid for the Canon on a landed estate on the border of North Yorkshire.

> Now the mistress of the house, she was one of these old aristocrats. I don't know how she'd married the Canon. She had three sons and two daughters and when I first went to them, even as a housemaid, I just treated them as though they were like my brothers and sisters. One April, I thought oh it's April Fool day. Well this Ella Lonsdale, she was a canny soul and I went up to her bedroom and I says, 'Hurry up, hurry up, there's two pheasants on the front door step.' Well she came hurrying down and she said, 'Eleanor that's lies.' I said 'Wey no, it's not lies, I said April Fool.' She just looked at me and tossed her head and away she went back and I was in disgrace for making a fool of one of the aristocracy.
>
> Then they wanted to get me in one of these starched rubber collars and cuffs to go and answer the door and I wouldn't. Well she said 'You are our housemaid and you'll have to open the door when we have a party.' I said 'I'm not.' But she said, 'Do it for me will you?' Well she was a canny person but her mother wasn't, she was just like all the damn aristocrats. Anyway she said, 'I'll put the

> collar and cuffs on for you.' Well I used to tear them off as soon as she went away. My mother put a nice little Peter Pan collar on the dress and I thought because my mother had made that, it was far better than these rubber collars and things. Well as soon as she went away, here the company comes up the drive. Well I kept these horrible things on until I was nearly at the door and I threw them behind the door, and she obviously saw me do that. Then they decided that I would become a cook because I was no good as a housemaid:

She was trained as a cook and carried on in that capacity but still on the 5s a week wages that she had had as a housemaid.

> I was cook and there were two kitchen maids. One of them used to dress up as a parlour maid and hand things around. They really had them on the cheap. I used to keep in my kitchen I wouldn't go anywhere else. I was boss of my kitchen but then the mistress would come in and say, 'Can I come and sit and put my feet on your fender?' I said, 'I don't mind, but you never ask me to come and sit in your armchair in the sitting room.'

Every year also the servants were laid off when the family took their holidays.

> We had to stop at home then, whether my mother could feed us or not, while they had about two months holiday. So when I was home on holiday my father said, 'Eleanor you're not going back there,' I said, 'Eh well I'll have to,' He says 'you're not you know. If you're doing all that work for 5s. and him a Canon. You can write and say you're not going back under 15s. a week'. And that was a lot those days. So I wrote, and they said they would meet me with the pony and trap at Barnard Castle if only I'd go back because they had been so disappointed.

Eleanor was to return to Chopwell—to marry a boy who worked at the pit.

Service at Home

The decision to get married often seemed to lead girls back to the pit village and thence from one family to another, from the position of servant to that of wife and mother. In Durham the family was the central social institution of the village: an institution built around a house which was a highly organised unit of production. A clear sense of this is conveyed by George Hitchin in his novel *Pit Yacker*:

> Once a week, 14 lbs of flour with salt, yeast and water were worked into a dough to meet the family's demand for bread. All the

> mixing, lifting and pounding involved was done on the same day as the weekly wash. This of itself, in days when pit-head baths were only dreamed of, was a major undertaking. Water for cooking, drinking, washing and the frequent hot baths had to be carried from a communal tap—each bucket, and there were many, perhaps a hundred yards along the unmade street. In winter the task became excruciating—always supposing, of course, that the tap had remained unfrozen. If it had not, an alarm signal was hurriedly sent to the colliery plumber while distraught housewives took up panic stations. Our drinking water was kept in the pantry in a specially clean pail covered with a board or a sheet of tin, and two or three times a day a fresh supply had to be hauled from the street.
>
> Our sole source of heat was an enormous open fire on which fuel was thrown by the bucketful. About a ton of coal was provided free each month. It was 'dirty' coal—that is, too full of stone to be marketable—and when this got hot, one was certain of a fireworks display complete with startling cracks as the flints exploded sending hot splinters ricocheting round the room. As someone said, the only safe way to burn this stuff was to put up the blazer and turn the pictures to the wall.
>
> On one side of the fire was a boiler and on the other a vast oven. On washday the fire was poked and stoked until the temperature was such that the kitchen had the atmosphere of a foundry.
>
> By late afternoon the clothes flapped on the line; dirty water was carried out to the street drain and, since under the stimulus of the roaring fire the oven was now hot, bread-making began immediately. The ingredients having been mixed, the dough was placed before the fire to rise. Then would begin the punching and the pounding until at last after hours of hot work seven or eight loaves and a yester cake would come from the oven. Meanwhile men were coming home from the pit and expecting cooked meals and hot baths and, miracle upon miracle, the women somehow dovetailed these into the washing and baking.[23]

The hours worked in the home were geared to the hours worked in the pit. As the men worked shifts so too did the women. Their domestic labour was not simply in addition to the men's work at the pit; it was a distinct, structural feature of the coal economy. Any alteration in the conditions, hours or wages at the pit directly affected them. Their stake in their husbands' jobs was therefore immense. Sidney Webb describes how changes in the shift system at the pit in 1910 affected their labour:

> to the wives of the miners, it is to be feared, the multiple shifts of the County of Durham have proved less of a boon. It was not

Washday: 'water had to be carried from the communal tap...By late afternoon the clothes flapped on the line; dirty water was carried out to the street drain.

found convenient—though no one seems actually to have made the attempt—to arrange so that all the men resident in one house, or at any rate all those of one grade, should always be working in the same shift, changing simultaneously from fore-shift to back-shift to night-shift. The consequence has been that where there is more than one man in the household, the labour of preparing meals and drying the pit clothes has to be undertaken every few hours during the whole day and night. With the progressive overcrowding of the colliery houses that, has nearly everywhere occurred, the pressure of work on the women has been intensified 'I go to bed only on Saturday nights,' said a miner's wife; 'my husband and our three sons are all in different shifts, and one or

> other of them is leaving or entering the house and requiring a meal every three hours in the twenty four.'[24]

In making these observations, Sidney Webb noted that the extent of 'domestic toil' did not 'seem to have been foreseen, or to have been adequately considered.' Domestic arrangements had been clearly established within the villages of the coalfield as a necessary part of the production of coal. Men who worked in the three shift pits like Horden remember how:

> my mother, would go months on end without going to bed through the week, because when my brothers got older and started work, they worked on different shifts. Two in the mine, another worked in a shop and my brother and I going to school. On night shift at the colliery, dad would come in about midnight. She got his supper ready, and he got bathed, because the bath was a tin one he had to get bathed in the middle of the floor in them days. She had to heat the water in pans, also the boiler, and pour it in the bath. Now one of my brothers would have to get up in first shift at about 2 o'clock in the morning, so it wasn't worth mother's time to go to bed, so she would just lie on the couch. Then, another one would get up probably two hours later, then at 7 o'clock one got up to get ready to go to the shop, then my brother and I would have to be up for school after that. So mother would not go to bed at all, just snatch a half hour or so's sleep.[25]

This multiple shift at home arose as a consequence of fathers, brothers and lodgers working at different times in the colliery. Mrs Turner's childhood home was of this kind:

> we had my mother and father, and we had an uncle stayed with us, my mother's brother, and another older brother well, it was like three workers. Well, you see they used to come in all different times. Some were coming in and others were going out and they all had to be fed. I've seen mother put a pudding pan—a big pan—on the kitchen stove...in the morning and it was after tea before it used to be taken off—different ones coming in you know, the lads.[26]

In Chopwell, George Alsop recalls how the superstitions of some men about *their* work affected work in the house:

> My father worked down the pit but he would never have his back washed. Never. It used to be filthy. His theory was—if you washed your back it weakened your back; you never washed your back. My mother used to go on to him about the bed clothes being filthy, about his clothes being filthy but no, he wouldn't wash his back. So she had to wash more sheets.[27]

This man wasn't typical, although there were a significant number with such beliefs across the coalfield. Generally though it was the case that:

> Being married to a miner was a full-time job for a woman, especially if she had sons who worked in the pit too. My mother had sons and lodgers! In those days it was considered the duty of the wife to be up to see that her man's pit clothes were warmed by the fire; his breakfast was ready. She'd just get him out to work and somebody would be coming in—bath in front of the fire, poss tub out [his pit clothes would be filthy dirty and sopping wet] in with the clothes, wash them and dry them. It's marvellous how they survived really; and my mother was just a little woman.[28]

When shift times coincided there could also be problems for women. Dick Beavis's brothers worked at the Dean and Chapter colliery in Spennymoor:

> Working eight hours, coming home black as the Ace of Spades, and as soon as I got home there was a squabble. Three brothers, all working in the pit—Who got washed first? What a carry on! My poor old mother, she had the big washing pan and the first one in got the water, the second one followed on, and the next got what was left.[29]

Women too remember how:

> It was a common sight to see a miner with only a pair of short trousers covering him getting bathed in front of the fire. His wife was on hand to wash his back and we were bundled into the bedroom till father got his behind washed.

Bathing the men, 'dadding' their heavy coats against the wall to remove the coal dust, washing their pit clothes, cleaning the mud-clogged soles of their pit boots. This was the ancillary labour of the home. This and childbearing, cleaning and, above all else, cooking. Because:

> a man coming in from the pit must have a good hot dinner. My dad used to always say that if you got one good meal a day you would take no hurt after that!

Shift times dictated meal times. Changes in the colliery (a change in job, in shift, in cavil) all had their immediate impact upon the routines of the women. The colliery hooter regulated the times of the day. People remember the precision of these routines which marked out their childhood lives. In Kibblesworth, Mrs Davies remembers her father as a good-living man who loved his garden.

> My sisters and I would go to meet him coming out of the pit, clutch his rough and dirty hands and eagerly tell him what kind of suet pudding was for dinner. These were always boiled in a cloth

> and he liked them on every day except Sundays. Strangely, we always had these puddings before the meat and vegetables irrespective whether they were sweet or savoury.

Bill McCabe came from another family with a 'good name'. He too writes movingly of the daily ritual at his home in Seaham:

> My dad was a coal-and-stone bargain man at Seaham colliery. He worked a four-shift cycle of shifts of first, back, night and tub loading...I can remember my dad coming home black, usually in the back shift, about 6 o'clock in the evening. He would walk up the street with the other lads in two's and three's, peeling off through their own back doors into their yards with a, 'See ya the morn', or 'See ya the neet'. The ritual was rigid: coat and cloth cap would be hung on the nail hammered into the brickwork of the yard wall away from the back door, so that the coal dust would not blow into the house. This area of bricks would be worn smooth by years of pounding from countless coats and caps. Then his tin water bottle would be stood, neck downward, to drain on the window ledge in the yard. The pit boots and stocking tops were then removed and then he would go into the house in his stocking feet. An enamel dish would be waiting on a little table behind the back door, half full of water (half full because it had to be carried, you see). Dad would then wash his hands and arms as far as the elbows, this done and dried, his meal was put on the table to coincide exactly with the drying of the hands: it was almost eucharistic. This meal, as I remember, was always a single person affair (the children having been dispensed earlier with jam and bread—and delicious it was too). I don't remember my Ma eating, I suppose she picked as she cooked—her labours didn't leave her time for the wasteful, time-consuming habit of sitting down to a meal.[30]

He continues with a description of the meals. Meals large enough to fill the stomachs of men who had spent hours underground. In Durham suet was the central ingredient.

> Every miner's house used suet. That was like the basic. Everyday you'd have something with suet in for the main meal of the day. To fill you up. You'd buy a big piece of suet from the butchers for tuppence and every day you grated a bit of the suet into the flour.[31]

Suet and bread; these were the staples. All cooked at home, and to a precise timetable. In most homes, Thursday was a baking day:

> I used to start on a Thursday morning, I used to bake eight loaves of white bread, four loaves of brown, a dozen tea cakes, spice and rice [cakes], I used to do a great big lump of ham and pease

> pudding. You have no idea what I used to make. I stood there from first thing on a Thursday morning till 12 o'clock on a Thursday night baking. We never bought bread, never bought a pie, we never bought anything.[32]

In the villages, with the exception of small houses where widows ('poor souls' as they are remembered) attempted to sell their wares, there was no commercial trade in bread or cooked foods. As Maurice Ridley has made clear:

> The miner's home had its own bake house. The oven next to the fire was a little bakehouse and, however difficult it was, the home-made bread, white or brown, the stotty cakes and the tea cakes were laid on.[33]

This 'bakehouse' reference is no fanciful one. Many of the descriptions offered by women of their work could be mistaken for a commercial enterprise:

> Those old-fashioned butter barrels, that had the hoops round—well, people used to line them out you know, with rice paper and that sort of thing, and scrubbed the outside clean and you kept your flour in that, stored in a big pantry. And you used to buy your yeast at the shop, you know, a quarter or two ounces or whatever you wanted. You generally did a big baking of bread, about twelve or thirteen loaves, big loaves, to a stone of flour. You used to bake a stone of flour at once.[34]

In these workplaces, like the pit, people will tell you how 'every day was mapped out'. If Thursday was baking day, Friday was left to the task of cleaning the oven and the stove. To clean a stove was dirty and arduous: 'it used to take me two solid hours to do that stove, and I was as black as any pitman'.

Cooking and cleaning formed just one part of the week. The clothes—pit clothes included—had to be washed, normally on a Monday. People remember their backyards and gardens being 'like Nelson's flagship' on that day with the pounds and pounds of washing flying in the breeze. Washing by hand, pounding with a 'poss stick', possing and double possing the clothes until they were clean—rinsing, wringing, drying and ironing with a flat iron, heated on the coal fire. George Hitchen wrote of how his memories left him 'with a more than normal abhorrence of wash day.' Generally people of his generation talked of how 'you dreaded washing days—you believe me—you dreaded it':

> Boys and girls irrespective of age, just when they were big enough, had to help their mothers with the poss stick, bash the old poss stick on the clothes in the tub. But the clothes used to be all washed, out on the line and dried, then on a Monday night, the

Durham aprons: 'this used to be the dress in those days...tied with a bow at the back'.

> old iron would be put on the fire till it got hot, because there was no electricity. There used to be two of them, and you would put like a shoe on the hot iron, while the other iron was getting hot on the fire, and keep changing the shoe, from the cold iron to the hot one. She would probably finish ironing on the Monday night or Tuesday morning, before she started to bake again.[35]

One woman remembers how:

> We had to poss and we had a great big wringer—great big heavy wringer and you turned the handle of this wringer, to wring the clothes out, and then you had to keep stooping down, in the poss tub, lifting the clothes up to wring them you know. Great big poss tub. And you had to wash that out. Oh, a big barrel it was. There

> was nothing like there is now, no ease in living like there is now, you know. You used to have your big pan on to boil your clothes on the fire...then you would have to lift that pan off and put your wash pan on. When you took your pan off for your washing...put your pan on to make your dinner, perhaps a meat pudding, if you had a bit of meat. Then you had to take that off when it was done, put your wash pan on again...you were on all day, slaving and washing, oh you were.[36]

These women would 'think nothing of heaving the coal through the small trap door in the coal house if their men were at work'. They made mats and rugs for the floor (hooky mats and clippy mats), they made and mended clothes, knitted pullovers and pit stockings. In all these activities the girls assisted—serving *their* apprenticeship:

> We used to knit all the socks, all the pit stockings, and of course I was taught to knit when I was very young. I used to say to her 'Can I go out, go out and play?' and she would say 'No, get some knitting done.' I'd have to get some knitting done. No, you weren't allowed to go out to play.[37]

George Hitchen has left us with an important reminder of the care, 'complete ruthlessness' and family endeavour which went into the activity of mat making.

> Hessian sacks were cut up, stitched together and nailed to wooden frames. Rags were dyed to the required colours and cut into suitable sizes called 'clippings', which were inserted into the hessian with steel 'prickers' like sharp spikes. Tea over on a Sunday, out came the mat, one end of the frame being placed on the table and the other supported by the sideboard. Two rows of chairs were then drawn up along the length of the frame and clippings were piled into the centre. Now the members of the family sat facing one another across the mat, pricking away for dear life, their tongues wagging, and their clippings creating a design which was roughly drawn in pit chalk on the hessian and which, as far as I know never altered in any significant detail, no matter how many mats were made.[38]

This, then, was a household economy of some intricacy. Based upon restricted company houses it drew upon the co-ordinated effort—the skills, the strengths, the organisation and perceptiveness—of the women. These people, denied any meaningful access to waged labour, education or social advancement, were the mainstay of the social fabric which made up the coal mining village. Their granddaughters described them to us as 'the slaves of slaves'. Often the memory is tinged with bitterness. June Davies:

> My memory goes back to Grandma Coxen and Gran Charlton,

> both were fine, hardworking women. Grandma Coxen was the closest to me. This little old lady with the same birthday as my own always was dressed in black with a white apron on Sunday and a hessian apron for weekdays. Her hair pulled hard back to a bun at nape of neck she walked with two sticks since her legs were crippled with pains. She was the mother of 13 children and she had had two husbands, the first was a miner killed in Chopwell pit. The day Chopwell pit whistle blew to let everyone know there was an accident was the beginning and the end of life as she knew it. Bill Gutridge was a fine healthy specimen of a man but after a heavy fall of stone all that was left of this fine man was put in a sack and brought to my grandmother's house and placed on the mat—a bundle of bloody rags.

Another account, sent to us, remembers 'treasured memories of a dear mother' and writes of how:

> We had a happy childhood thanks to the grit and bravery of a devoted mother who strove to bring up three children on a chronic shortage of money while afflicted with ill health. She would often sing hymns heartily as she went about her work, and she was always quick to laugh and see the funny side of anything.
>
> As I grew older I realised the terrific struggle she had had for at least twenty years. The war, ill health with father, then herself, and the worry of bringing us up left its toll of prematurely grey hair and lined face....She died in 1945 after a lifetime of hardship. Before she died she said she would not like to live her life over again. Her tragedy, and others of her generation, was that they were born too soon.

In reflecting on this 'tragedy' it is interesting to note that in the autobiographies of miners who lived through this period, repeated reference is made to the centrality of a 'mother' in their lives and to the arduous nature of housework. To quote from one:

> When I look back she was a proper slave to all of us. A slave and nothing else. She was a real good mother, she brought up a big family, and now I appreciate everything she did for us.[39]

Another contains a chapter entitled 'a queen who was supreme' and in this the miner writes of his need to pay tribute to the person who 'bore the brunt...the mother who was the Queen of Hearts'.[40]

These women also caught the attention of contemporary visitors to the coalfield districts. In the 1930s a report on *Motherhood in the Special Areas of Durham and Tyneside* observed that 'certain facts emerged again and again from amongst the host of impressions absorbed during these visits'. Principal amongst these was the fact that:

> the mother is the centre of the household, the mainspring on which all depend. It lies with her if the house is clean or dirty, the children tidy or unkempt, their health watched, the meals regular and as nourishing as possible. Yet the mother is the one who receives least assistance and for whom least is done.[41]

This absence of support was quite general. There was little or no advice on family planning and birth control. Equally antenatal care was primitive at best. In her speaking tours Dora Russell repeatedly noted that in the coal districts six out of a thousand births ended with the death of the mother: a death rate which matched that of the coal mines.[42] So acute was this situation that J.B. Priestley on his visit to East Durham as part of his *English Journey*, critically remarked:

> I am always hearing middle-class women in London saying they could do with a change—they should try being a miner's wife in East Durham.[43]

Priestley spent some time talking with a 'sewing circle' of 'worn but neat and smiling women' who were 'sewing on the razor edge of life'. They left an enormous impression upon him and he learned from them that, in mining villages, women occupy a situation of paradox. They were both central and marginalised: critical to the operation of the family and thereby to the husband and the mine, but often socially excluded and publicly undervalued. Living this paradox they became people of some substance:

> In these parts the women have far more influence than they appear to have at first. There is a matriarchal principle at work up here. It is generally assumed among them that although men have the muscle and perhaps, for contriving, arguing, book learning purposes, the brains, women have the *sense*, the *gumption*.[44]

In times of social crisis they could also be the most determined and wilful. The close relationship between the mine and the community meant that while they were excluded from the mine, women contributed to it (through their labour in the home) and were deeply affected by it through wages, accidents and the outcome of industrial disputes. Mining life involved more than the parallel coexistence of the sexes; it involved both in a struggle to live and survive in places which they came to know as communities. The struggles involved an important degree of mutuality, yet it also involved the women as 'slaves of slaves'. Another Northern novelist, Catherine Cookson, has made clear the significance of this in East Jarrow in this way:

> in those days a man went out to work and that, to his mind, was enough. The house and all in it was the woman's task, and it lowered the man's prestige if he as much as lifted a cup....Man's

> rightful standing in his house was a thing to be guarded, to be fought for; no weakness of emotions or kindly instincts must touch it. Our men didn't even mend their boots.[45]

In this though she is clear that the women were often actively involved in regulating aspects of this relationship. She recounts how her grandmother described a man as a 'nappy washer' because he had been seen in the house when his wife was confined to bed with her first baby. The neighbours usually did this chore.

In her novels, Cookson brings out the strength and the drama of these women's lives. The popularity of her novels relates to the ways in which they express the depth of women's experiences, and emotions that were involved in the industrialisation of the area. The first woman we interviewed enthused over the titles of Cookson's novels, insisting that we read them. Her favourite story was *Katy Mulholland*, and for a quarter of an hour or more we listened as she sketched the story for us with great feeling and dramatic effect, relating it to her own life and the lives of her parents and family.

Men and Women

Descriptions of the centrality of the household economy within the Durham coalfield invited the suggestion that some kind of matriarchal principle was at work in the colliery villages. Sid Chaplin was brought up in Ferryhill in South Durham and in the 1930s attended the Spennymoor Settlement. He writes:

> I seem to remember more women running the home and ruling their husbands than the reverse; but in between I'd say was a sizeable majority who split the responsibility, she the running of the home and the family, he the pit and his own leisure, meeting all reasonable demands.[46]

Maurice Ridley has also reflected upon these divisions of 'work', 'home' and 'leisure'.

> The men weren't involved in any of the so-called domestic duties. How shall I put it? Essentially the duties had been laid out beforehand; the miner or the iron and steel worker did his stint and was responsible for his wife and family. But the domestic side was completely under the control of the mother with the help of any daughters that might be there. Interference wasn't wanted and very rarely given. Mother was in charge domestically 100 percent and the man's role was as a breadwinner wherever it was and there was a clear division of labour. Very, very clear division of labour. And the pattern had been set generations before, you grew up and

> you had to conform. A male who involved himself too much in the domestic side was unfortunately looked upon as a bit of a sissy in the community.[47]

It is perhaps from a contemporary perspective that the nature of the social arrangements of village life on the coalfield gain greatest clarity. One miner at the Easington Colliery recalled how, when he grew up in Ferryhill:

> with my father and my mother it was ninety-five percent my father, five percent my mother. In fact it was a hundred percent my father. He would come home from the pit, bath, have his dinner. He'd sit and read the paper. If he was going out he would go out. It was his decision sort of thing.

Vera Alsop, a woman who grew up in Chopwell in the 1920s put it succinctly:

> In those old days...the man was the boss. He was the boss of the house. And if he wasn't the boss of the house he wasn't considered to be a man.[48]

The reference to 'the boss' makes clear the significance of power relationships and sexual identity underlying the separation of spheres of activity referred to by Sid Chaplin. Often marriages *were* worked out as partnerships. Some women did 'rule their husbands'; however in such circumstances it would be commonly understood that she 'wore the trousers' or was 'the man in that house'.

In the village, marriage and house tenure were irrevocably linked. This meant that a woman's hold on her home was her husband and, in an industry where fatalities were a commonplace this hold could be a tenuous one. Billy Simpson in Crook can remember 'only one woman who kept on her house after her man died'. Usually a woman:

> could only keep the house on if she had a son who was working at the pit. He could keep the house on in his name as long as his mother was alive, but as soon as *she* died he had to get out.

Billy Simpson himself worked through the 1920s for Pease and Partners at the Bowden, Waterhouses, and Wooley collieries. On the death of his mother, he found himself threatened with eviction.

> They told me to get out when my mother died. I was working every day at the pit but they told me to get out. So I went down the Registry Office and got married. They wouldn't give you a house on your own—they'd hoy you out. They didn't tell us we *had* to get married—they wouldn't give you a house if you weren't.

The position of the miner's widow, without a son living at home and working at the pit, was the most vulnerable. For women with a grown up family, the death of a husband most often involved moving in with a son or daughter. Many people, reflecting upon the past, have commented on the way in which these women 'grew old'. Often people say that women were almost forced to grow old—before their time, as if assuming the role of grandmother. One woman put it like this:

> In my mother's day I think people aged so quickly. Once their family got up and left they were content to get themselves sat in a nice little chair. My mother was fifty three when my father died and she was an old lady. That's the truth...I'll almost be as old as my mother was when she was widowed, and I'd hate to think I was an old lady with nothing better to do than sit at home.[49]

For younger women this was not an option. On the death of their husband the lodge might involve itself in the funeral arrangements and with a collection of money (this especially if the man was killed at work), but thereafter the union was of no further help. In these most cruel circumstances they were left with little choice: they could return to live with their mothers, or they could become housekeepers for other men. There were miners whose wives had died, and sometimes brothers would live together. But most of these men found it impossible to survive without a woman to organise the housework. Commonly, housekeepers were advertised for and hired; often to enter into ambiguous relationships which occasionally led to marriage. Fenwick Whitfield was born in 1898. He remembers that he was:

> three and a half years old when we came to Leadgate with my mother....My mother came to keep house for a chap—he was a blacksmith—and eventually he became my stepfather. So I was fetched up in that house...it was one up and one down and you went upstairs through a ladder; there wasn't staircases in them. Eleven of us children were fetched up there. The stepfather had started in the pit when he was nine....He was married three times. His first wife died in childbirth, and then he married her sister. And she died.[50]

Mavis Collins was born in 1926 in Newcastle. Her father was a miner and after he died, her mother moved with her seven children to keep house for a miner in Eleventh Street in Horden. This man had, like many others, advertised in the local newspaper. Her mother never settled in Horden, she:

> was a 'townie'. She didn't like the village. My mother never got used to it. She missed the markets and the town. We were always going back up to North Shields where we had relatives.

In Stanley (and much later in the century), Matthew Robinson, a single man, worked at the pit and upon the death of his mother, shared a house with his brother. His sister approached a friend of hers whose husband had died.

> She asked if I was working and I said 'No'. She said, 'My two brothers are living in number 12, do you think you could look after them?' So I said, 'Alright I'll come along and see'. She brought me along to see them....The house was filthy; really filthy. So I said 'I'll try and do what I can.' They said, 'Come to start on a month's trial'. Well by the end of the month I had the whole place cleared out. So I said, 'What about this month's trial—am I being kept on, or what?' And his brother Jack said, 'By, Maggie, I hope you're not leaving we couldn't do without you now.' So I looked after them for about five years. Then he asked if I would marry him. So I went back and I said to my father 'Matty's asked us if I'll marry him.' And he said: 'Well don't do anything that you'll regret; think it over.' He was a *nice* man, my father. So, I thought it over and I said, 'Well, I might as well. It might be better than turning out to work.' So I told my father and he said, 'Well please yourself—but do you think you'll get on together?' I said, 'Well, I think so, I can get on with anybody.' And in the August we got married. I wanted to wait until my boy had left school, but he wouldn't wait. And we haven't had one row. We got on really well together. We've had some good times.

Here then is a complex system of relationships based upon property and marriage which provided the framework for a rigid sexual division of labour. Generally, the term 'wife' is still used to apply in a universal way to women—as in 'that wife's shop on the corner'. It derives from Old English, and its continued usage relates to this period when the established place for women in a colliery village was in marriage.

The man's weekly wage, as with most things on the coalfield, was patterned by ritual: as the men were paid, so were the women. 'You always had a clean pinny on Satruday to get your money.' The marras, once paid, would divide the money amongst themselves. For many, these transactions took place in the club. At home their wives would wait, in their clean, white Durham aprons to be paid at the door. Mrs Allen remembers her mother:

> Whenever she'd finished her work or anything she always had a white pinny on, and this used to be the dress, more or less in those days, not just to keep the other clothes clean, but this was the dress at the time, tied with a bow at the back, you know.

Her husband recalls his own mother and how she used to sit in her white apron on pay day:

> In those days, £2 was really good money. He used to get about £6 a week at the docks at Seaham Harbour, and I'll never forget, me mother used to sit there, he would come in and he used to throw £2 into her lap. 'There you are, lass,' he used to say 'Do you want any more?' And she daren't say 'Yes', she used to make do with that £2.[51]

This incident is probably exceptional, and based upon the man's high earning on the docks. But it does exaggerate a common experience. One of the first themes of the early union organisers in Durham was that of family responsibility and the need for miners to be fair with the money they gave their wives. People we have talked with, who grew up and were married before 1930, all remember and refer to the issue of 'keepy-back'—the portion of the man's wages which he concealed from his wife; a strategy made easy by the fluctuations in piece-rate earnings. These accounts however almost always emphasise the subterfuge rather than the brutality implied in Mr Allen's account. Men talk of keeping their half crowns in their ferret's cage, in their caps, in their carbide lamps. Others describe the difficulties they had, when their clothes were off, bathing with a half a gold sovereign in their hands!

We talked to many women about 'keepy-back', and they all knew about it and accepted it as something which most miners did. 'Nay they all had "keepy-back", mine kept his in the peak of his cap.' Usually these discussions were patterned with laughter—'Yes', it went on; 'all the men did; we all knew they did it; it's a funny business isn't it.' These were the commonest sentiments which related to this general habit of the men to keep a (small) part of their wages secret, and for their own use, for drink, or gambling, or travelling to football matches. However there were limits, and these same women were most condemnatory of men who kept their wives and children in need through their own selfishness. Vera Alsop, for example, recalls how:

> when we were hard up, George used to do without. But at the club, men used to stand there drinking beer and their bairns were running around in bare feet. It used to sicken me.[52]

And of course there were marriages where the men and women attempted to operate on a basis of equality—with decisions being shared. There is no doubt that these arrangements went against the grain of the culture of the village or that they were difficult to sustain. Something of the tensions involved can be seen from an incident described by John Glenwright in his autobiography *Bright Shines The Morning*:

> Here I was, then, going home with a 'canny' pay—the best I'd had from the colliery—for I was on piece rate now, mending tubs and earning three pounds a week, a fortune to me. I went into the house whistling, and walked straight into trouble. I gave Edith

Men, women and children. Durham Gala, July 1935.

two notes and some silver. 'Don't I get a pay note now?' she asked, rather playfully. 'How am I to know how much you're really making?'

'Can't you trust me?' I asked, and down I went to unlace my pit boots with deliberate ease. I felt the prick of conscience, and the neat pattern of the hearth rug was very plain to me just then.'

'You've kept nothing back from me?' Edith asked, as she went to her purse to put the money carefully away. 'I hope you never do. I would rather you ask for it and have what you want rather than be deceitful about it.' 'I would never do such a thing', I maintained, rubbing my stockinged feet on the fender. 'Both pull the same way that's my motto.'

I could see without looking, that she stood with her arms folded, watching me, and that there was pain in her eyes. 'You haven't taken your cap off yet', she reminded me at last, the humour gone from her voice.

I laughed foolishly. 'Good heavens, so I haven't.' Peevishly, I got up, took off my cap and hung it on a nail behind the door. The next instant, Edith had it down and was examining the lining and, lo, there came to light three, shining half-crowns.

'Pull the same way, eh?', she cried, and the half crowns went

> flying across the table. She was hurt and angry and I was sorry for what I had done.
>
> 'It was money I had left from last week,' I said, trying to be calm.
>
> 'You are not content to deceive me, but you tell me a barefaced lie', she protested hotly. 'If it was money you had left, why hide it in your cap?' Two of the half-crowns had rolled on to the floor. I made no effort to pick them up. 'You can have half of it', I said.
>
> 'I wouldn't touch a penny' came the sharp answer and out she went banging the door behind her. She spoke very little to me all that weekend, but I guess I deserved it.[53]

The men, as Maurice Ridley has made clear, not only worked but also socialised together, not as members of a family but as hewers, putters or, as in the case of John Glenwright, blacksmiths. As men apart they worked their gardens, ran whippets and raced pigeons, often they gambled on the results of races or at pitch and toss. Always they talked. In Durham this kind of talk, discussion and story telling argument and banter between marras is referred to as 'the crack'. 'The crack' was always good in the club. The club, like the pit (and with the exception of the women who served the beer) was an all-male preserve or, as one man remembers:

> the odd old lady would go into the jug and bottle end with an old can. Now that would be for the husband coming in from work, but she would probably have a half glass for herself when she went in, or at home, but they never made a habit of going into pubs or clubs, they were all for men.[54]

For most women this meant either a social life without men or no social life. People from the Durham mining communities remember their mothers in this way:

> I don't know how she managed, you know, never mind, she did. She was quite happy poor soul in her work, and on a Saturday night...she used to wear her hair the way they wear them now, right on the top like the shaving combs and she would say, 'Oh, I'll put a clean apron on, and that's as far as I'll get, likely.' And she used to make this great big hot pot in the oven, because my uncle Bob would maybe's come back—one of my father's brothers, you know—and have his supper before he went home from the club...they would come up from the club and my mother would have this great big dish of hot pot, dishing it all out.

Often the returning men were in a bad temper. One woman recalls how:

> Some bashings went on. I often heard my granny talk about it. She was a midwife at Hamsterley and if anyone was taken ill they'd call for my granny. She'd come back and say 'Bye, so and so has

> been knocking her around again.' Men used to come in from the pub—big bullies of men—and they'd beat their wives if things weren't as they should be, or if the woman complained. They thought that was the proper thing to do. 'I can go out and enjoy myself but you're to stay in the house.' The woman was supposed to sit there with a little black shawl on and wait for him coming in. And that's what most women did.

These private beatings, exceptional as they might be, were rooted in arrangements which restricted women's access to critical aspects of public life. While in the nineteenth century we have noted accounts of women's direct (and occasionally drunken) involvement in public ceremony and display, by the twentieth century their spheres of activities had become more tightly regulated. In Crook—in the staunchly Methodist south west of the county—Polly Simpson remembers how in the 1920s:

> Very few women went into pubs. I once saw a woman coming out of a pub with a couple of bottles of beer and she was caught by her husband. He broke the bottles on her feet. He didn't like the idea of her going into a pub.

Remembering his childhood in Chopwell, George Alsop recounts:

> Any woman who went to the clubs was considered to be a floozie. But my mother used to like a drink of beer. She used to go out and, mostly on a Friday night, she'd slip over for a drink. She'd go across to the pub. She wasn't allowed into the pub itself. There was a little ducket place on the side where the women would stand and have a glass of beer. Maybe they'd take a jug of beer home. On a Friday night my mother would say to me 'I'm going across for a glass of beer don't tell your father mind.' I wouldn't tell him, if he got to know, good God, there used to be hell's flames around the house. He was a big fella.[55]

This regulation of women's public activities was felt most intensely by the daughters, for in a world where married women had very few rights, the daughters had none. In Ferryhill, Mrs Short remembers how her father was an extreme disciplinarian:

> He was very, very strict. We all had to be in by 9 o'clock, even when I was 17. In fact, the last good hiding he gave me was when I was just 17 only a lass. I was standing in the street talking to a young lad till half past nine. I was standing at the corner, making sure I could see up the street that he always used when returning home. I knew that I could get in before he saw me if I kept a close watch. But he came over by a short cut and caught me out. I ran into the pantry, and he followed me in and, this was the type of man he was, got hold of my hair and pulled me out into the

> middle room, took his buckle and belt off and lashed me to ribbons. I went upstairs to where my mother was lying. I was crying and she asked what was the matter. I told her I was standing at the corner talking to a boy. 'Why, you know you have to be in before he comes in.' I thought he was not going to come in before 10 o'clock. But I was wrong.[56]

In Horden, Mrs Turnbull talks of her father and how (without the violence) her social life was dependent upon his permission:

> No, I didn't to a dance until I was 32 years of age, my father would not allow it, in fact when I used to go out, even when I was engaged to be married, I had to ask permission if I could go. I many a time said that 'The Barratts' of Wimpole Street had nothing on him.' He wasn't cruel to us, you know. I would ask him on a Monday if I could go the following Saturday with Walter. He would say, 'I'll see.' And I wasn't told until the Friday night if I could go. He never stopped me though, but I never knew.[57]

Mrs Turnbull is clear just how dependent she was upon him, and how powerful was his sanction. Implicitly, she also recognises that cruelty *did* exist within family relationships. In Spennymoor several women remember an occasion when the Lodge Secretary 'upset his daughter's day'. She was pregnant and on her wedding day: 'he tore the ribbons off the car. Tore all the white ribbons off because she wasn't "clean". He was a terrible man.'

One man also told us of this incident. His wife was dead and he insisted repeatedly 'its a good job she isn't here now. She'd tell you the tale about him. She thought it was terrible. On her wedding day. She never forgot that, my wife. She always disliked him'. The energy involved in this account made it clear to us that on this occasion the Lodge Secretary (in his private life) had in the eyes of many of the women in the village transgressed. It also points to the extent to which men (as fathers and husbands) exercised power over women, and their sexuality. This, and further evidence of misogynous undertones, is illustrated again by Catherine Cookson in her autobiography:

> when my mother sick to the depths of her soul...had come home from 'her place' to say she was going to have a baby, The Father, as he was always called, was for killing her—she had committed the unforgivable sin. Yet when I was born and she had milk fever and her breasts swelled to bursting, The Father was supposed to have saved her life by sucking the milk from them. It seems incredible to me that she should have looked upon the act as something heroic for, remembering him as I do, I can see that he would have enjoyed this operation—he was a frustrated licentious

> man. His antidote against this...was drink and a dirty tongue which he used against all women...he had been known to make even the toughest women blush.[58]

Cookson's reference to drink is a common theme, and many women we talked to who had been politically active and radical in their youth were, like Cookson, strongly teetotal and opposed to 'the brewers'.

Mrs Short tells of how her father:

> got roaring drunk every Friday night, and every Friday night we slept in the out-house beside the old fashioned lavatory with a wooden seat. [Before then] mother used to come into the back bedroom where the three of us slept and pull a box across the door to stop him getting in. One night he smashed a panel in the door, so after that out we slept![59]

It would be a mistake to think women passively accepted behaviour of this sort. Vera Alsop remembers her mother-in-law as 'a little woman who always retaliated':

> My father-in-law was a very big man but she used to stand up to him. She used to go out. He'd say 'You're supposed to be in at such and such a time' and if she wasn't in by that time he used to lock her out. She was late getting home this one night and she got one of the lasses to let her in. She goes into the sitting room which was in darkness. Well he heard her and ran in after her saying what he was going to do to her. And he was a big man. Anyway she got up on a chair and she took this tray of toffee in her hand (she used to make toffee to give to the bairns). My father-in-law had a baldy head and every time he walked passed her she hit him on top of the head with the toffee. There was toffee all over the sitting room. Another time he came in drunk and started acting up so she got these rolls of paper. Hit him over the head with the rolls of paper. The next morning he couldn't remember: 'I don't know what's happened to me but my head's sore.' She says 'Will you look at all that paper! Mat got broke over your head last night'.
>
> This is what Women's Lib is all about you see. I don't go as far as they go perhaps but it's nice to know you have some rights. Because in those days you had no rights at all.[60]

What rights women had they made *privately* out of their personal relationships with husbands and family. In memory, the significance of a good husband for a woman is of central importance. The phrase 'a good man' crops up again and again in the assessment these women make of their lives and those of their contemporaries.

> The only entertainment around she got was if she had a husband who took her for a walk on a Sunday evening....They both got

> dressed, and they got the family dressed, and they went for a walk, up Ellison's Bank and around up Easington Village, and back home on a Sunday night. And she had a good husband.[61]

A 'good' husband was then a man who recognised the private rights of his wife, and who would publicly demonstrate this through his attachment to the family. A 'bad' husband was not only violent and mean he also, by such behaviour and in other ways, registered his lack of respect for and attachment to the family world which his wife had created. The public role performed by the men (union men, Chapel men, pigeon men, sports men, gambling men, dog men, drinkers) had profound effects upon the private lives of the women and the families they belonged to. A woman's fate was not only determined by the mine and being married to a miner. It was tied up with the complex patterns of social and moral practices which made up the mining community. Much of this was, of course, a private matter; women dealt with their own men and their family and people 'didn't interfere'. This phrase is a perpetual feature of mining life. But, there was also a degree of public regulation of these social and moral aspects, and in this the women played an active part.

A considerable amount of mutual aid existed between women, especially at times of ill health and childbirth. While their domestic work was a private affair, conducted in their own houses, they shared their experiences and discussed their problems. Of further importance is the way in which women were, to an extent, able to use ideas of domesticity in defence of their own position in the home. These women talked of not liking men 'under their feet' when they were cleaning or cooking and of the general unpractical nature of their husbands and of men in general. 'They're all boys really. They never grow up.' The women's practical support of each other was extensive during times of birth, illness and death. The frequency of all three fates meant that the support organised by neighbours and families existed as a permanent and indispensable feature of village life. This pattern of collective support was also brought to bear as a powerful regulating force within the community at large.

8
Community and Association

Within families and communities everyday life is one of 'proud and cruel publicity'...personal interdependence is not only benign but also extremely coercive; it fosters sentimental attachments but also the most intense personal hatreds; it encourages fraternity but also mutual surveillance and suspicion.

R. Bendix

IN SOCIOLOGICAL writing it is usual to distinguish, as provided by Tönnies, between two different kinds of social life, *Gemeinschaft* and *Gesellshaft*: forms of relationship based upon family and community and others based upon more formal patterns of association. Tönnies interpreted communities as 'unorganised collectivism', and this has influenced a great deal of writing about British mining—stressing the community forms of mining life and contrasting these with the more formalised and isolated patterns of urban living. While there is some truth in this, it is a truth which should be approached with caution for it can mask many important aspects of life in a mining village.

Power and Communication

To begin with it is important not to lose sight of the significance of power relations which related to the private ownership and administration of the mines. Mine managers often lived close at hand, and deputies and overmen lived in the village, in houses which were distinct from the houses of the miners. While managerial power had been corrected to a degree by trade-union organisation, this was only marginal. It didn't prevent men from talking in the mine about the nature of slavery and the extent to which mine labour was different from slave labour:

often we talked about that. And it's true you know. The power that the employers had in them days was almost a power of life and death. We always used to say that we were no better off than the slaves on the plantation.

This theme was echoed poignantly to us by Charlie Pick who had been checkweighman at Kibblesworth colliery in the 1930s and became President of the DMA in the post-war period.

The miner didn't get his freedom until 1945. You have to remember that. Under the private enterprise system the miner wasn't a free man at all; he was tied down by the employer.

In Easington, we met a group of old miners in the Welfare Hall in 1979 and talked to them about their early lives in the village. Immediately the discussion focused upon the power of a man called Charlton who had been colliery under-manager through the 1920s and 1930s. We were regaled with stories of how this man demanded deference in the mine and outside it; how you had to take your cap off in his office; how he operated as if he 'owned the village and everyone in it'. People in Kibblesworth talked in a similar way about their manager, George Strong:

It is difficult for people living today to realise the power that a colliery manager had in the Durham pit villages. He had complete power for the simple reason that everything in the village belonged to the coal owners....If you had a manager who took advantage of this situation then life could be very uncomfortable for certain sections of the community. In this village men had to be very brave to belong to the Labour Party or to play an active role in the union....You had to have lived in a colliery village with a manager like George Strong to understand the power he had. It was not until after nationalisation that things changed.[1]

The colliery manager at Langley Park in the 1920s is remembered as 'an old school type'. According to Herbert Cooper:

He was a man who was a cut above the average socially. He went riding on a horse to the hounds. He had a proper outfit. He went to the hounds with proper dress and a whip and a proper horse trained by the local horse keeper who was part of the pit personnel....They were all tied up to this upper-class school tie....I suppose in a way they were very important people. The village looked up to them as important. They came into the village and opened things like bazaars. Socially, there was the parson he was a shade below the doctor, then there was the doctor and then there was the colliery manager. Socially that was the order.

He adds:

> You've got to remember that in them days you could count the number of baths in Langley Park and flush toilets you could count them on one hand. In 5,000 people you could get them all on one hand. The doctor had one, the colliery manager had one and the fella at the post had one, and maybe the man at the store. I say 'maybe he had', I'm not sure about the store manager.

It is important to remember that while miners were by far the largest group in the mining villages, they weren't the only group of workers to be found there. The colliery office employed clerks, and many of the mines supplied local coke works, where a separate group of workers ('coke men') were employed. Amongst the coal miners the putters and the hewers formed distinct groups, and separate from both were the skilled men (the mechanics), and the engine men both of whom (like the coke men) had registered their difference through their own trade associations. These different groups lived together in the mining villages, but the 'community' they formed there was a complex one, which had within it considerable levels of formal organisation and no little internal conflict.

Equally important are the differences that related to the family and family circumstances such as its size, its composition and its political, moral and ethical outlook. We have noted how these patterns of 'moral differentiation' were understood in the 1870s. They were there too in the twentieth century and remembered in this way in Kibblesworth:

> The social lives of the villagers fell into two categories. The Chapel and Church folk, and the pub frequenters. You could not be both. I had an uncle who was told he could no longer be a Chapel member because he liked a drink. My family was Chapel and Sunday was truly a day set apart. Our best clothes were worn only on that day except for something special like weddings and funerals.

In Horden in the 1920s it was common knowledge that:

> Second and Third Street were notorious for drunks. You would know when you were in Second Street because a chamber-pot full of urine would come down, out of the window, straight on top of you.

There were also gamblers, and at a time when much of this was illegal, Mavis Collins remembers how:

> When I was growing up my mother always warned me to keep away from the pitch and toss men. They had a man watching for the police and you daren't go near them.

While a shared systems of values and understandings was developed by working-class people in mining villages, this community also operated as an aggregate of often very different families and households. In this way it is possible to understand accounts of community life which stress intolerance and mutuality, always matched by a certain degree of privacy, with 'the community' kept at arm's length:

> You knew everybody in the street to talk to, you saw them everyday, but you couldn't say that you were very close to them. The only time that I went into a neighbour's house was when I was playing with their kids. People were neighbourly, they would help if someone was ill and offer all the old-fashioned remedies and that sort of thing. But neighbours didn't go in and out of people's houses then.[2]

This is probably the most generalisable account of the experience of the street and the colliery row. To it should be added another, of a man in Easington Colliery who moved there soon after the First World War:

> In the colliery the areas were all different. Canada, east, south, you lived in one area and that was your area. There was always fights between the lads from the different areas. People are always going on about colliery people being together and getting along with one another. You are always seeing it on the television like, 'When the Boat Comes In'. But I don't remember anything like that. The pit was ruled by fear, so families stuck together, that was it. In the 1930s when you went down to collect sea coal off the beach you had to guard yourself all the way back home, otherwise you would lose it.

What accounts like this highlight is an awareness of the mining village as a collection of distinct social groupings. The basic unit in all this was the family and household, and these kin connections penetrated the workplace through the division of labour in the mine and the operation of the marra system.

The trade union played an important role in regulating these relationships seen clearly in the system of house allocation and tenure. To qualify for a colliery house you had to be a man, you had to work at the pit and you had to be married or living with your widowed mother. These complex rules were (in most part) endorsed by the miners' union with interesting consequences: a large part of the lodge secretary's time was taken up with the question of justice in relation to housing allocation and interpreting the 'Coal and House Agreement' made between the unions and the company. It also meant that the secretary dealt, on a regular basis, with people (wives, mothers, widows) who weren't formally members of his union.

The minute books of the lodges are full of detailed discussions relating to questions of housing and coal. To take but one—the Boldon Lodge. In 1919 a special sub-committee met 'to consider the list of applicant's names for colliery houses' and recommended that:

- married workmen claim their turn for a colliery house from the date of marriage;
- married workmen coming to work on the colliery, their claim for colliery houses to start from date of employment;
- in future when colliery houses are being granted to workmen in their turns we ask the manager if he will [mutually] agree;
- that no workman be granted a colliery house until he has consulted the lodge secretary and have confirmation of the same;
- secretary to compare manager's list of applications for colliery houses with his own list with a view of bringing them into uniformity;
- secretary to issue a notification urging applicants to give in their names to secretary before list is finally completed.[3]

These recommendations show that houses were tied to marriage and the union was itself involved in regulating the process of allocation. The houses were provided by the company, for their workmen alone and few men and women retained the family home after retirement from the pit. Dave Ayre recounts an occasion when Pease and Partners involved the bailiffs in implementing this rule:

> I remember—I was only five or six—and there were two old people lived at the back side to where I lived. I can remember their names now, Mr and Mrs Morrison, and they were tied cottages you see, and he'd retired from the pit, and they couldn't go on with the house. I didn't realise at the time, but I can remember going to school and when I came back, they were out on the streets. She was an upstanding woman, went to Chapel and so on. To see these old people—and they must have been between 65 and 70; to see the furniture, what they'd struggled for, in the rain, it had a really moving effect on us; even at that age I thought, 'There's something wrong that allows this to happen.' I remember all the people in the street booing when the bailiffs came, but that was it, they dragged the furniture out. The people were taken in by neighbours.

Incidents of this kind had led to the formation of the Aged Miners' Homes Association in 1896, the inspiration of Joseph Hopper, and from its earliest days the Durham Miners' Association was closely involved.

The first homes were opened by John Wilson in Haswell Moor in 1899 and '114 aged couples' were housed there. In the following year 65 houses were opened at Shincliffe—donated by Love, the coal owner. As a consequence other coal owners, the University and the Church involved themselves in a movement which they saw as being 'the most remarkable philanthropic work ever done by any body of workmen'.[4] In 1906 when a further forty dwellings were available the Association announced that places in the dwellings would be allocated by ballot—here was the cavilling system in operation once again. At Shincliffe, in the presence of the Shincliffe Homes Committees the DMA chronicled how Mrs Wilson, the wife of Alderman Wilson MP, General Secretary of the DMA, 'drew the whole of the ballots'. At that time the Association was pleased to announce that:

> We are glad to say that the Home for eight single old men which has been established at Haswell Moor, gives every satisfaction, and we are fully satisfied that it meets a great need. With a free home and his washing and cooking done free it leaves the single old man with his 5s per week for food, etc.[5]

The Chapel and the Store

Families were also linked to broader social and ethical groupings and organisations. The Chapel was one example of this. We have dwelled on the significance of Methodism in relation to the trade union; here it will be sufficient to comment on the additional social role played by the Chapel in the village. In these isolated places, the Chapel emerged as one place where women could visit and meet socially. There are many accounts of this; accounts too (in places like Horden and Easington) of young migrant workers seeing the Chapel as the place where they could meet single women. Generally these institutions had a role which extended broadly into the village life. In Kibblesworth one man remembered how:

> there was a small Chapel which we had to attend every Sunday morning, afternoon and evening. It wasn't a big place but it was the main centre of the village—everything that went on was at the Chapel. I remember that Mr Jefferson had a magic lantern that showed pictures from glass slides which was well attended. We once had a pantomime there...We had trips away. My father was a big noise in the Chapel and he used to run the brakes. It was a great day. We went to Tynemouth, Whitley Bay or Shields. We got a bag of sweets, an apple, an orange and a penny. You had games on the beach—it was really marvellous. Then we used

The two chapels in Kibblesworth—Primitive Methodist and Wesleyan Methodist: the Ranters' Chapel and the Managers' Chapel.

> to have the Sunday School treat....You had your own mug and you got a bag with a bun in it or a cake.[6]

In this village there were two Chapels, and this account refers to the first one, built in 1864 by Primitive Methodists. A Wesleyan Methodist Chapel was built in 1867. This was replaced by a new Chapel, designed by the colliery engineer in 1913. In this village, the two Chapels—Wesleyan and Primitive Methodist:

> were known as the managers' Chapel and the Ranters. It was common knowledge that if you wanted an official's job you went to the managers' Chapel.[7]

This link between Wesleyan Methodism and the employers is generally reported across the county and it reflects on the struggles taking place within the trade union in this period. For example in Langley Park, Herbert Cooper remembered how the officials at the colliery all 'went to Chapel and Church' and that 'the main thing about [them] was complete obedience to management. If the management said "turn" they all turned.' Similar stories were told to us by old miners in the south west of the county. In Crook, in the Roddymoor Colliery owned by Pease and Partners, 'all the deputies went to the Chapel—everyone that I can remember was a Chapel man. I think they had to be to get the job.'

Both Beatrice and Sidney Webb (writing separately) have commented upon the importance of Methodism and Chapel life to the development of mining culture in the north, and of the significance of this in relation to the emergence of quite *modern* forms of organisation in these isolated villages. Beatrice however was at pains to draw attention to another, highly significant, pattern of association in the mining villages. In writing about modernisation and the 'relationship between co-operation and trade unionism' she wrote that:

> when an intelligent foreigner asks me what there is most of interest in Northumberland and Durham I generally forget the Roman Wall, and sometimes the magnificent view from Durham Cathedral. The most significant thing about Tyneside in 1892 is that there are no fewer than 153 co-operative stores in the Northern Section, and that 470 trade societies flourish between Blyth and Middlesborough. No other part of the world can show so great a development of the two main forms of industrial democracy.[8]

The link she makes here between the co-operative movement and trade unionism as pre-eminently modern forms is significant and again shifts our attention away from a view of the mining village as one based essentially upon *traditional* patterns of community. True such traditional patterns were clearly at work in the mine and in family relationships. But equally clear is the fact that the working class developed new forms of association which built upon and occasionally transformed the traditional patterns of life. The co-operative movement is a very good example of this. In 1919, the Durham membership of the Co-operative Society stood at 270,000, the highest membership in the country. Total retail sales for

John W. White JP and Robert Simpson FCRA, president and secretary of the West Stanley Co-operative Society 1925.

that year were £17 million and by 1925 they approached £25 million. Sidney Webb commented that in Durham the:

> three score co-operative societies have something like 200 separate establishments, and hardly any Durham village, certainly no colliery village in the county is now without its branch store.[9]

Some of these societies were large organisations. Chester-le-Street and Mid Durham formed the biggest Association in the country and (with the Spen Valley division in Yorkshire) had the biggest turnover through its stores. As with trade unionism and its principles of collectivism, so too did co-operation establish itself more firmly amongst the miners of the north than any other group of workers in the country.

Jack Lawson recorded how his family's status rose with membership of the society:

> When we joined the Store, that respectable Society's cart came to our door regularly and proclaimed to all the world that we were real bona fide members who had paid for our groceries and looked the world in the face.[10]

To be looked up to in this fashion also linked in with the trade union. Lawson again:

> My father and brothers were known as good pitmen, and that means much for good standing. We were loyal trade unionists, and we were in the Store.[11]

The importance of the co-operative stores comes over in many ways. The institution is remembered and referred to repeatedly in the reminiscences of old miners and their wives. In his account of Craghead for example, John Hall writes of how the co-operative movement spread rapidly across Durham, influenced by the idea of:

> workers bonding together to purchase needed food and amenities then selling them to members and sharing the profits after allowing for expenses.

At Craghead:

> the co-op was built in the centre of the village on rising ground. The butcher's shop was at the corner, next on the rising ground was the manager's house and then the General Store. About these premises were the reading room and meeting hall, reached by wooden steps from the back yard.[12]

Here the store was given strong support and Hall notes that:

> Craghead society was one of the most loyal to the movement, buying co-op-manufactured food where possible, denying its members a choice of privately manufactured goods to their disadvantage. The principle of co-operation was to give the members a share in the profits in the form of a dividend....This was eagerly looked forward to by miners' wives with large families to cater for.[13]

For the most part the people who ran these societies were men. The history of the West Stanley and District Co-operative Movement lists the Committee Members and officials who organised the society from its beginnings (in 1879) to 1926. One hundred and seventy five men and four women are named, the first of these, Mrs Mary Bell, being elected in 1912.[14] These men were usually Primitive Methodists, strongly tied to the principles of trade unionism. In their official photographs they face the camera in three-piece suits and moustaches. They are clearly serious, confident and respectable men. The societies they ran so efficiently emerged as important centres of economic and political power in the villages. In 1881, the Crook Co-operative Society had a membership of 2,350, and by 1915 its total investments (placed in railway and colliery shares and in the national organisation of the Co-operative Wholesale Society Ltd) totalled £90,994 2s 11d.[15] West Stanley was a smaller operation with just 575 members in 1915, but it too was an organisation with substantial means. Both societies regularly made donations to the

The committee and employees of the West Stanley Co-operative Society, 1903.

Miners' Association and to relief funds associated with mining accidents and disasters. In times of industrial dispute their presence was a critical one—through donations to the miners' cause, and the provision of credit to its members.

These societies were also important employers. The relatively small Waterhouses store of the Crook Society employed 20 people and in the 1903 commemorative card of the West Stanley Store and committee there are photographic portraits of 96 people; most are men, but there are 21 women. The managers, as we have said, were exclusively men and in these times the store manager was a significant figure in the villages of the north. William Crawford, remember, worked for the Blyth Co-operative society in between the times as a union official in Durham. Before that, he had been the manager of the Ashington store. In Crook repeated reference is made to Roger Turnbull, who was for many years manager of the store, and 'a dedicated worker for the Russell Street Methodist Church'. These organisations also provided a strong basis for social solidarity in the villages. In Stanley, the official record notes how:

> each member got a visit from the Order Man, who read from a list of goods and ticked off the ones required by the member. These goods were then delivered to the house. In addition to this service

The West Stanley Co-operative Society: South Moor Branch opened in 1900—'no colliery village in the county is without its branch store'.

> the Greengrocer and Butcher carts came to the door at regular intervals.[16]

It was these 'Order Men' who spread the co-operative movement, travelling to outlying villages, building up orders to the point when it was feasible to open another local store. Linda McCullogh Thew, in her autobiographical account of Ashington in Northumberland, described these men as 'missionaries' of the co-operative movement who 'did more than take orders for groceries'.[17] They became highly significant sources of information and contact, as well as the people who spread both the idea of 'co-operation' and a strong degree of competition between potentially rival co-operative societies. Above all though she remembers:

> a solid brick wall led you to the corner where the premises of the Ashington Industrial Co-operative Society were to be seen in all their solid worth. First the stairs leading to the drapery department...Below and next to the drapery opening was the huge grocery department, then the butchery and, adjacent to it, the hardware followed by the greengrocery departments...At the top of the stairs on the left was the bespoke tailoring department and, on the right, a warren of rooms where meetings of all kinds were held for young and old.[18]

The details of this building (and others like it) are remembered acutely and in writing of the significant features of her life she identifies:

> my family, the Church, the school, the pit and the store. These were woven into the fabric of my life from the beginning. Allegiance to the Church might waver, schools change, our stay in various houses be short-lived, work in the pit unpredictable but our attitude to the store was steadfast. It claimed our wholehearted fealty and esteem. The Ashington Industrial Co-operative Society was the largest store in Northumberland, because it played such a large part in our considerable community.[19]

The significance of the store is recorded in other ways too. These co-operative societies were run by committees and frequently the secretary of the society would write a history of its development. Two excellent accounts exist of the Crook Society in the south west of the county and the West Stanley Co-operative Society in the north west. These books offer detailed insights into minutiae of the operations of the societies, and the place they held in the local communities. Through a reading of them it becomes clearer why Beatrice Webb attributed such significance to the trade society as examples of *modern* life in the coalfield districts. The societies were clearly scrupulously managed on co-operative principles. Their official histories provide evidence enough of this; of committee meetings, ballots, debates, and also public disagreements often conducted as arguments in the local press. They reveal in photographs and literary style, something of the character of these men who, as presidents and secretaries of local societies, administered the co-operative organisations. They stand out as earnest and respectable, dedicated to the interests of their locality and its people. They are cautious men, but men who strongly support the ideas of trade unionism. They record as a matter of course, the financial support given by their societies to the DMA in times of strike or disaster. Not short of business acumen, they see this to be best directed in support of 'the economic and industrial struggles of [the people] in their everyday lives'. This comes over clearly in the Preface written to the West Stanley history. Here the authors draw attention to the fact that:

> the true history of the society would be a history of the lives of all, rather than a record of the collective financial activities.[20]

And through all this comes a strong civic pride. A strong sense of both the economic and moral significance of co-operation as an elevating principle within mining life. A principle recorded through the mundane accounts of the opening of grocery and butchery departments, of committee meetings, elections and financial decisions and of the occasional 'event':

> we had never up to now [1903] launched a real co-operative exhibition into the district, and we remember with pride and

> pleasure the grand display given in our Co-operative Hall during the last week of February 1904. The chairman [Mr Hewison] opened the function and Mr Ritson presided, the CWS provided two speakers, whilst the committee provided an orchestra to render music.[21]

Clubs

There was another form of co-operation which exerted a major influence upon village life and this one was not mentioned with approval by Beatrice Webb. In the north, the working men's clubs built on the experience of the co-operative stores and created their own brewery. As with the stores, the Club and Institute Union (the now famed CIU) had its origin outside the north east, but it was there that it took firmest root. The CIU was established in London in 1862 by the Rev. Henry Solly and, as its official biographer recalls, started 'a pattern of social life hitherto unknown to the working classes, although enjoyed in a somewhat different manner by the gentry'. Initially it was seen as a union set up 'for the purpose of helping working men to establish clubs and institutes where they can meet for conversation, business and mental improvement with the means of recreation and refreshment, free from intoxicating drinks'. However under the Presidency of Lord Rosebery they became licensed premises. As he put it in 1875:

> Each club shall be free of all vexatious infantile restrictions on the consumption of intoxicating drinks and of similar matters—restrictions which tend to make these institutions moral nurseries, rather than clubs intended for the use of citizens of a great empire.[22]

At this time there were no clubs in the north, but as with the union and the co-operative store once established they rapidly grew in number. There was no club registered in Durham in 1898, six years later 58 clubs sent delegates to an inaugural CIU meeting held at the New Brancepeth Club, to the west of the City of Durham. The following year (21 October 1905) the first official council meeting of the Durham Club was held at Ushaw Moor Working Men's Club, presided over by the Alderman Robert Richardson, JP of Ryhope. Fourteen years later (and after the First World War) representatives of these clubs met in Prudhoe to determine they would establish their own brewery which would be co-operatively owned by the clubs it supplied. It would provide members with a strong, cheap beer, and it would remove the interests of the brewers and the coal owners. By that time, there were 220 clubs registered across the Durham coalfield, all of them administered by committees of workmen—most usually miners and the county was seen to be the place where the seed of the CIU had borne most fruit.

In his official history of the Durham Clubs, Ted Elkins has stressed the significance that coal mining, and the harsh labour regime of the mines, had for the co-operative principles which underpinned the development of the Clubs in Durham and Northumberland. As he puts it 'this was...mining country' and here men struggled against 'the tyranny of the mines'.

> This struggle, harnessed closely to the development of the trade-union movement, started in the first instance as a bid to get rid of slavery in the mines and progressed to become a day-to-day fight to get better conditions of work, safety and fair pay.[23]

Here:

> the life of a worker was cheap, his rights as a worker coloured by the desperate paucity of his role in society. But his anger against injustice and prejudice was mounting. At last the spirit of co-operation was stirring against the feudal class structure. The scene was set for the birth of a co-operative movement that was to break the bands of suppression and shake to the very foundations the society in which he toiled.[24]

This language is instructive and its account (of tyranny, progress, and co-operation) strongly parallels other accounts of the rise of trade unionism and the co-operative store, and to a powerful extent these developments were seen to be interrelated. Certainly they drew upon people with similar experiences and understandings. As with the co-operative stores, the men who ran the clubs were trade unionists, who developed a strong sense of propriety, of constitutionalism and the importance of rules to regulate behaviour. As the *CIU Journal* put in 1925:

> The club may be taken as a microcosm of the state. It is a perfect model of self-contained community. In it all men are equal and none hold position to exercise authority except by the will and pleasure of his fellows.[25]

However, as the *Journal* makes clear, this was a state of men apart. As Maurice Ridley has observed:

> The working men's club was another part of this division. These were the places where the male, generally at a weekend, sometimes during the week, used to go for their 'crack'—discussion, and drinking. The social life of the mining community, for the males, was centred around the club or the miners' welfare institute. And the club was a complete male preserve. No females. These clubs had very often been started in this area by Lodge

Syd Lavers.

> Officials and active miners and the same with regard to the steel workers and others. These clubs did a great job from the point of view of providing good quality beer, cheaper than the big private concerns could or would provide. The people who formed them, established the same rules at the club as operated in their own household. The division of labour was the same. A social club is for men, a place of work is for men; the women's role is in the home. And the pattern was established and it followed itself through into the social life. A great pity, and we've learnt how to do it much better since.[26]

The Methodist Chapels had provided centres for trade-union activities in the 1850s and 1860s; so did the club bar and committee room spawn another cadre of union leaders in the twentieth century. One such was Sidney Lavers. Born in Plymouth in 1890, Lavers had become a Socialist and joined the Social Democratic Federation as an unemployed seventeen-year-old. In ill health he had visited relatives in the north east where he eventually obtained employment at the Harraton Colliery near Chester-le-Street. After war service he started work at Blackhouse Drift near Birtley and became lodge secretary there. A committed member of the DMA, he became a Labour Party Councillor for Birtley Parish,

Chester-le-Street Rural District and later, Durham County. Elkins has noted how 'he supported the idea of the Federation Brewery from its conception'. His commitment to socialism involved him in political and industrial struggles and this was linked in with the fact that 'like his work mates, he was a clubman'.[27] This was a common pattern of activism associated with a general socialisation of trade-union activity in the early decades of the twentieth century. It helps to illustrate the fact that the position of the clubs within Durham mining life has many parallels with the store. Socially, the clubs became central to life in the villages. While the stores were frequented by the women, the clubs were the strict preserve of men. While clubs were never recalled to us with the same fondness as was the store, they had a ubiquitous presence in all of our discussions with the old miners; it seems men were forever 'going to' or 'coming back from' the club and there is no denying the pivotal role of these places in the organisation of men's social activities.

It was in the club that the men gathered to discuss their wages and the working conditions in the pit. Here men drank and talked. Here too, sports were organised. Most clubs had a quoits square and club members competed regularly in a County League. In Durham, pot bowling was a popular pursuit and this too was organised by the clubs. In addition the CIU in Durham co-operated with the Workers' Educational Association in the provision of educational classes. While the extent of this activity shouldn't be exaggerated it did have a significant presence in Durham with many of the clubs providing reading rooms on their premises. In 1923 at a quarterly meeting of the Workers' Educational Association at Burt Hall in Newcastle, detailed reference was made to the joint educational scheme set up between the Association and the clubs. In Durham 22 one-year classes were organised, and 13 of these were organised under the joint scheme. Alderman W.N. Smith, secretary of the WEA in the north east commented:

> This educational work forms a valuable and important part of the activities of the club movement in Durham County, and is already bringing beneficial results which more than compensates for all the efforts and costs expended...Branches of the club and Institute movement in other parts of the kingdom could with great advantage to the movement copy the example of Durham.[28]

In Durham, he said,

> the cost of this educational work amounts to several hundreds of pounds, but they have ungrudgingly found the money, and they are prepared to do still more to meet the educational requirements of their members.[29]

In the 1920s the club movement in Durham employed an educational secretary who spoke regularly at the local clubs. He had written the pamphlet, *What might be done* which focused on the role of working-class education. As a local reporter put it:

> The Union's endeavour in class work, lectures, etc., through the medium of the Workers Education Association and the Working Men's College [on both of which, as well as on Ruskin College, the Union is represented] is expected to grow, and the cordial relations between it and these bodies shows no sign of slacking.[30]

In that year the Durham Branch had provided five scholarships for its members to attend Ruskin College and was set upon a programme of expansion of education provision on its own premises. It is this local activity—reading rooms, books, occasional talks and lectures—which is most prevalent in popular memory. Hilda Ashby remembers the Chopwell of her childhood after the 1926 strike when her father:

> spent all his time in the Reading Room...it used to have all the Left literature. The *Daily Worker, Labour Monthly, Russia Today, New Statesman*—all this literature was there. And all the men met, played cards and read the newspapers and spent all their spare time in this Reading Room.[31]

Undoubtedly, throughout the county, the general pattern was one where these clubs, like the stores, became a significant economic and political power in the areas, and like the stores they were run by men who supported the union.

While the radical politics of Chopwell was not widespread through the county, the club movement generally supported a deeply egalitarian sense of democracy.[32] These sentiments, similar to those of the Co-operative Movement, were held in common with the now established trade unions. They had their impact upon the Mining Industry Act passed in 1920. This Act established a Miners' Welfare Fund at each colliery; under it, the coal owners were obliged to pay into the Welfare Fund a sum equivalent to 1d. for every ton of coal raised at the colliery. These monies could be used to establish pit-head baths and should generally 'be applied for such purposes connected with the social well-being, recreation and living of workers in or about the coal mines and with mining education and research.'[33]

These funds would be used to establish Miners' Welfare Institutes in each colliery village. These 'welfares' would be run jointly by the management and the union (through the Miners' Welfare Committees) and would mirror the range of activities provided in the CIU Clubs. Known as 'The Welfare' they became significant aspects of village life.

In Chopwell the Welfare is remembered as a comfortable place, well patronised and well conducted.

> There were dominos, draughts and chess played in the reading

room. The unwritten rule was that you had to be quiet. The same was true of the billiard room which had eight tables. The caretaker was in charge and if he raised his finger you were out. The company also provided the field for the village football team.

Accounts like these can be repeated from across the coalfield. They link back to the clubs provided by the employers for their workers in the nineteenth century; clubs built upon paternalism and a desire to influence and moderate the manners and moral standards of the miners and their families. In the 1920s they reappeared in a new form, backed by an Act of Parliament, with a clear recognition of the necessary and independent presence of the miners' own representatives. This often had unforeseen consequences. In Chopwell the colliery manager, Mr Imrie, acted as chairman of the Committee. The Institute employed an injured ex-miner as a part-time librarian who took on the task with great enthusiasm. By all accounts Imrie was a very liberal and democratic man, not uninfluenced by the significant rise in co-operative and democratic ideals on the coalfield, and he made no attempt to curb the activities of the librarian. By 1924, the library (which occupied a massive room in the building) was full.

> Every socialist publication was there, from Marx to all the old anarchist writers. The old socialists insisted upon this and they were all avid readers. All the standard English novelists were there—Dickens, Hardy, Thackeray—it was a wonderful library. Different speakers were paid to come to Chopwell, including many of the early socialists.
>
> It was often said that Mr Imrie...was to blame for the headway that was made with socialist ideas in Chopwell...when the big crack up came he got the sack and it just about killed him.

While Chopwell emerged as 'Little Moscow', in the east of the county, the Londonderry family continued to operate with paternal aspects of the Durham system, adapted in the context of independent organisations of miners. In this the family continued to fuse its relationship with the miners through a deep sense of nationhood and populist ideals of democracy. In Seaham, for example, the agents of the Londonderry collieries were directly involved in a range of local associations, most notably the branches of the conservative 'Primrose League', which they chaired. In December 1919, the *Belfast News Letter* describes how 'the Marquis and Marchioness of Londonderry had many engagements in the County of Durham on Saturday.' The first took place in the afternoon at the Silksworth Colliery where:

> her Ladyship opened a bazaar with the object of raising money for the Parish Church. She remarked that Silksworth was one of a

> happy family of collieries, the joys and success of which were her husband's and her own.

In the evening:

> Lord Londonderry visited the Dawdon Working Men's Club on the occasion of a social gathering of the members most of whom are employees of his Lordship's colliery. Lord Londonderry presented to Mr William Curry the Royal Humane Society's vellum and a watch from the Carnegie Hero Fund for life saving.[34]

These presentations were common events. Four years later at the same club, Londonderry attended a musical evening. Here:

> The health of Lord Londonderry and family was submitted by Mr P. Lavery, who said that his Lordship once told him privately, in the presence of their respected manager, that he was born in a fortunate and an unfortunate position—he did not know which. [Laughter.] 'But', continued the speaker, 'Lord Londonderry is a man.'
>
> The late Lord Londonderry gave them the site of that club on the lowest terms that could be arranged to satisfy the law. If they got many more bargains like that from Lord Londonderry they might claim the whole colliery.
>
> 'We keep tapping him and tapping him,' he added, 'and the more we get for nothing the more we want.' [Laughter.]
>
> Lord Londonderry, who had an enthusiastic reception, observed that his old friend, Mr Lavery, in proposing the toast had paid him the highest compliment that could be paid to anyone when he said that he was a man. He only hoped he was justified. [Applause, and a voice: 'He is.']
>
> After expressing regret at the absence of Lord Castlereagh who, he said, had been brought up in the full knowledge of his responsibilities, Lord Londonderry declared that whatever vicissitudes might come in the future, nothing would change the undying spirit of friendship between his family and the people who surrounded them, and with that complete understanding between them and that sympathy with each other in their lives he felt that there were few calamities which could befall the Londonderry collieries, Ltd. [Applause.]

In some places therefore the populist ideology of the clubs, readings of Robbie Burns and the deeply masculine nature of club culture combined to extend the influence of paternal employers in the twentieth century.[35]

Between 1869 and 1926 considerable changes took place in the social organisation of life in Durham villages, and the trade union played a significant part in this. In villages where once there were only Chapels and where they were dependent upon the patronage of the employer, there were now co-operative stores, reading rooms and all manner of clubs.

The impact of these developments upon the social structure of the villages and the sensibilities of their inhabitants was both far reaching and profound. Their influence can be seen in patterns of social interaction, and most dramatically in organised collective action—in ceremony and in the organisation of conflict.

9
Ceremony and Society: The Gala

Men cannot celebrate ceremonies for which they see no reason; nor can they accept a faith which they in no way understand.

E. Durkheim

The Annual Big Meeting of the Durham miners...has come to mean more than a demonstration of trade unionists. It is the great mining family on the march; the spontaneous expression of their communal life.

J. Lawson

'THE GREATEST unorganised ceremony in the world': this is how one old trade unionist described the Durham Miners' Gala to us. Like most other aspects of mining life in Durham, this ceremony has its origins in the nineteenth century.

At its first council meeting in 1871, the DMA delegates agreed that:

> the Council take into consideration the desirability of holding a general meeting of miners in the Central district, the expenses of such to be paid by the central fund.[1]

This general meeting was first held in Wharton's Park in Durham in 1871. The following year it moved to the Racecourse where it has met (as the Annual Gala or 'Big Meeting') on most years since. At the time of the first Gala 40,000 miners had joined the DMA, and 25,000 of these arrived in Durham on the third Saturday in July.

> In addition...not less than from 40–50,000 men, women and children were present, making a total of between 70 and 80,000. Each of the lodges and its accompanying friends marched in procession through the town from the railway stations at Shincliffe and North Road to the meeting place, and a great feature was the banners they carried.
>
> Mr J. Foreman of Roddymoor Colliery was called upon to

> preside. In opening the proceedings he said that it had been reported by many newspapers that they were met there for the purposes of inaugurating or agitating a general strike of all miners in the County of Durham [laughter] and it had given great alarm to the public, and more especially to the timid people of the City of Durham. Nothing was more utterly destitute of foundation than that statement, at least as far as they were concerned. Their object in meeting was to have a day's pleasure and enjoyment, to congratulate each other on their past success, to bond themselves more closely, if they possibly could, in the bond of brotherhood, and to show the country at large that the Durham Miners' Association was not a myth or a creature of the imagination, but a stupendous fact. [Applause.][2]

In the evening the delegates and principal officers of the union dined at a 'knife and fork supper' at the County Hotel and, like the Gala itself, this practice became an enduring tradition.

Banners

The following year another lengthy report appeared in the *Durham Chronicle,* and here the correspondent paid particular attention to the parade and the banners:

> The display of banners was a very prominent and pleasing feature of the demonstration. Altogether there were upwards of 70 flags on the ground. They were ranged around the full length of the field near the water's edge and thence across the end of the field opposite to that on which the platform had been erected and it is hardly necessary to state, composed as they were of every imaginable colour and hue, that they formed, as they fluttered in the breeze a very pretty and imposing spectacle. The greater proportion of them were indeed artistic productions both in design and execution.[3]

What is striking here is the speed with which the local lodges had designed and purchased these banners. The banner and its motif was seen to *represent* the lodge and the village, and the importance of this is reflected in the great care that was taken over the choice of image and of the words and phrases used. These issues were the matter of debate, and disagreements were settled by votes at lodge meetings. Generally absent on these early banners were paintings of leaders; a practice which developed later in the twentieth century. In 1872, only Alexander Macdonald's name is mentioned and in 1895 a giant banner from the Haswell Lodge portrayed Tommy Ramsay along with Macdonald and

This painting by Embleton depicts the 1872 Gala. The Lizzie Colliery banner was seen to have 'attracted unusual attention' with Alexander Macdonald defiantly standing with the 'Miners' Regulation Bill'.

Crawford. More usual then were themes which relate to work in the mines and to the advantages of union and unity. Overarching was reference to brotherly love, and the hope for cooperation in industry.

The banner of the Boldon Lodge, which was opened in North East Durham in 1866, was paraded at the first ever Gala in 1872. Its design mixed the themes of religion and justice: an arbitration scene—a female figure of Justice with scales standing between groups of masters and workmen. On the reverse side a religious motif in the form of two hands locked in a firm grip and the words 'Masters, know ye that ye too have a Master in Heaven'. The Mosley Colliery carried a 'fine view of the pit' on its leading side, with the words: 'We live for the well being of our fellowmen in order that they may live for ours'. On the reverse side was carried a representation of capital and labour. At the same Gala the banner of the Roddymoor pit, owned by Pease and Partners in West Durham, had on one side a representation of Master and Man emblematical of capital and labour, with the words: 'May we ever be united, let us love one another'. On the reverse was an emblem of Charity with the aphorism, 'An evil balance is an abomination to the Lord, but a just weight is his delight' and the words 'let brotherly love continue'. Similar motifs were on the banners of the other Pease collieries. The Stanley Colliery in Crook (Pease's West) was represented by a banner on which the two principle emblems emphasise 'Friendship' and 'Justice' with the motto 'let us love one another'. The following year this banner was changed to one which carried a representation of master and men emblematic of capital and labour, with the words underneath 'may we ever be united, let us love one another'— a theme often repeated. In the banners representing Pease's Waterhouses Colliery, the fair balance between capital and labour is emphasised and, if to make these words real, Pease himself marched to the Durham Gala with his workers in 1912.

However justice isn't always taken for granted in the lodge banners. As the *Durham Advertiser* noted:

> another banner from the same place had a portrait of Mr Crawford entering the House of Commons with the words 'we are resolved not to rest content, until a man to parliament we have sent. In justice we demand a fair share of the gain, which from the products of our labour you obtain.'[4]

While these motifs and themes change over time, what appears constant is the *form* of the Gala. In most of the villages, the banners would have been paraded on the Friday evening and the women would have cooked pies and prepared sandwiches for the following day. Early on the Saturday (often as early as 5.00 am) the banner would once again be unfurled and paraded through the village. The parade was led by the musicians of the brass band, playing hymns and marching tunes. Next came the lodge officials marching in front of the banner followed by the committee and then the miners and their families. All these people would then travel (sometimes on foot, mostly by train) into Durham City.

Hilda Ashby remembers it in this way:

> Gala Day was always a big day in Chopwell. At 7 o'clock in the morning they'd march with the banner around the village and

> then up to Blackhall Mill and Westwood station, and they'd all get on the train there and go to Durham. The Friday before ...everybody used to bake plate pies with meat in for people to take away with them.[5]

Jack Lawson provides us with an account of the parade in Durham which draws upon his memories of the early decades of this century:

> First comes the great banner carried by picked men, who must know how to carry themselves, or their strength will avail them little. Positing the poles in the brass cup resting on the chest, and held by leather straps on the shoulders, is a great art. The colliery banner is almost a personality. Much thought has been given to the colour, design, and size. Many have been the consultations with the artist and the firm chosen to carry out the wishes of the lodge in the matter of bringing this banner to life, and one of the great days in the history of the colliery was the unveiling of it. A colliery without a banner is almost unthinkable. Deep debate on design and the finance go to the making of it, and he is an honoured man who is chosen to cut the silken cord and speak to the great crowd which gathers at its unfurling. No regimental flag is dearer to the soldier than that emblem, showing the Good Samaritan tending the stricken wayfarer, in a setting of red, blue and gold, is to the miner. The officials of the lodge walk with pride beneath their banner, while behind comes the band and the men and women of the colliery. Down the main street they walk, between walls of spectators massed together on either side. Greetings are called by the onlookers to friends and relatives in the procession, and hands are gripped as they pass on. Sometimes the march is slowed down; sometimes it is stopped, marchers and spectators blocking the long street as far as eye can see.
>
> Above the fluttering banners, the old square castle, on its foundation of rock, rises clear cut against the sky, seeming to block further passage that way. But the procession moves on, and as it passes slowly over the bridge one can see the tree shadows like etched pictures in the seemingly still waters of the river below. Gradually the marchers wedge themselves into the narrow street which is called Silver, and past the mighty squat Cathedral, 'Half church of God, half castle 'gainst the Scot', standing there so grey and quiet in its own grounds. Turning and twisting round narrow hairpin bends, the procession sweeps into the broad street that leads past the handsome red Shire Hall, the great gloomy prison, until it finally reaches the wide, spacious racecourse by which the River Wear runs.[6]

Elsewhere he has written of how:

> You may see 50 banners in one sweep with their many coloured pictures and mottoes—portraits of old leaders who have passed on, portraits of present leaders, men known in local circles, the county in national and international life. And always on one side some picture wherein is a story.[7]

The Gala and the Union

Here too, the past was retained and reworked. Metcalfe in his assessment of the Gala and the purpose it fulfilled within the new union wrote:

> the idea of holding an annual Gala, or 'Big Meeting', was an inspiration which Crawford could readily appreciate in its vastness and eventual usefulness. This annual meeting, touched with emotion, and symbolic of the spirit of friendship and united action sealed the process of establishment.[8]

This sealing process drew upon a range of nineteenth-century tradition and practices. To some extent, the Gala can be seen as the symbolic replacement of the annual hiring meetings associated with the bond, but the meetings also had an important *social* function and were often treated as a holiday, the one occasion in the year when people from across the coalfield met and renewed old friendships. It was a family occasion too. Peter Graham reveals how:

> Every year people would sit in the same place on the Racecourse. Families you know. This was especially after people from the West of the county had moved across to the new pits on the East coast. The Gala was when they would meet every year—the Gala and Christmas Day. Every year in the same place—it was *ritual*—that's what it was.

Men and women have talked to us of being 'immersed' in the crowd and through this with the history of the miners. They talk of being carried through Durham as small children on the shoulders of their fathers. The language of social baptism is both striking and a general feature of these accounts. Lawson talks specifically of 'baptism' and others have used this expression directly to us. It resonates strongly with ideas of social solidarity in which miners and their families came together to publicly celebrate themselves. For while the 'Big Meeting' was a political meeting (with speakers and speeches on two platforms) it was far more than that. Lawson clearly saw it as an attempt by people in an industrial, rational world to retain and create customs that 'rouse the emotions and grip the heart'. It was, he wrote, 'more of an institution than a meeting, more

The 1937 Gala, 'one of the most impressive and inspiring experiences any man can have'.

social than economic, it is a combination of all miners' lodges, but the vast family eclipses everything.'

Here was a day, a public meeting, organised by the union which was a popular social occasion. People in the 1920s and 1930s remember the 'good day out' afforded by the 'Big Meeting'; for some Gala Day had a lasting effect upon their lives. Edie Bestford:

> In those days the streets were crammed; packed with hundreds of thousands of people. The Gala today is but a shadow of what it used to be. I can remember we used to walk two and a half miles from Annfield Plain down to Lanchester station, and on to Durham by train. That was when I was younger. Then, of course I had to go to work.
>
> I met George at a Durham Big Meeting Day. I was there with a friend. When we were young we used to go every year with my mother and father. And when the men went for a drink the women and the kiddies either had a picnic or they had tea which

> was served in some of the hotels and public houses. Well my friend and I went up Claypath and went in the *General Gordon* thinking we could get some tea. We walked through but there was no tea: the marquee was taken up with the men drinking. George came over and got us a seat each. He told his friend 'I'm going to marry that girl.' And so he did.[9]

In these and other ways, the Gala became patterned into village life. For if the Gala was a place to meet old and new friends and relatives, it was also the place where the dead were remembered and where death and loss were publicly displayed. In collieries where there had been a fatality since the last Gala, the banner would be draped with black crepe. As one man put it to us:

> it was a good day, the Durham Miners' Gala, but it was also a very sad day. You could see in those banners covered in black the terrible toll taken by this industry upon the miners. Sometimes it was terrible to see—banner after banner, draped in black. Terrible.

Sad, terrible, yet compelling. For Jack Lawson, a lodge official, Gala Day was:

> one of the most impressive and inspiring experiences any man can have. It is exhilarating to march with your band and banner, and also to watch this stirring spectacle from some high point of vantage, where you see it as a long, continuous whole. Officially this gathering is called a Gala, but to the miners and their wives, who come in from every part of Durham, it is 'The Big Meeting'.
>
> Banner after banner, band after band, followed by the members of the lodges and their wives. From remote places on moor and fell, and from huge collieries near the towns, they have marched; down from the boundaries of the coalfield, and up from the centre they have come keeping step all along the roads to lively tunes. Since eight in the morning they have been coming into the city of Durham, and even at noon the apparently endless march goes on.[10]

At the end of the day, the bands, the banners and the marchers returned home to their villages. And there:

> at night time, everybody who hadn't gone to Durham for the Big Meeting Day would wait around in the street for the banner coming back. They would get off the train and march all the way up with the band playing. It was always a big thing: 'Wait 'till the banner comes home'...'the banner is coming home.'[11]

The members of the Twizel Lodge (near Chester-le-Street) on the racecourse at Durham in 1924. The banner carries its black drape, 'A good day but a sad day.'

The tendency for miners to hold their own social festivals has been noted by Klaus Tenfelde in relation to central Europe. Here he sees that:

> the singularity of mining as an occupation, the unifying force of its special legal status and the town-like character of the mining settlements provided the essential structure for a separate festive culture.[12]

These festivals were 'saturated with practices derived from religion, communal and courtly festivals' and based upon:

> the desire of the miners' fraternities for a distinct and separate social life of their own [arising] first and foremost out of the special legal status of mining as an occupation and of mining society. Even outside the work situation the microcosmic world of the trade gave rise to ways of thinking and forms of conduct which soon proved a fertile soil for the idea of a separate miners' festival.[13]

Clearly, similar processes to those were at work in Durham and in this way the sense of exclusion *from* 'Durham society' was replaced by an exclusive occupational festival. Metcalfe's comments shouldn't be forgotten however. In the 1870s the Gala was linked powerfully to the union and thereby to the symbolic struggle within the reformed Durham society: it was, in the broadest sense, a *political* as well as a social occasion. It stretched back and drew upon those other occasions for mass assembly in the nineteenth century—strikes, demonstrations and religious meetings.

In 1831, for example, the miners of Durham and Northumberland were on strike and Richard Fynes provides an account of their meeting on Bolden Fell between Sunderland and Gateshead.

> During the forenoon, the roads in the vicinity of the meeting place presented an unusual battle, the men walking in procession from the different collieries, bearing flags and banners and accompanied by bands of music. The banners were numerous and of the gayest description, nearly all being embellished with a painted design and with a motto more-or-less connected with the recent struggle between the miners and their employers.[14]

During the strike which affected the coalfield in 1844, a similar meeting took place at Shaddons Hill, between Wrekenton and Birtley:

> many thousand miners were present and took part in the proceedings. On reaching the ground there was presented one of the most splendid and magnificent sights ever witnessed. The music of various bands was heard, and flags and banners were flying in every direction. The part of the Fell where the meeting was held was of the shape of an amphitheatre, at the bottom of which was placed a wagon, which served for a platform, from which as far as the eye could reach, was observed a mass of human beings, there being upon a fair calculation 35,000 to 40,000 men present.[15]

Certainly there is much evidence to support Moyes's view that:

> the idea of the mass meeting was well established before the first Durham Miners' Gala. Not only that, the essential elements of procession by collieries in order, distinguished by banners bearing colliery names and inscription, marked by black crepe to token fatal accident and accompanied by bands playing appropriate music, were all there—a well-established pattern of mass assembly.[16]

In these assemblies, the influence of religion and especially of the Primitive Methodists was clear. Ostrogorski, writing in 1902, commented on how:

> The field of religious propaganda and dissent long ago popularised outdoor meetings. The great founders of Methodism, Wesley and Whitefield deserting the consecrated places of worship and the respectable people who frequented them, preached in the

> open air, amid the fields, to thousands of brutalised miners, and it was there that they achieved their greatest successes.[17]

By the late nineteenth century this was the predominant form of the political meeting, and Ostrogorski's account helps to place the Gala in its historical context:

> These are large, extraordinary gatherings, the principle object of which is to convey an impression of the numerical strength of the party and its enthusiasm....Those who take part in the demonstrations arrive in a procession with flags and banners, to the sound of drums and fifes. Special trains were organised to bring people from the neighbourhood at reduced fares. If the meeting is a particularly large one, improvised speakers address the crowd which has not been able to get into the hall....When the demonstration takes place out of doors, several platforms are erected from which the orators speak simultaneously. The voting of the resolutions is sometimes accompanied by blasts from a trumpet....Every meeting of exceptional importance assumes the character of a demonstration.[18]

This was the form taken up by the Gala and one which John Wilson saw as being 'the demonstration *par excellence*' and one which 'incorporated us in the permanent institutions of the county'.[19] This was emphasised in 1896 when the miners were invited to a Cathedral service in the afternoon of the Gala by Bishop Westcott. Today, the Gala still ends with this ceremony, strongly evoking this sense of permanence.

However, it would be wrong to overstress the stability of the incorporation emphasised by Wilson. This political incorporation was based upon the DMA's organised regulation and control of the customs and conflicts which were endemic to the Durham system. The possibility for tension existed in the fact that within the structure of the union, an important degree of autonomy had had to be ceded to the local lodges and to the customary practices of villages and workplace. In Durham the county union organised the Big Meeting, but the attendance was 'organised' by the lodges. Thus, in May 1878 Crawford, a man who, as we have seen was capable of the most draconian control over the lodges on matters of county agreements, issued a circular on the matter of the Gala. In it he asked lodge secretaries to provide him with information as to the 'probable number of persons which will be coming from your place to the Annual Gala, and from which station they will come'. He adds: 'all we want is a good guess'. They would of course have got no more, and this says a lot about the occasion. So too do the speakers who were invited to address the meetings. Under the constitution of the new association these were nominated by the lodges and then elected by lodge votes.

Outside the General Gordon public house. 'When the men went for a drink, the women and the kiddies either had a picnic or they had tea which was served by some of the hotels and public houses'.

Over decades the 'Big Meeting' organised two platforms of speakers to address the miners and their families. In the 1880s and 1890s the Anarchist Prince Peter Kropotkin spoke at Durham, as did Joseph Arch, Charles Bradlaugh, Annie Besant and Tom Mann. Once the miners had joined the Labour Party its leaders (Keir Hardie, Henderson, Snowden, MacDonald and Lansbury) all addressed the Gala crowds, and stood on the balcony at the County Hotel. But always there was a radical presence, a presence at odds with the political integration stressed by the Durham leadership. This came to a head when Tom Mann spoke at the Gala. Interrupted by the President because of his implied criticism of John Wilson, Mann replied in anger that he would say what he wished, that he was there not as a guest of the area leadership—who would never invite him—but of the miners' lodges who had voted for him.[20]

The Gala, as a popular form, brought the union, the village and Durham society together but when these were in tension the appearance of stability could be overturned. From the earliest days members of 'Durham Society' were keenly aware of this 'other side' of the Gala—the occasion could be seen as the occupation of the city by the 'lower orders'.

The 'occupation' was symbolic but it raised the possibility of threat, something of which the inhabitants of that city had always been mindful. On the eve of the 1872 Gala, for example, John Wilson writes of 'the public feeling, and in many quarters, fear which was felt as to the consequence of bringing such a large number of miners and massing them in the City.' Tradesmen barricaded their shop windows and 'an urgent request was made to the Mayor to have soldiers in readiness.' Wilson, forever concerned to represent the moderate and respectable side of the Durham miners, and their fitness to occupy a place in the City was sensitive to the feelings of 'Durham society'. In his concern to placate these feelings and also to encourage sobriety amongst his members, he reveals an important edge to the integrative process. In a monthly circular, written before the 1897 Gala, he pointed out that:

> The Durham Miners' Gala is no mere formal affair; although it has become one of the fixed institutions of the county. If it were omitted, a serious vacuum would be made in the yearly gatherings, for it holds the premier place in those occasions. It has proved its fitness and, therefore, its continuance is more than a tolerated one. It is a clear instance of the survival of the fittest. It has borne down opposition; and by its character cleared away prejudices of long standing. Ideas of the crudest kind—which were surprising, because they were formed about people close at the doors of the citizens of Durham, and not of the inhabitants of some far-off savage land—have been modified and corrected, and fears founded upon those ideas have been turned into feelings of welcome.

He went on to outline these prejudices and ideas.

> The approach of the ruthless Goth upon the ancient City of Rome filling, as it did, the inhabitants with terror and dismay, was no more alarming than was the knowledge that the miners were about to hold their first Gala in Durham. The fact itself was synonymous with ruin. If so many thousands of those people were gathered together, there could be but one result, and it behoved the peaceful and more civilised and order-loving citizens of the city, to prepare for it. This was done by invoking the aid of powers, both civil and military, at least by requesting the chief magistrate, at the time, to have those forces in readiness for the outbreak, which was sure to take place; but our old friend, Mr Fowler [who was then Mayor] had more sense than to listen to such fearful and unfounded anticipations, and he refused, and at the conclusion, the City stood on its old site and no one suffered even in the smallest item.[21]

Ceremony and Conflict

In later years, however, especially in times of industrial strikes and conflict in the coalfield, the fears of the local inhabitants and the sensibilities of the union leaders led to the occasional cancellation of the Gala. This was the case, for example, in 1921 and 1922. Equally in 1926, the occasion of the General Strike and lockout, the miners' union desisted from holding its annual celebration and meeting; a decision which was influenced by an incident that had taken place on the Racecourse the previous year:

> during the week prior to the Gala the Bishop of Durham (Dr Hensley Henson) who had a seat in the House of Lords had roundly criticised the Labour County Council of Durham for what he described as their 'unexampled extravagance' in laying down six miles of new road between Durham and Lanchester. This pronouncement has been widely quoted, and it set up a feeling of resentment among the miners which was reflected in the atmosphere of the Miners' Gala, so much so indeed that in the procession through the streets on the Saturday there was one banner which bore the grim words—'To Hell with Bishops and Deans'.[22]

This slogan was quickly translated into action when the Dean of Durham (Dr J.E.L. Weldon) arrived on the racecourse to address a Temperance meeting. He was mistaken for the Bishop:

> He was always punctual at his meetings and he was there a few minutes before he was due to ascend the platform. He was tapping the miners on the shoulder as he came along and laughing and joking with them, little prepared for the drama in which he would so soon be the central figure.
>
> I never remember seeing him in a happier mood than he was at that moment: his bright red face beamed. 'Here's the Bishop,' the cry 'Here's the Bishop!' went up from scores of people, and then came a chorus of voices 'Hoy him i' the river!'
>
> Everybody on the platform heard the cry and must have been aware that something terrible was about to happen, but the speeches went on.
>
> The crowd surged towards the Dean who was then well past the allotted 'three score years and ten'. To the river he was going and I could see it all from the platform. A miner with a long cane was trying to remove the Dean's tall hat. Twice the cane got underneath it, but it fell back each time. On the third occasion it was toppled off his head and disappeared. This huge man was now being pushed and bustled by an angry, heated crowd

> towards the river. To this day I can still see him at the head of the crowd moving inexorably forward to the water and then he disappeared.[23]

The Dean in fact, escaped by motor launch to the safety of his home and a 'glass of lemonade...brought in on a silver tray'. To miners of that generation though (and everyone of them we talked with mentions the incident and being there) it was the Bishop who was 'hoyed in the river'.

In 1926, the cancelled Gala was replaced by an 'unofficial' massed meeting of thousands at the pit village of Burnhope. As one union activist recalls:

> The DMA executive Committee decided not to hold the Big Meeting at Durham in July; a decision with which many of the members disagreed and that minority decided to hold the Gala at Burnhope, and it proved to be an outstanding success....The preliminary and final arrangements were the responsibility of the Burnhope lodge and the major task of organising fell upon the shoulders of Jim Hobbs their secretary. The Gala followed much the same pattern as Durham Big Meeting, the bands, banner and followers sorting themselves out into single file order as they approached the field.[24]

The speakers at this unofficial Gala were A.J. Cook, Will Lawther, E. Edwards of Northumberland and the MP for Consett the Rev. H. Dunnico. Cook's speech took up the theme of the miner standing against the aristocracy:

> They know how Lord Londonderry's grandfather had worked against the miners of his day, but much as the present lord would like to have back the conditions of those days, he would go first.

And the church:

> If there was one man who had disgraced the cloth that he wore it was the Dean of Durham. He had taken the meanest possible position in taking the side of privilege against a lowly people. The Dean defended the rich against the poor and was a disgrace to his class and a betrayer of his master.[25]

Maurice Ridley, a young miner at the time, gives us his description:

> During the early weeks of the strike the Durham Miners' Gala was held. Usually, of course, the Gala is held in Durham but in 1926, for a number of reasons, it was held at Burnhope: a mining village in the Stanley area. I walked there with other young locked-out miners and our parents, and it was my first real experience of the leadership that was really in charge of our struggle. I should say that the speech of Arthur Cook, who was

the secretary of the miners, affected me for the rest of my life. His ability, the way in which he pointed out what was at stake, the role of the miners, and so on, left an impression on me that is still as strong today as at the time when I heard it, well over 50 years ago. Cook was without doubt one of the most outstanding trade-union leaders that this country has produced in the last 100 years. And the support which he got from the miners in Durham, and naturally of course in Wales and throughout the mining community, was probably greater than any other trade-union leader before or probably since. Arthur was a man of action, very similar to Tom Mann, whom I knew in later years. He could get to the heart of the situation and to the hearts of the people he was talking to in a way that politicians and others couldn't do. And you knew that he was a man who was dedicated to the cause of the mining community and to the improvement of the lot of miners. And this struck you as you listened to him. He was very eloquent. He had that tremendous ability that was as good on the public platform doing a job of work in politics as many of them were in the chapels.

There were at least 30,000 miners at the meeting. It was a magnificent turnout and of course they had to get there the best way they could and many of them walked from goodness knows where.

We walked 5 or 6 miles, but many of the people there that day walked much further. But that didn't matter. Even although it wasn't held in Durham, it was recognised that this meeting taking place at Burnhope was to be addressed by the leadership of the miners and the politicians within the labour movement who were supporting us. For any ordinary trade unionist it would have been a crime not to be able to go. I mean you just automatically had to go because you were in the midst of the struggle.[26]

The struggles of the 1920s had had their effects upon the political leadership of the miners' union and its local lodges. By this time the dominance of the reformist Methodist leadership was weakening. Socialist and Labour symbols had begun to replace religious motifs on lodge banners; most evident by the presence of the 'Little Moscow' lodges of Bewicke Main, Chopwell and Follonsby, each with revolutionary designs in their banners. Chopwell's banner, unfurled in 1924, carried images of Marx, Lenin and Keir Hardie. The Follonsby Lodge, strongly influenced by its syndicalist secretary and checkweighman George Harvey carried portraits of Lenin, Cook, Keir Hardie, James Connolly and Harvey himself.[27]

These, however, represent a minority. Interestingly they were located

Bewicke Main Lodge: one of the three 'red' banners unfurled in Durham in the 1920s.

in the north of the coalfield; larger more modern villages more open to the political ideas available in the urban centre of Newcastle. In Chopwell (the best known of the 'Little Moscow' villages) the public representation of revolutionary politics didn't pass without disturbance. Opposition there did not surface in the lodge, as in Boldon, but in the streets of the village itself. In 1924 at Durham the *Durham Chronicle* recorded how:

> one banner that attracted considerable attention was from the Chopwell Lodge, which secured a prominent place next to one of the platforms. It bore the portrait of the Prime Minister, Lenin and Karl Marx. Its unfurling at Chopwell on Friday had caused a 'scene', women pelting it with stones. On Saturday morning also, dislike was shown to the banner as it passed through Chopwell village to the station, some of those marching beside it being pelted with soot and other missiles. There was also a threat to set fire to the banner at Durham.[28]

Another reporter noted how:

> the police were close at hand during the progress from the station, in case of disturbance. The banner was jeered at nearly all the way but it reached its destination in safety and was returned to Chopwell in the evening without suffering damage.[29]

Commenting on this account he observed that the banner 'was by no means popular though', something which he considered to be indicative of 'the healthy outlook of the Durham miners'. Healthy or not, other banners in the county also reflected the changes that were taking place across the coalfields. Most common was a move toward secular images reflecting the achievements of cooperation or municipal socialism. The co-operative store, aged miners' homes and the local Welfare Halls were common motifs. However, religious motifs were also adapted in interesting ways. In 1920 the banner of the Gateshead Lodge had on its leading side a portrait of David with his foot on Goliath's neck, his arm raised in a triumphant, victorious pose. This image is supported by the words: 'He that would be free must strike the first blow.' The theme of 'brotherly love' is present on the reverse side, but here it unites with socialistic ideas of 'workers of the world' depicting workers from around the Commonwealth united together as 'comrades in every clime'.

Popular Culture

The Durham Miners' Gala was a dramatic event, and a quite exceptional one. Its historical origins in the nineteenth century, the Methodist influence on its banners, and the near medieval setting of the City of Durham combined to produce an extraordinary working-class occasion. It was a parade, family reunion, political and revivalist meeting. In 1927 and 1929, Oswald Mosley spoke there and the form of the Gala is said to have conveyed to him ideas about forms of political assembly which he attempted to implement at fascist rallies in the 1930s. However this was

Arm in arm on Gala Day, 1935.

based on a misunderstanding of the Gala and its relationship to mining life.

The democratic elements of popular culture displayed by the Gala are significant, as are its roots in pre-modern society. Yet it is easy (and tempting) to oversimplify any interpretation of this occasion. Certainly that is the case with the banners. In their motifs we *can* discern an important change from Liberal-Methodist influence to Labour-Socialist forms. But even here there is continuity. Until the pit closed in 1983, the East Hetton banner displayed the Good Samaritan, and the militantly socialist Wearmouth Lodge, until very recently, paraded behind a banner carrying the words 'In God is all our trust'. What this suggests perhaps is the need to consider the *diffuseness* of the image contained in the banner, rather than a strict formal political interpretation. The banner through the union provided the unifying element through which village life became established as 'community'. It had to embrace *all* the village; this was its purpose. This was the source of dissent from the women in the streets of Chopwell. The banner represented them all. This too is an important way to understand the parade in Durham.

It should not be thought that the social function of the Gala simply involved a public presentation of life as it was lived in the village. Certainly this dimension did exist: family groups met together, villages paraded as a group and honoured the men who had died in the mine.

Men dance with women, women with women and men with men. Durham Miners' Gala, 1935.

However there was also an element of carnival involved. The practice emerged of women parading in the clothes of pitmen, and of men dressing as women. Miners walked through Durham in top hats and tails; the symbols of their 'betters', the masters. Photographs of the 1935 gala capture moments when men dance arm in arm in front of their banner as they approach the race course. On the race course itself men and women dance together but so too do women dance with women and men with men. In the fairground, miners 'play' at being children on the roundabouts. While the Gala involved a public celebration of village life, it was also, and paradoxically, the one day in the year when the village was escaped.

In many ways, descriptions of the Gala mirror that of the Mardi Gras which takes place every February in New Orleans. Mardi Gras is a carnival with fancy dress, music and dancing. It is a parade in which the ordinary world is turned upside down. While there were elements of this on Gala Day there was order also. No more so than in the pattern of the parade. In Durham the miners' bands and banners congregated and marched down Silver Street or along Church Street to the focal point of the County Hotel. There they marched beneath the balcony upon which their leaders stood. It was almost akin to a military march-past. Unlike

Carnival it acknowledged a distinction between actors and spectators. It was always an occasion in which the leaders looked on. But they did not look on to a 'mass' of people. Some may have seen it like that, but the people themselves marched through with their friends and family as a *village*. The lodge banner represented them and their collective endeavours. On Gala Day the people marched behind their own banners and their own bands. It was those bands and banners which provided the pageantry in their colour and sound. It was the miners who played at the Cathedral service. As one old bandsman put it: 'it was an honour in those days to play at the Cathedral. You had to be a leading band in the county'. Their music, like the Gala, was in an important sense their own. And they adapted it, playing formal classical marches as they arrived and more popular tunes and marches, as they left—many of them drunk, most of them happy.

10
Riot, Rebellion and Strike

The riot as a normal part of collective bargaining was well established in the eighteenth century.

E.J. Hobsbawm

THROUGH trade unionism, coal miners and their families changed the pattern of life in the north. In this process they also changed themselves. The trade union (an organisation principally based upon the *instrumental* involvement of its members) emerged as their clearest source of mutual identity. Rituals and ceremonies were of great importance in this, as was the tendency for the mining villages to be involved in strikes and the spontaneous forms of collective action.

Riot and Insurrection

When Crawford called for the exclusion of non-unionists from 'ordinary, honest and respectable society', he was implicitly involving the women of the villages in the struggle for trade unionism. The women were not, of course, *members* of the union, yet they clearly became understood as a party to these struggles. One contemporary observer, writing in the *Sunderland Times* noted that in public disturbances women were more disposed than men to be mutinous: 'they stand less in fear of the law, partly from ignorance, partly because they presume upon the privilege of their sex and therefore in all public tumults they are foremost in violence and ferocity'. Jack Lawson made a similar comment in relation to the strike in 1892—'the women were the worst'. In 1872 they revealed their capacity for organised direct action in the 'food movement' in the colliery villages. Contemporary reports from the local press of the period have left us with vivid accounts of their activities.

> The agitation against the present high price of food, which was inaugurated on Tuesday by 'guild wives' of the miners of South Hetton colliery, appears to be rapidly extending throughout the

> entire mining district of North Durham, meetings of women having been held yesterday at Ryhope, Seaton Colliery, Wheatley Hill, Thornley, Murton Colliery, South Hetton and Silksworth. The good ladies at Seaton Colliery on Friday took part in a demonstration against a poor woman. The wife of a brakesman had committed a contravention of the general agreement by purchasing her usual quantity of beef. This led to upwards of 300 women turning up with fire blazers, trays etc. round the woman's residence, and for a lengthened time the greatest disorder prevailed. The miners, colliery officials, shopkeepers, innkeepers, and even the colliery doctor are prohibited from buying butchers' meat at the current prices. On Saturday the matrons of Seaton Colliery, taking advantage of the absence of their husbands at the Durham Gala, made another demonstration at the house of the unfortunate woman. They marched to the rendezvous with an effigy of their victim, which was placed in front of her dwelling, and soon reduced it to ashes amidst the wildest uproar and excitement. Not satisfied with this ebullition the 'ladies' vented their indignation upon the railings at the front door, which they pulled up bodily, a volley of stones being directed by way of a finale against the house. The butchers pursue their periodical rounds at the various collieries amidst a chorus of approbations, epithets and innuendos from indignant matrons, frequently accompanied by volleys of stones from the village 'loafers'. This was the case at Silksworth yesterday morning when the feeling manifested itself in the form of flying pots and missiles, causing a number of 'knights of the cleaver' to beat a hasty retreat.

The report goes on to give an account of a meeting which took place at Seaton Colliery in the evening which was attended by about 800 women.

> The movement appears to have taken this form, viz., not to purchase any more beef or mutton until these could be had at the workmen's own prices, namely 7½d. for choice pieces, 6d. for inferior and milk for a penny a pint; and at Seaton an association has been formed to defray all necessary expenses. The Ryhope meeting was attended by about 300 females in the field near the colliery. Mrs Robson who presided, said, 'It is no use your coming to the meeting unless you intend to act on your promises. If you don't do that all of you, we will strip you all stark naked, as the woman said at the Nack.' (Sensation and signs of appreciation.) If they adopted the course she had suggested namely, to refrain from the use of meat, the butchers would not get such grand livings out of them as they had hitherto. There were many poor families in the colliery, who had no doubt got a few

> shillings into the butchers' debt; and they would be put to trouble. She suggested that they should subscribe a penny apiece, and form a fund with which to help these poor people. They would never miss the pence and it is what they should do to support their kind. Mary Turner then ascended the rostrum and said she had lived with a farmer near Murton colliery (his name though mentioned for obvious reasons we suppress) who put eight pints of water to eight pints of milk. (Indignation.) At present if she bought a bit of meat for her man, her and the children had to subsist on gravy and bread. (Renewed indignation.) There was only a halfpenny worth of milk in a pint, for which they paid ld. They would give no more than 2d. a quart for new milk, 7d. for the best parts of their meat, and 4½d. and 5d. for the inferior bits. (A woman: 'What about the butter?) They could not do everything at once. The next meeting they held they should give everyone notice that the butter was only to be 1s. per pound. She then proposed that the articles to which she had referred should only be purchased at the prices specified, and a forest of arms was held up in its favour, followed by loud plaudits. The speaker concluded by saying that if any of them did not act up to that they would pull them out and strip them.[1]

Further meetings were held throughout the county. Mrs Robson appears to have emerged as the spokeswoman in north-east Durham. On 21 June she addressed another rally at Ryhope at which 300 women were present. By this time the demands had escalated beyond the idea of regulating the food prices to the idea of forming a co-operative butchery union themselves:

> She advised them if they wanted to get beef at the price they had decided upon, to start a co-operative store, appointing a man to go to market to purchase for them, and kill their own....If they would do that the money which at present went to the butchers would go to their own pockets....She thought that they should form a union and kill their own beast. She had killed many a sheep and pig, and had helped to kill many a beast. (Applause and a voice, then we don't want a butcher.)[2]

Similar meetings took place during the same week. At Shotton Colliery, there were 500 present, and at Oakenshaw, women passed a resolution prohibiting the people from buying meat during the same week. Women from all over the county were drawn into the movement. Activities were reported from Edmondsley, Lumley, Hatfield, Shincliffe, Newfield, Bishop Auckland and Spennymoor.

On 25 June the women of Ryhope, led by Mrs Robson, marched from their village to the neighbouring village of Silksworth. Mrs Robson again addressed the crowd. She made clear that it was a women's protest and a meeting for women alone, announcing that:

> Every man but the shorthand writers to go outside, or else we will twig them, for there is a bonny lot of them.[3]

According to the press report this brought loud cheering from the women, and the men withdrew some distance. A Mrs Green of Silksworth then addressed the crowd and amplified the need to resort to 'twigging':

> There were many that day who had got their meat at the old price. (A voice: 'We will twig them then'.) What did these women deserve? (A voice: 'Strip them.') Yes after the meeting was over that must be attended to and looked after. (Laughter and uproar and a voice: 'Strip them stark naked.') She considered they were all of one mind. (Cries of, 'Yes we are', and 'Aye, aye'.)[4]

There are reports across the county of women and men being thrashed and tarred and feathered. This 'petticoat strike', as the women called it, flowed directly from their concern with the household—their work—and it consciously excluded men. Interestingly, the strikers enforced their decisions by using the daily practice of *shame*, and imposing sexual humiliation on both women and men. Here, the sexual division of labour established as daily practice in the village, was used in a powerful way to fuse the women together as a group.

These outbreaks of rioting were not restricted to women. During the election of 1874, violence was widespread nationally, but it is agreed that Durham's experience was exceptional. In the run-up to the election, three men had been executed, and the local press were full of accounts of 'brutal assaults'. Feelings were running high in the coalfield because of Londonderry's attitude toward the 1872 Mines Act, and toward trade unionism in general. On polling day the miners (who were not entitled to vote) crowded into the polling stations to make a mockery of the ballot. Throughout the day Tory cabs were attacked, as were people who wore the *Tory* colour of red. Rioting took place throughout the county, and especially in Durham City and in Hetton. By late afternoon order had broken down in several places and 'mob rule' prevailed in one or two. At Hetton the police station was besieged and after a vigorous stoning was finally taken and sacked. Order was only restored after the arrival of the troops. At another Tory stronghold—Londonderry's own town of Seaham—the committee was put to flight, a cab hurled over the cliff into the sea and tar barrels lit in the street.

John Wilson has given his own account of these events in Hetton. While standing on a wagon in an attempt to keep order he was told by two young men to take no notice—'just watch and you'll see some fun'. It seemed that they were right;

> The police were returning from the lock-up after securing their prisoners when they were met by a shower of the whinstones. They were a dangerous missile, having very sharp edges, and when they struck would cut deep. The officers were taken at a disadvantage for the attack was well concerted and the stones were delivered with precision. The officers retreated and were chased to the lock-up. Their stay was short, for the crowd broke the windows, doors, all the woodwork, and the furniture of the resident officer, the estimated damage being about £100. The three prisoners were released. A visit was then paid to the houses of some of the leading Conservatives resident in the place, and the Colliery Inn, where in every case considerable damage was done.[5]

This violence can be seen partly as a consequence of the limited franchise. Certainly this was Wilson's own assessment. The rioting, he said, could be traced to the attitude and behaviour of those 'who are falsely our superiors'.[6] His solution was a wider franchise, for this would enable miners to 'lay aside brute force as a senseless weapon and fight with one more peaceable but no less sure—the ballot.' Electoral reform (achieved, politically, in 1884) was seen as a requirement for order and discipline on the coalfield. This view was shared by Beatrice Webb who wrote in her diary of the 'dark years' before electoral reform when socialism was linked to ideas of revolution and not constitutional reform.

Strike and Riot

In 1910, South East Durham was represented by the honourable F.W. Lambton who described himself as 'a Durham man bearing a well-known Durham name'. In the famous January election he was supported by the Londonderry family and had secured letters of recommendation from Lady Theresa Londonderry and the active involvement of the Pease family from Darlington.

The constituency covered that part of the coalfield from Sedgefield to the north of Seaham where capital expansion and development had been most extensive. A new kind of colliery village was emerging in this part of Durham with rows upon rows of brick terraces housing a mass labour force. The Horden Colliery had by 1910 established itself as the largest in the country, employing almost 4,000 workers. These men and their families were housed alongside the pit in rows of bricked houses numbered from 'First' to 'Thirteenth'. The owner of this new pit was the Horden Colliery Company Ltd, whose agent occupied a large mansion house called Hardwick Hall, situated some miles from the colliery. Near to their mine, the company had built a workman's club, costing £8,000,

The Horden Club, 1910: 'The rioters smashed everything breakable and left the place in sad confusion.'

and constructed on the 'most substantial and artistic lines'. The local press described it in glowing terms:

> It was replete with every convenience and includes a large hall, billiard rooms, meeting rooms etc, the whole building being furnished in a most elaborate state. It has a very extensive frontage and an imposing array of windows.

On 26 January this club was attacked in an 'outbreak of mad passion' and on the following day was burnt to the ground. The same press commented, 'for pure wantonness, the destruction caused rivals anything reported since the beginning of the present crisis'.[7] This crisis involved not only the election, and the meetings of the honourable Mr Lambton, but a strike—the unofficial eight-hours dispute—which had taken a firm grip upon these collieries in South East Durham.

The significance of Horden lay in the fact that it was a new pit, with a new young labour force employed on terms differing from the previous arrangements in the county. The customary two shift pattern of the area—the hewers working a six hour shift—was to be changed to a three shift system involving an eight hour shift. This system would disrupt not only the miners' lives but also the women and their domestic arrangements. The agreement, breaking the Durham custom and authorising a new regime of intensive working of the pits, was signed by the Durham agents on 13 December 1909, and was due to come into operation on 1 January 1910. The crucial clauses were those which allowed management to fix the times at which the various shifts descended the mine, removed any limitation on coal drawing time, and gave management the right to determine the number of shifts. At Horden the management demanded a three shift system, whereas at Murton Colliery, five miles to the north, they wished to push through one of four. On 1 January the Horden and Murton collieries, along with many others, came out on unofficial strike.

In commenting upon the strike, a reporter from the *Northern Daily Mail* made some interesting observations.

> The truth of the matter is that thousands of men, women and children are starving in the Durham coalfields.
>
> The chilling poverty is all the more keen for not being obvious. The miners are well dressed, they walk about in their Sunday clothes, their children are warmly and neatly clad, and the trim little houses are neatly kept. But there is no money and no food.
>
> The crowds that throng the soup kitchens are well-dressed crowds but nevertheless they are as hungry as the most wretched unemployed of the great cities. They differ from the City poor, however, in as much as they still possess their pride and their inexperience. They will not beg. The days of their prosperity are too fresh in their memory to make them beggars. But if they are ashamed to beg they do not hesitate to take. The local grocers have sought protection by giving largely to the relief funds formed by the colliers themselves.
>
> The pits are clamouring for work, but the miners sit and starve and refuse to hear the call. They are fighting for a principle, these men with blue streaked faces and sinewy figures. They are the pioneers of trade unionism, these miners of the north east coast. They had obtained their rights when other workers had only begun to grumble, and they mean to retain what they consider their rights.[8]

On Polling Day the new colliery village went up in riot.

> It was polling day, Horden being in the South East Durham division and this fact might account in some measure for the state of excitement of which the subsequent mad proceedings were the outcome. Whether, however, it was the colliery trouble or the election or both, the fact remains that some hundreds of the inhabitants completely lost their heads and in a burst of wild frenzy, utterly foreign to the Durham miner, gave way to

lawlessness and licence, the like of which has not been heard of in local mining annals for many years.

It would be about three o'clock when the riot began. The exact course is difficult to discover....The Conservative Committee rooms seem to have been first set upon and the windows demolished. The crowd then turned their unwelcome attention on the club....

Its windows were riddled with stones from without and there was hardly one pane left in. The rioters numbered hundreds and they simply took the place by storm. Not content with wrecking the outside they proceeded inside, and those in charge, and the handful of members using the premises, were powerless. In fact they had to seek refuge for their safety. The rioters smashed everything breakable and left the place in sad confusion. In the bar mirrors were broken and things strewn about. Beer was run to waste and carried away in buckets, and even the apartments of the caretaker were invaded and left in disorder.

The colliery offices, a fine suite of new rooms erected near the pit, were also visited and served in a similar manner. An inner door was pierced through as by a sledge hammer, and suggestively on one side was a workman's pickaxe. A telephone had been completely wrenched from its place on the wall and was left lying on the table.

Even the pithead was visited by the rioters, who in their lust for damage attacked the weighing machines and threw anything which was lying about down the pit.[9]

Mrs Turnbull remembers as a young woman watching as The Hall burned.

I was standing watching, it had been the Election you know, that is what started it, the people were coming out, men and women, with bottles. Women with their aprons full. There was one woman was nearly drowned in the cellar, somebody had turned the taps on and all the beer had gone down. Well I was watching, and do you know the front steps of that house, are still the same now, and that little window beside the front door, there was a man with some plates. He came out with a whole pile of plates, and he was throwing them out of the window.[10]

Police were sent in from West Hartlepool and Sunderland to assist the four policeman in the village but were unable to quieten the crowd. On the following day more rioting took place:

There was a wild day at Horden yesterday surpassing in many respects the previous days doings, for the club which was wrecked the night before was set on fire and completely gutted, and the colliery agent's house, Hardwick Hall, was attacked by the mob and great damage done.

Hardwick Hall is a commodious old manor house close to Hesledon and Blackhall rocks and some two miles to the south of Horden. It is the residence of Mr J.T. Prest, JP, Chief Agent to the Horden Collieries Ltd., an official who has charge of the various enterprises of the company at Horden, Shotton and Blackhall. Shotton and Horden are idle owing to the eight hours dispute and in common with other pits where the same dissatisfaction exists great feeling is exhibited against the management....

A crowd of about 300 men set out along the railway so it is alleged, to Hardwick Hall. Before they reached the house Mr Prest was informed and he telephoned for assistance to Horden. When the mob arrived they began to storm the mansion, and it is stated that Mr Prest fired a gun into the air, with the evident intention of showing that he was armed....

The crowd smashed the windows of the Hall and green houses were also riddled with stones, while other ornamentation about the ground was also damaged. It is also stated that Mr Prest's brougham was taken out of the coach house and thrown into the adjacent dene.[11]

Police were despatched from Horden, and charged the rioters with batons. But it was whilst they were at Hardwick Hall that the club was burned down. The press report goes on:

Then came the opportunity of the mob at Horden. Taking advantage of the fact that such a large body of police had been compelled to go to Hardwick a fresh disturbance broke out at Horden, and the club premises, so badly damaged the night before, were set on fire between three and four o'clock and were soon in flames.

The fire began in the gymnasium and soon spread to other parts of the building and by five o'clock it was fairly alight. There were no fire extinguishing appliances at hand and even if there had been there were no hydrants from which to draw the water, and the consequence was that the fire had simply to be allowed to burn itself out.[12]

That night further police reinforcements were dispatched from Sunderland but there was no renewal of the rioting. The press reported that this was due to a 'terrible snow storm'.

A little after midnight on 16 February a strong body of police went down into Horden Village and arrested several men. William Bowmaker, Jack Chambers, Pete Yore, John Scorer Raine, George Suggitt, Thomas

Fallow and John Robert Johnson were charged with 'riotously and tumultuously assembling with 5000 other persons at Horden on 26 January and doing damage.' All received prison sentences, and the miners were finally forced back to work under the new three shift arrangement on 11 April 1910.

Durham, of course, was not the only coalfield to experience disturbances in 1910. In November of that year a riot broke out in Tonypandy which involved the use of the Metropolitan police and troops in the South Wales coalfield, where there was industrial unrest and a strike. Here too the riot was interpreted as an unfortunate appendage to the dispute. Dai Smith's perceptive account of these events is helpful. In his view, the Tonypandy riots:

> should be seen as evidence of social fracture as much as industrial dispute. The crisis occurred within the framework of conventional industrial relations; the crowd's response, in both strike and riot, was strictly that of an already industrialised society, but they also chose targets symbolic of their discontent with a community which was supposedly their own natural form of being. Freed, via the strike, to reassess their own status, they ended by commenting on their relationship to a community defined for them in a graphic coda of selective destruction that was incomprehensible to those whose idea of the community was now threatened.[13]

In a similar way the riot at Horden can be related to the rapid phase of industrialisation along the south east coast of Durham, the sinking of enormous collieries, and the expansion of coke works. The new young miners were involved in *re*defining both their trade union and their community. In South Wales, the rioters directed their anger upon the shopkeepers and a growing commercial middle class; in Durham the rioters looted a club which was 'theirs' in name alone. The riot can be seen as a part of the erosion of the authority of the Durham system, and the assertion by free coal miners of their independence, as a class: an independence which was most clearly demonstrated in the organisation of their trade union.

National Strikes

In 1908, the Durham Miners' Association had re-affiliated to the Miners' Federation of Great Britain. In Page Arnot's words 'at last the hatchet had been buried'. Up to this point, the development of mining and of mining trade unionism in Britain had been subjected to strong statutory regulation and this related to a tendency for the union's leadership to follow a path of political constitutionalism. In developing this politics, however, conflicts emerged within the union over the need for a *national* organisation. The Durham officials were aware of the potential power that lay in a national organisation of miners, and to a degree they were fearful of this. They were also concerned about the potential for violence in any major industrial confrontation. The miners, as a populous and coordinated group of workers at the very centre of Britain's economy, were a group well placed to *dislocate* society. The tension implied here is between *industrial* power and *political* organisation. So long as the miners' union was linked into a constitutional form of reformist politics, and so long as this political strategy worked, the tension could be resolved. However, this resolution rested heavily upon the continued efficacy of the powers of control and persuasion developed by the union leaders. Ever present (with a national union and the peculiarities of the coal trade and industry) was the possibility of a leadership which emphasised the union's industrial strength. While a constitutionalist politics integrated the miners' union into the state, the path of organised industrial militancy would only lead to a confrontation with state power.

In the MFGB legal and parliamentary action was emphasised and strike action heavily circumscribed. The 1910 Rule Book committed the union to national strike action only in the event of being attacked on the general wage question. 'In the event of this happening all members connected with the Society should tender a notice to terminate their contracts, if approved of by a Conference called to consider the advisability of such joint action being taken'.[14] In 1911 this rule was changed to include situations such as where any Federation or District sought 'to improve the conditions of labour or to obtain an advance in wages' [then] 'a Conference shall be called to consider the advisability of joint action being taken'. At the 1911 Conference it was also agreed that the National Executive should have the power to call a national stoppage but only if a *two-thirds majority* was recorded in a national ballot of all the coalfields. The emphasis here therefore is upon caution and the need to preserve unity between the various coal districts, each of which had its autonomous organisation and separate interests.

The 1893 strike was held to demonstrate quite clearly that the basic problem of the miners lay in unifying the different coalfields under a single programme.[15] The two-thirds rule was an attempt to ensure that this unity was preserved without the breakaway of particular areas. In 1912 a sufficient majority voted for strike action. In Durham, despite the opposition of John Wilson, 57,949 (67 percent) voted for the strike; 28,504 against. The first ever national miners' strike began in February, 1912.[16]

The source of the dispute lay in the question of the payment of coal hewers working in 'abnormal places' in the South Wales coalfield. 'Abnormal places' were those sections of the coal face where, owing to geological problems, miners found it impossible to earn as much as men working in 'normal' places. This inability to stabilise the conditions of coal extraction led to the South Wales miners proposing the introduction of a guaranteed *minimum wage*. This demand was extended by the MFGB to include all underground workers whose earnings were reduced by delays caused by faulty services which were the responsibility of management.[17]

On 29 February 1912, in the middle of the strike, Prime Minister Asquith addressed the delegates at a miners' conference:

> He repeated that the Government were satisfied of the reasonableness of the principle of the minimum wage; and added that they did not intend that the resistance of a minority of owners should indefinitely delay the attainment consistent with justice and the best interests of the community; which if it could not be secured by agreement, the government would secure it by every means necessary for its effective attainment.[18]

From that point on the miners' executive stayed in London and negotiated directly with the Prime Minister. Asquith also invited in Ramsay MacDonald and three other Labour Party members to discussions.

On 12 March a tripartite conference of owners, miners and the government was established. Asquith himself, together with Sir Edward Grey, Sir George Askwith, Mr Buxton and four other officials met with twenty three coal owners and the nineteen members of the miners' national executive. The conference lasted three days but failed to reach a settlement. At this point, the Liberal government took the decision to introduce a minimum wage bill for the industry. In the face of the protests of the coal owners Asquith argued that the King himself was in favour of the proposal, and that:

> if their attitude remained unmodified, they might be summoned to Buckingham Palace, there to be confronted by the spokesmen for the miners. This seems to have brought the most obstinate to terms.[19]

It is also a commentary on the coal owners. George Askwith, Comptroller General of the Labour Department of the Board of Trade, described them as 'extraordinarily ignorant of all that had been happening in the miners' movement'.[20]

Dorothy Sells makes clear the historical significance of this piece of legislation:

> In its establishment of Joint Boards the bill resembled the Trades Boards Act. Its object, however, was quite different. Whereas, the Trades Boards Act aimed to protect unorganised, sweated workers, the purpose of the Coal Mines [Minimum Wage] Bill was solely to settle a national strike of well organised workers.[21]

Owing to the emergency, the Bill became an Act within ten days of its introduction and provided for District Boards to determine the minimum rates. The miners had won the principle of government protection for *organised* workers whose earnings fell below the normal level of earning through no fault of their own.

Although the 1912 dispute ended with rioting in Lancashire this was an isolated occurrence. Accounts of the strike emphasise the peaceful and orderly conditions in the coalfields, and the arrangements of football matches between strikers and management staff in some collieries. The sporting theme is characteristically English, and crops up again and again in descriptions of miners' strikes at this time. Writing of the 1921 strike in Durham, Jack Lawson reports:

> When the ponies were drawn out of the pit some of them had not seen the light of day for years, but they soon settled down in the fields. In due time officials and men arranged races, with the driver boys for jockeys, and rare fun they had in spite of the sad situation....To leave London with its flaming headlines at such times and arrive in Durham to find a whole village at a football match, or all the roads leading to a great pony-racing event, is an unforgettable experience.[22]

Clearly addressing a national (and parliamentary) audience he observed that: 'when the strike...began, as usual, there was alarm and apprehension of trouble in mining areas by those in high places'. Yet, he argued, 'between the miners' leaders and the police there were perfect relations, and there was scarcely an incident to remind one that a conflict was being waged.'[23]

Lawson goes on to reflect about the political philosophy which he had helped to establish in the Durham coalfield and beyond.

> There is no test of our national life in which British character is revealed as there is in the case of a lock-out or strike....For millions of men and women to remain patient citizens, marked by good conduct for months together, while they are engaged in silent struggle in which their whole livelihood is involved, is no small matter. That they should feel so deeply as to have taken action deliberately, yet curb their feelings and control their passions is a thing for wonder....If the country beyond the coalfield can hardly believe such a thing, the nations beyond the seas might well be forgiven for expecting news daily of a revolution which never comes. For in other lands, strikes are not of this kind. Such workers might be quiet for a few days, they may even live a normal life for a week, but a strike for months without violence is unthinkable.

Here he contrasts violence with the courage of 'patience', concluding that:

> it is hard to believe in the midst of suffering that violence is a sign of weakness, but the British miners long ago shrewdly came to that conclusion, so it is now the unwritten law.[24]

While this account is to some extent exaggerated, and clearly reflects Lawson's own philosophical viewpoint, it does offer an important interpretation of changes in the culture of political action amongst miners. In no small part this was a product of national trade-union organisation. National stoppages (with the total stoppage of coal production and the absence of strike-breaking miners from other areas) were far less inflammatory than county strikes, and they also offered a surer prospect of victory.

The Union and the State

Miners' national strikes revealed a power that was awesome in its implications. George Askwith's scorn for the coal owners was counterposed by his detailed observations on developments amongst the miners and the sense of a growing power of the new mining union:

> In the more powerful mining centres the Federation aimed at the inclusion of all workpeople in the Miners' Federation and the Miners' Federation only. The growing strength of the miners was proved by their power of enforcement of the Eight Hours Act [1908], the improvements of the Miners Regulation Act in 1911 and the passing of the Coal Mines (Minimum Wage) Act in 1912.[25]

For Askwith the miners in 1912 had shown the potential to place the state under siege, and this power threatened to destroy society if it was not harnessed by the employing class.

This concern was also expressed by miners' officials. William Brace was South Wales Miners' Agent from Monmouth; elected in 1892, he won a seat in the parliament of 1906. For the first ten years of the new century he was a member of the national executive of the MFGB. In 1912 he wrote an article for the *Contemporary Review* explaining the origin and nature of the 1912 Minimum Wage dispute. It is filled with a nervous awe at the extent to which the men he represented could disrupt and destroy society.

> The miners are a law abiding people, preferring much better to settle their disputes with their employers by negotiation and

> conciliation, rather than by strikes or lockouts. Their whole history goes to prove this.[26]

But on the other hand, their organisation had produced a dilemma, for:

> no power can be found to make such a body as the miners work if they decide, as a people, not to do so.[27]

And if they chose to strike, as they did in 1912, then the consequence would always be a crisis of 'grave national character'. How could this 'power' be answered?

> My own feelings are not of condemnation...but of gratitude to the statesmen who, by accepting the principle of a minimum wage, rendered the workmen a service of incalculable value at a most critical point in the proceedings.[28]

He added:

> the mines are privately owned and conducted, and if this fact is kept clear in mind, it will be realised what courage and determination was necessary for any Government or Prime Minister to take a stand in favour of the principle of the minimum wage, without being able to call in support of such a policy any similar action on the part of any government during the long history of this country.[29]

For Brace, then, the state was the necessary solution to the problem of the relations between capital and labour in the industry. Not in an ad hoc way through various interventions and arbitrations, but ideally through state ownership. That would put an end to such disputes:

> Were the mines the property of the nation, and worked and controlled on behalf of the nation, the Government's task would have been a less embarrassing one.[30]

Nationalisation promised both a solution to strikes and a consolidated minimum wage. Furthermore, it promised the security of the national union representing miners against a single employer. In 1912 Brace was arguing that only such a move could restore 'security' to the industry. There is little doubt that this view was considered the majority view amongst the leaders of the miners' union both nationally and in the local areas. However, it was not the *only* view, and the tension between industrial power and a constitutional politics gave rise to an alternative programme. This view was most clearly developed in the South Wales Coalfield. During the first decade of the twentieth century this coalfield experienced an enormous increase in production coupled with a tremendous influx of labour. There was no centralised area union, as there was in Durham, and so the amalgamation movement coupled with the move away from Liberalism pushed 'Mabon' and his heirs to the sidelines. It was the question of amalgamation and the constitution of any new South Wales Miners' Federation which stimulated the Unofficial Reform Committee to produce its classic tract *The Miners' Next Step*, advancing a view contrary to Brace's. For the Reform Committee the question of a new union constitution focused attention upon the need for an organisation (a trade union) which would lay the ground work for 'the emancipation of workers and the establishment of a democratic socialist society.' This syndicalist view argued that nationalisation, precisely because of the 'advantages' outlined by Brace, could not be seen as the way forward. It would, they argued, 'simply make a National Trust with all the force of the government behind it.' The most articulate of these men, Noah Ablett, elaborated this view in several speeches to audiences of miners in the Rhondda Valley. Borrowing the language of Hilaire Belloc, he insisted that nationalisation would 'simply place an important section of the working class in the hands of a state, servile to capitalists' interests, who would use the opportunity to increase the servility we abhor'.

This view gained in strength in South Wales in the post-war period, and until the 1926 strike it also had its supporters on the Durham coalfield, led by George Harvey. We have already noted the conflicts between him and John Wilson in Durham. After the publication of his pamphlet attacking Wilson he went to Ruskin College in Oxford, returning to Durham in 1910. At the college he had been involved in the student strike over the curriculum, which led to the formation of the Marxist 'breakaway' Central Labour College in London. In 1912 he was elected checkweighman at the Bowes Lyon colliery of Follonsby in Wardley; at 23, he was the youngest checkweighman in the county. He later became lodge secretary, an executive member of the union and a Labour Party councillor. At this time his principal energies were directed toward the syndicalist-inspired socialist Labour Party. He was its northern secretary, and editor of its newspaper *The Socialist*.

Harvey was closely associated with the activities of the Reform Committee in South Wales, and with one of its activists, Arthur J. Cook. Cook had been taught by Ablett, and almost certainly met him through the organisation of the ILP. While *The Miners' Next Step* was being published, Cook was studying at the Central Labour College in London. In 1912, at the height of the miners' strike, he spoke at a debate opposing the motion that 'political action is essential to the interests of the working class'. Cook gave overwhelming emphasis to the power of the union and of industrial organisation. Returning to his job as a collier at the Coedcae Colliery in Porth, he became lodge chairman and leader of the union committee for all the Lewis Merthyr collieries. His agitational speeches, especially during the war, earned him the close surveillance of both the Chief Constable of Glamorgan and the manager of the Lewis

Merthyr collieries, a Mr Percy Ward. Ultimately his politics were to put him in jail.

In 1919 Cook was elected as agent for the Rhondda No.1 District of the South Wales Miners' Federation, still advocating a strongly anti-parliamentarian approach for the miners and their union, acerbically criticising the established approach of the MFGB leadership. In his view:

> The MFGB, Triple Alliance and the TUC are fast becoming manufacturing centres for resolutions, glorified state institutions earning the praise of the capitalist class. We are led on the heels of the politicians, the atmosphere of the House of Commons is pervading the trade union executives. The very machine we have built up for our emancipation is being used to crush us.[31]

In the face of attacks of this kind Brace resigned from the South Wales Miners' Federation. His colleague Vernon Hatsthorn did likewise, describing Cook as 'the biggest fool in the coalfield', a view echoed later and more eloquently by Beatrice Webb when she described the miners' leader as an 'inspired idiot'. Yet it was to Cook that the miners turned for national leadership. In 1924, with trade in decline and an ominous gathering of forces amongst the employers, he was elected as General Secretary of the MFGB following the resignation of Frank Hodges, who had become an MP in the General Election. Cook's views clearly contrasted with those of his predecessor. Immediately he took office, he informed the press that he stood firmly for 'industrial unionism', and that he intended to continue carrying out his work 'with regard to Marxian Economics and Philosophy'. On the announcement of his election, Fred Bramley, the President of the TUC remarked:

> Have you seen who has been elected secretary of the Miners' Federation? Cook. A raving, tearing communist. Now the miners are in for a bad time.[32]

In part this assessment was based upon dislike for the new miners' leader, but it also involved an assessment of the forces that were stacked against the miners should they attempt to use their industrial strength in a time of recession. This was an assessment which Cook himself had made; as he put it: 'we are in for a battle.'

The 'Great Bust-Up'

By 1926 the miners' unions in Durham had obtained a near complete membership in the mines, and through the practice of fifty years and more established a pattern of behaviour which, if not *entirely* constitutional, was certainly keenly aware of procedural processes. Durham had become renowned as an area where 'loyalty was a big thing; it was a hell of a big thing in this county—loyalty to the union and our leaders sort of thing. Unity really.' This was expressed, in a different way, and from a different perspective, by Peter Lee, a DMA agent during the 1926 strike. In that year Durham miners remained solidly in support of the action, and in the end voted against the settlement and for continuing the action. In August Peter Lee explained to a conference of the MFGB that in Durham:

> There is no breaking away....I come from a county where you don't need any intensive propaganda. All you have to do in Durham is to put the owners' proposals on a piece of paper, and circulate them amongst the people....You need no more propaganda. That is sufficient for Durham.[33]

This solidarity rested historically upon the organisation of the union, and was maintained during the disputes by strongly developed local organisations. In Durham and South Wales the miners had gained control of local authorities, and had a considerable influence upon local Boards of Guardians. In 1921 the Durham council (taking advantage of the 1906 Provision of Meals Act) organised feeding centres for schoolchildren. This was carried forward in 1926, when the Durham County Education Authority provided free milk to children and expectant mothers on a greatly increased scale. In addition 309 feeding centres were set up for children which in all produced 19,387,504 meals at a total cost of £283,781. These meals were provided for all children. The County Medical Officer of Health made clear that:

> it is obviously quite impossible for the medical officers of the Health Department to personally examine every child aged 3-5 to ascertain whether, on medical grounds, provision of meals was necessary, but personally I am quite satisfied that but for the provision of those meals the health of the children aged 3 to 5 years would have materially suffered.[34]

These material changes (contingent upon own their political organisation) clearly affected the political temper of miners in Durham, as did the utterances and political viewpoints of their leaders. These activities were supported by local organisation, based upon the miners' lodges, and drawing support from those other associations which made up the mining villages—the clubs, the chapels and the stores. In times of dispute the form of the village altered. In normal times people lived separate lives, and the trade union relied upon no more than an instrumental involvement. As one old trade unionist has put it: 'all the men at the colliery belonged to a trade union, either the engineers' union, the mechanics' union or the miners' lodge. The union was so much an integral part of the life of the pit that you took it for granted, but the actual running of the union was left to a handful of men.'[35] But on Gala

Day, or in times of dispute, the village became an active community. In 1926 these communities set up their own 'Councils of Action' to organise the village during the strike. Chopwell was one of these, and George Alsop describes how:

> The Council of Action really organised the village during the General Strike. The leading trade unionists in the village—people like Harry Bolton, the Lawther brothers, Jack Gilliland, my father, who was Chairman of the lodge for some time, and so on—used to meet regularly in the working men's club. Most of the activities were organised from the club rather than the trade union branch meeting. The facilities of the club were put at the disposal of the Council of Action committee. They had big premises and they had the facilities for boiling soup and this sort of thing. They'd sit, have a pint or two, and plan out all the activities. The Council of Action really controlled the village. If a lorry came in with some produce or stuff on the wagon, they used to say 'What is it?' and they used to give them a permit into the village to go to the shop and drop it. If they didn't get a permit they couldn't come in. The Council negotiated with shops, asking that they allow people to have credit on the guarantee of the union that the people would pay it back monthly when they got back to work. And this is what happened. Some people shirked of course, some of them went away, but the majority of people conscientiously went to the shops and said 'tick that off the back'. This is how we all survived; without this credit we wouldn't have survived—neither would the shopkeepers of course. Also they knew, that if they didn't agree to this sort of thing, they'd come in one morning and there'd be nought in the shop!
>
> And then there were the soup kitchens. Everything was so organised that at least the children got something to eat. There was one thing that they were all bent on and that was that they weren't going to let the children either go hungry or without heating. The farms used to give them chickens and this sort of thing. (Of course they knew that if they didn't give them it, they would go and steal it.)
>
> I remember one lodger in our house, they called him Joe Herron. He used to sleep through the day and turn out at night. Right through the strike; he never used to turn out until midnight. He used to raid the farms—he'd get turkeys, geese, chickens—all sorts. They used to give some of the geese to the soup kitchens to keep the soup kitchen going. This is why some of the farmers used to say 'if you want a goose or a couple of chickens, come and ask us.' They used to willingly give it.

The defiant lodge at Chopwell—Little Moscow, 1926
Left to right: Jack Lawther, Will Lawther, Steve Lawther, Jack Gilliland, Ned Wilson, Jim Stephenson, Andy Lawther.

> The women folk used to make great sacrifices. They used to do the cooking and looking after the bairns and seeing that they got their proper share, and they used to see them to school. It was amazing to see the organisation behind it. While they were still restricted in the starving sense, it used to be a good feeling that you were all one family.[36]

These accounts reveal the detail of local organisation and control, and to these should be added the ways in which 'unofficial Galas' were organised in July. What is also clear however is the ways in which these local organisations of miners rested upon more than the stoical patience outlined by Lawson. Certainly—given the number of arrests and the active provocation involved in the owners' decision to lengthen the working day and reduce wages—the absence of violence is a notable feature of the dispute. However where the conflict was intense—over officials working in the mine, or the use of blacklegs—the men and women of the colliery villages protested violently.

In 1926 Chopwell, and north west Durham generally, was a centre of conflict. The coal mines of the Consett Iron Company had been on strike throughout 1925 as part of a dispute over wages.

> Chopwell was out on strike nine month before the 1926 strike

began. There was a local dispute over the prices in the pit. The men were advocating and struggling for an increase in the prices, and the only offer that they got from the management was that they were prepared to give one group a rise but in other parts of the pit they'd reduce the price of the tonnage. Robbing Peter to pay Paul. They struck nine month before the General Strike started.[37]

By this time the village had got a strong reputation for militancy. As a result of its banner (unfurled in 1924), and the street names introduced by Blaydon Council—Marx Terrace, Engels Terrace, Lenin Terrace—it had become known as 'Little Moscow'. Though many felt that 'Chopwell wasn't any more militant than other local villages', the name stuck, and events there were watched with some interest by the Home Office. In 1925 the colliery manager (a man called Hepburn whose father managed the Langley Park pit for the Company) wrote a letter to the Home Secretary which detailed the activities of the pickets and the involvement of the miners' wives:

It was only with difficulty and police supervision that officials were able to travel to and from the colliery, especially in hours of darkness, and during their absence their families were insulted and barracked in the houses by disorderly crowds. On 13 September a large crowd assembled at the west end of the village for the purpose of preventing an official named Winship from proceeding to his work.

He continues:

On September 15th a crowd assembled on the main road to barrack accompanying police to prevent them walking other than slowly to the singing of the 'Dead March' and funeral hymns. These officials were unable to attend work for the remainder of the week and have, since restarting, lived on the colliery premises.

Two days later two colliery officials were set upon and one of them was:

severely bruised and stabbed by hat pins and is still receiving medical treatment.[38]

This pattern of illegality and collective pressure bordering on violence continued during the 1926 strike.

The strikers used to raid the trucks, the coal trucks up on line, just above the tops of the trees there. There was maybe three, twenty-ton trucks of coal. They would drop the bottom boards and they'd have buckets, bath tins, bags and barrows.

They were fetching policemen down from Wales and Nottinghamshire: drafting them into the village. I remember one sergeant that came here. All the men congregated at the corner-end on the Sunday morning and he got onto a box and he introduced himself. He says 'I'm the new sergeant and there's one thing I'm gonna do in Chopwell, I'm gonna stop this raiding of coal from the trucks.' A week after he went to his coal house and some bugger had raided it—pinched all his coals.

The other thing that sticks in your mind is the blacklegs. They used to be escorted backwards and forwards to the mine: and I remember the processions very well. The whole village would be standing around; the lads used to be humming the dead march. There were hundreds of police there, escorting the blacklegs, and there used to be some heavy struggles you know.[39]

Looking back, people who lived through the strike in Chopwell remember how a 'system of apartheid developed in the village between the community of strikers on the one hand and the police, the company officials and the strike-breakers on the other'. As a school girl, Hilda Ashby remembers how she:

was going to the grammar school at Blaydon during the 1926 strike. We had to walk to Westwood Station to catch the train, and I can always remember sitting in the carriage full of girls—we were all miners' daughters. I was twelve and we were all talking about the strike and one of the girls said 'I hardly dare tell you this...' And we were just getting to know where babies came from and we said 'Are you going to have a baby?' And she said 'No—my father's going to be a blackleg.' Very shamefaced you know. I remember running home to tell my father 'Mary Wilson's father's going to blackleg' and my father saying 'By he's a "card joker", he'll get nae coal oot'.

After that strike we always remembered who the blacklegs were. You know, 'what can you expect—he blacklegged'. The whole village used to go out to see the blacklegs.[40]

Phyllis Short played an active part in dealing with the blacklegs. She was the chairwoman of the Co-operative Women's Guild in Chopwell and an ardent campaigner for birth control clinics. During the strike she was an active picket:

I took part in the strike along with the other women in the village. When we heard that certain persons were blacklegging at the pit we used to go up to the pithead. We used to wait on them coming out and then we used to sing them home or chase them home. One of them ran into his hen cree one day and we kept him there all day. Another thing we used to do when a man blacklegged. He still got his coal delivered; so when we saw the

> wagon coming we used to follow it, and every time it stopped we used to get our pails and fill them up and dish it out to the rest of the village; and his wife for the life of her dare not come out. We never badly used anybody; but we showed our determination that we wanted the miners to win.
>
> And then there was the parson's son who stood up and said he was going to be a miner and he was going to the pit and we went to the pithead and waited for him coming up and we sang him back to the vicarage through the church yard and some of the women put wreaths about his neck and he never went back to the pit again. He had to go and have treatment, he had a nervous breakdown. In fact I can't ever remember seeing him in the village again.
>
> We picketed the shops because the men stopped the vans from delivering the food to the gaffers' houses up at the pit. We picketed the shops to stop the gaffers' wives from getting their groceries, because *we* had no money to buy any. Of course, the police were there. But there were not many policemen for each area, so we could handle some of them as well. The policemen tried to get us to let the wives in to get their groceries and of course the manager of the shop; they had the money to but we would not let them sell the goods. One of the policemen came up to me at that time and said your mother should be ashamed of herself letting you out to do things like this. I was married at that time with two children.[41]

In 1912 the state was prepared to move against the owners and, in 'the national interest', meet some of the miners' demands. At the same time, cabinet ministers and permanent secretaries were aware that the state needed to prepare for a threat against itself. It was not until 1920 that the appropriate legislation to 'regulate' this new 'threat' was secured. *The Emergency Powers Act,* passed following the 1920 Miners' Strike, was used only twice: in the 1921 Miners' Lock Out, and in the 1926 General Strike. In 1921 the miners were worn into submission and the acceptance of wage cuts. In 1926, in spite of enormous resolution and the rhetoric of Cook 'not a penny off the pay, not an hour on the day' the result was the same. The miners, with their enormous organised strength, were isolated from the rest of the class, worn down and defeated. In defeat, however, the miners and their trade union revealed much about the way they and their political power had changed in the twentieth century.

11
The Checkweighmen's Party

They call the Parliamentary Labour Party, the Party of the Checkweighmen.

Beatrice Webb

BY 1920, Durham society was precariously balanced between the old and the new. The old power of patronage with its links to Conservatism was still in evidence. The Londonderry family retained control of Seaham economically and politically. The influence of coal owners in northern politics and in village life remained a large one. But there was another emerging force—organised labour—whose position had gained in strength and legitimacy during the war years.

In most parts of the country—especially in the urban centres—the previous three decades had seen the emergence of a new middle class. On the coalfields an altogether different phenomenon emerged. The class structure remained polarised between 'master' and 'servant' but civil society was largely regulated by a new layer of working-class committee men and officials rising through the trade unions, chapels, co-operative stores and working men's clubs. In the mines, many of these offices were established through act of parliament, and the 1920 Mines Act extended their number. These checkweighmen, mine inspectors, secretaries of stores, clubs and union lodges, executive members of various associations played an influential role in Durham society; their authority derived from acting as representatives of the men who worked in the mines. In 1924, Sidney Webb wrote of how the checkweighmen 'swarm on co-operative societies and Friendly society committees', and how they regularly funded 'working-class Justices of the Peace'. These men rose through political acumen, an ability to speak in public and to administrative competence. They can be understood as the political elite of the working class, and it was within this elite that ordered competition took place for key positions and offices.

A sense of what this meant for one of the officials, is made clear by Jack Lawson:

> With my pit work and county council, arbitrations for the men at collieries up and down the county, Executive and Conciliation Boards, and delegations to London and abroad, I was a real man of affairs.[1]

This 'man of affairs' was at the time checkweighman at Alma Colliery and a member of the Durham Miners Executive, the ILP and the Methodist Church. Writing of men such as himself he commented:

> that which drives them and holds them, is the respect, esteem and standing that they have in their own community; but above all the spirit of service.[2]

The combination of offices in one person was typical in Durham, and served an important social function. It facilitated social cohesion among the officials, who met regularly. Their disagreements were conducted (for the most part) within established rules. Where new organisations or activities were established, they provided an immediate list of potential committee members. But their coherence also served to effectively limit the involvement of non-officials, and the entrance of newcomers. County Durham had become an officials' society, and this was most clear in relation to party politics.

The Labour Party and the Union

The 1918 Constitution of the Labour Party has been called a Fabian document. Miliband has argued that its piecemeal collectivism was in fact a 'Fabian blueprint for a more advanced, more regulated form of capitalism'.[3] It would be more correct perhaps, to characterise it as a trade-union document. For it was in the rules governing the new Party that the most important political innovation could be discerned. McKibbin has argued that this constitution (in spite of clause four): 'confirmed the triumph of the unions and the defeat of the socialists'.[4]

With the new party came the establishment, for the first time, of constituency parties of individual members. As such, much attention was paid to the question of membership, registration of committees, and rules governing voting at party conferences. Arthur Henderson had considered 'the foundation of a political organisation depending only upon individual membership',[5] but he could not imagine 'saying to the trade unions upon whom the Party had depended that they had no further use for them'.[6] The trade union leaders were equally clear that such a situation would not be acceptable. Their view was particularly significant given the Labour Party's total dependence upon trade union finance. The ILP warned that a political party:

> dependent upon the financial support of powerful and wealthy

Table 11.1 The Mining Vote in Durham c.1910[7]

Constituency	*Electorate*	*Estimated no of miner voters*	*Miners as a % of electorate*
N.W. Durham	18,361	11,280	61
Mid Durham	15,832	9,550	60
Houghton-le-Spring	17,504	9,930	56
Chester-le-Street	23,906	13,160	55
Bishop Auckland	14,552	5,570	38
S.E. Durham	18,880	7,070	37
Barnard Castle	12,212	4,220	34
Jarrow	18,292	4,790	26

> trade unions can never be a democratic party in the true sense of the word.[8]

This fear was strengthened as the new constitution grafted the constituency organisations onto the old federated form, of the unions and socialist societies.

The balance between the trade unions and individual membership varied widely. On the coalfields the rising occupational density of coal mining had by this time produced many constituencies in which coal miners could exert a decisive effect in elections. These 'mining seats' became an established feature of British electoral geography for much of the twentieth century. In 1910, for example, miners represented 10 percent or more of the electorate in 86 constituencies. Across the eight constituencies on the Durham coalfield, miners represented between 26 percent and 61 percent of the electorate (see Table 11.1).

In the parliamentary election of 1918 the MFGB put up a total of 51 Labour candidates, 24 of whom were elected. This number of MPs (increasing in subsequent elections) established the miners as *the* dominant trade-union organisation in the Labour Party. It drew from G.D.H. Cole the comment that the Labour Party was 'overwhelmingly a Trade Union Party, and half of the trade union representation was drawn from a single union.'[9]

It was the trade union constituencies which provided the initial hard core of Labour MPs, and a great deal of the symbolism of the new party. Groups like the miners, with their banners and galas, provided not only organisational and ideological support for the new party, but helped to establish the popular image of 'Labourism' and its own self-image as it became established as a national force in British politics.

Durham Labour Politics

The Durham division of the Labour Party was inaugurated at a meeting of trade-union organisations, labour bodies and co-operative societies at the Miners' Hall in Durham on 9 February 1918. The DMA, as the founding host, was naturally the most influential trade-union organisation involved and it was not surprising that W. Whiteley, one of the miners' agents, became the first president of the new divisional party. Whiteley, a Methodist, along with three other Methodist agents, Robson, Richardson and Batey, had clear political ambitions. All four men were on the Labour Party list of prospective parliamentary candidates as miners' MPs. In total this list recorded thirteen politically ambitious members of the DMA. Along with the four agents were the names of John Gilliland, the political agent of the union, seven checkweighmen and one rank and file miner. This parliamentary list was informally replicated at the local level as members of this official group sought office in local elections.[10] The new party, then, was still dominated by trade-union leaders but the re-organisation involved the established power of the checkweighmen—the 'new men'.

The circular issued by the DMA executive 'to the members' makes clear, in its tone, the changes that had accompanied Labour affiliation. Referring to the new Franchise and Representation Act it argued that:

> it will add greatly to the number of working-class voters, and in this way will give them greater power if rightly used....For the first time in the history of the country, working men and working women will have the opportunity of using their combined votes in electing members of parliament. At the present time, Capital is strongly represented by several hundreds of members, whilst Labour has only forty-odd representatives....Capital has captured the political machinery with the result that profiteering goes unchecked; voting interests are made secure....The workers must realise that if their interests are to be looked after they must use their political power in conjunction with their industrial power and capture the House of Commons for Labour.[11]

The circular pointed out that a new vigour and determination was needed, for although eight of the Durham constituencies had supported miners' candidates in the last election, only three of these were elected: Swan for Barnard Castle and Richardson for Houghton le Spring (both checkweighmen); and the established member for Chester-le-Street, J.W. Taylor. Taylor had been the first MP in the north to take the Labour Whip after his election in 1905. At that time he was General Secretary of the Durham Mechanics' Association and an active member of the ILP. He had publicly resigned from the Liberal Party before he was nominated to

W.P. Richardson, General Secretary of the DMA 1924–30.

fight a seat made vacant by the elevation of its sitting member (Sir James Joicey, the coal owner) to the House of Lords. Votes of confidence in Taylor were carried in every miners' lodge in the constituency, and he was elected with 45 percent of the poll (the Conservatives and Liberals polling, respectively 28 percent and 26 percent). By 1918 the constituency had become a safe Labour seat, and on the retirement of Taylor (through ill health) Jack Lawson was overwhelmingly successful in the by-election.

This transformation of the old Joicey constituency into a Labour stronghold says much about the pattern of political change in the county. Chester-le-Street, situated in the north of the coalfield, was more radical than other parts of Durham, but the pattern became quite uniform in the 1920s. At the 1922 General Election the new Party won ten of the eleven county seats, and the DMA was successful in filling six of these with their own members. At Blaydon, Whiteley, a DMA agent, defeated F.R. Simpson, the head of the Stella Coal Company; at Durham, Ritson; at

Sedgefield, Herriotts, while at Spennymoor, Joe Batey defeated Anthony Eden for a seat that had been in the Eden family for three hundred years. As Eden's biographer noted, whilst:

> Eden had strong local connections here and it was his home ground...the choice of the Marquess of Londonderry, a coal owner, as his principal supporter was slightly misjudged.[12]

This elimination of coal owners and landowners was completed by Richardson retaining Houghton-le-Spring and Lawson being successful once again at Chester-le-Street. Labour candidates were also elected at the steel town of Consett, the shipbuilding town of Jarrow and in Bishop Auckland, a town with railway connections. The constituency of Seaham elected the Fabian author of the 1918 constitution, Sidney Webb.

In 1924 this pattern was repeated, both locally and nationally. The DMA lost one seat whilst nationally the MFGB lost one more, reducing the number of MFGB-sponsored MPs to forty. The local seat lost was that of Herriotts. He was defeated by just six votes at Sedgefield in a contest with L. Ropner, the Conservative candidate and Director of Ropner Shipbuilding and Repair Company (Stockton) Ltd. The Barnard Castle seat was also taken by the Conservatives by Cuthbert Headlam, a former Clerk in the House of Lords. Labour then held nine of the eleven seats. The DMA's election expenses that year were £47,958. The political fund of the union prior to the election had stood at £71,156.[13]

With this record of success the DMA had effective control of the new Party in Durham. They financed it, and a central group of individuals (agents and checkweighmen) provided the Party with its candidates and speakers. These in turn were financially supported by the union during their electoral campaigns. The union employed a number of political agents (four in 1919) responsible for promoting political activity across the coalfield. In addition miners' representatives were paid a salary by the trade union, making them 'much of the best financed of all Labour candidates'. The union was also active in the direction of the Party's programme and the selection of candidates loyal to the union. The centralised form of the union worked to produce a centralised Labour Party. The union mobilised financial and voting support for the Party through its lodges and at the same time it directed the Party's affairs through its regional officials.

In circulars issued to their members the DMA made support for the Labour Party central to its political programme. It urged the electors to vote for their own candidates who were, as they stated, usually the checkweighmen standing against colliery managers. Their 'own candidates' understood their problems of life and labour:

> If the circumstances of life compel the widow or workless man to apply for Poor Law Relief, let it be to men and women who

> know and understand the hardships of life, and not to those whose continuous cry from year to year is 'keep down the rates'.
>
> On this question of relief, need we again remind you of what employers are prepared to do as evidenced in the Usworth case, where the men have been idle 26 weeks resisting the attempts of the management to scrap every agreement on the colliery; and because the men refused, the Owners journeyed to London and before the Umpire succeeded in stopping the men from getting their Unemployment payment, and if it had not been a Labour Board of Guardians in this area they would also have succeeded in stopping their relief. It is Usworth today! It may be you tomorrow.[14]

This literature stressed that the political struggle was the very condition for the industrial struggle. This emphasis can also be quite clearly read in the electoral addresses of the County Labour Party. In 1925, Circular no.19 of the Durham County Federation of Divisional Labour Parties linked the question of wages, working hours and political control of the county:

> In face of the coming battle with the employers of Labour and the united forces of Capitalism, that on the question of Wages, Hours, and your political machinery, it is of great importance that your defence should be the strongest possible.
>
> Your opponents are not BABIES AND WEAKLINGS and will put forward every effort to penetrate your ranks.
>
> They will measure your strength or weakness by the result of the Local Elections. Are Landowners, Independents, Land Stewards, Colliery Agents and Managers, Overmen and Representatives of Big Business through the channels of the Reaction Party called 'Moderates' best fitted to control the Administrative Councils of the county? If the Election decides that they are, then you can take it for granted they will use the result to claim that they are best qualified to determine your wages and the number of your working hours.[15]

This circular was signed by the President, W. Whiteley, MP for Blaydon, former agent of the DMA and W.P. Richardson, General Secretary of the DMA.

In the DMA, the first step in the career of a 'union man' lay in securing the position of lodge secretary or checkweighman. This was the beginning of his political capital, which could accumulate with experience. Jack Lawson describes this process. In 1910 he was invited to stand as checkweighman by the hewers of Alma Colliery:

> I was not only assured of election, but also that I would be given

John Swan, General Secretary of the DMA, with Stafford Cripps at the Gala, 1935.

> support and opportunity for useful public work....I would still be a miner, yet free to speak and work for the things I desired.[16]

Establishing himself in his position he soon discovered that:

> my work as a checkweighman was a mere detail and by no means my real work. I was their business man, watching closely and attending to every detail affecting their wages and conditions. I was adviser on domestic questions, lawyer and executor. So are all checkweighmen.[17]

At this level a move into the local or district councils was possible or, for Lawson, a move to the county council. It could also allow an entry to the union executive, where the 'King Makers', the agents, the men with political influence in the union, discussed policy. This 'arena' was not, however, unified. As we have seen, the agents and the checkweighmen had different interests, and increasingly different views. The ILP checkweighmen aimed to reform the union in ways which would increase their influence. In October 1917 for example, it was finally agreed, after many attempts, that any agent elected as MP would be requested to resign his union post. This was of course in the direct interest of the checkweighmen. It enhanced the turnover of agents, and with it their chances of moving to Durham, as is clearly revealed by examining the turnover of agents and checkweighmen in the inter-war period.

In the 1919 DMA elections for agent the successful candidate was Peter

Lee, who was at the time checkweighman at Wheatley Hill. Amongst those unsuccessful were Gilliland, Herriotts, Lawther and Ritson. The next election took place in 1922 and this was directly caused by the operation of the 1917 rule. Whiteley, who had become MP for Blaydon, had resigned and he was replaced by John Swan. This election is of interest for the part played by Swan. A former checkweighman from East Howle Colliery, he had only just been defeated in the parliamentary elections having held the Barnard Castle constituency for Labour for three years. In his trade union election Swan defeated Herriotts, who had failed in three previous elections for the agent's position. Herriotts then stood for parliament and was elected as MP for Sedgefield. Swan went on to become General Secretary of the Association on the death of Peter Lee in 1935. The interchangeability of trade union and political positions is clear and significant.

At the next agents' election (held in 1925 as a result of Cann's death), James Gilliland obtained the position and so joined his brother Jack, who was already a political agent for the union, at Redhills. Once again the loser was Herriotts, who after losing his parliamentary seat at Sedgefield in the 1923 General Election had again attempted to move back into the union. Herriotts' case raises the important practical question of the subsequent career of defeated miners' MPs. Once separated from their jobs in the coal mines, these men were dependent upon the political institutions for their livelihood. The agents of the union had guaranteed job security. Their tenure was for life, and they would move upward to more powerful positions in the Union Hall at Redhills. Councillors and MPs were more vulnerable. For example Herriotts stood, and was again defeated, at Sedgefield in 1924. In 1929 he stood again, this time being successful. However, in 1931, when the union returned only two of their seven sponsored candidates, he was defeated once again. It was in this year that the question of defeated miners' MPs was resolved. Positions were made available for these men at the union headquarters, carrying a salary of £150 a year. In return they were required to carry out propaganda work for the organisation. This can be seen as a political elite operating in defence of its own interests, but also shows that the Durham Miners' Association had become a sophisticated political bureaucracy.[18]

Of the original 1919 list of checkweighmen candidates, only two are unaccounted for. Ritson, having failed in 1919, was to be elected as MP for Durham in 1922, and Lawther (the only non-Methodist amongst them) was finally elected as agent for the union in 1933.

The integration of the trade union and the Labour Party thus laid the foundation for Labour control of the region for decades to come; other forms of socialist activity on the coalfield were displaced. For example the Women's Labour League, founded in 1906, had been quite active in the north. Its main aim was to politicise women and 'obtain direct Labour representation of women in parliament and on local bodies.' To this end the Durham members of the League organised large numbers of meetings for women on issues as various as women's suffrage, infant mortality, married women as workers, old age pensions, socialism and the child, baby clinics, food prices, the Minimum Wage and William Morris.[19] Yet the League found difficulty in organising on the coalfield. Mrs Simms (the wife of the ILP organiser) noted that 'where branches seem to be most needed, as say in the mining villages, where women in politics are almost an unknown quantity, there it is most difficult.' Here, the League came up against 'the great answer up here—"women's place is in the home". Women have heard it so often they believe it now.'[20] As Maureen Calcott has recorded, the League was able to establish thirteen branches in the North East, but the majority of these were in the urban districts of Tyneside and Sunderland. In 1918 the League was replaced by the women's sections of the Labour Party. In Durham, women's sections were set up across the coalfields and organised under the umbrella organisation the Durham Women's Advisory Council. It could be argued that within this framework of the Labour Party far more women became involved in political activity.[21] However, their role was clearly a subordinate one, as is made clear in the pattern of local and parliamentary elections.[22]

Local Control

In 1919 the Durham County Council went Labour, as the new Labour Party took fifty-six out of the total of ninety-nine seats. It was the first time anywhere in Britain that a county council had ever been won by the Labour Party. The majority of the councillors were members of the DMA, having their expenses met by the union. The elected Chairman of the new council was Peter Lee, Councillor from Wheatley Hill. In that same year he was also elected agent for the DMA; in time he was to become General Secretary of the Association and through the 1920s and 1930s the major voice of the miners in the north.

The Party lost control in the subsequent council elections of 1922, only to regain it in 1925. They were never to lose control again. An examination of these election results (and those for the positions of magistrates and colliery guardians) reveal the extent to which the coal miners (through their officials) had wrested political control of public life from the coal owners. In villages throughout the county colliery managers, undermanagers and engineers stood for election against checkweighmen, store managers, club secretaries and committeemen.

In the 1919 election the five divisions of Stockton (then in Durham County) returned unopposed members. On the coalfield proper eleven seats returned unopposed councillors; seven of those were either miners or checkweighmen. In the remaining seats interesting contests ensued. In Willington the sitting member Llewelyn Weeks, a mining engineer, was defeated by Matthew Reed, a coal miner who polled three times as many votes as his opponents. In Hetton another miner, Thomas Glish, polled five times as many votes as J.B. Doxford, the local science teacher. In Birtley, Jack Gilliland, a checkweighman, polled 1,837 votes while his opponent, a retired building contractor, polled just 639. In Ryton, Thomas Addison, a miner, beat the local colliery manager, but in Stanley's No.1 division Harry James, a coal miner, was defeated by the sitting Councillor, Thomas Welsh, an engineer at one of the local mines. In Houghton le Spring Tom Husband, the secretary of the miner's lodge, defeated John Foster, a local grocer. This pattern of electoral contests was repeated at the more local levels of district and parish councils as the social structure of the coalfield became politicised.[23]

In 1922 the political power of the Labour Party was checked slightly, but it was still a formidable force. The full strength of the Council was 99, and in that year there were 60 contests in the 74 divisions. On this occasion the Labour candidates faced greater opposition and of the 14 candidates returned unopposed 12 were members of the newly formed Moderate Party. Only two women stood in these elections, neither of them for the Labour Party. While Labour lost overall control in 1922, the pattern of local elections was firmly established. For the most part they were fought out between men who represented the Labour and Moderate Parties. In Durham both these parties were strongly attached to the coal industry and in local elections the two sides of industry argued their views on the political hustings. So it was in Thornley when Peter Lee, the ex-chairman of the council and miners' agent, defeated Mr M. Barnas, colliery manager and representative of the Moderate Party in a straight fight. Lee polled 2,715, Barnas 1,801.[24]

In 1925 the Labour majority was restored for good, and the Party set up camp in the red-brick Shire Hall on Old Elvet in the City of Durham. The miners' agents and executive committee held sway at the other side of the city in their imposing Redhills Villa. Durham, the citadel at the centre of the county, had become taken by the forces of labour.

This was already clear in 1919, when George Peart, agent for the Durham Colliery Engineers' Association, stood as a candidate in the Durham City Number Two Division. He was well beaten by the sitting candidate, W.A. Lord. Durham City was the preserve of the Moderate Party, backed by the influence of the church. Beneath the shadow of the cathedral, however, considerable poverty existed and this had been Peart's main concern. At the count

> Mr Peart...said that he made up his mind at the outset that he would fight clean and straight. He stood for ideals and his protest was against the living conditions of the working people in that

> city (hear, hear). He had visited some of the homes. Men had told him that homes are made by people who lived in them. They also said that if a pig were put into a palace the palace would become a sty. He had seen some of the sties, but none of the pigs. He had seen men and women, working people like himself living under undesirable conditions. It was because he wanted to lift the standard of living that he had fought that contest. The fight would not end with the defeat. It was only beginning. The Labour Movement never acknowledged defeat, and they would continue to fight until the city moved for the interests of the working class.[25]

Thomas Cann, the General Secretary of the DMA, soon issued a circular in which he strongly criticised the role of the church in Durham City, and for its interference in the recent election. This circular brought a reply from the Dean of Durham Cathedral, Dr J.E.C. Weldon. A former Bishop of Calcutta, Weldon had not long been in Durham, and this was to be the first of his open disagreements with the DMA and the Labour Party. His letter, printed in the *Durham County Advertiser*, expresses 'so much respect for Mr Cann', but defends the role of the church in the elections. While accepting that housing conditions in the city need improving, he argues that:

> the provision of houses rests with the municipal authorities. It does not rest with the ecclesiastical authorities, and what is wanted is that the municipal authorities should make full use of the Housing Bill when it passes into Law.

The Labour Party, he writes, 'are now the power in the county' and as such the Durham Miners' Association:

> possesses far greater political power than the churches. It is not at all indisposed, as has been sometimes shown, to make full use of its power.[26]

In this exchange (the precursor to many others) the new political reality is recognised. Support for the Labour Party steadily extended to groups whose economic activity had previously developed under the political patronage of the coal owners and their political parties. The Labour benches in Durham became leavened by the presence of shop keepers, school teachers and the occasional doctor. Overwhelmingly, however, the Labour group in the Shire Hall remained dominated by men who had come to power and prominence through the DMA.

Tom Benfold offers a good example. Born at West Stanley in 1882, Benfold went to the pit at the age of 12. At twenty, he was converted to Methodism at the Oxhill Chapel, and became a successful local preacher for the Primitive Methodists. In 1910 he began his life in politics by being elected to the Ferryhill Parish Council. In 1922 he was elected President of the Miners' Lodge at Dean Bank Colliery. In the same year he was elected to the county council where he was also elected as vice-chairman of the Labour group under Peter Lee. Benfold's career, ending in the county council, was quite typical. The council was dominated by Methodist miners and officials of the union. In the thirty-four years after the first Labour victory in 1919 Methodists held all the key positions. This is made most clear by examining the names of the people who were Chairmen of the Council. With the exception of two years when Labour was out of office, this position was held by a Methodist: Peter Lee, 1919-21; John Lazenby 1921-22; T.F. Brass, 1924-25; T.C. Major 1925-26; W.N. Smith, 1926-1929; Peter Lee again from 1929-1932 and W.N. Smith again from 1932 through until 1942.[27]

Moving down to the level of the rural and district councils we encounter the same links. The 1934 election addresses of Robert Hunter and John Joyce illustrate both the style of politics and the way in which the link between union and party was assumed:

> LADIES AND GENTLEMEN,
> On Monday, the 26th March next, you will again be called upon to elect two members to represent the interests of the Parish of Broom upon the Durham Rural District Council.
>
> Having once again been invited by the *Ushaw Moor Miners' Lodge,* and the Local Labour Party, with its affiliated bodies of organised workers, and endorsed by the Durham Divisional Executive Labour Party to be the Standard Bearers for Labour, it affords us a great pleasure to come forward as Official Labour Candidates.
>
> Three years ago, in consequence of your wonderful solidarity, we were greatly honoured by you by being returned at the head of the poll, and during that brief period, we have made further endeavours to carry out the numerous duties entailed for the social and moral development of the Parish, with regard to Housing, Highways, Health, and Sanitation.[28]

Having made their association with both the unions and the party clear they went on to announce themselves as coming from the people in order to serve the people. Further they reminded the electorate of the role of the Labour Party as welfare agent in the General Strike:

> We appeal to you for your earnest consideration and support, and our advice is that you, as electors, should use your franchise in the interests of your own people, and when these people, who are opposed to us, and entirely against any reform for the mutual benefit of the working class come along to solicit your vote, tell them you are going to send your Town men back, who have been

> trusted and tried, men who have been schooled in a hard school of experience, men who are primarily concerned about human well-being, men who are true economists, because our first concern is in your interests for the improvement of Social Life and Conditions, Public Health and a reduced Death Rate, which are the most essential factors at all times, and ask you to remember that it was the Labour Party who fed the children during 1926, and also provided them with footwear, no assistance being offered or given in any form by our opponents.[29]

The Party was the union. At Shire Hall, as at Redhills, both institutions represented 'our kind'.

The officialdom of both was generally composed of self-educated Methodists who believed in the union as a method of advancement for the working man. As the Liberal agent John Wilson had put it in the first decade of the century: 'for a working man single in opposition to a capitalist is in an unequal position'.[30] The Labour agents who followed him spoke no differently and in the Labour Party they had their own organisation. In this coal mining district, and despite the 1918 constitutional changes, the nature of the class structure did not promote the establishment of middle-class constituency parties or the election of middle-class Labour councillors. The union's hegemony was almost total in this respect. The Labour Party served the purpose not of preaching an evangelical socialism, but of extending the influence of a narrow-based Methodist union officialdom in the county.

Constituency organisation was extremely limited and individual membership low. It was taken for granted that the union man—the 'big man' in the mining village—would be the Labour Party man also. The new Party was, then, part of a *machine* in the sense that it provided security in office and openings for union men. It was systematically controlled by the union: the loyalty and discipline granted to the union were simply extended to the Party. As a result of this success the county was characterised by two different power structures. The political power structure was controlled by the union, but economic power remained in the hands of the coal owners. This disjunction produced a Labourist society increasingly characterised by the contrasting ideologies of this newly established officialdom and that of a decadent aristocratic elite.

12
Local Leaders

All the bare days of childhood, the sweaty wrestle in the pit, the years of battle for a definite place for the toiler in the social and political life of the nation, all the dreams and work of years was crowded into that moment. I sat down and looked at the assembled company. This was the House of Commons.

Jack Lawson

By our silent vote in the ballot box we shall change all this system of gold and greed.

Peter Lee

FOR FIFTY years and more the Durham miners produced their own political leaders. Crawford and Wilson were dominant figures but around them, in the local institutions of council, trade union, chapel, co-operative society and club, leaders of great acumen and oratorical style emerged. In the various council chambers and meeting halls across the coalfield these men developed their political and administrative skills dealing with, and regulating, the economic and political issues associated with the social organisation of a capitalist coalfield.

We have seen how, in this early period, the union's leaders were Primitive Methodists and how this survived the change from Liberalism to socialism. In 1914, for example, when the parliamentary list of the DMA was drawn up all the candidates were ILP members and all were Methodists: Robson had already moved to Durham as miners' agent in 1911; Batey and Richardson would be elected to the same position in 1915 and J. Gilliland in 1924. Jack Lawson would become Labour MP in 1919 and Batey would follow him in 1922.[1]

The ILP and Methodism

Jack Lawson is of particular interest; a checkweighman at the Bolden Colliery, he was a member of the Durham County Council from 1909 and MP for Chester-le-Street from 1919. His autobiography *A Man's Life,* is widely recognised as a classic expression of the English Labourist tradition. It was this text which James Callaghan, as prime minister, gave to US President Jimmy Carter on the occasion of his visit to Durham.

At the turn of the century Lawson had been a key member of the group which had strongly opposed Wilson's association with the Liberal Party. He identified himself deeply with the socialist cause, and with the ILP. For him, socialism was both practical and ethical. On the practical side he declared that he:

> preached no abstract economic theory, not even Marx. I knew the problem better than any theorist, and had plenty of material at hand from day-to-day experience to point the moral.[2]

On the ethical side there was a romantic rejection of industrialism which 'may spell progress, but it destroys the poetry of life.'[3] This view he combined with a strong assertion of the value of labour, and of the work of the miner in particular. He argued:

> that a man might be proud of his dirty work, all the more proud because it was dirty, so that instead of esteeming the man who had a 'good job' we should most esteem the man who did good. And who does better work than a miner?[4]

In this reversal of accepted values he held that 'the humble manual worker is first, the very soul of the body national.'[5]

Lawson, like Wilson and Lee, had experienced a conversion to Christianity. He notes that from '12 to 20 years I would gamble my shirt'. His conversion to the Methodist faith was linked to his discovery of the classic works of English nineteenth-century literature. He writes of how he immersed himself in the 'great tradition' and that Dickens had placed him on the 'literary trail'.

> And didn't I follow [it] once I had found it!...Scott, Charles Reade, George Eliot, the Brontes, later on Hardy, Hugo, Dumas and scores of others. Then came Shakespeare, the Bible, Milton and the line of poets generally.[6]

His life became consumed by the desire for books:

> I did not drink or smoke, nor did I worry about dress. I only wanted books.[7]

With these interests Lawson was attracted to the sober, rational Methodists and the chapel which: 'took the "nobodies" and made the most humble and hopeless somebody.' In his view he pays his respect to 'the society':

> from this society there went men and women to all parts of this country, and indeed of the world. Miners and the sons of miners became school teachers, headmasters, university professors, managers, ministers, musicians, social workers and public men and women.[8]

These 'nobodies', like Lawson himself, were converts from the hedonistic culture of drinking and gambling. Methodism had allowed them to moralise and rationalise their actions and had made them an 'elite' in the villages; it also prepared them to leave for higher things. Lawson was to leave for Oxford where he continued his education at Ruskin College and, after two years, returned with his wife to Boldon Colliery. He notes: 'That I would do any other work than coal we never dreamed.'[9]

At the same time his return to manual labour was coupled with the idea that:

> a just order of society implies an educated manual class as well as educated professional men and workmen...for the manual worker knowledge is the key to social justice.[10]

He now viewed his life 'as a revolt against the low estimate placed upon the hard-driven manual worker'[11] and his programme in life was to gain 'greater esteem' for the manual worker. Thus from being 'noted queer by the people' that he grew up with, for his reading and his religion, he now wished to serve them with his acquired knowledge: 'I held that no man needs knowledge more than he who is subject to those who have knowledge.'[12] At that time, Lawson was well aware of the affinities which the ILP had with both the chapel and the union. It was for him a synthesis, but with Methodism as its grounding:

> One great force held the field in matters of personal development and that was the chapel. And looking back now, I see that it was inevitable that I should ultimately seek the company of the serious-minded people who gravitated together to form the 'Society'.[13]

The chapel was his first organisational base and there he: 'was encouraged to express myself, to preach and to speak....No longer was I queer or alone.'[14]

Through his membership of the ILP, Lawson declared himself to be a socialist. That organisation absorbed the ideologies and practices of these earlier movements and as such he could still argue that: 'the Gospel expressed in social terms has been more of a drawing power in northern mining circles than all the economic teachings put together.'[15] As such he continued to preach and his new belief in socialism complemented his

Methodism. The ILP capitalised on this symbiosis. In Lawson's view the Party's speakers:

> appealed directly to the moral and religious sentiments and in terms familiar to those who had been reared in the non-conformist chapels, called for a 'change of heart'.[16]

In 1919, Lawson entered parliament as a miners' candidate:

> I was convinced that the workers were right in shaping their course to capture this citadel, for it is a place of great strength and power, just as capable of great things for the humblest in the land as it has been for the wealthy in the past.

And if the workers were right it is also the case that Lawson saw virtue in them. Like himself, they too had progressed:

> Better and better have they grown in my lifetime in all those things that matter to men and nations.[17]

Lawson's account is typical of the labour leader: it charts his rise from obscurity, by way of hard labour and reading, to local and then national success in the very 'citadel' of power. The account is moralised throughout, and associated with a corresponding 'rise' or 'progress' in the moral position of the worker. In this version the accession to power is the completion of the programme of service. What Lawson has given us is an ideal typical version of the ethical doctrine of labourist officialdom. It is not a doctrine of self-interest, nor of trade-union bargaining, but of *solidarity* and selfless *service* to the cause of labour. It is a doctrine of the dignity of work and worker whereby, as in the Methodist religion, virtue is found in labour and thrift. It is an ordered doctrine constructed after passing through the hierarchy and experiences of the mine and community and it is traditional, resting on family and community as much as on status and service. These ideas predominated amongst the north's coal mining MPs. They were also present in local government.

Municipal Socialism and Service

In the inter-war period the most significant member of this Durham Labour Party and the political leader of its officialdom was Peter Lee. Lee chose not to take up a parliamentary career but instead held a series of significant local offices. In 1919, a year of considerable unrest in the coalfield and the year in which Jack Lawson went to Westminster, Peter Lee became both a Miners' Agent and Chairman of the County Council; dominant positions at Redhills and Shire Hall. He was in the words of Will Lawther: 'one Methodist who never changed'.[18] Lee died in 1935 at the age of 70 and was 'canonised' by the local movement when, after the

Peter Lee.

Second World War, the first miners' new town on the east coast of Durham took his name.

Lee's biography was written by Jack Lawson. It is a history written out of respect, recording the life of a converted drinker and gambler who had also heard and obeyed the calling of service to his community. Like his autobiography it is characterised by a high moral tone and a complete absence of any suggestion of calculating self-interest or dilemmas on the part of the 'hero'. It is a biography of conversion, achievement and selfless work, in which the 'hero's' life is held together and given meaning by the renunciation of his own self and the dedication of his life to service. Lee's life is held to mirror that of Lawson's own. Portrayed are ethical and exemplary lives united by ideas of social progress and service to the community. They present ideal-typical versions of labourism. However, what they do not reveal is how both men used and deployed the power they wielded. The political machine of the trade union and Labour Party remains silent.

Lee was born in 1864 in Trimdon Grange. He was to make the passage from the 'devil-may-care drinking, fighting man' to that of a sober, respectable Methodist miner.[19] He entered Littletown Colliery, Sherburn Hill, at the age of ten and became a hewer by the age of sixteen. But he was not to stop at this colliery and between 1879 and 1886 he worked in thirteen different pits in Durham, two in Oldham and two in Cumberland. In 1883 he claims that he discovered himself. Lawson quotes him:

> I was seated one night in the 'Lanky' House, or Colliery Arms Inn, Wingate, when the unexpected happened. I cannot say how it came to pass, but I remember saying to myself 'Peter is this to be the sum total of your life?' You have no education, little real knowledge, and apart from coal hewing and drinking, little real experience of life. You can make men laugh with jest, and entertain them in other ways, but what is the end of it all?[20]

Lee was then nineteen, and he decided to educate himself by going to night school:

> I made way to the Master and said Sir, 'I wish to come to your school.' I thought to myself, Peter, this man will think you are a strange sort of scholar, with your cap in hand, a large muffler on, a small black-and-white check coat and corduroy pants all filled with six feet of strange manhood. I said, 'I know that it is unusual for you to have a man in your school, but I wish to learn and I am sure you will help me. My desire is that you will look upon me as one of those boys and whatever you tell me to do I will endeavour to do it.'[21]

Like Lawson himself, but under more difficult circumstances, Lee began his union career with a struggle for knowledge. It was a struggle against a sense of worthlessness, experienced as a will to control his own life and to achieve. Like Lawson, his life would later merge with the Labour movement and became a mission to serve.

In January 1886, at the age of 22, Lee left Durham for the USA: 'with the intention to learn to read and write and see if I could do better'.[22] He took his books, including the Bible and Shakespeare, and travelled to Pittsburgh. After a short stay he moved on to the mines in Ohio and from there, via Indiana, to Kentucky. In March 1887 he arrived back in England, and took up mining again at Wingate Colliery. He was soon elected as lodge delegate and attended the DMA council meetings in Durham. In these meetings he was deeply impressed by William Crawford 'a man after his own heart, straight speaking, decisive, ruling with a rod of iron' and 'he felt as never before, pride of class and the value of his calling.'[23] Lawson is clearly reading into this event an understanding of his own past but it probably has validity. It marks the first time that Lee involved himself publicly. In 1896 he again left Durham to travel to South Africa, where he worked in the gold mines for a year before returning home overland, via Naples, Rome, Turin and Paris. At the age of 33 he became a convert, and subsequently a preacher, for the Primitive Methodists. In Durham, Lee was to take up the ideas of Methodist Christianity as a *social* religion, and translate them into a belief in municipal socialism.

According to Lawson, Lee was an autocrat and this fitted well with his adopted religion. The rationale of Primitive Methodism was to require obedience of believers and to make all men believe. In the small groups (which were the essential units of the religion), all members were invited to speak and to confess their temptations. But it was the leader who asked the searching questions on these matters. It was in these small, face-to-face groups (which enquired into the lives of individuals who then gave voice to their inner faith) that Lee emerged as a leader. He would transfer this system of 'benevolent despotism' into his trade-union and Labour Party work. In this, Lawson describes Lee as a striking, charismatic figure: 'Few who saw Peter ever forgot him. His form and face electrified men so that their eyes opened wide and he was photographed on the mind.'[24] Over six feet tall with long, curly black hair which turned white in later life, he possessed the ability to move men: 'the very sight of him stirred emotions like unto the appearance of a prophet'.[25] And this 'force' inevitably brought him followers:

> this effortless power of personal attraction, and the capacity to will those around him to the need of making something of themselves, or doing something useful, had the inevitable result of gathering around him those who were young, inquiring of life and eager.[26]

He attempted to force others to make something of themselves through conversion, just as he had made himself. A convert from drinking and gambling he, like Lawson again, was to pursue literature and knowledge as ends in themselves. His love became his library: 'He was frugal to the point of self denial but was unconscious that he lacked anything except books.'[27] Another redeemed sinner.

Following his conversion to sobriety and the adoption of an ascetic mode of living his career in public life began. In 1902 he was elected as checkweighman at Wheatley Hill Colliery and in 1903 he became Chairman of the Parish Council. As a parish councillor,

> he fulminated against the social evils that he saw on all sides and with the strength and zeal of a crusader he set about addressing the many wrongs.

This eulogistic account of Lee makes clear that:

> the road was far from easy. The authorities treated Peter Lee with the greatest suspicion. He was described as a Bolshevik, as a revolutionary, as a 'red'....Attempts were made to side-track his many schemes, always on grounds of 'cost to the voter'. Peter Lee argued that anything that was for the public good, could not be too costly.[28]

In Lee's view the principle of a property tax was sound as it was 'a taxation system on the distribution of wealth'. To those who complained he would argue 'while you think of high rates, think also of better conditions'.[29] It was, he thought, a 'Christian approach' and on this basis he organised the building of roads, and he established a cemetery in the village. As a district councillor he pressed for running water to be delivered to houses (previously people had shared out-door taps), for sewage schemes to be introduced and street lighting installed. In Wheatley Hill when the street lights were first lit: 'people danced around the lamps all night'. In the space of five years Lee's endeavours had turned Wheatley Hill 'from a hotch potch shambles of a village into a respectable community'.

In 1907 he was elected to the Rural District Council and became Chairman of the Wheatley Hill Co-operative Society where he argued strongly in favour of spending on developing the Co-ops' property rather than paying out dividends. In 1909 he was elected to the County Council as one of ten Labour members and ten years later Lee became the Council's first Labour Party Chairman:

> Peter Lee had not only become Chairman of the County Council, he was chief of civic life in Durham and the leader of its people.[30]

He was a clear thinker who was dedicated to the idea of municipal socialism. In a carefully worded document he spelled out what he considered to be 'Labour Ideals' in relation to the development of a party programme for office. (Like Crawford he contributed such documents regularly to the local press, and often involved himself in fierce debate over the moral superiority of socialism.) In his view, the theoretical assumptions of Municipal Socialism were based upon the idea of 'social provision on the rates'. In this, councils were empowered by act of parliament 'to do collectively what had been before left to the individual'. This had grown since the Municipal Corporation Act of 1835 so that 'after many years, the parish, district and county councils are all working on the collective principle'. For him the Labour Party, in pursuing these collective principles was a 'people's party' and not a 'class party'; he thought a politics based upon class to be a selfish one, which was 'one sided'. Such a people's party had a number of aims. Of these he listed (a) health; (b) free education; (c) mental health care; (d) law and order—'we shall see that the police are well housed and well paid'; (e) raising the moral standards of the community; (f) collective ownership of all basic services—water, electricity, transport, etc. All of this would be held together through 'the brotherhood of man and the fatherhood of God', as represented in the Bible 'the most democratic book in the world.'[31]

For Lee the powerful claim for Labour lay on ethical grounds, upon the fact that the capitalist system was based upon corruption; upon the degradation of working people, housing them 'in the cheapest homes possible, crushing out the more honest'. It related to the fact that 'dear old England' was in the wrong hands, but 'by the vote we have the power to rule the land'. He frequently turned to the past and pointed to:

> the suffering of our forefathers: the treatment dealt out to them by employers and the neglect of the state and those who were supposed to administer the laws for the general welfare.[32]

In 1919, writing in support of the Sankey Commission and the nationalisation of the mining industry he wrote:

> Does it seem strange, even after nineteen centuries of Christ's teaching, that any part of a Christian nation should try to practice the law of truth? Do the people know that under the system of private ownership in nine years, 1909 to 1918, over 12,600 miners were killed at their work? Do they know that each year about 160,000 are injured—nearly one of every six of those working? Are they aware that we are the worst housed and most overcrowded, and have a high death-rate in our homes, and that if we were out for self we should organise with the mineowners to make wages follow prices, and with them, like Shylock, drive a hard bargain at the expense of the consumer? That is not our plan. We know by the report of the Commissioners that the present system stands condemned and we believe national ownership will mean better conditions and homes for the miners, cheaper heating power for the consumer and more wealth and prosperity to the nation.

He would frequently extol the virtues of the miners and their moral standing in society:

> the Durham miners are a great and noble class of men...let him search the land amongst all the classes and he will find no class that has done more to increase production, and one which has done so well to contribute to those out of work.[33]

Once in office with a clear majority Lee established a determined programme of action, generally understood as a 'sweeping experiment in municipal socialism.' It contained a number of elements. Public health had a central place, the Labour members building upon the statistical evidence of the County Medical Officer—Dr T.E. Hill—to the effect that, had the death and infant mortality rates in the county between 1913 and 1917 been as low as the average for England and Wales, 7,500 adults and 3,250 children would have been saved. A scheme was set up for the training of maternity nurses and for the provision of medical attention for young children. Education was also prioritised, as was transport. As part of the new council's agricultural policy, a number of experimental allotments were to be set up, to be worked under the advice and direction of scientific officers from the Council.

This programme came under repeated and prolonged attack from Conservative supporters across the county: none more strident than the Dean of Durham Cathedral, Dr J.E.L. Weldon. Lee's relationship with Weldon had none of the accommodating calmness that Wilson shared with Westcott. Frequently Lee and the Dean of Durham argued in print and at public meetings, Lee making reference to the social conditions of the miners.

> Let me tell the Dean that in the ages to come, people will be proud of the miners—those men who worked in the darkness of the mine and yet were the first large body of labour to hold up the light of true brotherhood to the world.[34]

In a debate, organised by the Durham branch of the Middle Class Union and the Durham City Chamber of Trade in 1921, Lee was again criticised by Weldon for extravagance with the public purse. In reply he said this:

> The Dean in an amusing spirit said that he was in favour of education for some of the members of the County Council. (Hear, hear.) Let me tell the Dean that at the age of 10, I went down the mine to try and produce the wealth that he was talking about. When he left his school and started to work, I had been putting in nearly a quarter of a century of hard labour in the mine. Then I had to start as a man to try and get some little education, and nobody is more aware of the fact than myself of how ignorant I am tonight, because in the past the greed for gold had stopped the education of the people and neglected the health of the people.[35]

Weldon's views were strongly supported and developed in the local press. In March 1922 the *Northern Star* carried an attack on Peter Lee, the Labour council, and the idea of a 'Labour' party. In reply, Lee drafted an 'open letter' made available to the northern press. On the question of a *Labour* Party he asserts:

> who sent us to the Council? Surely not the coal owners' middle-class union and the other people who joined them in opposing

> us. One would have thought it right to take the name of the parents [Labour]: we are the outcome of the workers' votes.

In defending the policy of the council he drew, once again, upon a defence of Labour:

> we are a body of men who have toiled in the mine and workshops for our daily bread—men who in the hard school of experience learned of the bad housing, bad streets and bad sanitary conditions under which people exist; also how disease, which is ever with us is largely the outcome of these conditions. We have the sad knowledge that education has been kept from the people. We also have some knowledge of the wealth produced in the county in the past and we feel that these things could have been made a great deal better if those in power had looked after the interests of all instead of the interests of the few. We in the Labour Party and those 88,000 who voted for us believe a change should be made, not by disorder and revolt but...by law and order.[36]

In a lengthy speech to Sunderland Rotary Club in 1925 he returned to this theme reflecting on the history of the Durham coal industry. In this he argued that:

> a great many people wonder why Durham is so strong for Labour and how the Labour Party should hold power on so many councils...no body of miners in the world is better organised and none have done more for the old and the young as seen in the Aged Miners' Homes and the freeing of Secondary Education. Those who are inclined to blame us and say we stand for class distinction should remember it has been bred in us, not because our fathers had a desire for it, but because the educated and the rich left us very largely alone in our village life.[37]

When Lee took office as Chairman of the County he was 55 years old. In the same year he was elected agent of the DMA. He began as financial secretary; in 1923 he was Joint Committee secretary and took on the additional duties of Executive Committee secretary in 1924. In 1930 he became General Secretary. He lived in a specially built house, paid for by the union, on a plot chosen by Lee himself in order that he might have a view of Durham Cathedral. He named the house 'Bede's Rest', after St Bede whose remains were kept at the Cathedral. This desire to live high over the city in view of the Cathedral seems strange for a Methodist but perhaps Lawson himself provides the clue. In his autobiography he details how the cathedral affected him:

> As a miner, Methodist and socialist I cared little for its ornate or its ecclesiastical side. But I felt myself so turned and enlarged by

> this place of strength and beauty, with its setting of toilers, that I was carried in a vision beyond the things of today.[38]

Through election Lee had entered into the Durham establishment and the Cathedral was one of its greatest institutions. Having achieved respectability he embraced it, adopting its most famous Saint for the name of his own house. In such ways was the new officialdom associated with the power, prestige and tradition of the past.

Lee took his inspiration from his religion. His sermons at the pulpit linked this religion with his politics. One of his major themes was the classic nineteenth-century theme of service. Lawson writes of how:

> his sermons were saturated with it. We are all members of one body, and men and women have their personal duties to society as well as rights to claim from it. Service, always service, was on his lips, not as a sentiment but as a fact of life. He loathed idleness and the kind of society which made it possible. Whether it was the idleness claimed by wealth as a right, or that imposed by economic circumstances upon masses at the other end of the social scale, it made him sad to contemplate a situation where men gave no service.[39]

A sense of Peter Lee's view and understanding of the world, and the role of political leaders, comes across clearly in this report of his speech to the Stanley Brotherhood in January 1922.

> They were living in very strange times, said the speaker. The world seemed to be wrapped in the power of materialism; the British nation, equally with other nations. The material seemed to be everything, and high and low seemed to be centring their hopes upon the material forces of life. There was a need for spiritual vision and power for he was fully persuaded that the ills the nation was suffering from were the results of materialism. A craving for pleasure had seized upon the people, the speaker went on, and gambling through coupons in newspapers or tickets of the bookies and other sources was rampant. Many of the competitions were arranged by proprietors of newspapers, who ought to set a better example to the nation. The drink bill of the nation was over £450,000, whilst trade seemed to be wrong altogether. They never had more unemployment and a darker outlook industrially than to-day. This position, in his opinion, had been brought about by materialistic forces and through people lacking thought and losing vision. There were some of his friends who believed that the wrongs they suffered from could be righted by materialistic forces. He did not.
>
> His remedy, Mr Lee went on, was to bring in a new state with spiritual forces as the driving power. It needed no prophet to tell

> that the nation was on the road to destruction unless she changed her life. No nation could exist in the state that Britain was today, and unless they changed they were doomed like the Empires of old. They were all lovers of their nation and wanted to see it stand strong in the day, which would surely come, when the world would be linked in the brotherhood of man. The church was often caught in the materialistic spirit and that was why their churches were so often empty. Wycliffe, Luther, John Wesley, General Booth and all other reformers had been men who stood out from the general order of things. They, who believed in the uplifting force of the unseen power, must catch that force and use it to help their fellow men.

He concluded that, as Methodists and leaders:

> They must oppose the power of drink; destroy the power of gambling and the system of commercialism which was sapping the life blood of the nation. They must be prepared to suffer and sacrifice for the sake of humanity just as others in past ages suffered for their sakes. The new force that they must work with was love and sacrifice.[40]

This Protestant conception of personal duty produced a powerful leader, but Lawson notes the paradox that is often central to an understanding of such men:

> he himself was of the very stuff of which dictators are made. He could listen, weigh and balance reasons before he arrived at conclusions, but once his mind was made up he could be intolerant of other views if it was a matter of deep import. It was also true that he was a stern disciplinarian, but he demanded of others no more than he imposed upon himself. Further he had a high conception of a citizen's duty to the State. And he had the courage to fight for, and the driving energy to give effect to, the things he held of worth.[41]

In these ways he was characteristic of the Methodist lay preacher. Currie has commented in a less reverential manner than Lawson:

> The Preachers, often undistinguished by class or education from their members, endeavoured to control the people by rigid imposition of discipline, and assumption of far-reaching pastoral prerogatives that often degenerated into petty tyranny. The contemporary reputation of Methodism for Jesuitism and intolerance was not entirely at variance with the realities of an authoritarian organisation, driven by the effects of its own growth, to assert its principles in ever more extreme form.[42]

Viewed in this way, Lee presents us with another side of Labourism very different from the ethical core outlined by Lawson. It is a 'professional ideology' of service combined with an authoritarian discipline which in turn characterised Methodist practices. Taken from Methodism, it had shaped Lee's generation.

In these terms the aim of trade unionism remained no different from the time of Crawford and Wilson. Labourism, under Peter Lee, stressed the need to raise up the standing of the miner in society: 'to give him pride in the service he renders mankind':

> the day will come when he gets not the 'leavings' but the first fruits of all his labour, when he is counted first amongst the nation's citizens because he renders more courageous, exacting labour than most.[43]

Wilson had argued it this way: 'Position, rank, title, wealth are all useless, for the true index is manliness and useful service.'[44] With the same emphasis as Lee and Lawson he had claimed: 'Sobriety, education, association. These used, the darkness will disperse, the down-trodden be raised, and England made truly a home for her people.'[45] Similarly he had seen ethical progress in his own lifetime: 'Taken in the bulk, and as compared with our start, the miner has been raised on to a pedestal of respect. That is a result of his own self respect.'[46]

Lee's politics revolved around ideas of trust and community. As late as 1934, he addressed his members in his union's monthly circular in the following way:

> We must work together in a co-operative spirit if civilisation is to endure. The difference between trust and mistrust is the difference between life and death, between civilisation and barbarism. I hold this true of nations today and in a smaller way, but equally as powerful in its results, to our industry if it is pursued between mine owners and miners. By trust and co-operation, coal can once more be made a great and powerful asset and play a greater part in bringing prosperity not only to miners and mine owners but to the nation.[47]

Through trust Lee sought an accommodation with capital, in which labour should be granted recognition and place. Ten years earlier in a period of conflict he was invited by the Thornley Lodge to unveil its new banner. In his speech, Peter Lee recognised that the Thornley Lodge was one of the first to form a union and had sent a delegate to the first meeting in Durham. He:

> thanked the Thornley men from his heart for asking him to unfurl their new banner.... The 'banner' was given in the old days to a man who became a knight and he was supposed to keep his

> banner flying. It stood for truth and right—according to books—but in practice it was not always so. The banner had been sometimes used for very unworthy purposes—and often for gaining more and more power. That is not our idea said Mr Lee. The idea was to show that they stood for right and justice and that their aim was to leave the world richer and better than they found it....In unfurling the banner Mr Lee said that when they followed it they should remember that it stood for what they were striving for.

Sidney Webb had also been invited to speak; he was forced to send his apologies, along with a message to the Thornley miners:

> I wish I could be with the Thornley Lodge on Saturday at the unfurling of the new banner, but my work here absolutely prevents my getting away this week. With all the will in the world it is impossible to be in two places at once. Let this letter carry my best wishes for the prosperity of the lodge and for the success of your gathering on Saturday.
>
> The Durham miners have still a hard time to go through; but with patience and loyalty they will surmount their difficulties as they have done in the past. Their one chance is to stick together, and to fight collectively. If every man in Thornley is true to the lodge, and if every lodge in the county is true to the Durham Miners' Association, they will certainly achieve all that is possible under the existing conditions of the industry.
>
> But, in my judgment, the adverse conditions cannot be righted until there is a scientific reorganisation of the industry in the direction of getting rid of the separate private ownership and direction of all the collieries. This means adopting the Sankey Report, or something like it. It means bringing the political power of the miners to reinforce their industrial power. It means voting together as well as working together.

Webb was pointing to something that was becoming clear: an accommodation with capital would be increasingly difficult, and not something that could easily benefit the miners. This theme was taken up by Joe Batey, the miners' MP for Sedgefield, who spoke in place of the DMA's General Secretary, T.H. Cann, who was unwell:

> the old kind of lodge banner pictures figures which represent Capital and Labour—with Capital smiling at Labour. The fruit of the coal industry was pictured as falling at the feet of the capitalist, and the mere blossom fell at the feet of Labour. He believed with Mr Sidney Webb MP, that a complete reorganisation of the industry was necessary to prevent industrial owners from carrying on the collieries just as they pleased. It was all very

> well for an owner to say 'This is my pit, and I have a right to do with it what I please,' but the fact that he had brought hundreds of men and their families together in a colliery village gave the latter a moral claim for work and decent wages, and no employer ought to be allowed to cause men to be thrown out of work by stopping pits, districts or seams which were not paying.[48]

He was to return to this theme 14 years later when he moved a Private Member's Bill for the nationalisation of the industry.

In 1925 as conflict in the trade increased Peter Lee came under repeated attack. In a letter to the *Evening Chronicle,* Harry Bolton, the Delegate of the Chopwell Miners' Lodge, wrote of reading:

> your report under the heading 'A Straight Talk to Durham Miners', of the speech by Mr Peter Lee on Saturday. We are told that Mr Lee informed us 'we would have to accept some new things which are not very palatable to us'. We hold Mr Lee in very great respect, and we admire him for his great administrative ability; but, depend upon it, the man will be a foolhardy chap who comes along at this time of day, after years of semi-starvation and living on the borderline of poverty while working hard, as we miners have done, and are doing, if he suggests we have something we can, or will, give up. We have lost millions of pounds in wages since the war for liberty and democracy, etc., and yet last year £19,000,000 clear profit on coal and royalties went into the coffers of the investors in human flesh and blood.
>
> The tears, the blood and the agony of the past are not going to be forgotten so lightly, no matter who gives weighty advice, for other people to give away things which have been so dearly won.[49]

A further sense of Lee's relationship with the miners is provided in Ned Cohen's autobiography:

> The first time I met Mr Peter Lee was at Bewicke Main one Sunday. Eight of us were playing 'nap' when a tall man got off his bicycle and came across the railway to us. We asked him if he would like to play cards. He refused, but said that his reason for coming was to invite us to the chapel anniversary to hear the children saying their pieces. Before teatime most of us were 'smashed' so we decided to go to the chapel at night. Then we saw this tall man in the pulpit, Mr Peter Lee. In later years I met him often and found him a good adviser, whenever there was a dispute his advice was always the same: 'get the men back to work and then we will talk it over with the employers'.

Cohen emerged as a senior member of the DMA and the local Labour

Party. He recalls one occasion when on the Executive Committee he had attended a dispute at the Dunston Colliery where the manager (a man 'of a bullying nature') was clearly in breach of the agreement with the union. He recommended the miners to withdraw their labour. However at the next meeting of the Executive Committee, Peter Lee:

> reprimanded me in front of everybody, and threatened to have me thrown off the Executive Committee. I agreed that I was wrong in stopping the pit. However when the case was heard at Newcastle the decision was given in favour of the lodge and the owner-manager was told that he must honour agreements between the coal owners and the DMA. But I had learned the lesson that I could not behave on the Executive Committee as I could at my lodge.[50]

Methodism is often discussed in the context of nineteenth century work and labour. Working-class Methodism supplied diligence and moral self regulation which eased the 'labour problems' of the early establishment of a capitalist society.[51] However, whilst this may have been true for the nineteenth century, for the twentieth century what we observe is a moralisation of working-class politics itself. The conventional moralism and discipline provided the ethical core for the officials who staffed the trade unions and the emergent Labour Party. In its content and its latent authoritarianism it did not differ from the labourism of the earlier period in the twentieth century; however this ideology did have a more representative structure. The Methodists, the organisers of the trade union in the nineteenth century, and then, through the ILP, the Labour Party in the twentieth century, had survived both transitions in Durham.

This evidence contrasts strongly with a common view, that the rise of trade unions and the Labour Party at the end of the nineteenth century coincided with an increasing secularisation as: 'the possibility of working-class aspiration being expressed through religious media declined considerably'.[52] However this assessment underestimates the interpenetration of religion and socialism in the ideology of the ILP, as well as the continual influence of religion in the mining unions. Hobsbawm refers to the Durham leaders who were drawn from the chapel and mentions the fact that John Wilson remained in power until 1915.[53] However, the fact that Peter Lee did not take up office until 1919, makes clear that greater ideological continuity existed. Certainly the Methodist link extended well into the twentieth century and any examination of miners' officials, at every level in the coalfield, up until 1935 confirms this point. While the miners might represent the 'modern' through their trade union their social existence was strongly regulated by the traditional side of community life. As such Stark's view that Methodism: 'bore in itself a latent liberalism, and indeed a latent labourism, which asserted itself with increasing vigour, and in the end linked Methodism to the political left', seems justified.[54] To this he adds the rider that by the end of the nineteenth century: 'Methodism had become the creed of an aristocracy of labour, a foreman's religion.'[55] To this we should add that in Durham it was also the religion of an officialdom produced from within the working class.

A Secular Tradition

In Durham Methodism can be seen to have survived and in fact organised the formal transition from Liberalism to Labourism. It left its mark until the third decade of the twentieth century. From then on though, the mining community would be defined not by the chapel but independent socialist societies and increasingly the Working Men's Clubs. During Lee's lifetime this tradition was best represented in Durham by R. Richardson.

A former checkweighman from Houghton-le-Spring, Richardson was elected to parliament for the same constituency in 1919, and became the national Treasurer of the Labour Party. He combined this position with being a County Councillor and President of the Durham branch of the Club and Institutes Union. A local newspaper reported his speech at the National Executive of the CIU at the Three Tuns Hotel in Durham in 1920. In this he argued that, 'I want to make men thinkers, not drinkers.'

> They had no desire to indulge in excess, but they had the strong conviction that nobody should come along and tell them what they had to do. He trusted that they were not going to allow any infringement on individual liberty in that county.[56]

Richardson's career, like those of Lawson, Lee and Wilson, once again shows the degree to which the significant institutions in the county were monopolised by the same men. In Richardson's case the chapel is replaced by the Working Men's Clubs but his involvement in the union and the Labour Party followed a similar pattern.

It was also the case that like the Methodists, Richardson and the CIU had links with Durham society. At the Conference that Richardson addressed there were alongside him on the platform the Mayor of Durham, the Dean of Durham, Mr A.J. Dawson, Director of Education for Durham County and the Conservative MP for Durham City, Major Hills. In his Presidential address Richardson went on to report that the CIU had the backing of a gentlemen friend of his who unfortunately was unable to be present at the conference. The gentleman friend referred to was the Vice-Chancellor of the University of Durham.

Such connections with the principal figures of Durham society point to the manner in which the leaders of the working-class institutions had been endorsed by the 'old order'. Significantly it was those sections of the 'old order' that were most removed from direct economic interest. The guardians of morals and culture were prepared to tentatively associate themselves with the working-class movements but whilst this granted legitimacy and 'place' to the officialdom it did not, of course, reconstruct the class relations of the society. The social contacts, however, seemed to confer a new respectability upon the officials of the new institutions. Richardson, as a representative of three of these institutions, easily found his place within these arrangements. His speech could have come from the platform of any of the institutions which he represented. He went on to say that he did not want the Working Men's Clubs:

> to be political agencies but wanted members to be true citizens of a great country. Democracy must and did govern, and he wanted his friends in the union movement to know their Country and to do the best for it always (Hear, Hear). He wanted to build up a happier, noble and more beautiful England for he loved his country and his county, and because of that he would always be pleased to offer his services to his fellow countrymen. 'Those people who come along in a humbugging manner, trying to take away the individual liberty of the subjects will find an enemy in Richardson'.[57]

Rhetoric apart (and with it the significant habit of referring to himself in the third person) it is clear that Richardson conceived of working-class institutions as having negotiated a space of freedom for their members, an autonomy whereby the working man could assert and raise himself up as he had done. The context of this view—a civil society historically dominated by the practices of the coal owners—is both clear and instructive. In Durham, a working man's opportunities to rise were limited to his own organisations. These organisations, at one and the same time, forced the recognition of the independent claims of the miners *and* established an officialdom as a countervailing power group. Richardson's career reveals the strengths and limitations of these arrangements. His description of a negotiated freedom within an hierarchical society was clearly not a total, or revolutionary, critique of that society. It was one which stressed the value of the working man, and gained strength from the conviction that these people should be recognised for their worth, both in work and in their social life. As such it shares many of the features of the Methodist view; not least the secondary importance attached to the activities of women.

Richardson's affirmation of identity and liberty in the face of the patronage of Durham 'society' was a claim that staked out the autonomy of the miners' organisation within a class society. This was the voice of a secular Labourism, a unity of clubs, union and party. Together with Lee's professional ideology of service and trust it provides us with the two poles of Labourist thought and their organic links with Durham society.

Both were rooted in community and ideas associated with the moral recognition of the labourer and his place in society; both were concerned with the individual. In Lee's formulation the individual was to serve the community, in Richardson's he was to be given the right to determine his own liberty. What both viewpoints asserted was that, for the first time, working-class individuals should have the right to determine their own needs. This right, or this freedom, was linked to the establishment of working-class institutions that defended the claims of a particular occupational group. In some respects it can be seen as a reconstructed liberalism voiced through the collective institutions of the working class. This ideology was linked to a strong sense of corporate identity, one earned in manual labour by the individual miner and expressed through trade unionism, 'the best workman was always a good trade unionist',[58] and the community. Politically it had resulted in the establishment of a trade-union party within which the miners pursued their own corporate interests.

These two strands within Labourist thought represented the official and the popular. On the one hand there was, in both, the belief that working-class people could be released from the personal dependence and subjugation of the practices associated with aristocratic rule. On the other, the recognition that this release involved a struggle to form their own associations: civil, political and religious. It was in working out principles by which the miners as a corporate group should govern themselves that quite different emphases appeared.

Lee shaped a moral code of Christian ethics that extolled the virtues of the labourer but subordinated the individual to the service of the community. This ideology could be seen to correspond with the closed communities in which the miner lived. But Lee himself had not been contained by this world; he had wandered three continents as a miner. It was as if Methodism had enabled him to close off the arbitrariness of his life, taming his freedom and independence and pressing him into a vocational routine. In his talk and actions he always stressed the integrity of the group and the value of service, not as deference—as in the aristocratic era—but as free men who had chosen this path. For Lee, religion, service and trust united with the Labour movement could improve the moral standing of the miners and the whole of society. Like Lawson and Wilson he believed that he had witnessed this change in his own lifetime. The authoritarian impulses of these men derived from this need to assert the moral principles of community over and above the rights of the individual.

In Richardson we find elements of a popular tradition which were separate and distant from the 'preachers' and the 'prophets'. This tradition bluntly asserted that a man had the right to determine his own life, to make his own choices. In Durham it was regularly expressed through the words of Burns: 'a man is a man for all that'. In this view the certitudes spoken of by Lee, Lawson and Wilson, were simply a part of a cloistered, official world (in Durham or Westminster); a world detached from 'real life'. This popular tradition was at home in the pubs and clubs and it contrasted strongly with Lee's sacred duty and the idea of service drawn from the chapel.

These two different traditions existed side by side in Durham. The official and 'sacred' version asserted the dignity of man and his labour; the popular and profane version emphasised the right to liberty. Together they supported and drew upon different elements within local culture. They represented the tension in the mining community over the hierarchy of internal control and regulation organised by the group's own officialdom. In the struggle for the miners' community and the establishment of the miners as a powerful corporate group the 'official' tradition of Methodism was crucial. But this religious tradition would pass. Within Methodism it had already passed to conscious socialists by 1910. In the 1930s and 1940s it would be secular socialists who would articulate the ethic of labour and carry forward the official symbols of Labourism.

13
Seats Safe for Fabians

Arthur Henderson bridged the gap between the unionists and the intellectuals, so that he could confidently ask the Webbs to prepare a new constitution for the Party.

Emanuel Shinwell

AS THE political organisation of Labour established itself on the Durham coalfield, so too did many of its constituencies emerge as 'safe seats'. These soon entered into the folklore of British politics. In Seaham in the 1930s Emanuel Shinwell was to say that the votes for Labour were weighed and not counted. Alongside stories such as these emerged the desire (amongst ambitious, national Labour politicians) to represent a mining constituency. Shinwell, of course, was a beneficiary of this process but before him Sidney Webb, Ramsay MacDonald and Hugh Dalton had represented Durham constituencies in parliament. The phenomenon of the Labour grandee in the north is interesting in itself—it also illustrates the developing relationship between the new National Labour Party and mining trade unionism, and the communities upon which it was based. In this the role and influence of the Fabian Society was of considerable importance.

Established as a debating club and research organisation committed to dispassionate investigation, the Fabian Society had not wanted the responsibility of building or running a socialist movement. They preferred professional politicians to establish the reforms which they advocated. In general they had opposed the idea of working-class, direct action and instead sought to educate the middle class towards collectivist proposals for change. The Fabians argued that socialism was a product of the *middle* class and that its attention to state reform and planning derived not from working-class experience but of a middle-class administrative tradition. As early as 1898 Beatrice Webb noted in her diary the success of 'their' London School of Economics and the importance of their role in London politics:

> we can feel assured that with the school as a teaching body, the Fabian Society as a propagandist organisation, the LCC [Labour Coordinating Committee] progresses as an object lesson in electoral success, our books as the only elaborate and original work in economic fact and theory, no young man or woman who is anxious to study or to work in public affairs can fail to come under our influence.[1]

This emphasis on the significance of the middle class for a socialist project was linked to their view of socialism as the product of gradual reform accomplished through the refinement of state policies. In this they differed powerfully with other socialist organisations such as Hyndman's Social Democratic Federation and William Morris's Socialist League. They were especially at odds with Marxist and syndicalist currents which emphasised the working class as being at the centre of any socialist project. This difference led the Fabians to include reference to the middle class within their own policy programme:

> In view of the fact that the Socialist movement has been hitherto inspired, instructed and led by members of the middle class or 'bourgeoisie', the Fabian Society protests against the absurdity of Socialists denouncing the very class from which Socialism has sprung as specially hostile to it.[2]

From this standpoint, notions of 'workers' control' and 'direct action' were clearly anathema; but so too were the trade unions. These organisations were seen as defenders of the corporate interests of particular groups of workers and as such, potential obstacles to progress; privileged interest in need of reform by the state. They were certainly not viewed as creators of a new party.

The Fabian conversion to the idea of an alliance and then active membership in the working-class Labour Party was both pragmatic and opportunist. It was the result of a combination of factors. These included the electoral successes of the new Labour Party and the election of trade union officials into the corridors of state power during the First World War. Sidney Webb's election to the executive of the Labour Party as the Fabian representative in 1916 was both significant and illustrative of this conversion. There, he was to make close friends with Arthur Henderson from the north east who was at that time Labour Party member of the War Cabinet, and key organisation man of the new Party.

The meeting of these two men was, for both of them, the fulfilment of their political projects. Henderson desired to expand the Party—as he wrote to C.P. Scott, his policy was 'to enlarge the bounds of the Labour Party and bring in the intellectuals as candidates.' Webb was not only willing to be co-opted as an intellectual leader for the new Party but was also prepared to offer the party the full resources of the Fabian Labour

Arthur Henderson ('Uncle') 'trade union leaders trusted and liked him—he was not regarded as a socialist...but an old fashioned radical.'

Research Department. The 1918 constitution of the Party, written by Webb in collaboration with Henderson, was the first significant product of this relationship. It revealed the Fabians as 'clerks to the Labour movement', it also opened up the prospect of their members serving as Members of Parliament. This double role was to be represented most vividly by Sidney Webb himself. In 1922 he was elected as MP for the mining constituency of Seaham, County Durham. He was introduced to the constituency by Arthur Henderson, formerly MP for Barnard Castle, whose links with the area were critical and the relationship between Henderson and Webb took on a general significance in the Party. Elie Halevy, a friend and frequent guest of the Webbs, confirms this perception of their role:

The 1924 Labour Government. Sidney Webb stands on the left of the back row. Arthur Henderson sits at the right in the front.

> Every ambitious young man knew that if he got into touch with them and convinced them of his ability, they would be in a better position than anybody to assist his career and place him where, in their opinion, he was best fitted to serve the state.[3]

Henderson had first been elected to parliament in 1903. The Durham Miners' Executive, while noting the importance of the election, had refused to support his candidature at that time, since they continued to support the Liberal Party. In many respects this was quite odd, given Henderson's own associations with Liberalism: a Liberal trade unionist from a non-conformist background whose links with the early Labour Party were a product of circumstance. To the Fabian intellectuals he was a strange figure. He constituted their lifeline to the Labour Party and its social base in the trade unions; but he remained for them a distinctively working-class character and continued to attend Labour Party conferences as a delegate for the Foundry Workers.

The official histories of the Labour Party describe him as a trade unionist:

> He is one of the most representative labour leaders of our time: a Trade Unionist of long standing, a practical and sagacious politician standing midway between the extremes of right and left on matters of policy, a socialist without doctrinaire rigidity in his views, a Free Churchman with austere standards of

> personal conduct, a temperance reformer....Men of his type and character have made the British Trade Union and Labour Movement the sanest, steadiest, and most united working-class movement in the world, largely because they have imparted to it their own qualities of mind and spirit.[4]

Official histories are, of course, given to sentimental rhetoric and selective recording but in this account we have at least something of the man. His distinctiveness from all the other early leaders of the Labour Party was that he came not from the ILP, like Hardie and MacDonald, but rather directly from the trade unions and Liberalism. It was not until 1912 that he joined the Fabians.

In her book, *The Makers of the Labour Movement*, Margaret Cole also refers to Henderson's working-class credentials. He had attained:

> the highest achievement of the typical Trade Unionist brought up in the tradition of Liberalism and Non-Conformity. His plain living, his bourgeois standard, even his lifelong interest in football, were characteristic of his class—unswerving loyalty to the organisation and to the people with whom he had worked is one of the distinguishing marks of a good trade unionist.[5]

This repeated reference to a 'trade unionist' representing and loyal to his class was elaborated on by Beatrice Webb:

> Arthur Henderson is a magnificent, moral stalwart and a sound party manager—but he has little or no intellectual gifts—no imagination, he is dull and slightly commonplace; within the Party he is trusted and even loved, but outside the Party he is a nobody.[6]

These characterisations, by middle-class socialists, are worth commenting on for they express a very fundamental 'class division' within the new party. Henderson was a senior figure in the new Party and a Fabian; but in these accounts he is quite clearly understood as someone whose class background placed him in a role that was subordinate to the party's intellectuals. He typified the trade-union side of the party which they believed would have to be overcome if Labour was to establish itself on the national stage. Raymond Postgate's description adds to this:

> a silent, unimaginative man, loud-voiced, stiff, red-faced, with deep pouches under his eyes, an iron-founder by trade, a nonconformist preacher from an early age; patiently hard working, but rather rough and short tempered in politics; a rigid teetotaller with few individual characteristics beyond a trick of shooting out his white cuffs at subordinates he rebuked.[7]

In spite of this consideration he was the only manual, working-class trade unionist ever to lead the Labour Party. For twenty years he worked in tandem with MacDonald, taking over the leadership after MacDonald's early resignation, and again after the defection to the National Government in 1931. Together they were linked (as 'a tiger and elephant') in harness.

Henderson occupied the role of go-between: a leader of the Party with a trade-union background yet prepared to carry the Party towards a new alliance and a new national role. He could manage the two sides of the new Party and be loyal to both. Like the Durham miners' leaders, his past was deeply rooted in working-class non-conformity. He also had a keen interest in sport and was directly involved in developing association football amongst the workers of the north. Indirectly, he was one of the founders of Newcastle United, as well as being a prominent figure in lawn bowls.[8] Born in 1863 he had begun his working life as an apprentice iron moulder; he was to become a union official with the Friendly Society of Iron Moulders. It was in this position that he acquired his organising skills. As an industrial negotiator he had acted as secretary and senior workers' representative on the North East Conciliation Board for the Iron Founders. At home in non-conformist circles, he was a trade-union leader not unlike Wilson or Lee. He was twice president of the National Council of the Brotherhood Movement and an active member of the United Kingdom Alliance and other temperance organisations. Henderson's background was characteristic of English, working-class institutions of the last quarter of the nineteenth century: institutions which were formed before, and remained outside, the socialist influence at the turn of the century. Henderson was a Liberal and from the beginning of his political career was sponsored by Liberal patrons in the north east; it was through their influence that he became secretary/agent to Joseph Pease, Liberal MP for Barnard Castle. From this influential position in the Liberal Party, Henderson launched his political career with the Labour Party.

This early career in non-conformist Liberal circles had marked and shaped him. Typically as the trade unionist it would be his organisational skills that would make him the organiser, the Party manager of the national Labour Party: a position he achieved without changing his ideology. Emanuel Shinwell described the appeal of the man to the trade unions:

> his influence came from the fact that trade-union leaders trusted and liked him—he was not regarded as a socialist in practice or in theory but as an old-fashioned radical.[9]

Arthur Henderson then, had no socialist faith to compromise. He was a man of the political machines; first Liberal and then Labour.

Henderson shared with the Fabians a belief in compulsory arbitration on strikes. His skills in trade-union arbitration had been recognised early in his career. In 1911 he was brought in by the Liberal government to negotiate on the railway strike, and in 1913 he mediated in the Dublin transport workers' strikes. For Henderson the Labour Party was:

> in politics, not in the interests of a class, but to further the interests of the Community as a whole. The Labour Party...is a National People's Party.[10]

Henderson was well aware of the significance of class in Britain. He saw the rule of property as deeply inimical to social progress, and his experiences in the War Cabinet reinforced his awareness of the low status attached to manual labour in British society. However, he opposed the selfishness of propertied, class interest with a grander and more selfless ideology. In his view the politics of the new party operated on a higher ethical plane. He was fired by an intense loyalty to 'the Party', and by an equally significant awareness of the need for the pragmatic development of organisation forces, linked in a way which would allow the Party to endure. As secretary of the Party he provided an organic link between the world of the working class and the trade unions from which he had come, and the middle-class politicians who sought to represent them in parliament. In this he was indispensable. It was not for nothing that he was referred to as 'Uncle Arthur'. In this role he exercised a significant influence in the selection of Labour representatives for the Durham seats of Seaham and Bishop Auckland.

Sidney Webb and Seaham

Unlike Henderson or the leaders of the ILP like Hardie, Snowden and MacDonald, Webb was not from the provinces, nor had he risen through the provincial Labour movement. He was a political intellectual who had spent his life in London. Henderson and Webb did, however, share some political views. Webb was a member of the English middle class who identified closely with the idea of an emerging rationalised state, a state freed from the trappings of aristocratic privilege. This identification was so strong that Webb proposed that the state itself should eliminate private property in the interests of society as a whole: a conviction he placed at the heart of the Fabian programme, and subsequently the programme of the Labour Party.

These views apart, it is difficult to imagine anyone less like Arthur Henderson. Sidney Webb, Professor of Public Administration at the London School of Economics, was born into a lower middle-class family in London in 1859. According to Beatrice the family upbringing:

> did not encourage class bitterness, nor lead to the conceptions of class war; there was certainly no consciousness of family failure; and, as it happened, there was so far as he and his brother were

> concerned, from their early youth upwards a growing consciousness of personal success.[11]

Webb's father (an accountant) and his mother (a shopkeeper) arranged for him to be educated at private schools in London and Switzerland, and in the family of a German Pastor. On his return to England he began a conventional commercial career, at the age of sixteen, as a clerk in a colonial broker's office in the City of London. Two years later, in 1878, he entered the Civil Service as a lower division clerk in the War Office. At the age of twenty-two he competed for and obtained a second-class clerkship in the Colonial Office. His acceptance into this post, as a public servant of the British state, was exceptional. Of all the candidates accepted for office in the early years following the introduction of examinations for Civil Service positions, Webb was the only non-university entrant. Of the eleven clerks who entered office between 1871 and 1889, seven were from Oxford, two from Cambridge and one from Aberdeen. Webb's achievement as the eleventh was therefore remarkable. It is even more so when it is understood that the entrance examinations, by determining half of a candidate's marks in Latin and Greek, were designed to ensure that the new clerks possessed both a public school and university education. Webb finished second in the examination entrants for his year and, as was to be expected, he had chosen the Colonial Office as not only the best paid but also because it, along with the Treasury, was the most prestigious office.[12]

In 1891 he resigned his post. He had married Beatrice Potter, the daughter of a railway magnate (who he had thought to be too beautiful, too rich and too clever for him) and was thereby able to choose an independent political career. Six years earlier he had joined the Fabian Society and had already established himself as their most prolific author. He was not without direct political experience. In 1892 he had stood for and won the London County Council district of Deptford and he was to stay in London politics for a further sixteen years. Webb's world was that of the political intellectual. He was also a man with contacts at the very centre of the British state, one who was constantly called upon to provide evidence for Government Committees and Royal Commissions. Between 1903 and 1906 he was a member of the Royal Commission on the Trade Unions.

Webb's world was one of political influence, of dinner parties, holidays in the country with friends and meetings at his home in Grosvenor Road, Westminster. The house was ten-roomed and served by two maids and a full-time secretary:

> There you would meet mingling with the intellectual Fabians, high officials, politicians belonging to more moderate sections of the House and representatives of fashionable society.[13]

The hosts of this political 'salon', 'the firm of Webb and Webb', constituted an ascetic, intellectual and working partnership which was not disrupted by the claims of children. It was the home of an upper-middle-class couple who (whilst living on Beatrice's rentier income) modelled for themselves a professional lifestyle of social enquiry and public activity, strongly influenced by the late Victorian traditions of service and scientific efficiency.

Webb's membership of political dining clubs further enhanced his influence. One such club, set up by himself, was named 'The Co-Efficients'. Writing to H.G. Wells in 1902, Webb characterised it in the following way:

> It is proposed...to arrange for about eight dinners a year, mostly at a restaurant at the members' own expense; that the subject of all discussion should be the aims, policy and methods of Imperial efficiency at home and abroad; that the club is to be carefully kept unconnected with any person's name or party allegiance.[14]

The original idea behind the group was the creation of a potential 'brains trust' for a new national party committed to the Empire and the idea of national efficiency. Webb's field at these dinners was municipal affairs; Leopold Amery, war correspondent of *The Times*, the Army; and Commander Bellairs, the Navy. H.J. MacKinder, Reader in Geography at the University of Oxford, and W.A.S. Hewins, Director of the London School of Economics, represented the universities. Wells was invited for his concern with the need for new elites to regenerate the nation. Bertrand Russell, a close friend, was also a member. Russell recalls that both he and Wells later resigned from the Club because they disagreed with Imperialism.[15] The nature of the Club, however, is a good indication of the political and social circles that Fabians mixed with, as well as the social dexterity of the British upper class. Within this world, Webb played the role of an intellectual theorist of the new science of administration and social reform. As a former civil servant he had acquired and continued to exhibit the habits and mentality of an administrator. Characteristically he held popular claims and opinions in contempt whilst exalting the claims of professionals. The civil servant was his model of what man should, or rather could, be and as such his decision to seek election to parliament at the age of 63 was somewhat anachronistic.

The offer to run as a parliamentary candidate sprang from his reputation as a writer for the Labour movement. Beatrice and Sidney Webb had been perhaps the most important documentors of the institutional history of the working-class movement in Britain. The Webbs' writings had provided an important contribution to the first generation of those working-class socialists who were to form the Independent Labour Party and subsequently, the Labour Party. Jack Lawson, in an admittedly eulogistic and a very exaggerated piece, refers to the influence of their writings on active militants. According to him they:

> gave that sense of purpose and unity to the young leaders and potential leaders, which enabled them to wean the industrial masses from the two great political parties that had long held their eyes.[16]

and again with reference to Sidney:

> were we not all in one way or another, his pupils? Despite his distant, diffident ways, despite his lack of personal impact upon us, we were all 'permeated' by him. He was not so much a person as a mind; and few minds have rendered such great service to the working classes of Great Britain as that of Sidney Webb.[17]

Their two most famous books *The History of Trade Unionism* and *Industrial Democracy*,[18] plus their numerous pamphlets were recommended reading by the ILP. However, it was Webb's membership of the Sankey Commission of Inquiry into the Coal Industry which brought his name to the attention of the miners. G.D.H. Cole, writing at the time of the Commission, recorded its effect. The Commission:

> held its first meeting on 3 March 1919, in the King's Robing Room at the House of Lords...its proceedings were reported at length and frequently 'starred' in the press. There passed before it as witnesses an extraordinarily varied collection of personages—great landed proprietors such as the Duke of Northumberland and the Earl of Durham, great industrial leaders such as Benjamin Talbot, bankers such as Dr Walter Leaf, Mr Ryan, the Prime Minister of Queensland [Australia], Civil Servants from the Mines Department, Professors of economics professing all manner of opinions, journalists, experts, labour and co-operative leaders as well as the representatives of the various associations of coal owners and colliery workers...all these and many more received an amount of publicity never before accorded in the Press to the discussion of the fundamental issue of industrial politics.[19]

It was here that Webb made his name among the miners by successfully accusing private enterprise of inefficiency.

Jack Lawson confirms this:

> During that time, every miner devoured the Press reports of the Sankey Commission. At mass meetings the proceedings supplied text and sermon. Every coalfield was in ferment; the miners' representatives on the commission were almost demi-gods. Seaham wanted a candidate, so they sent for Sidney Webb.[20]

Emanuel Shinwell, in a more precise analysis, records the favourable change that the Commission brought to Webb:

> His emergence as the hero of the practically minded men who had hitherto regarded him as an adversary occurred as a result of Webb's work on the Sankey Commission of 1919. The Miners' Federation could appoint three of their own members and nominate three experts from outside the industry. Webb was of the trio they nominated.
>
> In the event the miners learned that their moral victory was entirely due to Webb...the facts came from Webb. Cool, calculated statistics devastated the owners' and Government's case.
>
> The Miners' Federation were not ungrateful. They saw that Webb topped the poll for the Party Executive and were the leading group which put him in the chair in 1923.[21]

On the Sankey Commission, Webb had acted as an advocate of the miners because he was in complete agreement with the case for nationalisation. In 1916 he had edited a book, produced by the Fabian Research Department, entitled, *How to Pay for the War* with the sub-title *Being Ideas Offered to the Chancellor of the Exchequer*. The nature of the venture clearly indicated the Fabians' overwhelming concern with the British state, rather than with the British working class, but the central concerns of the book were nationalisation and efficiency:

> We suggest in fact that the only effective way of meeting the new burdens is, not by increasing imports but by making the nation, as a whole more productive.[22]

Part of the suggested programme involved the nationalisation of coal:

> The ever increasing dependency on the continuity in the coal supply, not only of the railways and tramways, and of the greater part of our systematic heating and lighting, but also of practically every trade, makes it imperative to place this industry outside the control of private individuals or separate classes whose interests are not necessarily identical with those of the community.[23]

and Webb made it quite clear that:

> One important benefit of the Nationalisation of the Coal Supply would be to take this fundamental national service out of the arena of perpetual strife between Labour and Capital.[24]

His idea was that:

> the transformation of miners from wage earners struggling in the

> Competitive Labour market into Government employees discussing their terms of service, would really be to the advantage of all parties.[25]

The key to the programme was located in the need to reorganise the trade unions. First, the proposal included state recognition of the MFGB:

> In order not only to secure a genuine representative organisation, but also to obtain from every workman his co-operation in the common control of his industry, the state would necessarily be led to make membership of the Miners' Federation of Great Britain, through its constituent Unions for several coalfields, a condition of employment.[26]

Second, the necessary recognition and acceptance by the state that:

> the Trade Union, thus transformed into the legalised representative organisation of the manual working wage earners in the industry is, it need nowadays hardly be explained, really indispensable to the smooth working and efficiency of the administration.[27]

In Webb's usual manner the book was packed with statistics and organisational recommendations. It was this information which he used whilst on the Sankey Commission, and his domination of its discussions was complete. It was a domination which led to his election as MP for Seaham in 1922.

Seaham

Seaham Harbour was the very centre of the Londonderry family's political power. The constituency stretched beyond Seaham itself, extending west and south to include the mining town of Murton and the new mining settlements of Easington Colliery, Horden and Blackhall. It was a constituency that was deeply entrenched in mining, and the growing conflicts and tensions of Durham society were well illustrated there. The District Council was controlled by the Labour Party after the 1919 elections and its chairman, Robert Broad, was checkweighman at Dawdon Colliery, and insurance secretary of the miners' lodge. This rise of a political opposition was viewed as a real threat by the Conservative Party, and its attendant association the Primrose League. In October 1919 it announced that 'the next few months will be a period of great activity for the League'. This was due to 'a campaign against socialism and Bolshevism', and the increase in the electorate associated with the extension of the franchise to women.[28] In Seaham, the attack on Bolshevism was linked to Londonderry's support for the expanding

Comrades Club, and drew upon the patriotic ideology of ex-servicemen. In January 1920 he opened a new club for the Comrades of the Great War:

> Lord Londonderry, who had a hearty reception, said they could all take a great pride in the part Seaham Harbour had borne in the Great War. They remembered the numbers who volunteered in the early days of the War, and who went out to the front and played men's parts there. The Durham Light Infantry, the Northumberland Fusiliers and the Tyneside regiments were all filled with Durham men and the Seaham men took their share with the rest. Through the War, they had lost a great many friends, and to those who remained there was left a great duty and a great responsibility. It was the duty of those who remained to show that they valued the sacrifices made, and that they were determined in their lives in the future that those sacrifices had been made in a good cause, for which they were determined to do their utmost. The Comrades of the Great War was an institution, he felt it was not only their pleasure but their duty to support. It was an association of men who had been allied in a common cause, and who would meet together as the months and the years rolled by for the purpose of refreshing their memories as to the reason for the inception of the association. He was delighted to give his support to an organisation resting on that basis. It was refreshing, too, that there was nothing political about it. He knew that the word politics had sometimes an unpleasant savour in their minds, but he thought that it was quite wrong that should be so because the meaning of politics was, after all, the government of a country, and politicians were men who wanted to take part in the government. They were anxious and desirous that in those clubs there should associate together men of varying opinions and men who might not see eye to eye with each other as to the manner in which the country ought to be governed. He was not asking that in the ranks of their comrades they should include those who during the war were Pacifists and in peacetime Bolsheviks. These were not the people they wished to enlist in their ranks, but as the years went by, and as opinions governing the country might develop along different lines, so long as these lines were patriotic there was no reason why anybody should be excluded from the Comrades of the Great War on account of ordinary political opinion. He sincerely hoped that the branch would grow.[29]

Three months later:

> at the Comrades Club on Saturday night and in the presence of a large attendance, Mr Malcolm Dillon, presented to the members,

> on behalf of the Marchioness of Londonderry a suitably framed photograph of her ladyship as a commander of the Women's League. In a letter addressed to Mr Dillon, Lady Londonderry said 'I feel I am speaking in the name of many thousands of women who enrolled in the League that they were all proud and pleased to have been given the opportunity of serving and helping the men in however small a way during the Great War.'[30]

In order to make plain the linkage between war and peace, an address was given by Major C.W. Fryers on 'the advantage of industrial harmony'. Earlier that week a new stand, a gift of Lord Londonderry, had been opened at the Seaham Harbour Football Club. This had been designed by Londonderry's surveyor, and marked a further aspect of the family's desire to regulate the life of the town through their direct involvement in all its aspects.

This was the world Sidney Webb entered in 1919. In September of that year a meeting of the Seaham District branch of the Labour Party was held at Horden to consider:

> the future representation of the Seaham Division. The following names were put forward from which to make the selection: Mr Sidney Webb, Dr Rutherford (Newcastle), the Rev. J.R. Herron (Seaham Harbour), Mr James Robson (Durham) and Mr Henry James (West Stanley). A further meeting will take place on Saturday 13 when...the final selection [will be] made.[31]

This shortlist pointed to a major complication for Webb's candidacy. While the miners' lodges in the constituency supported him, the established procedures of the DMA insisted that the union, and its affiliated lodges, only supported candidates from the DMA's parliamentary list. In this case it was clear that the lodges should support Robson. Their refusal to do so (and support Webb) brought them (and Webb) into conflict with the DMA in Durham.

In an attempt to construct a compromise, Webb offered to pay for his own election expenses and made it clear that he was prepared to act according to the decisions of the DMA executive. For its part the DMA was determined to stick to its established procedures and on 18 February 1920, Beatrice Webb recorded in her diary that the matter had been resolved. Sidney had accepted the decision of the Durham executive and refused the nomination.

The Seaham miners, however, were not prepared to accept either the instructions of their union or Webb's acquiescence. They persisted with their request and Webb, provided with an introduction from Henderson, decided to visit the constituency for two weeks. At the end of that period he agreed to abide by the decision of the local Labour Party.

During this time in the constituency Sidney and Beatrice gave several talks and answered questions at meetings. On 17 June, Sidney spoke at Thornley. There he commented on how:

> some members of the Labour Party—especially the younger men—were inclined to 'pitch into' the Liberals. He preferred to say that he was very grateful to the old Liberals for the fights and votes they had won for the progressives of today.

At the end of the meeting Webb made his position clear in another way:

> replying to a vote of thanks and the expressed wish of the Chairman that Mr Webb would be adopted and returned to parliament, Mr Webb said it was for them to say whether they wanted him to take up that new job. He could go on quite comfortably doing what he was doing. If they wanted him to take up the candidature they must make their wish quite clear.[32]

On 20 July 1920, Webb accepted his nomination. This was the first, and significant, chink in that otherwise sealed group of local miners' officials. That it was broken 'from outside' rather than 'from below' says much about the ordered reality of mining politics. In his letter of acceptance, Webb wrote that his own reluctance to 'assume a new responsibility' should not lead him to oppose:

> an invitation emanating from the lodges of the Durham Miners' Association and nearly every other Trade Union and Labour Organisation in the Division...and conveyed to me as the unanimous decision of the Divisional Labour Party.

As part of the new responsibility Sidney and Beatrice undertook another lecturing tour of the constituency in December of that year. In travelling around the constituency and through his contacts in the Durham union Webb also collected the material for his short *History of the Durham Miners.*[33]

In June, at Ryhope, Webb had received a barracking from some miners and members of the Conservative Party. He had begun his address with the view that:

> All workers should belong to the Labour Party (A voice: 'Are you a worker?') 'Yes', replied Mr Webb, 'a skilled worker. I teach economics in a University'—'Oh!'

That meeting had been brought to a close:

> The Rev. J.R. Herron (Seaham) said that the Unionists had not paid toward the cost of that meeting, and they had no right to take part in it....The Reverend gentleman left the stage and the Chairwoman invited all their friends to tea in the Miners' Hall.[34]

Two years later Webb returned for the Election. His opponent, representing the Conservative Party, was Captain T.A. Bradford. An audience at the New Seaham Conservative Club was informed by Mr Malcolm Dillon that 'this was not a contest on the lines to which we have been accustomed in the past, but was a fight between the government and Bolshevism.' Captain Bradford, for his part, argued that:

> he was out for...a better England. [The Conservative Party] wanted to work together for the good of the country. If they all worked hand in hand he was sure there was a better future before us.[35]

Lord Londonderry was clear that:

> he should not think the arguments of the Labour Party would have very much weight in a place like Seaham Harbour which had been made by private enterprise.[36]

Furthermore:

> Mr Sidney Webb...was a theorist and an author. He seemed to take very little interest in the management of coal mines or the management of a business, to judge by the answers which...[he] gave to the Coal Commission.[37]

In spite of the attacks, and the potential splits amongst the miners, Webb was elected as MP for the constituency with an overwhelming majority of 10,624. He was in the first of a growing cohort of middle-class MPs to be elected for the National Labour Party. On that day, the 3,000 workers at the Murton Colliery 'abstained from work' for the Election.

On the issue of nationalisation then, Webb was at one with the miners' leadership but as a parliamentary politician however, he made it clear that he would not be a sponsored MP. The miners, who had developed the strategy of the sponsored MP, could not expect him to operate in such a manner. Webb would not reside in Durham, although when in the constituency he would be responsible for his travel and accommodation costs. He would not be responsible for the local party or the organisation of elections and he further made it clear that he did not wish to be involved in the local political, charitable and recreational affairs of the constituency. In a letter to R.J. Herron, Congregational Minister and secretary of the Seaham Harbour Labour Party he explained that his relationship would be of the parliamentary form:

> A parliamentary candidature is of the nature of a Partnership which cannot be successful unless the burden is duly shared between the candidate and his supporters. You may count on me doing my part without stint, although I must warn you that my work in London will compel me to concentrate my meetings in

> the Division in successive visits of a few weeks each. Those who have pressed me to stand—the members of the Miners' Lodges and other Trade-Union branches, women's societies, the Divisional Labour Party, and all the various bodies concerned—will I am sure, not fail in their part of organising every separate local centre, and getting into communication with every elector.[38]

In this detailed effort to free himself from direct dependence upon, and accountability to, the people of Seaham, Webb drew upon the English parliamentary tradition and the eighteenth-century meetings of Burke. As with Burke, Webb made clear that:

> Your representative owes you not his industry only, but his judgment; and he betrays instead of serving you if he sacrifices it to your...authoritative instructions.

In Webb's view, such instructions were 'utterly unknown to the laws of the land, and against the tenor of our constitution.'[39]

In true British parliamentary fashion Webb the Fabian would represent the miners. But he would not be bound by them.

Miliband has argued that it is this type of relationship which chained the Labour Party to a pragmatic politics:

> The Labour Party has not only been a parliamentary party, it has been deeply imbued by parliamentarism. And in this respect there is no distinction to be made between Labour's political and industrial leaders.[40]

In Durham the 'industrial leaders' had affirmed this parliamentary tradition from the beginning. But as agents, acting as Liberal MPs, they had retained power within their trade union, thinking they were not dependent upon the patronage or discipline of the Liberal Party. Their powerbase lay outside it. In the new context of a 'checkweighman's party' the power of the union was enhanced by its control over a party it had helped to create. Webb's demands however made clear the weakness of its democratic structures. Previously the 'independence' of the parliamentary representative was regulated through the operation of the trade union. Webb was seeking to extend this tradition to middle-class MPs who had no accountability to or dependence upon the structures of power in the county. His request was granted, and it set an important precedent for mining representation in the north.

This question of representation was a serious one for the new party. Formed from a social movement operating outside of parliament there was a natural tendency for it to operate as a system of functional delegation rather than indirect parliamentary representation. This was more true of the miners than other groups given their experience of trade-union representation in parliament. Webb, himself, had written of this problem two years before winning the election at Seaham:

> The predominance in the Labour Party of the vocational organisations, notably the great Trade Unions of miners, railwaymen, textile operatives, engineers and general workers, and the paucity of funds available for the election expenses of other parliamentary candidates has led, down to the present, to the selection of candidates, in too many instances, on a vocational basis. Whatever may be urged in favour of the choice of a representative actually because he is a miner or a cotton spinner, to an assembly having to do with mining or cotton spinning, it is plain that there is a loss when what is in question is the Democracy of citizens...the place of the vocational representative is where the affairs of his vocation are being dealt with.[41]

The tension here went to the heart of the new party and the problems associated with it; becoming a working-class, trade-union party with middle-class members of parliament.

From Beatrice's diaries a very clear picture emerges of their relationship with their working-class constituency. On her first visit to Seaham she recorded her impressions of the working-class culture of the miners, and the account is a familiar one:

> There is a lot of money flying about and much spent on alcohol and betting. The life seems to be in fact completely materialist, though fairly respectable. There are groups of fervent chapel folk. Here and there is a bookish miner, usually with quite a large bookcase filled with the well known poets and classics—a little philosophy and more economics. It is to these 'bookish miners' that is due the pertinacity with which Sidney's candidature has been pursued. How far they represent their rough and stupid fellow miners is doubtful: though probably they will vote in herds when the day comes....There is little or no organisation in the constituency.[42]

She went on to talk of the miners 'as children in politics; they are not critical and they are solid trade unionists'. Their union was viewed as 'a mechanical black-leg proof' organisation.[43]

This description would have been supported by Sidney Webb, whose views on workers and their 'working-class luxuries' are well known. For him, 'there is good reason for preventing consumption in excess, and even for restricting consumption in moderation.'[44] Such measures would, in his view, improve the 'intellectual and moral hygiene'[45] of the coal miners.

Beatrice's political and organisational comments were supplemented by more personal statements concerning the area. On 30 November 1922,

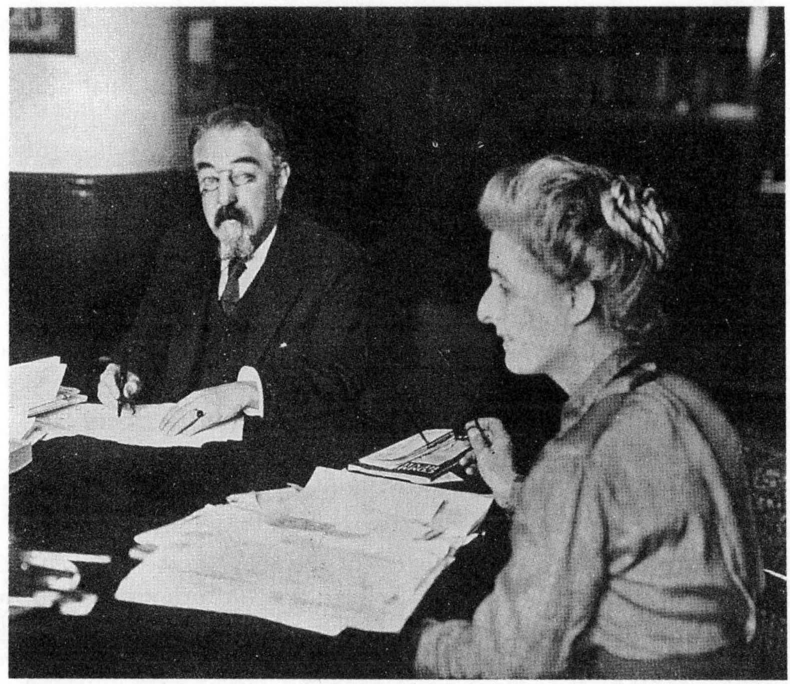

Sidney and Beatrice Webb

she noted how she was haunted by 'the vision of those pit villages and those strained faces of the miners and their wives listening to our words'. She went on to question 'how we get into an intimate and sincere relation to them, so that we may understand their lives?'[46] As the 'Member's wife' or as she described herself 'the helpmate of the Member for Seaham Harbour',[47] Beatrice attempted to produce a 'sincere relation' by addressing a monthly letter to the women's section of the Seaham Labour Party. These letters were aimed at informing the 'ladies of Seaham' of the ways of parliament and the habits of her's and Sidney's lives in the capital.

In the December she wrote to the 'friends of Seaham Harbour':

> My husband and I live a very regular life. Every morning at eight o'clock punctually we have each one cup of coffee and bread and butter on a tray in our workroom; we read our letters and skim through *The Times* and *Herald* newspapers, and then we get to work, and work steadily until our midday meal at one o'clock. In the first place there are letters to attend to...when these letters have been attended to we set to work on the book that we happen to be writing. Writing books is very hard work....In the course of the last thirty years we have written about twenty books. I am afraid you would find them very dull and difficult reading.[48]

Beatrice's guilt was however, tempered by the knowledge that, as she put it, as 'far as we are concerned we are on velvet in this constituency'.[49]

Sidney's relation to the constituency consisted of occasional visits. In the crucial year of the General Strike—which he considered a lunacy—he chose to absent himself entirely. Whilst the strike paralysed the coalfield, he spent his time researching through the Poor Law archives at the Ministry of Health and the Public Record Offices.

Beatrice recorded in her diary what the strike meant to both of them. It was,

> the weak side of the Labour Party constitution—its organic dependence on the Big Trade Unions—has been discovered by the events of this year. The sooner the remnant of the Liberals throw themselves into the political Labour movement and transform it into a constituency party, the better for the Country, assuming that it could be done without the trade unions forming another party of their own.[50]

This Fabian dilemma was also shared by the Liberal intellectuals of the period. They could find no replacement for the unions as a social, organisational and financial base. They were drawn towards the new Labour Party yet reluctant to join, fearful of the other side of trade-union reformism. Hobhouse argued that he could not feel at home 'in a body governed by trade-union members and their finance'.

> It seems to me that there is possibly a distinctive kind of socialism, being one based not on the Trade Unions but on the Community and Social Service. The constitution of the Labour Party binds it tight to the Trade Unions and their sectional selfishness, a most serious defect. I have once or twice written in the MG [*Manchester Guardian*] that the Liberal Party might teach true socialism in the point of view of the community as a whole, but I don't think hitherto they have shown much enthusiasm for this role.[51]

This is all too reminiscent of the Webbs' complaints regarding the trade unions, and their own promotion of the ideals of both service and the community. In truth not much divided the political views of these Liberal and socialist authors. Hobhouse argued that 'it was party that got in the way'. In truth though, it was trade unionism—the organisation of material interests—which divided them and the peculiar terms under which the constitution of the Labour Party gave trade unionism control. This 'fact' of British politics and the dilemma of the politicians within the Labour Party, whether they were of a socialist or liberal kind, would remain as the core of the problem of British Labourism. In both the liberal and socialist versions these 'interests' should be subordinated to the society, or the community. Such thinking gave rise to much moralising on the issue but it could not overcome the basis and rationale of the party: the promotion of trade-union interests in a capitalist society rather than service to the community or the state.

Sidney Webb's attempts at politics were to end in disaster and demoralisation. If it was the Labour Party which had projected him into the national political arena in the first place, it was now this same party, and 'the generation of mediocrities' which surrounded him, that failed him.[52] Owing to advanced years (he was now 70 years old) and the general recognition, both by those who knew him and himself, that he had not managed well the transition from civil servant to constituency MP, Webb decided not to stand for the 1929 Parliamentary Election. However, together with Arthur Henderson, he managed to fix the Seaham constituency as a seat for the leader of the Labour Party, Ramsay MacDonald. It is significant, and revealing, that he needed to warn MacDonald that his friendship with Lord and Lady Londonderry would be resented in the constituency and it would ruin his electoral chances if it became public.[53]

Beatrice was to write in characteristic fashion of the 'fixing' of the Seaham seat to her lady members in the constituency:

> If a devoted wife may be excused in saying so, I think you did precious well when you got Sidney Webb to represent you in parliament. But in persuading Ramsay MacDonald to take on the task you have made one big jump to the top of the political ladder.[54]

Beatrice was quite clear that this jump was only possible because of the 'Ladies' who turned in the vote on the appropriate day. Furthermore, that MacDonald needed such a safe seat:

> What the Seaham Labour Party has done in providing Mr MacDonald with a safe seat and, as I can testify, with a most loyal and intelligent body of supporters, may well mean years of added service from him to the state.[55]

MacNeil-Weir, MacDonald's biographer, was to refer to the offer as:

> a gift sent from the miners to the Labour Party—an acknowledgement of MacDonald's services to the movement and a tribute to his personality.[56]

MacDonald happily accepted this 'gift' and in so doing he argued for the same conditions as Webb. He, too, had no intention of involving himself in the constituency and he had, in fact, released himself from his Abervan constituency precisely because of the pressures being brought to bear upon him there by his constituents. In going to the old Londonderry seat of Seaham he knew that he was going to a constituency in which he would have no local responsibilities. His views on this were clear:

> they offer me a constituency which I need not visit more than once a year and where, at a General Election, three or four speeches at the outside would be all they asked of me....They guarantee no subscriptions will be asked for and that the whole organisation is maintained from local sources.[57]

On his arrival in Seaham he, like the Webbs, was also horrified by the lack of organisation but pleased to discover that even the minimal demands he expected upon his services were not pressed. In fact he received 'the homage of his cheering admirers like a film star making a personal appearance at a premiere',[58] and his majority at the election was 20,794. In the subsequent 1931 national government election, in which MacDonald stood against the Labour Party as the leader of the National Coalition, he was re-elected but with his majority reduced to 6,000. Four years later, and after visiting the constituency only twice, he was to be ridiculed at election meetings and lose the election to another 'outsider' Emanuel Shinwell. The seat returned to Labour and has been so ever since.

Hugh Dalton and Bishop Auckland

The miners, and mining seats, had, by the election of the second, minority Labour Government in 1929, come to be seen as being able to provide seats which did not have to be 'worked' since union loyalty secured the vote. In cases like Webb's, where MPs were introduced from the outside, this proved to be a convenient arrangement. It was also extended to leading Labour politicians who were temporarily without a seat or to those who, like MacDonald, wished to find another 'home' in a mining area. The acceptance of Webb's and Henderson's advice by the Seaham Labour Party is both illustrative of this process and clearly revealing of why mining seats were so crucial to the Labour Party. The new Party exchanged the paternalism of the nationally known figures for the deference of the voters. In such ways was the relationship between mining areas and the Labour Party built, and for such reasons the miners themselves became central in the political rhetoric of the Party.

In the same election that MacDonald was first returned at Seaham, Hugh Dalton was elected in the Bishop Auckland constituency in the south-west of the county. Dalton, a close friend of the Webbs, was a second-generation Fabian with a degree from Cambridge. He was a recruit from what Beatrice termed, 'the nineteenth-century Governing Class of England'. She added that he was also a member of the London School of Economics Group and one of Henderson's bodyguard of intellectuals.[59] Dalton was to be an important carrier of the Fabian tradition.

The Bishop Auckland constituency was not a miners' seat but was split between the miners and the railwaymen. This produced a constituency which, while once considered the safest Liberal seat in the country, was by the late 1920s solidly Labour. Yet, as if by arrangement the local MP, Ben Spoor, an ILP member, was not drawn from either of the two occupational groups that dominated the town. Spoor had joined the ILP in 1902 and from 1903 was active as a Bishop Auckland Urban District Councillor. As a builder's merchant with his own business he was described, in almost religious terms in the official history of the Labour Party, as 'a middle-class apostle of working-class liberty, an advocate—worthy to plead the cause of the people in the great councils of the nation'.[60] This most working-class constituency had then, already elected a member of the local middle class before it chose the national figure of Hugh Dalton. In doing so it switched from the ethical socialism of the ILP to the practical statism of the Fabians.

Dalton, son of the tutor to King George V, was brought up at Windsor Castle. His father had been chosen by Queen Victoria to supervise the education of her grandsons but Dalton himself was provided with the more traditional training of the 'English governing class'. He was a pupil at Eton and then passed on to King's College, Cambridge. J.C.C. Davidson, who was also at Cambridge at the time, and later became Chairman of the Conservative Party, remembered Dalton in his memoirs:

> Hugh Dalton was the great man in my day at Cambridge and for the rest of his life whenever he greeted me he always used to boom out in that horrible voice, 'of course, we were at Cambridge together'.[61]

As a student Dalton, with his Fabian convictions, must have mixed in different circles to Davidson so this observation from a Tory is interesting. Dalton was active in university politics, holding the post of secretary of the Fabian Society. The Fabian Society was also his route to joining the Labour Party. It was an unusual route for a member of the 'governing class' to take but he was in close contact with the Webbs and they had provided the key introductions which gave him credibility in the new Party.

In 1918, after campaigning for the Party in the General Election Dalton recorded his impressions of the likely future of the Party:

> Four years hence Labour ought to poll a tremendous vote, and meanwhile win a lot of by-elections. What is chiefly needed is: (1) improved organisation in the constituencies; (2) an influx of brains and middle-class, non-crank membership. It is very weak now in knowledge on foreign and imperial policy, and army and navy. Also it will want some good lawyers (but not too many).[62]

In fulfilling this, Dalton saw his own role as supplying the 'middle-class

Hugh Dalton with Harold Laski, 1934.

brains' which would 'court' the working-class trade-union leadership. His biographer, Ben Pimlott, describes Dalton as a:

> child of the Webbs; pragmatic, paternalist, collectivist, a pre-war critic of property rights. He disliked liberal high mindedness almost as much as he disliked the rich, and had no difficulty in identifying wholeheartedly with the trade-union leadership.[63]

For Dalton's generation, the trade-union leaders were confirmed Labour Party men and any new, middle-class entrant had to come to terms with them. In the Webbs' day the unions were only just moving towards the Labour Party and they retained a hostility toward middle-class intellectuals. For Dalton's generation the link between the trade unions and the Labour Party had become firmly established, and this had been accompanied by the emergence of a new style of trade-union leader. Less intolerant of 'outsider intellectuals' and more predisposed to creating a new political class based upon an alliance of workers of 'hand and brain', these new trade-union leaders were easier to deal with. It would seem that this was an arrangement which Dalton thrived upon, and operated with the developing style of a patrician. Bishop Auckland and the Durham coalfield was vital to this, providing him with a stage and also the symbolic props through which to project himself as a natural Labour leader.

Dalton's first parliamentary campaign was a Cambridge by-election in 1922. He lost this but he had gained a reputation as a good performer and, more importantly, gained the friendship of Arthur Henderson, who made clear to him the route to parliamentary success. He gained credibility from another campaign in a Tory seat—running third at Maidstone in the 1922 General Election. In 1923 he fought and lost Cardiff East, and in July 1924 again lost in a by-election at Holland-with-Boston. In the October election of the same year he was at last successful in being elected for the marginal seat of Camberwell/Peckham, in South London, becoming the constituency's first Labour MP. The local Party was an active one and had expanded in numbers. But Dalton, who was chairman of the local party, clashed with his agent over its political direction. This conflict reached the point of Dalton placing the demand that either he or his agent should resign. Dalton lost and decided to withdraw from Peckham at the next Election to rid himself of the 'hairshirt' of a troublesome local Party.[64]

After this experience—four elections in three years, followed by the difficulties of an activist Labour Party constituency—Dalton was looking for a safe seat, an inactive local party and a supportive agent. He was to find these in the Bishop Auckland constituency of County Durham. His manner of obtaining first the nomination, and then the seat itself, reveals the degree to which the Labour Party had, by 1928, become a national party which organised its local branches. The leadership of the national organisation was by this period bonded by links of personal friendship. Dalton's successful introduction to the constituency was guaranteed by a letter of recommendation from Arthur Henderson to Peter Lee. Having gained the crucial backing of the Durham Miners he was then selected by the Bishop Auckland General Committee of the Labour Party at the beginning of October 1928. As he recorded in his diary for 7 October, he knew the 'value' of this selection:

> I have got Bishop Auckland. This should be a seat for life barring grave accidents. Voting at selection conference: Dalton 108, Fenn 17, Rutherford 4. Then a unanimous vote for me. Clouds pass away.[65]

However, at the time of this election Dalton was still the sitting MP for

Peckham and despite his optimistic view of an 'easy ride' future events were to prove bizarre, if not difficult.

The General Election was due to take place the following year, but Ben Spoor, who was by this time a chronic alcoholic, died on 22 December 1928. A by-election was necessary and Dalton was faced with a major problem. If he went to Bishop Auckland he precipitated a by-election in Peckham where to further complicate matters, the prospective Labour candidate, John Beckett, was also currently representing another constituency. Dalton's move would therefore have forced two by-elections and this was not seen to be in the Party's interest. The Bishop Auckland constituency did not want to switch candidates again, and as Pimlott records, the solution lay with them:

> It was against this background that constituency officers put forward a solution which Dalton, even at his most ingenious and artful, would never dared to have suggested. That it went through without a word of protest is a reminder of the discipline, and perhaps the deference, of delegates in the mining constituencies in the 1920s.[66]

The solution was put to Dalton at Spoor's funeral. It was as follows: Dalton should request that his wife Ruth should fight the by-election but agree to step down in his favour at the General Election. This idea was backed by Henderson and, as a consequence, the Bishop Auckland constituency, without reactivating a selection committee procedure, named their new candidate as Ruth Dalton. Dalton noted in his autobiography:

> She is willing—though she says she has been more interested in an Edgar Wallace thriller than in the prospect of being an MP.[67]

Ruth Dalton's parliamentary career was to last for only three months. She became MP for Bishop Auckland on 8 February 1929 and parliament was dissolved on 10 May. She was glad to leave.

Dalton's own election was, as he had anticipated, a foregone conclusion. In his diary covering the election week, he recorded:

> This election is the easiest thing I have ever had. It seems hardly fair to take the money. Aaron Park, our agent, is almost too calm, and everything is a bit late and casual. But it all comes out well in the end.[68]

His career was made. When much later, in 1948, he was looking back on the event and noting the key men and women who had helped to make it possible, he recorded:

> Keir Hardie converted me to socialism, when I was an undergraduate at Cambridge, and when I helped to protect him in a

> street scuffle after a meeting broken up by Tories. Sidney Webb and his wife I saw often, both at the University and elsewhere, over many years. He taught me as he taught so many others, not any theories, but the practical economics of socialism in modern Britain. Arthur Henderson showed me great kindness, when I was a young man entering practical politics. In that field he was my guide and my leader.[69]

Here we see the practical, intellectual traditions of Webb coming together with the organisational skills of Henderson to deliver up-and-coming members of the Fabian Society to the miners' union on the instructions of the national office. Webb's case at Seaham had been unusual; Dalton's, although bizarre, would become typical.

Dalton, like both Webb and MacDonald, chose not to live in his constituency and his appearances in Bishop Auckland were infrequent. His duties were carried out for him by Will Davis, the Bishop Auckland secretary. Davis was a miner's son who had become a local headmaster. He was in perfect agreement with Dalton's view that a 'healthy party was an inactive one'.[70] This principle was carried out. Pimlott quotes a regional official on the Bishop Auckland Labour Party as saying: 'the less Bill gathered the Party together, the happier he [Dalton] was.'[71] Under Davis's rule the local party would pass through a year without the executive meeting. He would claim that there was nothing to discuss. In the absence of such discussion, and to Dalton's liking, membership fell. His role as an MP was to fix things in London. He did not have to have to meddle in local affairs, or to serve as a representative of his new constituency.

In addition to Davis, Dalton relied upon the support of Bob Middlewood, a railway stationmaster, leader of the Bishop Auckland council, and locally known as 'Mr Bishop Auckland'. Within the local party he shared with Henderson a liking for the familiar; like Henderson too he was a master of the Party's organised structure. While Henderson ran things from London, Middlewood was a man of the local machine. His style typified the local party:

> Uncle Bob Middlewood's relationship to civic affairs was based on a mixture of paternalism and patronage that had long been the hallmark of Durham politics. Feared and respected, Middlewood ruled Bishop Auckland Council through a network of personal contacts, and a system of favours given and received. 'If Uncle Bob recommended you for something, you got it', was an accepted local principle.[72]

This local style was complemented by Dalton's. Increasingly the MP operated more as 'a patrician grandee than a tribune of the people'.[73] Within such an arrangement a constituency party was not essential. Both local and national political control was effectively carried by the networks of significant individuals in the local labour movement. The key to their power was the organisation of the unions, especially the DMA. Fully aware of this, Dalton took great care to be on good terms with the local lodge officials. These men represented separate power bases and, in an emergency, they could be called upon to swamp a local party meeting and stamp out opposition.

Pimlott sums up the relationship between the Fabian MP and his constituency:

> Dalton also gained much from his connection with the north east. County Durham provided him with a powerful political base and one which allowed him to get on with the job. For a middle-class southerner, the backing of the miners and the important northern group of Labour MPs was a vital source of strength. MPs and miners' leaders such as Will Lawther, Jack Lawson, Will Whiteley and Sam Watson became his friends and allies. His own presence at the Durham Miners' Gala became an annual attraction reinforcing the support of one of the most influential trade unions in the Labour movement.[74]

This relationship worked well for Dalton and would work well for others in the future, and it brings to mind the image of a political machine; an image often used in the National Labour Party during this period. In the words of the National Committee of Constituency Labour Parties:

> Many of the largest parties have just become electoral machines relying on an automatic Labour vote to return their candidates in all elections but holding practically no meetings.[75]

The application of this to Durham is clear. Even where there was an occasional split between the railwaymen, the miners and the local middle class, this organisation was able to operate quite successfully. The more so in the other constituencies where the miners dominated. In Bishop Auckland, the unions supplied the vote, Middlewood the patronage and the headmaster Davis acted as the link man between these groups and Dalton himself. Such an organisation (through the astute political and committee skills of these officials) became an extremely effective machine; capable of delivering the vote and of stamping out internal opposition and dissent.

In Durham, the Labour Party was established as an extension of the trade unions and in this the miners' unions were central. After 1918 (and with the single exception of 1931) constituencies on the coalfield were 'safe' for the Labour Party. Writing of this phenomenon Dalton put it like this:

> The greatest power in this great Durham Community are the

> Durham miners—stormtroopers in peace and war, in industry, in politics, in the armed forces and on the football field. They have a succession of leaders, many of whom have been my personal friends. I count conspicuous among these Peter Lee, W.P. Richardson, Jack Swan, Will Lawther and today Sam Watson. And among the many good men and true who have come from the Durham pits to parliament, I have known no two finer characters than Jack Lawson and Willy Whiteley.[76]

Dalton's list, which moves rapidly from the 'storm troopers' to their leaders, contained the key men who controlled the Durham Party machine in the inter-war period. They were the leaders of the most disciplined and organised group within the working class, a group which could guarantee both support and safe seats for the Labour Party. They could do so because that support was grounded in the mining village; the authority of these men drew upon the traditions of these communities and was backed by that nexus of institutions which gave them their name. The *political* fusion of party and the union with the *social* fusion of work, family, store and club produced a powerful system of officialdom. It was this system which created the Labour Party as a new route to power in the coalfields and in turn placed the miners in the centre of British policies. The careers of Sidney Webb and Hugh Dalton are testimony to the ways in which the legitimacy of this system could be conferred upon honoured outsiders. These men had none of the capacities necessary to organise the working class: they simply occupied positions that had been created by the trade unions and the ILP.

14
A Tory Seat

Everything is politics in this world and politics is, above all, a problem of legitimacy.

Carlos Fuentes

IN THE electoral record of the Durham County Labour Party there was one flaw. The Party had consistently failed to secure Arthur Henderson's old seat of Barnard Castle as a safe miners' seat. It is to this seat, but from the very different perspective of its Tory MP, Cuthbert Headlam, that we turn to provide further clues as to the changes that had taken place in Durham politics, as control was transferred from the Londonderry and Pease families to the DMA and the Labour Party. Headlam, like Dalton and Webb, was an outsider to the county and, like them, was an especially astute witness to the impact of the Labour Party on the coal owners and their interest in the county. Like his political opponents he kept a diary and was a close chronicler of the triumph of Labour in what he described as the 'miserable, miner-led County of Durham'.

Barnard Castle constituency covered an area of nearly 600 square miles, mostly in the foothills of the Pennine Range in the west of County Durham. Within it was farmland and coal mines; Weardale farmers and members of the DMA—different classes who lived entirely separate lives. The industrial, mining villages of Esh Winning, Quebec, and Langley Moor could not have been more different than the market towns of Barnard Castle, Stanhope and Middleton. In the past they had shared a common religion in Methodism and this had placed the constituency in the Liberal camp but this unity had been split with the assertion of the independence of working-class organisation and the extension of the electoral roll (in 1910 it stood at 12,212 and in 1918 at 19,949). In the 1918 election the farmers attempted to run their own National Farmers' Union candidate against the miners' candidate, J.E. Swan, a checkweighman. The Liberals lost and for the farmers this had meant coming to terms with the Conservative Party.

In the constituency, miners made up 40 percent of the population and, in any election involving more than two candidates, their votes determined the outcome. Barnard Castle was an exception—for whilst it could be won by the Tory Party, it could also be won by the Labour Party. The condition for the Tory victory was the withdrawal of the Liberal Party from the constituency; the condition for Labour a Liberal presence to split the Tory vote. Cuthbert Headlam won the seat without any Liberal intervention in 1924 but lost it in 1929 when the Liberals participated. In 1931 he won it again in the exceptional circumstances of the National Government election. In 1935 he was to lose it, again as a result of Liberal intervention.

The Making of a Tory MP

It has been said of Headlam's generation of Conservative MPs that:

> its enemy was Liberalism, and it was bitterly hostile to any version of the higher thinking. Its intention was sometimes traditional, sometimes paternalistic, occasionally English or Nationalistic, and in Chesterton's shadow, Christian.[1]

Cuthbert Headlam fits this bill exactly. Throughout the 1920s and 1930s he kept diaries which provide us with a unique and detailed account of what Cowling has termed a public doctrine: a 'loose combination of interlocking assumptions about politics, economics, science, scholarship, morality, education, aesthetics and religion which constitute the basis on which decisions are made about public matters.' Such a doctrine is fed from many sources and is expressed with varying degrees of openness and sophistication. 'It does not need to be articulated in order to be effective but it needs to be articulable when deep changes of direction suggest that articulation is desirable.'[2] Headlam's doctrine came out of his experiences in Durham where he witnessed the political decay of the coal interest in the county, and the rise of organised labour. He was both a representative of and witness to a declining segment of the dominant class in English society. His experience as an MP was constituted by an encounter with decadence, and his diaries reveal his innermost thoughts on this condition.

Cuthbert Headlam's one desire in life was to become a Conservative MP. It was, as he admitted in his diary on 29 September 1922, a strange ambition:

> I hanker after a public life and long to measure swords with all the vulgar and most second-rate people who throng the Houses of Parliament. It is odd because I see what a hollow mockery their whole performance is and how little worth is their world.[3]

It was at the relatively late age of forty-seven that he realised his ambition, when he was elected for the Labour-held constituency, Barnard Castle. The 1924 electoral return gave Headlam 9,465 votes and Turner-Samuels 9,152. On winning the seat, Headlam, the only Conservative MP in the county, took up permanent residence at Holywell just outside Durham City.

Headlam—or more formally, the Rt Hon. Cuthbert Morley Headlam—1st Bt, PC, DSO, OBE, TD of Holywell Durham—was born in 1876, the son of John Francis Headlam, a stipendiary magistrate of Manchester. He was educated at King's School, Canterbury and then at Magdalen College, Oxford, always describing himself as a 'Magdalen man'. On leaving Oxford in 1897 he became a clerk in the House of Lords. The twenty-three years of service that he was to provide for this institution he describes in his diary as years of 'ineffable boredom and futility'. They represented time spent in a 'lamentable hole'[4] from which he sought escape.[5] The war provided such an escape and his professional career was then with the military, one of the older of the state professions. He was a proud member of the 'officer class': Lieutenant-Colonel on the General Staff of the Bedfordshire Yeomanry. It was for these services that he was awarded the DSO in 1918 and the OBE in 1919. His connection with the Army was to continue through his appointment to the editorship of the *Army Quarterly*, a post he held for twenty-two years. He was also to write a two-volume *History of the Guards Division in the Great War.* He described this project in the typically romantic terms of a military officer:

> My task has merely been that of a faithful chronicler who, with a profound admiration for the heroes of whom he writes, sets down the events as they occurred throughout the campaign and by doing so hopes to give to his readers the true picture of the great deeds that were performed and the sufferings that were endured.[6]

Headlam's romantic inclinations also led him to publish, in 1922, an adventure novel called *Strange Delilah.* This was followed in 1934 by a similar novel called *A Knight Reluctant.* Both novels were published under the pseudonym, B.B. Unlike the heroes of his novels, Cuthbert Headlam was, on his own admission, a failure and judging by the scarcity of references to him in the biographies of his contemporaries, or in the political histories of the period, this judgement would seem to be correct. However, his diaries do provide us with an understanding of a member of the upper middle class in London and, after the war, as a Conservative MP in the Labour Party stronghold of County Durham. In them his own analysis of failure is painfully recorded against the background of the decay of the codes of his class.

Middlemas has described the paternalistic code that characterised this class and its world view, seeing it owing:

> conformity to a code, experienced from birth, in family upbringing and at school which was designed to inculcate a set of common assumptions about the position and role of the upper class in society, its historic mission of national leadership, and its relations with inferiors—the middle and working classes The code carried an obligation to live in a certain style, to spend, patronise the arts, encourage good farming, horsebreeding, to fill public offices without taking pay or perquisites, to serve in the armed forces in peace and war.[7]

In Durham, Headlam discovered a class that had broken the code. In the face of the political organisation of the miners—their 'inferiors'—landholdings and their coal ownership no longer guaranteed public office or promoted public service. Whilst they remained the social leaders and arbiters of 'taste' for county 'society' they no longer supplied the leadership of the county. In the face of this they had retreated to their own spheres of private splendour on their county estates. There was no longer any public honour, dignity or integrity in their presence in the county. They had created a society of deference and in face of opposition, ruptured it, rendering it futile.

It is not hard to see how on being thrust into the sealed world of Durham society this 'Magdalen man' discovered a place where things were deeply 'out of joint'. The Shakespearean reference is both revealing and appropriate. Images of Hamlet's plight in a rotten, corrupt court, where almost everything needs to be put right fit well with the state of affairs over which the Durham coal owners and the Conservative Party presided. That Headlam should, implicitly, cast himself in Hamlet's role ('O cursed spite that ever I was born to set it right') tells us a lot about him too; thrust as he was into a society that was 'a sorry place for the possessors' and where 'one has not even the consolation of feeling that things are much happier for the masses'.[8] Elsewhere John Galsworthy, the chronicler of upper-class decadence and another of Headlam's favourite authors, had referred to the same phenomenon as: 'The condition of England, that nightmare of its...public men.'[9] Headlam shared in and lived this nightmare. A 'nightmare' that was made real in claims made by the working class in the years following the First World War. It was this phenomenon that created that 'mood of disillusionment' in the upper classes and which in turn produced the ostentatious display of luxury by 'the men about town', those whom Headlam referred to as the 'Dandies' or, as Evelyn Waugh described them, 'the bright young things'. His disgust with these types (who 'seem to perform no useful function in life and are a perpetual reminder of the inequality and futility of society'), was complete.[10]

In Headlam's view, meaningful political change had to be a process of adjustment to the claims of the working class and its political party, the

Labour Party, and it was not possible that change could produce a better future for himself and his class. They contradicted Headlam's view of the social order and could not be legitimate for they in no way perfected the character of society. It was not that he held the character of that society to be perfect, indeed he presented it in the opposite way, but it could only be perfected through the established class relations: 'the introduction of the working man into the Government will not change the system of compromise...but rather extend the ladders of corruption.'[11] Social order existed to serve the needs of his particular class and to preserve his particular culture; any other needs could have no rational basis as they must necessarily threaten both. The giving way to such demands had to be resisted. This was the role, as he understood it, of the Conservative Party. Yet at the same time there also existed within British politics a will to accommodate, to 'give way', represented by Lloyd George and the Liberal Party, especially through the Liberal reforms of 1906–1914. Headlam thought these reformist actions had transformed the class relations of British society and had raised the expectations of the working class. This was the context of his sojourn in Durham, where he attempted to understand what could be maintained of his class and his culture in a world 'out of joint'. Or again in Galsworthy's words, 'what were they to hold on to in this modern welter of democratic principle'.[12]

It is perhaps ironic that Headlam moved to County Durham and a mining constituency for, in the years between 1919–25 it was here that Labour was most deeply established. Here, all that he stood for was under scrutiny and whilst this move was to energise him he was to be faced with a daunting political reality and one in which the local bourgeoisie and landowners were unlikely to rise to support. As a result, he became a public critic of Labour and a private critic of Durham 'society'.

Headlam moved to Durham at a time when the alignments of British politics were in a state of flux. In Durham the balance had been decided in favour of Labour. Nationally, however, this was not the case; Headlam decided that Labour had displaced the Liberals and that British politics would henceforth be conducted on class lines. In his view, Durham prefigured a national change and not just a local situation. As he noted in his diary on 11 December 1923: 'There is really no room for the Liberals nowadays, but it is difficult to get rid of them.'[13]

This opinion had been formed as a reaction to the national strikes of miners, railwaymen and dockers between 1918 and 1924; strikes had shown him that the demands of Labour were too great to be allowed to stay outside of the legitimate, political arena. He noted, 'they are better in, than out, of the House of Commons'.[14] Though this might be acceptable it also meant a necessary transformation of British politics and on 12 February 1924, he wrote: 'if MacDonald can keep in his wild men, the future before the Labourites is a bright one.'[15] A view not so much of a Tory reformer as of one who had come to recognise the realities of class politics.

Headlam had accepted the inevitability of the vast extension of the electoral roll in 1918, not because he was a democrat but because of expediency. In his view it was a claim that was impossible to resist, and a further product of being 'led by such damnably cowardly, vastly incompetent, and amazingly crooked statesmen.'[16] The major villain of the piece being Lloyd George: 'The little Welsh Wizard has proved himself to be England's curse.'[17] This 'curse of England' had not only raised the 'common man' by giving way to his demands, he had also raised their trade-union organisations to the level of bargaining with the state:

> How ridiculous it is that the Government itself now has to meet Labour directly—in the good old days the Government came in as an arbitrator—now Mr Pott and Mr Bloggs and Mr Smoggs, representing or claiming to represent many thousands of dull, harmless, working men are immediately brought face-to-face with the Prime Minister who should be too highly exalted a being to have truck with such microbes—and the very existence of HM's Government is in jeopardy the moment a few extremists decide to force a big strike. Such is nationalisation—such is the new order of things which makes anything like stable Government wholly impossible.[18]

Ridiculous or not, by 1919 Headlam recognised that this 'new order of things' had to be accepted and he was astute enough to apportion some of the blame upon the owners of industry. In a remarkably open statement for a man of his views and Party he privately advocated:

> Letting the work people know the true facts about business, explaining to them exactly how trade is run etc. It seems to me to be the only solution to the present impasse. It should lead to co-partnership and an era of some work and good trade—but of course some of these fools of employers won't see it.[19]

Headlam not only recognised that the 'distinction between employee and employer is too great' but also that such class distinction could lead to the 'great danger' of nationalisation.[20]

These projections were not a symptom of weakness but a balanced, commonsense recognition of what was possible, given the circumstances of a mass electorate and an organised working class. He remained well aware that in the last instance the political outcome of any particular struggle rested on the force of the state—and he was blunt about that too: 'Call it what you like, force must be the ruling intelligence.'[21] And: 'I doubt whether the moral force of the law would be very effective if it were not backed up by the material force of the police.'[22]

However, as a member of the upper class he was wary of using this power for he was fearful of the consequences. Better to carefully prepare for the integration of Labour into the political processes of the state. Thus he could declare that 'the world has gone mad'[23] and also calmly note that he had 'no objection to the [Labour] party as a party provided that we can keep it on commonsense ground.'[24]

For Headlam, the problem that Conservative politicians faced in the years following the First World War was one of organising and defining acceptable forms of rule in a situation where political equality was so blatantly contradicted by vast economic inequality. This meant that he accepted the legitimacy of the Labour Party even though he hated what it stood for. As a political man, sure of his own class role, he had risen with passion to offer his services to the state against the railway strikers in 1919:

> I telegraphed to Basil Thomson, this morning offering my services in any capacity—but I don't suppose they will be accepted. It is rather hard not to be in a position where I can do some good work—it is delightfully peaceful here, but one ought not to be lying fallow in this secluded haven of peace when the forces of disorder are so busy in the land. It is likely that every good man may be required—even an infirm old derelict like myself and it is not for Achilles to sulk in his tent even if he is not given a job worthy of his powers![25]

But in 1919 he was still cramped by the confining sterility of the House of Lords. There he serviced his class but in doing so suffered from complete boredom. There he played no determining role, but nursed the idea of becoming a parliamentary figure—doing a 'job worthy of his powers'. Industrial conflict had charged his class instinct and he longed to translate it into activity on the political stage. He was aware that he suffered handicaps such as the lack of a sufficient independent source of income to buy himself a candidature or the lack of good political contacts that could forward his career and because of these disadvantages he suffered setbacks in his attempt to get a recommendation in 1923. But, in the following year, on the invitation of Lord Barnard of Raby Castle, County Durham, he was offered the opportunity of fighting the marginal seat of Barnard Castle. The challenge was taken. Cuthbert Headlam moved north to take up what he later came to call 'the unequal fight against Labour'.

Barnard Castle

Headlam first visited the Barnard Castle constituency in June 1924 as a guest of Lord Barnard. His first impressions of the constituency were not hopeful:

> We visited several of the mining villages and the gloominess of the pit managers we saw was very disheartening. They clearly think that it is a hopeless business to try and induce the miners to vote for me. In some places seemingly a man dare not admit that he is a Conservative. There is no one to help one—I mean no local gentry. The clergymen are usually socialists and the few people who are not Labour are Liberal.[26]

Fortunately for Headlam, the Liberals were not putting up a candidate. Even so, he recognised the impossibility of winning the miners' vote for, as he put it, 'the grip of the trade union is too strong upon them and the moral obligation to vote with their class is a strong one for the majority of men'.[27] Headlam's task then was to 'give courage' to the coal owners and to those outside of the mining industry. This prospect he viewed with some distaste as he had no sympathy for the practices of the coal owners of the county. He felt that 'as long as coal mining existed...no one could really do anything to make the lives of the miners more agreeable'. Good management practices and sound political judgement could have alleviated the situation but in Durham the 'business methods' of the coal owners had merely aggravated the miserable condition of their workers.[28] As he saw it, it was the coal owners of this and previous generations who were responsible for the divided political condition that the county found itself in. He noted that:

> all this unrest would never have occurred if only the employers had behaved better to their own people in the past.[29]

As he came to know the coal owners better he was to push this view further, arguing that, 'If big employers are so dull and unforthcoming they must expect to be dispossessed.'[30] In facing his first election therefore, he was already distanced from the people he was to represent, and upon whose support he would (as a Tory in Durham) need to rely heavily.

This distancing was necessary. Gone were the days when coal owners could directly represent their interests in parliament. The Pease family had virtually owned the seats of South Durham up until 1880. Even after the electoral re-organisation in 1884 Barnard Castle had remained in the family until Henderson's victory in 1903. In the election of 1880, two coal owners, Pease and Lambton, plus Surtees, a major landowner in the county, stood for election in the two seats of Durham South. But the bitterness in the coalfield after 1910, the separation of working-class organisations from their Liberal links and the 1918 Electoral Reform Act had changed all that. It was now no longer possible for a coal owner to stand and be elected. The political conditions required them to be represented by men, such as Headlam, with no interest in the county and no financial interest in coal.

The coal owners and landowners had been removed from what they had considered their natural political functions by organised labour. Now they, like Labour, required other people to represent them. Where they had once made politics a part of their natural leadership of the county, they now needed to deal with people who made politics a career. Headlam's tie to these families was not through the interest of coal; they were the ties of class and its institutions of politics, church and army. As such he could distance himself from the coal owners; he could also resent them for their direct withdrawal from politics, and for their role in stimulating the independence of Labour. But, in a real sense, he was to be their MP and as such he remained trapped in the circumstances which *they* had created. The further their confidence was sapped, the harder *he* had to struggle. His was an overwhelming task—one of constructing a popular basis for Conservatism in a district split between the interests of the coal owners and organised miners and farmers who continued to hold strongly to their Liberal sympathies.[31]

The absence of a Liberal candidate guaranteed Headlam's success in 1924. But it was a rough ride. He had witnessed the 'violent socialism' of the women and he had been shouted down at meetings in Quebec, Cornsay Colliery, Burnhope and Langley Park. His diary makes us aware of the background of 'cowardice' of the mine owners; the weakness of their public support and the narrowness of their social vision; something which was made most clear in their failure to articulate the philosophy of Conservatism as a philosophy of the propertied class as a whole. He had won nonetheless, and it was not only his victory, it was also a class victory. His 'heart was full'. He noted in his diary:

> People in the South can have little idea of what a victory such as we have had up here means to all our party in a region such as this. We have been so long the underdogs that the change of atmosphere one now sees is not surprising. 'We can hold our heads up now!' said one man—'we can just laugh at them', said another, 'we can say what we think and snap our fingers at them down the pit' etc. etc. It is very satisfactory.[32]

The satisfaction was to be shortlived. In his first year of office the crisis in the coal industry nearly resulted in a general strike. His was *not* going to be a safe seat. Unlike Webb and Dalton he was a career politician who had to live in his constituency.

As a Tory MP, Headlam found that he received little help from Durham Society and its leading families—the 'upper ten' of the county. Only two months after the election he had decided that it was 'hopeless to expect any help from the bigger people up here'.[33] This, however, complicated his task for building up Conservatism as a force in the area. In his experience in the villages 'the little people are not fit to run themselves and immediately start quarrelling if they have no leaders who are socially their superiors'.[34] He noted the rough equality of village life, and saw this to lie at the root of the tragedy:

> there is no natural leader—therefore, each individual is always striving for the leadership with the consequent result that they are all at sixes and sevens.[35]

Headlam recognised that his position as a Conservative MP in a mining district was one of impotence but, as we have seen, it was a measure of his own failure that he had been forced to take such a seat at all.

Headlam's impotence was clearly expressed in local Conservative politics. These were 'led' by Lord Londonderry, a figure who did not rank in the Conservative Party nationally. In the opinion of J.C.C. Davidson, National Chairman of the Party, Londonderry:

> had the reputation of being a rather soft, regency-beau type of man. Although he had a certain amount of cunning and capacity, he was not really equipped for thinking. As a mine owner in Durham he had quite a good reputation, but people who were his agents were regarded as a pretty hard lot. He was never really fit for Cabinet rank....But Londonderry took himself very seriously and that was in a sense tragedy, because others didn't take him at all seriously....He owed his preferment really to the fact that Ramsay MacDonald greatly enjoyed standing at the top of the great staircase in Londonderry House, as the first Minister of the Crown, in full evening dress.[36]

In 1919 Londonderry encouraged the local Conservative Party organisation in its attempt to change from an exclusive party of notables and social superiors. We have seen how organisations like the Primrose League had been developed to this end. However as a general strategy these groups lacked the coherence and organised strength of the miners' lodges and this strategy failed as the Party lost the control of Durham County Council to Labour. For local elections from then on, the Tory Party was disbanded and presented itself under the banner of the 'Moderate Party'.[37] This new party was set up with offices in Old Elvet, Durham City, on 9 August 1921, and held its first meeting on 5 September of that year. The organisations contributing to it were the Durham County Unionist Association, the Anti-Nationalisation Society, the Durham and North Yorkshire Federated Chambers of Trade, the Middle Classes Union, the National Farmers' Union (Durham County Branch) and the North Eastern Area Coalition Liberals. In spite of this fusion with the Liberals, and the clear backing from regional business interests, the party lacked organisation. Officers for the 'Moderate Party' were drawn from the organisation of the Conservative Party. Whilst Londonderry remained simply President of the Conservatives, the position of President of the new party was taken up by W.E. Pease, of the

Pease family, who was chairman of the Conservatives. His Party Chairman was another coal owner—Stobart—who was vice-chairman of the Conservatives. Another prominent Conservative held the post of treasurer—J.H.B. Forster, colliery agent of the Weardale Iron Company—so the Moderate Party was, in effect, the public front for the Conservatives. The organisational aims of the new Party were formulated in response to the strength of the Labour Party in the county. Point 7 of the Constitution declared:

> Propaganda work to be anti-socialist and in advocacy of the necessity of supporting 'Moderate Candidates' in local affairs but not to advocate the claims of any political party.[38]

In Point 11 the object was made quite clear:

> The County Committee to take all possible steps to prevent any split in the anti-socialist vote through the nomination of more than one anti-socialist candidate.[39]

The Moderate Party was the sole organiser of opposition to the new Durham Labour Party formed only one year earlier at the Miners' Hall at Redhills. Established in defeat it was to have little success.

In 1924 the Moderate Party received most of its funds from the coal owners and the brewers. In that year the coal owners donated over £2,500 and the brewers £770. Other contributors included the North-East Coast Engineering Trade Employers' Association, and the North-East Coast Ship Repairers' Association. Up until 1925, when it appointed three, the organisation had no full time officials and, unlike the Labour Party, they did not pay their own councillors. Professionalisation of the party machine had hardly begun.[40] Apart from a single victory in the 1922 County Council election the Moderates were overwhelmed locally by the Labour Party. Throughout the inter-war period they attempted to reorganise their own base through the encouragement of local ratepayers' associations but even this proved unsuccessful. After 1925 their officers were admitting that they could never seriously expect to win the County Council again. The minutes of the organisation refer repeatedly to 'difficulties in the coal trade' being the main reason for their failure. Unlike the Labour Party, the new Moderate Party was not a modern, centralised, disciplined machine which could automatically mobilise for victory; it remained a party of the 'old order', one that was dominated by the propertied families of Durham. This, combined with the absence of a middle class which would have served as the organising base in the county, meant there was little possibility of expansion. Durham (along with South Wales, Yorkshire and the East End of London), became known as no-man's land in the Conservative Party. In all four areas indigenous Conservative Party organisation became simply ritualised affairs with little impact on local politics.

It was out of necessity then that Headlam became involved with the Moderate Party and represented them as a member of Durham County Council from 1931. His verdict on the Party was that it was: 'a fraud because it was wrong to say it was not political.'[41] Furthermore, he: 'took strong exception to keeping alive the Liberal Party, which possessed no real live organisation.'[42]

Nationally, the fortunes of the Conservative Party seemed healthier, and as an MP, Headlam (like Webb and Dalton) records the complex inter-relationship between national and local events. In 1925 he notes that the ability of the government to stand up to a general strike (in his view brought about by the bad tactics of the coal owners) was not clear and therefore should not be risked. On 28 July he recorded:

> My own opinion is that a strike should be avoided—because it would be such a costly draw on our financial resources and its consequences could not be gauged—at the same time I am convinced that if Parliamentary Government is to be retained in this country, a stern fight will have to be fought against trade union dictation.[43]

On the offer of a subsidy for the miners the strike was avoided but for Headlam (as for everybody in the coal industry) this was only a stop gap. He noted:

> a subsidy is a subsidy by whatever name you choose to call it. Still a subsidy will cost less than a strike and one could not have risked a general upheaval of Labour (and presumably that was inevitable) without being convinced that the great mass of public opinion was against the miners.[44]

Locally, however, his impression of the coal owners was further diminished. Following the crisis he noted:

> Here we have come and won the seat for them and here we are gallantly fighting their battles for them against overwhelming odds—and scarcely anyone of them has gone out of his way to offer us any civility or to help us in any way. Truly they deserve to be left to stew in their own juice—to be beggared and put down by their work people. Indeed I don't see that the majority of them are worth keeping. Every day that passes I realise more and more that they have had their day and, if only there were anything better to put in their place, I should resign the unequal task of defending them.[45]

But his contempt for the coal owners is not matched by his recognition of any of the claims of the miners: he saw himself representing the class interests of the owners which, at critical moments, involved being against the miners. For the reasoning that lay behind this stance we have to return to the national focus. Headlam put it this way: 'it is because one believes in existing institutions and the social system under which one lives that one wishes it to survive.'[46] However much he resented them personally as individuals or as a group, they nonetheless represented capital and the interest of private property. The coal crisis, which had been brought to a head by the resistance of the miners, had raised doubts about the status of their private property and by extension about 'existing institutions' generally.[47] In 1925 these institutions survived through compromise and subsidy; in 1926 it was to be the defeat of the miners through lock-out. On both occasions the existing social system withstood the 'threat', yet paradoxically such threats tended to confirm the view that, in the case of coal, private ownership was necessarily coming to an end.

During the 1926 strike Headlam's view was clear: it was a fight against the extremists—a question of the supremacy of parliament or trade unionism. Yet he recognised that to defeat the General Strike would not defeat the miners; they would remain as a class on the coalfields and the problems of the industry would remain unsolved. This view was sustained as the miners stayed out, refusing to go back on the owners' adjusted terms. On 24 May 1926 he noted in his diary, that:

> I can see no way out of this coal mess except some form of Government interference in the management of the pits—and I don't see how that is going to solve the problem.[48]

This consideration of state regulation of the mines was not a positive recommendation but rather a solution of despair. Nevertheless, it records a process of adjustment on Headlam's part to the changes in the organisation and regulation of the economy brought about by the class struggle of the inter-war period. His diary entry for Saturday, 17 July gives further testament to this view:

> The coal business has taken the guts out of our people—and no wonder. The situation appears hopeless and the Labour crowd is growing more and more bitter in this part of the world—and more objectionable. It is a bad state of things and one can really do little or nothing to make things happier for our unfortunate supporters in the mining area. It is a humiliating position.[49]

It was also a position which Headlam realised could not be restored even if the miners were defeated. His reflections on the end of the strike make this point very clear:

> It has been a sorry business throughout—a political business—nothing more nor less than an attempt by Cook and his friends to ruin the industry and force nationalisation on the government. If only this failure would lead to peace—and politics could be kept

out of the business. All this loss of money and the inevitable trade depression might have been worth while. But my own opinion is that we have not got through our troubles yet and that the working men have not learnt their lesson—why should they have learnt it when day in and day out they are being taught to believe that once they can down the employers they will live in peace and contentment, and earn good money—or be given it—whether they work or remain idle?[50]

In Headlam's opinion therefore, the miners' defeat had not solved the problem and nor could state control. In his view it was the enforcement of the workers' subordination that was at stake. If private capital could not achieve this given the demands of the miners, could state control achieve it?

It is all very well saying that the men's attitude would be quite different if the state ran the industries: it would not because their only idea of state control is that it would bring with it higher wages and shorter hours—and this is clearly out of the question.[51]

After two years in Durham, Headlam had been educated by local circumstances to see the necessity for state control but at the same time could not grasp its mode of operation. Both emotionally and intellectually he rejected it.

But in 1929, he was himself rejected by the electors of Barnard Castle, thanks to the intervention of a 'psalm-singing' Liberal candidate. Headlam lost the seat to Will Lawther, the miners' Labour candidate:

It was a bitter blow because we had hoped (and until yesterday had believed) that we should pull it off. The Liberals did the trick. Their wretched man polled over 4,000 votes, the majority of which in a straight fight would have come to me and put me in by a '4 figure' majority. As things were Lawther won by about 800 votes.[52]

In defeat, Headlam at least had the satisfaction of knowing that it was the Labour candidate Lawther, rather than the Liberal Spence, 'the fat unctuous town councillor from Middlesbrough', who went to parliament. With this victory, however, the Labour Party was dominant as local and parliamentary representatives of County Durham.

The eclipse of the Conservative Party in the area led to considerable tensions in relations between the local organisation and Conservative Party Central Office. Lady Londonderry, writing to J.C.C. Davidson in her capacity as President of the Northern Area in 1929, asserted bitterly that her husband and herself ran the Party and:

Considering it is I who organised the Ball which produced all the money for the anti-socialist campaign in the north, and that it is

> to my husband that you owe everything in these quarters, the only time there has been a failure was in the last election when the Central Office ran the Campaign and they lost nearly every seat. I do not accuse the Central Office nationally of any intentional discourtesy but of gross ignorance in the management of affairs of this sort.[53]

While Headlam might have agreed publicly with Lady Londonderry, in private he had supported Central Office. As his diary reveals he did not see the Londonderry family presenting a viable basis for Toryism on the coalfield.

> There is no doubt about it that one must be a confirmed optimist to try and be a Conservative leader up here—if only one could count upon a keen body of followers, their lack in quantity would not matter so much—but when one's followers are so cowardly, apathetic and disgruntled as they are in Durham one is inclined to lose heart and to tell them all to go to hell. Even the so-called leaders—Northumberland, Londonderry, Alexander Leith, etc., only seem to care about themselves and their own dignity—there appears to be no loyalty to a cause or enthusiasm—what chance have we against the well-disciplined forces of Labour?[54]

In the wake of political defeat, Headlam began a new phase of his career—concentrating on the search for directorships. For all his criticisms of business and a professed lack of knowledge of business affairs, to live and retain his political life he needed directorships and he was prepared to use what influence he had in the north to gain them.

Five days after the election results were announced he was offered and accepted a director's seat on the board of the Timber Trust. Directorships on the boards of the Brankford Power Company, the Priestman Power Company and the Newcastle Electricity Supply Co. Ltd followed.[55] Yet principally Headlam remained a politician and in 1931 he was to return to the political arena by fighting three elections. In March he presented himself for the County Council elections as a member of the Moderate Party and was elected with a majority of 795. In June he fought and lost Gateshead in a by-election and then in the National Government election of the same year he stood once again for Barnard Castle and was successful in a straight contest with Will Lawther. With this, Headlam began what were to be his last four years as a Conservative MP in Durham. It saw him remain as a political activist in the county during the critical years of the 1930s. In this time his view of his political masters became more and more acerbic. In 1940 he stood successfully as an Independent Tory to represent West Newcastle and remained in the House of Commons until 1951.

15
The Beginning of the End

The Crisis consists precisely in the fact that the old is dying and the new cannot be born; in this interregnum a great variety of morbid symptoms appear.

A. Gramsci

IN THEIR epic strike in 1926 the coal miners were defeated. In Durham, the miners never voted to return to work. Nationally the position became untenable and across the coalfield 'it ended; it just ended.' But its effects were enormous. Union activists were blacklisted, and men returned to work demoralised and disorganised. Fenwick Whitfield describes the strike's end at the Eden Colliery near Consett.

> We'd been out seven months [and] I remember the final meeting prior to signing on for the pit at the Miners' Hall. Everybody was that eager in case they didn't get a job. When it came to the time that they were released from the meeting to fall in and march away and go down to the pit in an orderly manner, they smashed the doors off the meeting room in their hurry to get out. When I saw that I said: 'Well that's the finish as far as Fenwick is concerned.' So I went and sat on the platform of the hall and watched the struggle. Then I went out and turned down to the house, and the first person I met was the wife. She said 'Where are you going?' I said 'I'm going home for my tea'. 'But,' she said 'they're all signing on.' 'Ah, but I'm not going with them; I'm not going along with a mob like that, even if I never work again. We've managed seven months, we've struggled through. I'm going back decently when I do go back.' So I went home and had my tea, and then walked up to see what was going on. Well, they were around there, all milling around. So I said 'to hell with them and their pit!' I didn't go in until the next day. I went to the office and the manager was sitting there. And there was a policeman there—I don't know whether they were afraid of the boss being attacked! 'Come in' the boss said 'You've been a long

> time coming along, Fenwick—I'm sorry I've nothing for you.' But seven days time I was sent for, and I was stuck at the pit ever since.[1]

In many collieries far fewer men were rehired than began the strike. At the Langley Park Colliery only a thousand of the 1,800 work force was re-employed.[2] At the Waterhouses pit of Pease and Partners, young men were forced to migrate to the company's more prosperous collieries in South Yorkshire. In many villages managers recruited in a way which settled old scores, as militant miners and those active in the strike were turned away.

George Bestford recalls how:

> It was hard for a 'politician' to get a job....If he was a 'politician' he had to keep it under his cap, because if it once got out that he was an agitator, and fighting for better conditions, there was no chance of a job for him. There were a lot of good workers who never worked after the 1926 strike, you know. In fact I had an uncle who was involved in the 1921 strike and never worked another day in the pit again. Anyone who was a bit of an agitator couldn't get a job in the pit.[3]

During the strike Chopwell village had maintained its reputation as 'The Reddest Village in England'.[4] In June 1925 the lodge officials had argued strenuously against the new pay and conditions approved by the Consett Iron Company. A strike ensued affecting all the collieries owned by the company, and this lasted until March 1926. At that time the DMA officials recommended a settlement, but again the Chopwell Lodge refused to accept the terms, and in a ballot the miners agreed rejecting the offer by 1,100 votes to 286. The pit remained on strike until the onset of the national dispute. In March 1926, the Consett Iron Company complained bitterly about the leadership of the lodge, and the level of poor relief provided by the local guardians: 'as long as payment of relief is made, the men will not go back to work, even though work is available in as good, if not better terms than are being worked at many collieries in the country.'[5] In November 1926, they had the opportunity to take issue with the local lodge officials; at that time, and in spite of the poor relief:

> the miners' deprivation forced them to submit, as on previous occasions....The men were forced to accept worse terms than they had been offered in March 1925. They were now asked to work eight hours at the face and piece work rates were reduced. The Consett Iron Company, like the coal owners in general, showed no mercy towards the leaders of the strike. Jack Gilliland, Chairman of the lodge, was not restarted, and the company refused to meet him on union business because he did not work at the pit. None of the Lawther brothers were given work: Eddie

moved to Kent, Herby joined the local bus company, while Andy and his younger brother Jack emigrated to Canada. Henry Bolton and Vipond Hardy remained unemployed. Trade unionism suffered a setback; in the enginemen's union there were seventy-three members before the strike and only four afterwards. The miners' union suffered a similar fate in Chopwell. In 1927, Jack Gilliland was appointed full-time secretary to co-ordinate what remained of the union.[6]

The attacks upon the new militant trade union leadership would continue in the years that followed, as would attempts (locally and nationally) to curtail the control which miners and their sympathisers had obtained over the level and distribution of relief.

These attacks were not restricted to Chopwell, or to the centres of militancy in the north. They appear to have been quite general. Kibblesworth, for example, was known as a 'moderate' village; yet in November 1926 their leaders, and others who had actively supported the strike, received firm treatment from the local company.

> When the General Strike finished there were some sad days ahead for some families, as none of the men who had taken an active part in the Labour movement got their work back again.... Those families who were victimised—that's the only word you can use to describe what happened—were forced to leave their homes. Families like the Loweries, the Potts, the Bouchers, the Armstrongs and many more were forced to get out of the village—families who had been born and bred in Kibblesworth were put out onto the streets.[7]

This account blames the power of the manager George Strong ('you had to live in a colliery village...to understand the power he had'). It also shows that Primitive Methodists were victimised, while Wesleyan Methodists maintained their alliance with the employers. In the view of Charlie Pick (a union activist in this part of the Durham coalfield) the 1926 strike and its aftermath 'marked the end of Methodism's influence in the union. After that no Methodist won an election for office in Durham.'

In Chopwell, Hilda Ashby remembered how her 'father was a member of the Labour Party, but he and a lot of people became disillusioned. Not that they'd ever vote Tory, but with all the strikes they became disheartened.'[8] Her husband Henry recalled how, at the pit:

> on bad cavils you couldn't earn anything. You were working on the minimum. The minimum rate was about seven shillings, and the piece rates were so low that you had to work very hard to earn more than that seven shillings. A lot of men in bad places couldn't get near the seven shillings. And so it was left to the colliery manager, and he could say to them: 'You haven't worked

> hard enough so you are not going to get the minimum. You're only going to get what you've really earned according to the piece work rate.' Which meant four, or five, or six shillings. And every Friday night there was a queue at the manager's office—men who hadn't earned enough to earn the minimum....You had to go begging, cap in hand, to ask him, to plead with him saying you'd worked as hard as you can so could you have the minimum rate. Men used to dread that...it was heartbreaking to see the men on the minimum begging at the manager's office.

In these changed circumstances, the employers were able to use the cavilling system to force down the wage rate and their overall wages bill.

> At the end of three months, with the new cavils, you'd have a revision of prices. And if someone had worked hard, and been at a good place and earned say fifteen shillings a day, that was too much. They'd chop the rate, take threepence or tuppence a ton off that place and put it on a place where they were earning four shillings a day. You knew it wouldn't make any difference because the men wouldn't get above the minimum anyway. So altogether you'd earn less for the same work.
>
> The union was so weak then, you see. They used to ride rough shod over them. There was no fear of the men going on strike again after they'd been flattened down in the 1926 stoppage. There was no possibility of the men being about to resist.[9]

This was the dominant response by the Durham coal owners in the 1930s. Another miner remembers how he was sacked by Bolckow Vaughan, the owners of the Dean and Chapter Colliery, for hitting a blackleg during the 1926 strike.

> When the pit got started up the undermanager was prepared to take me on, but the manager said 'no: he's been interfering with one of my men.' He wouldn't allow it. The dole was only eighteen shillings a week. You had to sign on on a Wednesday and paid out on Friday. A lot of weeks you didn't get it. You had to go to this colliery; go to that colliery and show you'd been looking for work. This day, we went over the Sherburn Hill and we went into the institute—that's the Reading Room you know—to talk with some of the lads, pit lads. I said we've been sent over by the dole; they want some hand putters. 'By lad—don't go, don't go. They're taking on two or three a day and they're all packing it in. It's bad work—tubs that catch on the top, tubs that catch on the side. Up to your knees in water' 'Oh Ay' I said 'but we've got no chance of getting the dole at all.' The boss had to sign your card you see. Well we went to see the boss and he said 'you're the likely lads. I want some hand putters', and

> I daren't say no. Then he said 'Where do you belong'—'Spennymoor: Bishop Auckland way.' So he said 'are you fixed up for lodgings?' Well the women weren't taking any lodgers. And I didn't blame them. Lads were coming there on the Friday and getting set on. The women would keep them for the weekend, for nought, and on the Monday they'd leave. Because of the job. The boss said 'you cannot travel.' So he ummed and ahed. I think they called him Mr Foster. I said 'Mr Foster will you do us a good turn' just like that you know. 'Sign your name to say that we've been.' 'Eh,' he said 'you've put me in a funny hole...I want lads. But if you cannot get lodgings it's impossible. You cannot travel...I'll be shot at dawn.' And that's how we got away from Sherburn.
>
> Shortly after that a drift started—just over the ridge from Ferrybank. And that's where I got a start. That pit worked just in the winter months. In the summer months—about May—he couldn't sell his coal. He used to take it around the streets in a pony and cart. Then the back end of October he'd want the men again. Give them a start. You always had your summer holidays! He just wanted you in the winter months so he could get shot of his coals.

This practice of irregular work and intermittent colliery closures became quite general in Durham, especially after the major slump in trade in 1930. It applied to the small drifts and mines in the west, and also to the largest of the county's collieries. Kit Robinson remembers how 'between 1924 and 1934 there were colliery closures all across the county.' He was brought up in West Auckland:

> and my father and three brothers were working at the St Helens pit and I was working at West Auckland. The St Helens pit was owned by Pearce and Partners and West Auckland by Bolkow Vaughan. In those days they just gave you a fortnight's notice, and you had to vacate your colliery house. They were hard times. This was before the big strike mind. The St Helens pit closed in 1924, and we all decided that we would try to get a start at Horden or Easington. In the end Easington sent word for us. In those days if you had two or three workers you could get a job—if there was only one of you they didn't want you; they wanted a family.

They started 'as a family' at Easington Colliery. After the 'big strike' Kit remembers how:

> Easington was the funniest pit in the world. It never closed down but it didn't run regularly for over ten years. I remember I was married in 1933 and the first wages I drew were 23s 9d. The pit had only worked three shifts and with my 'off takes' I had 23s 9d.

> And I was always one of the big wage group. If you were making 11s or 12s a day you were on a big wage.

Others recall how the company alternated the production from its various seams in relation to the demand for different kinds of coals. The colliery hooter would blast out once, twice, three times depending upon which seam was about to work the following day and which of the miners would be employed.

'Worms, Fools and Cowards'

So intense had been the antagonisms unleashed by the 1926 strike that what remained of the traditions of paternalism in the county could not be sustained. In some villages paternalism's darker side showed itself, in exclusion through the black list, and the introduction of harsh punishment for recalcitrants. Dick Beavis started at the Dean and Chapter Colliery in 1928 as a boy of fourteen. He recalls with feeling how:

> It was private enterprise then in its most ruthless form. It was coal, King Coal and the devil take the hindmost. If anyone got lamed then, hurt or anything, the only bandages that were kept were at the shaft bottom. So you had to tear a man's shirt to bandage him. And if there was a fall of stone you can bet your life the man would come and say 'How is the pony?' It wasn't the men it was the pony. As a kid I used to think that there ought to be police down the pit to see some of the things that went on. It was terrible under private enterprise in the 1930s...terrible....You were penalised from going down to coming out....To me you were nothing else but wage slaves.[10]

Another option was open to the employers in Durham however. Given the breakaway of the Nottinghamshire trade union under Spencer, the Durham owners could have sponsored a new paternalism linked to a Spencerist 'non-political' union, a strategy which was adopted with some success in South Wales.

In Nottinghamshire, the Spencer Union was vigorously supported by the coal owners. In an odd way they repeated the nineteenth-century experience of the Durham coal owners. Political and economic paternalism became dominant. The breakaway Spencer Union was recognised, and developed by the owners in the expanding new coalfield to the north of Nottingham, known as the Dukeries. In 1927 the *New Statesman* wrote:

> The balance of power in the mining industry is shifting inevitably from South Wales and Durham to South Yorkshire and the Dukeries. The foundations of the most important and profitable coalfield in Great Britain are being laid down with an enormous

> emphasis on the 'Butty system', on company unionism, on the company village. A new industrial foundation is being erected in the Dukeries side by side with which Trade Unionism can at present find no place.[11]

Yet this 'new system' clearly recalls aspects of the old 'Durham system'—a monopoly of employment in isolated villages, company housing, and a paternalistic domination of village society.

Between 1918 and 1928 seven new mines were sunk in the Dukeries. This coalfield, along with its extension into South Yorkshire, was the most productive and profitable in the country. Again, it involved the industrialisation of a previously rural area where the land was owned in the form of aristocratic estates. In Nottinghamshire the Dukes of Newcastle and Portland Saville were the principal land owners. Though this landed nobility did not involve themselves directly in production, and relied on coal royalties, the coal companies deliberately sought not to disturb the local political arrangements:

> the coal owners' model villages were characterised by a respect among the miners for the aristocratic hierarchy, a respect encouraged by the companies themselves who had every reason to preserve the principle of due order and degree.[12]

The Marquess of Tichfield remained the Conservative MP for Newark throughout the inter-war period. In the villages of the Dukeries the Conservative Party established its own branches, led by company officials' wives. In local elections their representative or an independent was returned. Not until 1943 did the Labour Party manage to establish itself within this system.

The company villages of the Dukeries can be seen as sophisticated versions of the old Durham system. Employment at the pit was a condition of occupation, the companies ran their own shops and pubs and, as in Durham, the companies helped to build churches of all denominations. They sponsored cricket and soccer teams, horticultural associations and prize colliery bands. Order was maintained in the villages of the Butler Coal Company by a uniformed company police. Neither the union nor the Labour Party were allowed to operate in the villages, as it was not possible to book rooms for meetings. The split in the Nottinghamshire Miners' Association over the continuation of the 1926 General Strike allowed the owners to open up a new part of the coalfield and provide critical support for Spencer's new union. All miners who signed on in the new Dukeries pits were required to join the new union, and union dues were deducted from wages.

The new 'non-political' union spread through the British coalfields. Branches were established in Durham, first at the East Tanfield pit and then at the Esh Winning colliery in December 1926, where it took the name of the Esh Winning Miners' Industrial (non-political) Society, and explicitly barred funds from being used for political purposes. More significant, perhaps, a branch was formed in Chopwell. In January 1927, branches of the non-political trade union were established at Eden Colliery and St Hilda Colliery. The union (the Northumberland and Durham Miners' Non-Political Association—NDMNPA) claimed a membership of 10,500 on formation, rising to 14,000 in forty branches across Northumberland and Durham in April. These figures were much higher than those reported by the Chief Registrar of Friendly Societies, who reported membership at 3,911 in 1928, rising to 4,081 in 1929 and falling slightly in 1931 to 4,068.[13]

The new union was successful in the north-west of Durham, where it was supported by several coal companies. However, it failed to secure the support of the Durham Coal Owners' Association. Whilst the Consett Iron Company had given support, Pease and Partners refused to recognise it where it emerged in its collieries. Equally, Lord Londonderry had responded to a circular issued by Havelock Wilson, in the north-east, calling for £30,000 to establish non-political district mining unions, by giving £50 as a contribution, adding that this subscription should not be publicised for fear of antagonising the DMA. Cuthbert Headlam, who had been giving strenuous support to the new union, was appalled by the attitude of the coal owners.

> This morning I went into Newcastle—I saw Mr Duncan, the non-political union secretary at Armstrong's office. After a very gallant fight he has come to the end of his tether and cannot carry on much longer—the question is what is to be done? Old Sir George Hunter is ready to go on helping him if other people will also help—but in my opinion it is hopeless to expect anything of the Newcastle businessman or Durham coal owner. If they would not support the union when it started, still less likely are they to do so now that it is to all intents and purposes down and out. Besides they waste their money in running the Economic League which they fondly imagine is converting the masses to sound Capitalist ideas—I cannot see Mr Duncan pass out—and yet I cannot see what I can do to help him—it worries me.[14]

Mr Duncan and the non-political union did 'pass out', and its failure in Durham is interesting. For Headlam, the post-1926 period confirmed his view that to operate as a Tory on the Durham coalfield one had to be 'an optimist or a fool'. His view, continuously expressed in his diaries, is of a class of coal owners who:

> have made all the trouble for themselves—they and their fathers—and they will not see that their only chance of redeeming the

> situation is by vigorous political action and themselves getting down to it.[15]

Such an appeal proved hopeless in the early 1920s. After 1926, Headlam's view of the owners (as 'worms, fools, cowards, etc.') was simply confirmed. They would not act decisively. They would not entertain the risks involved in the struggle to establish a new union in the county. They were clearly aware of the formidable institutional structures that the DMA had built over sixty years. Even in the wake of a terrible defeat, the framework of the union remained intact, and with it its political grip on the county. In 1928, the DMA in Chopwell took legal action against the company for agreeing a wage reduction with the new union. This made clear its determination to resist the emergence of a 'blackleg union'. Recruitment to the NDMNPA was never as great as publicised, and even the publicised figures were quite small, especially in the large and critical collieries in the north and east of the coalfield. The result was an impasse. Investment in the Durham coal mines lagged behind the other major coalfields. Cuthbert Headlam was an inside observer of these changes. He had arrived in Durham at the end of the political dominance of a socially archaic landed class. The ownership of coal had refreshed the landed class with a fresh injection of wealth, and so preserved their social prestige, customs, traditions and even their rural lifestyles for over a century. But the passage of time had worn thin their paternalist claims. Their presence as the leading figures in the new and unsuccessful Moderate Party combined with their lack of parliamentary representation had rendered them politically redundant. The landowners no longer ruled politically, their coalfield was old (after 1918 only one new coal mine opened), and the industry suffered from both under investment and mass unemployment.

As this decline accelerated, so did Headlam's assessment harden. In 1926 he strongly supported the non-political union, and vehemently opposed nationalisation, which he thought of as conceding power to the trade union. By 1932, however, his views had changed. To put it more accurately, they had been changed by his experience of the Durham coal owners. As he wrote in his diary:

> There never were such difficult people to try and help as coal owners—and my own impression is that they are individually too much obsessed with their own particular interests to ever take a broad view of the industry as a whole. Many of them, too, are sick and tired of trying to compete with modern conditions of Labour, etc., and political changes, and would be only too glad to get out of the whole business if they could be adequately compensated. Sooner or later, therefore, it seems to me that some form of nationalisation of the industry is quite certain.[16]

In Headlam's view, the coal owners were finished, and they acted as if they were. However, their farewells would take a painful decade and more.

The 1930s

In the General Election of 1929 it seemed as if the consequences of the General Strike had been clearly resolved in favour of the Labour Party and the working classes (though as Pimlott has noted, the election result 'seemed to establish what was to become a trend' of Labour governments inheriting economic crises). In Durham it seemed as if Peter Lee's faith in democracy had been sustained. Seven miners' candidates were returned as Labour MPs from Durham constituencies, and although the local press reported 'very little interest' in the campaign, the vote for the Labour Party was overwhelming.

In Seaham, Ramsay MacDonald replaced Sidney Webb as the leader of the Labour Party. A.J. Cook supported him, and he was returned with a majority of 28,794. The Communist Harry Politt stood as a part of a campaign which had built up around the strike at the Dawdon Colliery. He lost his deposit, as did the Liberal candidate, and this seemed to leave Labour with the undisputed hegemony of the coalfield. In Bishop Auckland, Hugh Dalton took up his seat, and was appointed as parliamentary under-secretary to Arthur Henderson, the new Foreign Secretary. Further west, in Barnard Castle, Cuthbert Headlam was defeated by Will Lawther. Lawther had been a leading activist during the 1926 strike and, as checkweighman at the Victoria Garfield Colliery he had been arrested (with Harry Bolton, the Chairman of Blaydon District Council) and imprisoned for two months in Durham jail. Lawther was from a political family. His father was born in 1854 in Blyth and his grandfather in 1812. Both were strongly influenced by Methodism. His grandfather had been an active Chartist and his father and uncles were all powerful supporters of trade unionism and cooperation, serving as lodge and co-op secretaries. He moved to Chopwell in 1906 when it was a new colliery village and where, in the words of Andy Lawther 'a very good union pit (had been established) with fellas of a similar type. Many of them involved in the Methodist Chapel.'[17]

Will Lawther typified the new secular working-class socialist tradition emerging in positions of leadership in the county. In Chopwell, a Socialist Sunday School had been established in 1913, and Will Lawther had been a leading speaker. Like George Hardy, he had attended the Central Labour College in London, and became closely involved with new Socialist thinking. Through his contacts in London, an Anarchist Club was formed in Chopwell. In the Socialist Sunday School, Lawther and others had preached the gospel of class inequality and rational thought. This mode of thinking seemed set to reorder the politics of Labour on the coalfield in the late 1920s.

But it was to be undone. Dalton records in his diaries his occasional fleeting visits to the constituency. On Friday 14 February 1930 he notes that the constituency secretary, the Rev. William Hidgson, thinks of MacDonald as 'a frightened man'. In his judgement this was 'a shrewd comment'. A month later Dalton, who had entered the government with such high hopes, was writing:

> the Cabinet is full of overworked men, growing older, more tired and more timid with each passing week. Pressure from below and within is utterly ineffectual. High hopes are falling like last autumn's leaves. There is a whisper of spring in the air, but none in the political air. One looks at the political platform and one wishes we had never come in. We have forgotten our programme or been bamboozled out of it by officials. One almost longs for an early and crushing defeat.[18]

Such a defeat came, of course, but in an unexpected manner. The Labour Government could produce no policy to deal with the central problem of unemployment. Faced with the Tory and Liberal parties combined in their agreement on the need to cut unemployment benefit, Ramsay MacDonald went to the country as the head of a new National Government, fighting the Labour Party which he had previously led. At Seaham, the Party secretary requested that MacDonald not continue in the constituency. MacDonald declined, and in Dalton's view:

> arranged for his deserters all to stand their ground and fight their present constituencies with the aid of the Tory machine and a private fund supplied by 'certain friends'.[19]

In Durham, this arrangement backed by an electoral pact between Liberals and Tories, produced a complete turnaround in fortunes. MacDonald was returned, Dalton and Lawther both defeated. The majorities were narrow in each case, but the result was clear; so was it across the coalfield. Jack Lawson and Joe Batey retained their seats in Chester-le-Street and Spennymoor, but the other miners' representatives were defeated. Garside summarised the situation:

> the General election....proved a miserable defeat for Labour. The seven miners' candidates who had fought the 1929 election had again been elected to fight in 1931, but only two were retained. Will Lawther was defeated in Barnard Castle by his previous opponent, C.M. Headlam....W. Whitley, who had held the seat at Blaydon since 1922, was defeated by a narrow margin by the Unionist candidate, T.B. Martin, a private secretary....In Durham, W. McKeag eventually succeeded in securing the seat

> from Ritson by a majority of only 270 votes....At Houghton-le-Spring the Unionist candidate, R. Chapman, a member of South Shields Town Council and a Deputy Lieutenant of Durham County, defeated R. Richardson...who had sat for the division since 1918....J. Herriotts lost his seat at Sedgefield to the Unionist candidate R. Jennings, a chartered accountant and a director of several companies associated with the mining industry in the north of England.[20]

In interpreting this defeat, Garside explains how, in the crisis 'nationalism spread throughout the north east', and he draws upon Peter Lee's view that the election was 'the worst fought...in modern times for abuse and misrepresentation.'[21]

But none of these accounts adequately explain why Durham stood out in 1931 for the depth of the defeat of the miners' MPs, although local control was maintained over the district and county councils. It seems clear that the presence of MacDonald as the representative of Seaham was a factor. In Dalton's much-quoted view, 'the contagion of Seaham spread like the plague'. It also seems likely that the collaborative sentiments of earlier times were reawakened by the claims of a nationalist government to be offering a national solution to economic problems. In the view of a Labour Party organisation in the north east, the 1931 election:

> was a strange, disconcerting, bewildering experience. The electorate was not then the more educated body it is today....Meetings everywhere were packed, but numb—almost at times deathlike: no hint of response. MacDonald was the National Labour candidate in Seaham: the Labour candidate was Will Coxon, a local teacher. Many ordinary voters felt that they must support MacDonald; yet could they desert their Labour candidates? How could they calm their consciences on an issue such as this?[22]

The bewilderment and conflicting loyalties point to the demoralising effects of the defeat of the strike, and the splitting of the parliamentary Labour Party. At the Dean and Chapter Colliery in Spennymoor, Dick Beavis recalls that:

> The men were very demoralised during the 1930s. They had stood together in 1926 and held out for almost a year, but they had to go back to longer hours and huge debts. The older men would never trust anyone again. It was as if they lost faith....From then onwards Durham became politically dormant. Creeping paralysis, I've called it.[23]

A further point: the DMA's conversion to the cause of Labour and Labourism was complete. Yet, as we have seen this was achieved without the development of vibrant constituency parties. The Party was very much established as the political arm of the trade union.

These factors, allied with 'the contagion of Seaham' and the area's liberal tradition help to explain a lot about 1931. They come together repeatedly in our recorded discussions with old miners. We were often told that: 'Ramsay MacDonald was re-elected by the wives. That's how he got back in, he took the votes of the women.' These comments, it must be said, were most often couched in terms of the political illiteracy of the women. What they ignore is the process whereby women in the Seaham constituency, encouraged by Beatrice Webb, had become involved in the politics of the Labour Party and were both loyal and sympathetic to MacDonald and his political views. In this way the split which the National Government created, also highlighted the need for the Labour Party to take seriously all of its supporters and not simply the unionised men. Margaret Gibb, who took up her appointment as Party organiser for the north east in 1930, was well aware of this. With her support:

> Women's organisations went forward in leaps and bounds. In Durham County alone in the 1930s there were some 150 women's sections (Chester-le-Street constituency had 23)...the women, conscious of their lack of experience and political knowledge, organised conferences, two Session schools, weekend schools and week schools. Each year there was a full week school and often two. They organised Round Table conferences, TeaTime Conferences, Question and Answer gatherings and paid particular attention to their conduct at meetings and procedure in general in party events.[24]

The shock of 1931—the numbing of the senses—made clear that solidarity was not enough. Victory required a more comprehensive form of political organisation. Thus defeat set in train a process which transformed the Labour Party, and finally moulded it into the working-class life of Durham. In 1931, as the economic crisis worsened, Dalton records his visit to the Miners' Gala. As with all his references to his constituency, it is a clipped, sparse note:

> At Durham for the Durham Miners' Gala. Maxton and Cook the chief speakers. A downpour of rain, but crowds stood patiently, with or without umbrellas, listening for hours.[25]

This patience and attention was moulded into a deeply Labourist attachment. The support for left-wing speakers reflects the dynamic within the DMA and Durham Labour politics, and developed as the dole was cut and the Means Test applied. It also produced amongst some, a thoughtful reassessment of politics. As one woman recalls:

> My father was a union man: he was Treasurer of the union. He

> was interested in politics and so was my mother. They always took newspapers and my father always used to explain things to us. For a long time I wasn't very interested in politics so when I had the vote he explained to me who I should vote for—he explained the reasons. He explained that the Labour Party was the party of the working class: as far as it went. I remember clearly the first time I went to vote, 'Well, Edie,' he said, 'the best one for you to vote for is the Labour Party, it's nearer the working class. But it's socialism we want, and the Labour Party isn't socialist.' I can remember as if he told me it last week.[26]

As the slump deepened, the mining regions of Britain suffered—nowhere worse than in the small villages of West Durham. In 1932 thirty-five percent of all coal miners in Britain were unemployed, and the national unemployment rate stood at 22.7 percent. In West Durham 45.8 percent of the workforce registered as unemployed. Ernest Armstrong remembers attending a Labour Party meeting in Crook at this time. Joe Batey gave a particularly gloomy report, to which the chairman responded:

> Well Joe man the way you're talking it's about all finished; we might as well blow the whole place up. It couldn't get much worse.

Cuthbert Headlam supported MacDonald's policy of cutting the dole, and argued that the unemployed miners in his constituency should be regimented and disciplined. As early as 1928, he had viewed unemployment as a problem of surplus population: 'What can be done except a reduction of rates and the removal of the surplus population?'[27] To assist in the 'removal' he supported an agency established by his wife Beatrice, for sending the daughters and sons of miners south to work as domestics and servants in the homes of the rich. This was justified by a characteristic rationalisation:

> So far as I can make out none of these people is starving. The truth is that they have been so much better off than most working-class people in the past that they cannot adapt themselves easily to the present bad conditions.[28]

Further, this failure of 'adaptation' (or more appropriately submission) meant in his view that what Headlam referred to as an 'entirely economic problem' was dragged into politics and became: 'Inextricably bound up with political fads and policies that obviously no kind of political agreement on the subject of industrial organisation can be expected.'[29]

Such views were representative of the political consensus in 1931. Headlam himself attempted a further development of his unemployment 'policy'. Again, rather than solve the problem of unemployment he was concerned to categorise and discipline the unemployed.

> My plan of dividing the unemployed on an age basis implies—at any rate according to the way I want it worked out—a great change in our Poor Law administration, because it means that a certain section of able-bodied workers should be a charge on the rates. But as a matter of fact these days men over 45 years of age stand very little chance of getting jobs once they are on the dole unless they are skilled men—and so they might just as well be placed in a different category from the first. I think that they ought to be the care of local authorities—because they are difficult to move, and can be more easily supervised by local relief officers than by the Labour Exchange people.[30]

This scheme did not come to pass, but it should not be seen as an extreme view. In the pages of the scientific journal *Nature,* sterilisation was discussed. On 11 January 1936 an article by Professor E.W. Macbride maintained that while it would 'be a libel to accuse the working classes as a whole of over-breeding....When we came to consider unskilled labour, we find reckless breeding still going on. Dock labourers and miners figure prominently in the over-production of children (and) this level also receives social failures from the higher grades.' He quotes Bishop Weldon of Durham who had: 'recently mentioned the case of a worthless pair in Durham, both of the tramp class, whose only means of support was the dole and who have not less than seventeen children, and every time a new baby arrived the maternity benefit was spent on drink', and concluded that: 'there is only one remedy for the over-production of children that we can see and it is very unpopular, so that it will probably be some time before the necessity for it forces itself on the public mind. This is compulsory sterilisation as a *punishment* for parents who have to resort to public assistance in order to support their children.'[31]

In real life, discipline was extreme enough. George Bestford remembers how:

> they had everyone taped. They knew what you were—if you were a bit of a shouter they didn't want you there. So you'd go to the dole: 'Where have you been today Bestford?' 'I've been to Trimdon and I've been to Tudhoe and I've been here and there.' I'd never been because I knew there was no point in going! We used to meet men coming back and they'd tell you there was no point in going there. So you could walk your feet off and there was no bloody chance of a job. But you had to tell the dole you'd been because you had to be 'looking for work'. There were some men—'dole clerks' who had worked with you down the pit and yet were bloody awful. They'd make you take your cap off before you came in. 'Have you forgotten anything?'; 'No, I'm looking for work.' 'Well take your cap off.' In a nasty, snotty way you know. Just to show their authority. It used to vex me. But you

> had to be careful you know. If you used any violence they soon picked you up. At that time, my father was getting about 35 bob, and my brother 15 bob. Under the Means Test, if your father was earning, you got less, and they got my dole down to nine pence a week. We had two sisters and a younger brother and we all had to live on that. It was a bit tough. So I went to Durham and played hell about it. They told me that if I didn't behave myself they'd send for the police and I'd be in trouble. So, I just had to keep quiet you see.[32]

Henry Ashby worked in the west of the county:

> The 1930s were a period of abject poverty whether you worked or didn't work. I worked for some of those years at the Derwent Colliery in Medomsly. Mostly we were on short time; on three or four days a week. I remember going around the countryside looking for motorbike tyres. You couldn't afford to send your shoes to the cobbler, but if you could get a piece of rubber from a motorbike tyre you could repair them.
>
> I was a miner, but I can always remember that the job of someone sweeping the roads was the envy of everybody. It would be a big step up in the world if you could get a job as a council road man. They had about £2.10s a week. Which was to us, a decent wage, and security as well, without working like hell like we were down the pit.

Henry experienced unemployment regularly after 1931, and he remembers how:

> In those days if you'd been on the dole for so long you had to go on what they called the Tribunal. A man would come down to the house to interview you. So you went up before the Tribunal. And he would say 'Where have you been looking for work?' If you weren't 'looking for work' they'd suspend your dole or stop it altogether because you weren't trying to get work. Well, looking for work then was absolutely farcical. Because we used to get a bicycle and go all around the district and, everywhere you went, there were hundreds of men sitting around. There was no chance for you—all unskilled men—when there were men on the spot. Anyway we had to go in front of this chap to explain. And he'd say 'Where were you on Monday?' and you had to have the name of the place where you'd been 'looking for work'. 'Where were you on Tuesday?' right through the week. Then they'd try to trip you up. 'Where were you on Tuesday again?' And if he tripped you up and you couldn't remember or give the same name, he'd scratch your name off and stop your dole. So I had a little square piece of cardboard with a name on for every day of the week and I

> used to carry it here inside the cuff of my jacket. 'Where were you on Wednesday again?' And I'd look out of the corner of my eye. They never tripped me up....You'd go to places and ask 'Is there any chance of a job here?' And they'd look at you as if you were daft.
>
> We thought of these people, the Tribunal and the Means Test, as the enemy.[33]

His wife Hilda lived at home in Chopwell with her unemployed father:

> This was the Means Test period too you know. And my father was unemployed and I had this job at the picture hall, and my father never reported it because if they knew I was earning 12s 6d. a week they would deduct that from his dole. And I had a sister who was working in an office in Newcastle and she had it down that she was lodging at Blaydon—somebody we knew at Blaydon. This Means Test man used to come periodically and we used to be terrified of him. We just had a big living room and a pantry where the tap was. And as soon as this Means Test man came I'd go in the pantry. 'Your daughter isn't working?' And my father would say 'No.' He never turned a hair and I was terrified that we'd be put in jail! And people did all these things you see. All the sons were supposed to be lodging elsewhere because you'd lose your Dole.[34]

In Cornforth:

> Because of the Means Test, there were men who were leaving home to live in sheds in the allotments in order to get the dole. They wouldn't allow their fathers to keep them so they just left. Quite a number used to live in the gardens. Sometimes they'd go home to have a meal—unofficially! That's what they had to do if they didn't want their fathers and mothers to suffer. They did some awful things around here.[35]

At Easington and Horden, men talked of living 'on the beach banks' and in caves along the coast, or in the gardens:

> if a man or his son fell off work, or if one could not find work, well, his family had to keep him, so to show his independence, he would say, 'Oh, I'll get a little hut up in the gardens.' He would put up a little hut, with a bed or settee in, and would grow vegetables, flowers, have a few hens, keep a few pigeons, and sell them to make a couple of shillings a week by living up there, and when he wanted a bath, he would go home, and have one there.

In spite of the harshness of these experiences, it seems that in Durham the political representatives of the miners were able to exercise some control over the operation of the Means Test. This was especially the case in the north of the coalfield. In Stanley, for example, Bart Kelly, a county councillor and a member of another 'political family', argued at a meeting of Lanchester Public Assistance Committee in 1932 that:

> Durham can hold its head up and say that there have been no unemployment demonstrations or marches in the county such as have occurred on the Tyne and Merseyside and Belfast.

He went on to explain how it was that:

> Durham has not suffered these things because the Means Test has been administered on humanitarian lines, and I am one who absolutely refuses to act in the brutal manner laid down. We will show the people that, as working-class men and women ourselves, we are going to stand by them until the last ditch.[36]

This level of control and support was important. So too was the sense in which Durham society provided a form of continuity. While the coal mines closed (wholly or partially) they were not shut down. For many of them there was every expectation that they would re-open, and re-employ the men who had once worked there. For these men, unemployment (no matter how upsetting and demeaning an experience) involved a break from pit work; and it didn't imply that they were no longer coal miners. The hardship was real, and the observations of the Pilgrims Trust in Crook mirror the account which Huxley provided of the lives of coal miners in the east of the county. The researchers found that the hardship was most often borne by the women, who were 'intentionally starving themselves in order to feed and clothe the children reasonably.[37] In this regard we have seen how in contrast to urban workers, the miners (via their gardens and poaching) had some independent access to food.

One sign of this can be gleaned from George Hitchin's autobiographical account *Pit Yacker*. 'Even at its worst I doubt whether the poverty in the mining villages was as acute as in the larger communities like Sunderland. Certainly, no one at Seaham begged in the streets for food'.[38] The Pilgrims Trust researchers contrast Crook with the accounts of Liverpool, where the social and cultural lives of the unemployed seemed to have been most deeply disorientated. In Durham villages unemployment was something to be endured yet characterised by 'a sturdy refusal to give up', 'a determination to see it through'.[39] Many things remained the same. To remain in Crook, unemployed, was to remain a part of a familiar world, lived out amongst equals with a common past and likely futures. In contrast, to leave (in search of employment) was to invite the possibility of social disruption, loneliness and distress. One women noted how her husband was planning to leave Crook for the south of England. This caused them both considerable anxiety. For her it created a problem of resources so: 'Every week that there's an extra shilling, I've bought a little extra cocoa or sugar or something to help me over the time he goes.'

However, her husband was, 'in a sweat about going, for he's heard that the people are not friendly.'[40]

However discontent *did* develop in the coalfield in the 1930s. The Ministry of Labour suspended County Durham's Public Assistance Committee and replaced local officials with commissioners. Headlam had recognised that the application of the Means Test was politically dangerous, and especially so in Durham. He appreciated the logic of the County Council.

> I understand that the idea is to 'make the buggers see what it means to have voted for a national government' and of course from the Labour point of view this is quite an intelligible policy. They will score hands down because obviously if the Means Test is applied at all rigorously it is bound to create a lot of ill feeling and press very hardly on the people.[41]

He worried about the political consequences for the Conservative Party in the area:

> As things are today up here, I would not give myself any odds on keeping the seat if we had an election and certainly we should lose all the other seats in Durham that we won last year. The policy of the national government has certainly done nothing so far for the workers in these parts—increased unemployment and the Means Test are not exactly the two things one would like to fight an election upon![42]

An Alternative Tradition

In Durham unemployment demonstrations did occur, but most of these were organised by members of the Communist Party and supporters of the Minority Movement. The Communist Party had been active in 1925 and 1926. Page Arnot spoke in Newcastle at the beginning of the General Strike and in 'words spoken...quietly, without heat' he had outlined a strategy for resistance based upon Workers' Councils.[43] In spite of the Labour Party's decisions in 1924 and 1925 to separate themselves from the Communist Party, members of the Labour Party in the north west of the coalfield carried Communist Party cards until the 1940s, and Page Arnot's talk in 1926 was chaired by Will Lawther. Following the defeat of the strike, the Communist Party gave support to the unofficial strike that took place in Durham, most notably the one at Dawdon which lasted for fifteen weeks in 1929. An activist noted that 'the lodge officials made a vicious attack' on the Communist Party and refused its offer of help. In a manner which is deeply reminiscent of John Wilson's account of the 1850s, Jim Ancrum described their attempts to find a headquarters in which to set up a 'feeding centre' for the striking miners. Refused the

Lodge premises, they obtained access to the Parish Hall but 'the Lodge officials had been to the vicar and persuaded him that as the WIR was a communist organisation he should not allow us to use the Hall'. Finally 'as a regular feeding centre we were able to obtain the cooperative Hall.'[44] On the basis of this organisation, the Communist Party fielded a miners' candidate in the 1929 election, and again in 1931. At that time George Lumley, checkweighman at the Rythorpe colliery, was also a member of the executive committee of the DMA. In spite of strong opposition from the union officials he stood against Ramsay MacDonald and the official Labour candidate W. Coxon—a local school teacher and divisional secretary of the party. In this election Lumley polled a derisory vote, 677 (in contrast to MacDonald's 28,978 and Coxon's 23,027), yet one which veiled the growing influence of communists within the local lodges, similar to that of the ILP a generation earlier. Much of its activity was devoted to the creation of a new cadre of leaders who would democratise and transform the union. In this, it allied with a growing number of Labour Party members and disaffected lodge officials who sensed that as the old arrangements of class compromise had passed, the time had come for the Methodist leadership to give way to a more secular orientation; one which gave greater emphasis to the material, and used the language of class in a less compromising way. These people had had a growing influence in the county throughout the 1920s. These were the people who organised unofficial galas in 1921 and 1926, and who controlled the Councils of Action during the General Strike. Several of them had spent time in Durham Jail.

In 1921, an editorial of the *Durham County Advertiser* identified this as a growing menace within the Durham Miners' Association: 'The fact is that the Durham Miners' Association has more to fear from attacks within than from without.' It drew particular attention to the developments in the South Wales Miners' Federation and the influence of the syndicalist Noah Ablett in that coalfield and beyond. In its view, in Durham: 'The Abblettites have had a sufficiently long innings, and when they realise there is no room for Soviet methods in the Durham Miners' Association a great step will have been taken towards that solidarity of which we hear so much nowadays.'[45]

What was seen to be under threat was the kind of solidarism which had established the miners and their institutions within Durham society. But Durham society was changing irrevocably. In Seaham, and especially after the 1929 Election result, the Londonderry family attempted to refashion the paternalist arrangements that had characterised its control of the district before 1926. In Londonderry's correspondence, however, reference is repeatedly made to the fecklessness of the miners, and their lack of trustworthiness and loyalty.[46] The old social arrangements could not be re-established. The 'circumstances of class' had come to dominate over the politics of patronage. In the disputes of 1921 and 1926 two coal owners had prosecuted miners who had 'abused the privileges' afforded to them. Sir Timothy Eden, for example, had allowed his miners to 'gather fuel in the woods of his Widley Stone estate during the coal stoppage', but took to court four who were found guilty of 'game trespass'.[47] In the west of the county many of the Pease collieries were idle for six years, between 1931 and 1937. The company had long objected to the system of 'tied cottages'. In 1910 Pease had informed his fellow coal owners that they were all 'cursed by the system of free homes for miners.'[48] In 1934 the company sold off the majority of their houses. For Londonderry, these were all disturbing signs and they became the more so when in 1935 the hall and pavilion which he had provided for 'his miners' were used to house packed meetings for Emanuel Shinwell. Shinwell had spoken in the town during the 1926 strike and bitterly attacked Londonderry and the coal owners. In 1935 the 'Red Clydesider' was chosen by the local Labour Party to fight the seat against MacDonald.

It is useful here, perhaps, to recall what Antonio Gramsci was writing about Italian society at about this time. In his view social groups often:

> for reasons of submission and intellectual subordination [adopt] a conception which is not their own, but is borrowed from another group; and it affirms this conception verbally and believes itself to be following it, because this is the conception it follows in 'normal times'.[49]

This state approximates to the position of coal miners, in 'normal times' under the paternal rule of the coal owners. As a system it had been modified by the recognition of the miners' trade union and also by other aspects of their organised social life in the twentieth century. However the lock-out of 1926 signalled an end to 'normal times', and they could not be recalled.

Meanwhile coal-face mechanisation was, more extensively, introduced. Although Durham (along with South Wales) was significantly less mechanised than the other coalfields, this did involve considerable change, especially in the larger collieries. Beavis recalls the introduction of cutting machines into the Dean and Chapter Colliery in Spennymoor. He describes how the machine was moved along the face, making a cut underneath the coal, adding that 'the noise and dust from it is better imagined than described'. When the cut was completed, the face would be drilled and the coal blasted down ready for the hewers to fill into tubs:

> However there was such a vast amount of roof exposed when the coal was blasted that the roof invariably broke away. This made it extremely difficult for the men to get the machine set up again. It was worse still if 'droppers' of water started coming through the broken roof. The two men working the machine were black

> as the coal they cut. They got one shilling and 6d. [2.5p.] a ton for filling it into tubs, plus 10d. a day for working beneath the 'droppers'.[50]

Note the stress on piece rates. Men who talk about working in the mines inevitably talk about money—the rates they were paid, and the fines and deductions imposed upon them by the employer. The system was complicated enough without the introduction of geological hazards and disturbances. The miners, through custom and through union agreements, had attempted to regulate these processes; but while customs reproduce themselves through daily encounters, agreements need to be regulated and enforced—not easy after the humiliation of 1926.

> At that time, men seemed very hesitant about going to the offices where the foreoverman sat with all his overmen and deputies. The man I was working with was much older than me and he was worried about the price of driving a cross-gate up. The price used to be about three pence a yard but we weren't sure. So he asked the union man. Well this union man said: 'If I tell you, you will go and tell the overman I told you. No sir, you go and ask yourself.' This was a typical example and I realised then the fear of the backlash some men had.[51]

Fenwick Whitfield out of the Eden Colliery recalls similar experiences, with men allowing their names to be put forward to union positions but not turning up for the meetings. 'They weren't taking any chances. People were afraid to do trade union work you know.'[52] Without leadership and representation miners were frequently 'on their own'. Men like Dick Beavis learned caution. Working on a face:

> twelve of us on a hundred yards long surface of coal, stretched out in two's, heaving the coal and filling it onto shaker pans....With pneumatic picks and stone above, the roof would come away before we could get the props to hold it. I was told we could get extra money for this—'inch mining it was called'. So I led the way into the office, no foreoverman was going to frighten me—or so I thought. There he was sitting at this desk, the back shift overman beside him. At each side of the room sat the various deputies. 'We have come to claim some pay for stone coming away at the coal face and having it to shift. We want some inch money.' 'Well', he snapped 'how much?' 'Well, I said, there's some coming down here and somewhere else.' 'Well' he snapped again 'what do you want?' I could feel my colour coming up. I just did not know how much I wanted. I was stuck. Then one of the older men behind me said 'We want inch money.' The foreoverman snapped back again. 'Yes I know, but how much?' Then each one of the men started to tell the tale about the stone

> coming down. The foreoverman turned to his deputies who were obviously enjoying our embarrassment: 'Fancy men coming in here and don't know what they want.' We were being made a laughing stock, and I was wishing I had never gone into the office. I felt humiliated. I was.[53]

In the 1930s, then, the coal owners owned the collieries and the miners were subordinated to the owners. As one man put it, talking of his father 'he was a big man, a strong man and a hell of a worker, but he was cowed; he'd been that nailed down by the employers in the 1930s that he had no spirit. No spirit at all.' Such effects are important ones. But this exercise of economic power ('take your cap off', 'get your cards') did not provide the basis for an accommodation which could reorder the industry. It produced a stalemate, one which infuriated Headlam, and set in train a profound pattern of change within the trade union; one which mirrored the changes that had taken place earlier, in the 1830s, the 1860s and the 1900s.

Fenwick Whitfield became a lodge Delegate in 1929, and represented the Eden Lodge at Council meetings in Durham up until the war. He recalls how:

> As a delegate to Durham in the 1930s it was very difficult. There were some progressive-minded people, but there were some queer fellas going there at that time too. We had people who took religious objections to any fight we were putting up. They threatened to withdraw their membership from the union if certain ideas were put forward.[54]

Strikes did occur, but they were rare, and received little support from the area organisation of the union. In 1935, for example, the Follonsby Lodge went on strike in protest against the company's attempts to lay men off and rehire them 'without conditions' thereby breaking established agreements in the mine. The Lodge secretary, George Harvey, wrote an 'open letter to the DMA Agents and Executive Committee' on behalf of the Lodge officials. This drew attention to the fact that 'for a long time now men in the Durham pits have been attacked pit by pit. Even the strongest Lodges have been attacked'. It protested that:

> Failing to smash us up, the management appealed to you as Agents, but on the old lines—Divide and Conquer. You the Agents fell for it, ran away from the fight, and upon no settlement at all, advised resumption of work....This the lodge refused....Since then without recognising the lodge at all, Major Kirkup, Agent, writes to 'Durham' to further divide us; and without asking our version you, the DMA agents, accept his letters as Gospel Truth. He never wrote to us, but to you....Why we should suffer this we do not know. There is a fight all over

> Durham; selecting and rejecting men, weak and aged Union officials; refusing to meet any deputations; unemployed and rejected lodge officials; imposing day-to-day contracts; refusing the minimum wage, terrorising men; selling colliery houses; extending winding times;...closing pits and restarting on reductions; interfering with the old Deputy system; replacing men with boys and youths. There is a war on, and you as agents and committee quote the war maker's word against that of your own class. You expect men to follow it. Your arguments are weaker than used by any other leaders.

In reflecting upon this period Beavis recalls how:

> the union was very weak. They were more like collaborators. Looking back now I wouldn't tolerate them for a moment. They were all 'yes men', more liberals than anything. They didn't like to be interfered with. When I started to go to Lodge meetings I used to ask questions. I remember one day this chap said to me 'Oh you're the little fella who dared to attack Joe Sutch.' All because I had dared to stand up and criticise the outstanding Lodge Secretary who was a very prominent person at the time. I used to say: 'I don't think he was right, that's all.'[55]

But there was also change. Beavis recalls how, after his humiliating experience with the foreoverman he was able to turn to a lodge activist called Billy Todd who was a member of the Communist Party.

> I made it my business to see Billy Todd....I met him as the shift changed in bye. He had done his shift in another district. I told him what had happened: 'sit down here' he said 'and before you go away you will be able to go into the office and never again be made a fool of.' Then he started going through the prices with me. 'Half penny an inch per ton, the face of a hundred yards long, one inch of stone coming down all the length of the face means one farthing on the price of every ton produced.' Then he gave me sums to do 'if six inches of stone comes away for twenty yards—how much?' Never in all my life did I want to do sums so badly, but getting it right was difficult. He said to his marra who was waiting to go home: 'Leave me, I'm not leaving this lad until he knows exactly what he's talking about.' And teach me he did. It was a lesson I never forgot.[56]

Over the hill at Cornforth, George Cole, another Communist, played a similar role.

> At Cornforth the money was always better. The checkweighman there was a Communist and he was a hell of a fighter. The Cornforth Colliery didn't start right away after 1926—they

> blacklisted the lot! But when the demand for coal increased they opened it and the men wouldn't go back without George Cole, and they elected him checkweighman. The pit closed a few times but when it started up the men voted George checkweighman again. He was checkweighman for years and years.[57]

In 1934 the average wages paid to Durham miners were the lowest in all of the coal districts.[58] This, in the wake of all other deprivations, put in train a powerful pressure for change. In December 1933, the MFGB called a special conference. At this time, Peter Lee had been elected as chairman to work alongside Ebby Edwards of Northumberland as General Secretary. This reintegration of the northern unions into the leadership of the MFGB says much of the changes that had affected the industry and the union. At that conference Lee concluded the debate in this way:

> Let us plod on. Let the chaos caused by the coal owners, mismanagement, and indifference of the government deepen as it will deepen, then public opinion will see that the endurance of the miners has been great under great difficulties.[59]

In Durham, the County Federation strongly endorsed the decision by the MFGB to launch a campaign for a national wage increase, and local newspapers noted how across the county 'meetings are constant and arguments are widespread.'[60]

As this resistance developed, the lodge activists tried to change the union and its rules. The rules relating to the position of the officials were subject to closest inspection. In Durham there was no maximum retirement age for agents and officials who normally died in office, as did Crawford and Wilson. In 1933 a new rule was passed which established a compulsory retirement age of 70. This was reduced to 65 in October 1937. The rule requiring officials to have worked for five years in the Durham coal mines was amended, and the qualifying period doubled. These changes in combination aimed to ease out the old officials (Lee and Robson particularly), and also disbar many of the 'unemployed MPs'. They were not however immediately necessary. The President, Robson, died in 1934, and Peter Lee in 1935. Garside has recorded how in the 1930s Lee had begun to openly question his views of trade unionism and human development. In November 1933, at a meeting at Ferryhill he observed how:

> War as a rule is a hard and cruel way of settling disputes, but there are times when injustice, poverty and hardship are worse to bear than to fight in endeavouring to remove those evils.[61]

Five years earlier, he had 'thought we had reached a period when human life would be of greater value than profits, but as far as these two counties

Listening to Swaffer, 'Crowds stood patiently...listening for hours.'

are concerned we have been mistaken.'[62] His death marked the end of the continuity which had been sustained through the Methodist Chapel. By 1935 the elements of a new tradition were being put in place.

In that year, Hannen Swaffer was an invited speaker at the Durham Miners' Gala. In the *Daily Herald* he wrote of how he, Herbert Morrison, Stafford Cripps and the leader of the Labour Party, George Lansbury, had spoken from two platforms:

> We had watched before that, the marching into the city of the mining families, who had come from all parts of the county to take part in their Annual Gala. There were certainly over 100,000. There may have been nearer 200,000. It was the greatest turn-out since 1924. It was the largest gathering of its kind in the world—and who can count a great multitude.
>
> There were over a hundred banners—and most of the banners were followed by a band. Many of the banners were hung with crepe. Since the last Gala not only the beloved Peter Lee, the General Secretary, but James Robson the president have passed on....Last year 107 Durham miners were officially reported killed while at work. This does not include the many who died in consequence of injuries. Still treated as a race apart, and still condemned to ill-paid slavery, the brave miners of Durham

> marched. The banners were a defiant symbol of their determination to establish, one day, sound justice—their bands a proud sign of their long struggle for a culture denied them in the schools.

This account is appended to a photograph album presented by Swaffer to the DMA and lodged in the reading room at Redhills. There, surrounded by the bric-a-brac of the past, the photographs of James Jarché portray the earnestness of the men and women who listen to the speeches ('silently for hours'); there too is the power of the march and the banners, and the conviviality of fun fairs and waltzing on the green of the Race Course. They portray people who are far from defeated. Swaffer describes how the villagers:

> passed through the narrow cobbled streets—old men, young men and women, mothers and grandmothers, children on foot and babies in arms. We saw on the banners the painted form of former leaders, Keir Hardie and Arthur Cook, the most revered of all, symbols of comradeship and mutual help, pictures of the aged miners' homes.
>
> 'G.L.' told me that, during the previous night he had scarcely slept. 'I am so fearfully conscious of my responsibility,' he said. 'This great army, properly led, is a power for infinite good. I think of my own unworthiness. I fear lest my message shall not be worthy of our Cause.'

As the procession left the city, passed the Royal County Hotel:

> someone saw our Leader in the window. A cry went up: 'There's Lansbury!' Cheers began—cheers that lasted for over two hours! For there went by one solid stream of bands and banners, miners and their families. Lansbury had to stand up to take the salute—and there he stood for over two hours! Everyone in the procession cheered! Every now and then it stopped, to cheer longer. Old men cheered, young men, mothers and grandmothers—and babies. Sometimes a band would stop to play George a special tune. One band insisted on halting to play the 'Red Flag', lining up, meanwhile, in front of the hotel.
>
> Lansbury, obviously, is the idol of all these workers and their women-folk. He has moved, in his time, in proud places. But his heart remains with the people.
>
> Both Cripps and Morrison were deeply affected by what they saw. Now and then there was a cheer for them. But it was Lansbury's day!
>
> One miner's leader, a tall, husky man, who has, nearly all his life, braved death in the pit, cried like a child with mother. 'I

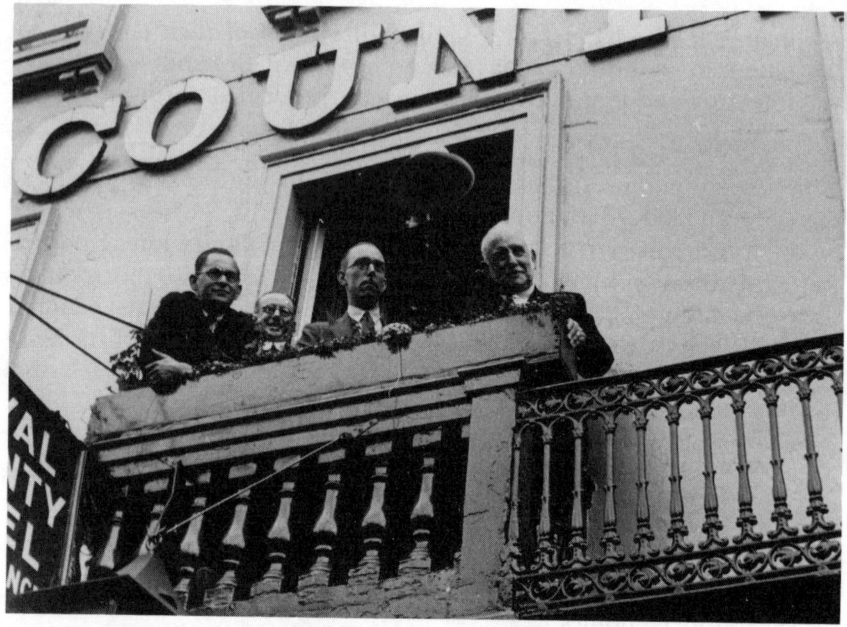

'There's Lansbury...' On the balcony of the County Hotel.

> can't help it,' he said, moving away from the window where Lansbury still stood, taking the salute of a vast multitude.
>
> Then a policeman came up into the hotel room and asked Lansbury if he would move from the window. 'We shall never get the people home,' he said. 'You're holding up the traffic.' And so there passed out of Durham for another year of toil, or unemployment, the army of the miners, whom 'civilisation' treats as slaves, although they are the salt of the earth.[63]

Ironically, Lansbury would not last out the year as leader. In speeches delivered at a time of economic crisis he was aware of an impending election and spoke passionately of the need for government to take control of industry.

> We want power to use all the available money for the service of the community as a whole...what should be done with the great industries of the county can only be done when the credit of the nation is at the disposal of the government. We cannot allow anyone, not even Mr Montagu Norman (Governor of the Bank of England) to determine the policy of Labour as to how these things shall be accomplished.[64]

In the election of 1935 Labour was again defeated, but the Durham coalfield returned a powerfully Labour vote. In Seaham Ramsay MacDonald was defeated comprehensively by Shinwell, and across the county the seats lost in 1931 were regained. In Barnard Castle, Headlam was defeated, but not by Lawther. In 1933 (and out of a total of 111 nominees!) Lawther had been elected to a newly created position for agent at Redhills.

The careers of the new Left leaders are worth documenting. In 1907, at the age of 17, Lawther had been elected as vice-president of the new Chopwell pit. In 1918 he was elected to the executive committee of the area union and, as we have seen, became a parliamentary nominee for the union. He then fought and lost the 1922, 1923 and 1924 elections in the South Shields parliamentary constituency. In 1929 he was successful in the Barnard Castle constituency. However he was only to hold the position for two years before being defeated in the 1931 national coalition election. His return to the union was by way of election as checkweighman at the Wheatley Hill Colliery, following in the path of Wilson and Lee. In 1934 he was elected as vice president of the MFGB and in 1939 he became President. In 1944 he became the first President of the NUM.

The death of Robson and Lee created openings for two new officials. Robson was replaced by Edward Moore (Treasurer of Harraton and Durham County Councillor). In the election to replace Lee in 1936, George Harvey and Sam Watson, the secretary of the Boldon miners' Lodge, were on the final ballot paper. In this Lawther intervened:

> I helped to make Sammy an agent. I did what no other agent did in Durham. You're not supposed to take sides in the election of another agent, and I claimed the right as a rank-and-file member of the union. I paid my money and I had as much right to say what I was going to vote for as anybody else. I made a lot of enemies with that.[65]

In the 1930s, Watson was certainly on the Left, but rather detached from the inner circle of the DMA. He had never been elected to the county executive committee yet he had established a strong reputation across the coalfield as an opponent of the employers and a committed supporter of unemployed miners. He was born in Boldon in 1898. His family had been miners on the Durham coalfield since the eighteenth century, and his was the fifth generation of Watsons to enter the mines. That was in 1912 when, at the age of fourteen, he started work on the screens, and then trapping. Like many other boys and girls in the mining villages, Watson showed real academic ability at school, and his school teacher resisted his move into the mines. Watson's wife remembers:

> When Sam was fourteen the teacher from the local school begged the family to find the money to let him carry on with his schoolwork and go on to university. But the money wasn't there.

George Lansbury, 'We want power.'

> He had to leave and go down the pit. That's all there was in those days.

This did not however prevent him from continuing in the reading class the vicar—an ex-Eton tutor—had set up in the village. When the Boldon miners established the Miners' Institute Library he became the secretary, and he was to 'read widely for the rest of his life'.

Watson's father broke his back in the pit and was invalided out of work for the last fourteen years of his life. The local lodge assisted with his case, providing money for a wheelchair, and for the widening of paths into his house. Sam was to stay with his father in Boldon up until 1935. In 1923—one year after Boldon Colliery had established the first pit-head baths in the county—he was elected on to the lodge committee as a hewers' representative, and five years later in 1928, at the age of 30, he was elected lodge secretary by an overwhelming majority. He held this position until 1936, and was also elected assistant checkweighman, and in 1935, as a lay member, to the National Executive of the Miners' Federation. In that year he published a pamphlet on unemployment in the Durham coalfield. Boldon lodge purchased 1,000 copies and distributed them free to its members. Ned Cohen remembers it as 'a very useful guide as to the amount of benefit eligible under the Means Test.'[66]

Watson was by now a man with a considerable reputation, and a man with powerful friends in the Durham union. Bill Blyton, then the secretary of nearby Harton colliery remembers:

> He had a first-class brain and he was a good negotiator for the men. Sammy wasn't connected with the Labour Party much before 1934 until his ambitions were building up to be an Agent. The man who made Sammy an agent was Jack Summerbell, the chairman of Boldon Lodge. He was very prominent in the Executive Committee and used his influence for Sammy.

He also remembers how:

> it was in the days of chronic unemployment. Boldon had closed and there were only a few hundred employed there; so Sam was unemployment secretary as well as corresponding secretary. And every case he won, he used to publish the Referees' reports; and he became known as the unemployment expert. And that was the way he built himself up. He was very left wing in those days, very left wing. He became very right wing when he got in with Gaitskell, but in the 1930s he was very left wing. I remember one time we refused to let the Communist Party join in with the Harton colliery contingent when we were demonstrating against the Means Test. And when they came to the top of Stanhope Road from Boldon, Watson invited the Communists to join in with the Boldon men. He was very left wing in those days.

Durham University professor Teddy Allen put it like this:

> one of the things that he attacked really very strongly was the attempt on the part of the then unemployment assistance board

> to cut the rate of assistance to long-term unemployed people. This would have affected Durham particularly harshly. So he attacked the UAB, and this gave him a reputation for being fierce and to the left, and against officialdom and all the rest of it.

Maurice Ridley, at that time an active member of the Communist Party in the Durham coalfield, remembers how Watson was:

> a very good secretary at Boldon Colliery. He did his work the hard way you know, and he did an enormous amount of self study. He was on very good terms with both members of the ILP and the communist party. I've always respected his ability.

That he was on good terms with the left and aware of the political debates of the day was also revealed in the lodge minute books which contain his personal writings, including references to both Lenin and the Communist Party.

The early banners of the Durham miners had clear religious motifs, and that of the Boldon banner figures in this number. By the 1920s however, the lodge had moved to secular Labourist themes of cooperation and union. On one side the banner featured the Boldon Miners' Hall, built in 1891, and on the other the Wheatsheaf emblem with the slogan 'Each for all; all for each'. In 1932, the lodge decided to commission a new banner, and Watson gives his account of the prognostications.

> The sub-committee recommended that the photo of Lenin should be put on the banner and the Miners' Hall on the other, but owing to the new departure by putting a photo of an international working-class leader on the banner it caused dissent, in spite of our so-called desire for Socialism, so it was decided to call a special meeting. The meeting was small, but very divided. At bottom it was the clash of a new idea against the old. The philosophy of Socialism as at present being pursued in this country by the workers as against Communism is being propagated by a very small minority. Like all new ideas when they arise, all the old shibboleths, all the old prejudices, religions, social, etc., were trotted out. Most of them in a purely prejudiced way. The photo of Lenin didn't matter in the least, what really mattered was that the philosophy of Lenin was not understood by more than six men. It is a sad reflection that in this year of grace 1932 the majority of members of a strong miners' lodge should run away from the idea that a leader of a new world order should adorn this banner. The question arises, are we really sincere in our belief in Socialism? Are we sincere when we say 'If only the working class would vote Labour at the election all would be well', or is it just an excuse for our own cowardice in not facing up to the real issues of the class struggle? After a very

> lengthy discussion for and against the Committee's recommendation it was put to the members as to whether they were in favour of the Committee's recommendation. The vote was put and they voted nineteen for the committee recommendation and twenty nine against. Therefore the photo of Lenin will not be put on the banner; and the new idea of communism must be spread more widely, more scientifically and more sincerely before it can hope to succeed. We take heart from the fact that the new idea is arising. That is something. It is up to us to help it on.
>
> After the committee's recommendation had failed, a resolution was moved that the emblem of Labour and the Co-operative Movement be put on the banner and the miners' hall on the other, an amendment was moved that we put a representative of the working class from each county on the banner and the miners' hall on the other. The resolution carried, and the banner will have on one side the miners' hall and on the other the emblem of the Co-op Movement and Labour.[67]

Watson's account is interesting evidence of the competing political traditions in Durham in the 1930s, and of the deep significance given to the banner as a representation of the village and community. It is also a revealing insight into his own thinking at this time, and the strong link between Lawther and Watson. At the Labour Party conference in 1936 Lawther spoke strongly in favour of the Communist Party affiliating to the Labour Party. The election of Watson and Lawther marked a critical shift in the leadership of the DMA; secular rather than religious, practical rather than ethical, it had been produced out of a period of severe industrial conflict and material deprivation. It was to be men like these who would fashion the reconstruction of the industry and the union in the post-war period.

This was not to mark too dramatic a change from the past, as was made clear by Lawther soon after his own election. Along with the other officials in the MFGB he was appalled by the impact of the 1926 strike upon the union and its membership. As they struggled to re-establish a national union against the encroachments of both the employers and non-political unionism, they became determined that the experience would never be repeated. As Lawther put it:

> we'd had such a bitter experience in 1926 that we made up our minds that in our lifetime there'd never be another one.[68]

They 'got it accepted by the coalfield that no executive had the power to call a national strike without a national ballot supported by two-thirds of the membership'. When he argued this case in the council chamber at Redhills, Lawther was criticised with a rhetorical question: 'Is this the Lawther of Chopwell, of Little Moscow and the General Strike?' He answered firmly that it was not. It was the Lawther who had learned a lot from the hardship of the intervening ten years, and that anyone who hadn't learned their lessons was a fool. This was to be the legacy of 1926 and the slump.

Conclusion

To understand and judge a society, one has to penetrate its basic structure to the human bond on which it is built; this undoubtedly depends on legal relations, but also upon forms of labour, ways of loving, living and dying.

M. Merleau Ponty

MINERS form an interesting and unusual occupation, one which bridges feudal and capitalist societies. The organisation of mining was based on landholding but because of its primary role in industrialisation, coal miners gave a lead in the organisation of the emerging, urban working class. This double exceptionalism has given focus to our study of the Durham coalfield.

Capitalist expansion took place earlier in Durham than in most other parts of the British coalfield, and its development there was organised through the paternalistic-aristocratic form of domination which we have termed the 'Durham System'. *Pre*-capitalist forms of labour contract were maintained; and with them, the continued ascendancy of aristocrats and bishops—the land and the church. Within this system coal miners and their families lived out their lives, through what Thompson has referred to as the 'old culture'—a culture which drew upon its rural past and expressed itself in customary practices in the pit and the village. These partly determined the ways in which the industry was managed and the nature of its trade unionism.

The miners were able to form *unskilled* labourers' unions in the nineteenth century, when skilled workers were forming model unions. No other unskilled group was able to organise so early and with such completeness as the miners did. However, where skilled groups built their organisations upon exclusion and the apprenticeship system, coal miners relied on political action to produce solidarity.

The difficulty of building what became successful trade unions in the context of hostile employers should never be underestimated. The approach in Durham was exceptional, and involved processes and activities not normally associated with 'industrial relations'. In arduous and often brutal working and living conditions, the miners combined to form a stable union, supported it with regular subscriptions, and invested in banners which symbolised their involvement. The village as a 'community' became a vital aspect of their identities, but this development was not simply inevitable, and should not be taken for granted: solidarity had to be *built*.

In a world where economic security was transient and death or serious injury were all too common, it would be a brave or foolish person who stood apart from the neighbours; but as Weber noted:

> neighbours do not necessarily maintain 'brotherly' relations. On the contrary: wherever popularly prescribed behaviour is structured by personal enmity and conflicting interests, hostility tends to be extreme and lasting.[1]

In isolated mining villages every aspect of life became public. As in the mine, people were watched and tested by their fellows. In this process 'communities' were created out of *distrust,* and the *solidarity* that was established was often very localised. Barrington Moore has argued that such communities imposed suffocating sanctions against deviance from the established norm: 'There is hardly any refuge from the disapproving eye of the upholders of tradition'.[2] To survive while challenging tradition required membership of a sect capable of making a stand before the community. This is the context within which trade unionism was established in the nineteenth century in Durham.

Any detailed account of mining villages in the nineteenth and early twentieth centuries reveals lines of potential conflict: between different occupational groups employed in the mine; between men and women; between people of different ethical and political persuasion. In the 1850s and 1860s Primitive Methodists committed to trade unionism were often mocked and ostracised by villagers who were antithetical to the idea of a union of coal miners across the county. On one occasion in the 1860s, John Wilson visited a village called Hagglescote in the west of Durham:

> I was passing up the street when a band of women, who had been informed of my coming, made an attack upon me, and threw various kinds of missiles at me.

They missed, but:

> If, however they could not throw a stone accurately, they could say queer things. They were not choice but they were emphatic. The sum of their epithets was that they did not want an agitator there stirring up the minds of their men folk and inducing them to strike.[3]

As late as the time of the First World War, Moore has recounted how the funeral of an ILP miner (a conscientious objector) was stoned by fellow villagers.[4] Such conflicts were not unusual, nor are they surprising. They remind us that social solidarity and community feeling did not flow easily from the establishment of coal mining. Calhoun has raised critical questions about the relationship between economic interests and social identity, and thereby the structural features of life which help produce feelings of solidarity. He raises a variety of issues, but concludes that 'organisation is the crucial factor which may make a community...out of a mere aggregation of people'.[5]

This process of 'organisation making communities' was not a simple one. The early activists operated as a religious *cadre*, established the trade union, and developed it through drawing upon community solidarity. Once organised, they *extended* the nature of this solidarity. Under the umbrella of trade unionism, life in the mine and the village took on a different form. The chapel not only provided the basis for early trade-union organisation and activism, but gave it a particular moral code which endured much later in the north than elsewhere. Primitive Methodism was the context in which men like Wilson, Lawson and Lee became redeemed sinners, changing from itinerant drunkards to sober, respectable, and highly accomplished trade-union officials and political representatives.

Through trade unionism, the Methodist preachers established themselves in positions of authority in the village and the county, exerting a new kind of discipline upon the men in the coal mine. It also affected the seasonal pattern of village life—most especially with the annual Gala in July. But this cultural change can be exaggerated. Thompson, discussing the cultural dynamics of the organised introduction of Methodist sects into the social order of a village, points to an initial 'sharp confrontation' between the old culture and the new, followed by the selective adaptation of both. While chapels became acceptable as a part of village life, Methodism did not *envelop* the community. 'The old and the new culture, dramatised in "the pub" and "the chapel" continued to coexist and to compete'.[6] In Durham, Methodist trade unionism provided a framework within which aspects of the old culture (cavilling in the mine; drinking clubs etc) could expand and develop. Equally, the Gala always had its 'disreputable' side. Against the county leadership's wishes, radical and revolutionary speakers addressed the crowds on the race course.

Nevertheless, the changes were real enough, and can be seen in the position of women in the villages. The rise of the trade union, and its dominance over chapel, club and store, limited the roles available to women in an increasingly complex institutional structure. Aspects of the 'old culture' continued through neighbourliness and social solidarity in times of distress, and this was reinforced powerfully in times of strike and industrial unrest. In the end, the cultural dynamics associated with the *formation* of communities at the end of the nineteenth century saw a reform of the position of women in village life. The chapels—through their development of Victorian ideals of respectability—played a strong role in this. This pattern was repeated, with the shift from Liberalism to Labourist and socialist politics on the coalfield.

At first, women had only a limited recognised public role in political change. Their sphere was the private one—the family. The *miner* had proved his worth, and won recognition through his trade union; but in this context the question of the recognition of women did not arise. The symbolism of the system emphasised the importance of mining labour. Women's *labour* did not constitute *work*. The working man's club, the most popular institution of the society, did not extend membership rights to them. Under Labourism the enforced segregation of the sexes and the rigid control of sexuality was to continue. Mothers continued to raise and send sons to the pit, sons for their part continued to assert their masculinity by resisting the claims of women. In this way the two worlds were kept separate; and as the father had played little role in the home, so too did the son when in turn he married. This syndrome has often been commented upon in the case of male dominant societies. Elshtain notes that in societies and social groups where fathers are regularly absent from family life 'the more severe are the conflicts about masculinity and the fear of women'.[7] On the Durham coalfield the need to 'be a man' became one of the strongest sources of labour discipline in the mine. Equally, the most powerful jibe made against blacklegs related to their status as men. Ironically, these jibes were most often made by the women; but though they fought for their men, they were left largely on their own when they campaigned for their own political voice. On 'women's issues', especially in relation to family planning and birth control, the northern representatives of Labour were deeply conservative.

This account has stressed the idea of the formation and reformation of coal mining communities, and the ways in which various kinds of organisation reinforced the development of community attachment and feeling. The chapels, together with the clubs and co-operative stores, were the most significant of these, and were involved in the creation of communities. They also produced a stratum of officials and committee men within the villages. These were the people who organised the trade union and the political party; the political process on the coalfield most often involved competition and struggle within this group of officials.

The early Methodist leadership, through organising themselves as a *cadre*, exerted a deep and lasting impact upon the organisation of the union (its rules, its election procedures, etc.). In important ways, *their* leadership closed off leadership opportunities to others. Crawford—the architect of the union—laid down the structure and organisation for the county. Under his leadership Durham was effectively unionised, and after his death no significant groups of workers in the mining industry needed to be brought into trade unionism: the union and the community was 'sealed'. So too were all questions of succession. Crawford was duly replaced by Patterson, and he in turn by Wilson. From then onwards, internal struggles were fought out under rules established in the 1870s. For this reason each of the subsequent *cadres* became involved in a struggle to change these rules and in this process the union was slowly reformed. Nevertheless important aspects of the original edifice remained, and the county-wide union (established early in Durham) adapted to dramatic increases in coal production without radical reform. This stability was reinforced by the procedure whereby the miners' agents, once elected, progressed through an unchallenged sequence of offices until they became General Secretary or President. In other coalfields these offices were directly elected, and therefore more responsive to changing political and economic circumstances. Seniority ruled in Durham—both in the pit and in the chapel—and the union was, in effect, always run by an earlier generation. This helps explain the extended period of Methodist control, and its ending with a change of rule and the coincidental death of the General Secretary and President.

After this petrification, the 'rebirth' of the union in the 1920s and 1930s was a dramatic one. Yet the 'same' union continued. Many of the procedures and practices remained unchanged, and within the rooms of Redhills Villa—that most remarkable of Miners' Halls—meetings, communications and forms of address retained a deep familiarity. The new men were still union men, with a strong commitment and emotional attachment to the DMA; and in spite of important differences in political persuasion and personal sensibilities, these men shared similar experiences and outlooks. As leaders of the miners, they arrived from 'outside' society, something which was made very clear in their new home—the Cathedral City of Durham. Each group of leaders (Crawford, Wilson, House, Cann, Lee, Lawther, Watson) fought a broad defence of miners, of mining culture and of the political organisation of labour. They fought their campaign in the local press, in seminars and speeches, at University debates and meetings in Cathedrals. Initially, they were socially isolated in Durham, though surrounded by 'communities'. As time passed, however, they became involved in the practices of the city—most notably with the Cathedral and the University. Wilson became a guest at the dinner tables of the Bishop of Durham and the Professors at the University. In later life he was rewarded with an Honorary Doctorate of Civil Laws (a title which was later to be given to Watson). Commenting upon the social position of trade-union leaders in this period, Bauman has observed their concern to 'occupy a legally sanctioned place in capitalist society—a place of honour'. This concern was not simply self-seeking, it reflected a deeper wish for capitalist society to 'recognise their stratum as an integral component of that society'. This concern with *social* recognition had its roots deep in the 'Durham

System', and the spatial and political arrangements which had kept coal miners (an essential economic group) separated from the rest of society.

The miners in their villages developed a deep sense of occupational and community identity, and this often separated them from other workers. They offer the clearest example of Anderson's critique of British working-class politics which through:

> the very intensity of its corporate class consciousness, realised in and through a distinct hermetic culture, has blocked the emergence of a universal ideology in the English working class. It has not been the lack of class consciousness but, in one sense, an excess of it which has been the obstacle to the commitment of the working class to socialism.[8]

This view appears to have strong support from the evidence. Coal miners have all the makings of a separate corporate group within the working class; but there are problems (or dilemmas) in this analysis.

To begin with (and again paradoxically) we have seen how the *universal* ideologies of religion and socialism were necessary to the building of the union, and to subsequent change. Anderson underestimates this, and indeed the enormity of the struggle involved in establishing trade unionism and the deep structural and political constraints placed on the 'first' working class. In examining the 'corporate' practices of the coal miners it is easy to lose sight of this fact. Equally, too much emphasis upon community (and, by extension, the idea of the miners as a separate and powerful corporate group) can mislead commentators into neglect of politics and political action. A central feature of mine workers' organisation in Britain has been a concern with political action, and by extension, with the state; yet this is rarely commented on.

As an occupational group based upon communities of solidarity, the miners had the power to appeal to the state for regulation of their own industry; but their power and solidarity were often also seen as a threat to society. The great functionalist sociologist Talcott Parsons has observed how in advanced industrial societies:

> too close ties of community solidarity, which are inevitably diffuse rather than specific, can be a serious threat to the main system.[9]

He was not, of course, the first to point this out; but coming from a man most concerned with the maintenance of social equilibrium, it serves to emphasise how the separate culture of the mining villages made them an object of indifference and also of fear. For the authorities, the thought of a miners' strike was a source of concern and worry. Ironically these misgivings were often shared by the miners' leaders; they feared the disruption associated with the use of the union's economic power. To preserve order, they sought to regulate the economic and social position of coal miners through the state. From its beginnings, the DMA petitioned parliament for changes in legislation relating to mining, and elected its own MPs. This concern with parliament and with legal enactments flowed directly from the nature of the industry.

The miners formed an easily recognisable political group in society. The Liberal Party had recognised this, and in the last quarter of the century attached the union to their party by promising and carrying through reforms directly aimed to serve its interests. In this respect the 'constitutionalism' of the miners was successful. The first miners' agents became Liberal MPs, and the different miners' unions were to remain loyal to the Liberals until 1908. What attracted the Liberals was the very size of the miners' electoral bloc; the alliance made the miners at one and the same time the most legally regulated and the most politically powerful group in the working class.

But it was an alliance of convenience rather than political conviction. The overlap of the collieries with industrial communities and electoral districts operated to produce electoral representation virtually monopolised by the miners; and it remained so irrespective of the party which mobilised their support. In the years following their affiliation to the Labour Party, the introduction of county councils and parish and district councils extended their dominance even further. From the beginning, and equally after party labels had been switched, it was the trade union which achieved and guaranteed political control. The miners represented a new kind of power in British society, not simply the market-regulated scarcity exploited by the old craft unions. After they switched their support to the Labour Party, this power and its associated traditions of fraternity, community, banners and galas came to be symbolic of the labour movement as a whole, and were assumed to be at its heart. Yet these elements were brought to the Party not produced by *it*. Miners' entry into the Labour Party secured the party's survival; at the same time, it sealed its fate as a *trade-union* party. The mining trade unions were the leading *political* unions. This flowed in part from the tripartite arrangements that the state established in relation to the coal industry and from the way the miners established their political strength *within* the state. It is ironic, but certainly not coincidental, that the miners' union went on to produce a militant brand of anti-state, syndicalist politics under the leadership of A.J. Cook. In 1926, the union's industrial muscle was flexed in an all-out conflict with the state. It left the miners defeated, and once again divided. This opened the way for a return to the reformist path, to a redevelopment of the union relationship with the Labour Party and to a reaffirmation of the value of nationalisation, the logical end of state intervention.

The demand for nationalisation can also be seen as a logical conclusion to the attempt to form a national union, capable of regulating all the different coalfields in the country, and so create unity among the miners. The mass strikes of the nineteenth and twentieth centuries revealed the awesome power of the miners to disrupt society, but also revealed the frailty of national solidarity. For these reasons, nationalisation had been the solution adopted by the early reformist leadership, and it was the policy which fused the union with the Labour Party.

The fusion was an uneven one, however. In Durham, where the links with the Liberals lasted longest, the remnants of Liberal ideology survived within the union as well as amongst the coal miners and their families; yet it was here that the most powerful support for the Labour Party was established both locally and in parliamentary elections. Durham became a haven of 'safe seats' for Labour which (excepting the severe hiccup of 1931) extended through the 1920s and 1930s. Here the tradition of the miners was expressed in a language in which 'communities' and 'class' were interchangeable as ideas of solidarity. It is this which found expression in 'Labourism' and municipal socialism, and in an emphasis upon community development, and the moral superiority of the lives of the labourers. These ideas and traditions owed more to Wesley than they did to Marx and they provided the cultural cement which linked the Party's programme to daily life. They were to exert their influence most strongly in the years that followed the Second World War.

Appendix

Presidents and General Secretaries of the Durham Miners' Association 1872-1939

General Secretaries

1872-1890	William Crawford
1890-1896	W.J. Patterson
1896-1915	John Wilson
1915-1924	Thomas Cann
1924-1930	W.P. Richardson
1930-1935	Peter Lee
1935-	John Swan

Presidents

1872-1900	John Foreman
1900-1917	William House
1917-1934	James Robson
1935-	James Gilliland

Notes and References

Prologue

1. Sir John Colville, *Those Lambtons: A Most Unusual Family*, Hodder and Stoughton, London, 1988, p.27.
2. T.J. Nossiter, *Influence, Opinion and Political Idioms in Reformed England: Case Studies from the North East, 1832–74*, Harvester, Brighton, 1975.
3. I. Leister, *The Sea Coal Mine and the Durham Miner*, University of Durham Occasional Publication, No.5, Durham, 1975.

Introduction

1. E.P. Thompson, 'The Peculiarities of the English', in Ralph Miliband and John Saville (eds), *The Socialist Register*, 1965, Merlin, London, 1965. p.345
2. Michael Burawoy, *The Politics of Production*, Verso, London, 1985, p.8.
3. See, e.g. R. Page Arnot, *The Miners: A History of the Miners' Federation of Great Britain, 1889–1910*, Allen and Unwin, London, 1949; *The Miners: Years of Struggle: A History of the Miners' Federation of Great Britain from 1910 Onwards*, Allen and Unwin, London, 1953; *The Miners: Crisis and War*, Allen and Unwin, London, 1961; *The Miners: One Union, One Industry*, Allen and Unwin, London, 1979.
4. Richard Fynes, *The Miners of Northumberland and Durham: A History of their Social and Political Progress*, Blyth, 1873, republished Thos. Summerbell, Sunderland, 1923; John Wilson, *A History of the Durham Miners' Association: 1870–1904*, J.H. Veitch & Sons, Durham, 1907; John Wilson, *Memories of a Labour Leader*, J.H. Veitch & Sons, Durham, 1910, reprinted, Caliban Books, London, 1980; Sidney Webb, *The Story of the Durham Miners (1662–1921)*, Fabian Society, London, 1921; W.S. Hall, *A Historical Survey of the Durham Colliery Mechanics' Association 1879–1929*, J.H. Veitch & Sons, Durham, 1929; E. Welbourne, *The Miners' Unions of Northumberland and Durham*, Cambridge University Press, Cambridge, 1923.
5. W.R. Garside, *The Durham Miners 1919–1960*, Allen and Unwin, London, 1971.
6. P. Abrams, *Historical Sociology*, Open Books, Shepton Mallet, 1982, pp.X, 16–17.
7. The Easington Past and Present collection is an archive of interviews with men and women of the mining district born around 1900. It is housed in the offices of the Easington District Council. It originated within Peterlee new town where an attempt was made to link the past with the present via the Peterlee Artists Project. In Durham, the County Council sponsored its own interviewing programme. Transcripts of these topics are held in the Durham County Record Office and at the Beamish Industrial Museum. Where we have used these transcripts, we have indicated with footnotes. Otherwise, the interviews are our own. In operating this way we were influenced by the South Wales Miners' History Project and the publication by Hywel Francis and Dai Smith, *The Fed*, Lawrence and Wishart, London, 1981. While we felt that this book paid too little attention to the process of work, and the position of women and the

Labour Party in mining villages in South Wales (see H. Beynon, 'Props of the pit', *New Society*, 14 June 1980) it nevertheless contained many similarities with our researches in Durham, and important points of potential comparison between the two coalfields.

8. Strong Words was a publishing group set up in 1978 with the aim of documenting working-class lives and experience directly through the words of the people themselves. The group produced a number of exhibitions of photographs and text which were the basis of meetings and discussion in the coalfield. It published a series of books and pamphlets two of which (*Hello Are You Working?* and *But the World Goes on the Same*) contain material which relate directly to the history of the coalfield.

1 The Old Establishment

1. E. Welbourne, *The Miners' Unions of Northumberland and Durham*, Cambridge University Press, Cambridge, 1923, p.18.
2. W. Sombart, *The Quintessence of Capitalism: A study of the history and psychology of the modern businessman*, Howard Fertig, New York, 1967, p.78.
3. K. Marx, *Capital*, vol.1, Penguin, Harmondsworth, 1976, p.626.
4. W. Sombart, *The Quintessence of Capitalism*, op.cit., p.81.
5. E. Welbourne, *The Miners' Unions of Northumberland and Durham*, op.cit., p.18.
6. Thompson uses this phrase in 'The Peculiarities of the English' in R. Miliband and J. Saville (eds) *The Socialist Register*, Merlin, London, 1965. It is taken up by P. Corrigan and D. Sayer, *The Great Arch*, Blackwell, Oxford, 1985. Interestingly, in his criticism of Thompson, Perry Anderson has pointed to the fact that in *The Making of the English Working Class*, no detailed attention is paid to the workers of the coal and iron industries—see *Arguments Within English Marxism*, Verso, London, 1984, pp.34-5.
7. Quoted in W. Fordyce, *The History and Antiquities of the County Palatine of Durham*, vol.1, A. Fullerton and Co., Newcastle, 1857, p.292.
8. Quoted in G. Purdon, *The Sacriston Mine Disaster*, private publication 1979, pp.2-4.
9. Sir T. Eden, *Durham*, vol.2, Robert Hale Ltd., London, 1952, p.395.
10. Ibid., p.599.
11. E. Welbourne, *The Miners' Unions of Northumberland and Durham*, op.cit., p.19.
12. Sir T. Eden, *Durham*, op.cit., p.397.
13. Ibid., p.537.
14. See for example H.R. Trevor-Roper, 'The Bishopric of Durham and the Capitalist Reformation', *Durham University Journal*, Vol.VIII, No.2, 1945.
15. See W. Fordyce, *The History and Antiquities of Durham*, op.cit., p.292.
16. Sir T. Eden, *Durham*, op.cit., p.553.
17. Ibid., p.319.
18. Ibid., pp.619-20.
19. T.J. Nossiter, *Influence, Opinion and Political Idioms in Reformed England: Case Studies from the North East, 1832-1874*, Harvester Press, Brighton, 1975, p.51.
20. Quoted in D. Spring 'The Earls of Durham and the Great Northern Coalfield 1830-1880', *Canadian Historical Review*, vol.XXXIII, No.3, 1952, p.239.
21. Quoted in H. Montgomery Hyde, *The Londonderrys*, Hamish Hamilton, London, 1979.
22. D. Spring, 'The English Landed Estate in the Age of Coal and Iron 1830-1880', *Journal of Economic History*, vol.XI, No.1, 1951, p.6.
23. Such a list would take the following form. *Church*: Bishop, Dean and Chapter, Ecclesiastical Commissioners; *Dukes*: Northumberland, Portland, Hastings, Ravensworth, Windsor, Handen, Carlisle, Grey, Durham, Londonderry, Eldon, Dunsany, Waterford, Boyne; *Baronets*: Hazelrigg, Blake, Ridley, Musgrave, Clavering, Eden, Millbanke; *Squires*: Towneleys, Claytons of Chesters, Ellisons of Hebburn, Bowes of Streatham, Blacketts of Wylam, Edens of Beamish Park, Shaftos of Whitworths, Salvins of Burn Hall, Surtees of Redworth, Riddels of Felton Park and Swinburne Castle, Wilkinsons of Hulam.
24. J.T. Ward 'Landowners and Mining' in J.T. Ward and R.T. Wilson (eds), *Land and*

Industry: The Landed Estate and the Industrial Revolution, David and Charles, Newton Abbot, 1971.
25. The irrationality of this form from the standpoint of *capitalist* production was clearly argued in the report of the 1925 *Royal Commission Into the Coal Industry.* It put it like this: 'the error was made in times past, in allowing the ownership of coal to fall into private hands and should be retrieved. The mineral should be acquired by the state'. The 'error' spanned 400 years as the judgement of 1568 was overturned with the nationalisation of the Coal Royalties 1938.
26. *Commissioners Report of Mining Districts,* 1850, p.45.
27. R.W. Sturgess, 'Factors affecting the expansion of coalmining, 1700–1914', in R.W. Sturgess (ed.), *The Great Age of Industry in the North East,* Durham County Local History Society, 1981, pp.16–17.
28. Ibid., p.13.
29. Letter from Humble Lamb to John Buddle, Buddle Collection, Durham County Record Office, DRO/NCB1/JB/838.
30. Ibid., DRO/NCB1/JB/852.
31. J.T. Ward, 'Landowners and Mining', op.cit., p.67.
32. J.W. House, *North Eastern England: Population Movements and the Landscape Since the Early Nineteenth Century,* University of Durham, Kings College, Department of Geography research series 1, 1954, p.29.
33. Mr Hewitt, quoted in T.H. Hair, *Views of the Collieries of Northumberland and Durham,* J. Madden & Co., 1844 (reprinted Frank Atkinson, 1969).
34. Quoted in D. Spring 'The Earls of Durham and the Great Northern Coalfield', op.cit., p.239.
35. In J. Ginwick (ed.) *Labour and the Poor in England and Wales, Vol.2, Northumberland and Durham, Staffordshire and the Midlands,* Frank Cass, London, 1983, p.17.
36. 1851 Census, Enumerators Returns for Kibblesworth. For a detailed discussion see R. Dixon, E. McMillan and L. Turnbull, *Changing Kibblesworth: The Study of a Mining Community,* Gateshead Metropolitan Borough Council, Local Studies Series, n.d.
37. Quoted in K. Wilson, *Political Radicalism in the North East of England 1830–1860: Issues in Historical Sociology,* PhD Thesis, University of Durham, 1988, p.172.
38. Lucinda Fowler, 'Marriage, Mining and Community: Four Durham Parishes', MA Thesis, University of Durham, 1984, pp.37–8.
39. Ibid.
40. G. Ginswick (ed.), *Labour and the Poor in England and Wales,* op.cit., pp.36–7.
41. T.J. Nossiter, *Influence, Opinion and Political Idioms in Reformed England,* op.cit., p.82.
42. *Durham Chronicle,* 1 January 1859.
43. R. Moore, *Pitmen, Preachers and Politics,* Cambridge University Press, Cambridge, 1974, p.84.
44. Ibid., pp.84–5.
45. D. Roberts, *Paternalism in Early Victorian England,* Croom Helm, London, 1979, p.8.
46. A.J. Heesom, 'Entrepreneurial Paternalism. The Third Lord Londonderry (1778–1854) and the Coal Trade', *Durham University Journal,* 1974, New Series, Vol.LXVI, no.3, p.252.
47. Quoted in R. Colls, 'Oh Happy English Children: Coal, Class and Education in the North East', *Past and Present,* No.73, 1976, p.97.
48. Quoted in A.J. Heesom 'Entrepreneurial Patriotism', op.cit., p.249.
49. Ibid.
50. Quoted in R. Moore, *Pitmen, Preachers and Politics,* op.cit., p.84.
51. *Durham Chronicle,* 24 November 1871. Quoted in ibid., p.79.
52. *Poor Law Commissioners' Report 1834,* quoted in A. Redford, *Labour Migration in England 1800–1850,* Manchester University Press, Manchester, 1964, p.57.
53. Buddle Collection, Durham County Record Office, DRO/NCB1/JB/852.
54. Ibid.
55. Letter from Buddle to Londonderry, 16 May 1842, Londonderry Collection, DRO.D/LO/C/42.
56. W.P. Bourne to A. Saltmarch, 24 September 1859. Cited in R.S. Storbin, *Industrial Slavery in the Old South,* Oxford University Press, New York, 1970, p.74.
57. Ibid.

2 Bonded Labour and Independent Miners

1. H. Scott, *The Miners' Bond in Northumberland and Durham,* MA Thesis, University of Newcastle, 1947, Newcastle Central Library, p.23. Marx was aware of this practice and referred to 'a boorish clumsy form of bondage in the County of Durham'. In considering the position of the northern aristocratic capitalist he notes a Public Health Report to the effect that 'the very dung of the kine and bondsmen is the perquisite of the calculating lord...and the lord will allow no privy but his own to exist in the neighbourhood and will rather give a bit of manure here and there for a garden than bate any part of his seigneurial fight', K. Marx, *Capital,* Vol.1, Penguin Books, Harmondsworth, 1976, pp.723–4 fn.
2. Ibid., p.23.
3. J.U. Nef, *The Rise of the British Coal Industry,* Vol.II, George Routledge and Sons, London, 1932, p.158.
4. J.L. and B. Hammond, *The Skilled Labourer,* Longman, Harlow, 1979, p.10.
5. S. Webb, *The Story of the Durham Miners, 1622-1921,* Fabian Society, London, 1921. These certificates were introduced into the South Wales coalfield fifty years later in 1841. See J.H. Morris and L.J. Williams, 'The Discharge Note in the South Wales Coal Industry, 1841–1889', *Economic History Review,* 1957, 2nd Series, Vol.X, No.2.
6. Quoted in S. Webb, *The Story of the Durham Miners,* op.cit., p.6.
7. Quoted in W. Bainbridge, *A Practical Treatise on the Law of Mines and Minerals,* 2nd edition, Butterworths, London, 1856.
8. T.J. Nossiter, *Influence, Opinion and Political Idioms in Reformed England: Case Studies from the North East 1832-1874,* Harvester Press, Brighton, 1975, p.127.
9. *Colliery Guardian,* 5 October 1867.
10. *Reynolds' Political Register,* 1850.
11. P.E. Hair, 'The Binding of the Pitmen in the North East, 1800-1809, *Durham University Journal,* 1965-1966, New Series, Vol.XXVII.
12. Durham County Record Office, DRO.D/X.36.2. For a full discussion of the significance of the bond and binding ceremonies see Robert Colls, *The Pitmen of the Northern Coalfield, Work Culture and Protest, 1790-1850,* Manchester University Press, Manchester, 1987.
13. Ibid.
14. Letter from George Hill to John Buddle, Durham County Record Office, DCRO/NCB/JB/695.
15. T.J. Nossiter, *Influence, Opinion and Political Idioms,* op.cit., p.12.
16. Londonderry papers, Durham County Record Office, DRO/LO/B. For an account of this dispute see R. Fynes, *The Miners of Northumberland and Durham: A history of their social and political progress,* Thos. Summerbell, Sunderland, 1923, pp.19–23.
17. Quoted in R. Challinor and B. Ripley, *The Miners' Association, A Trade Union in the Age of the Chartists,* Lawrence and Wishart, London, 1968, pp.133–4. This account is an extremely helpful one in relating the politics of Chartism to mining unionism, and the continuity which extended into the 1850s and 1860s. The 1844 strike was of critical importance in Durham, and nationally. Locally, the bond—described in a miners' pamphlet as 'the most disgraceful documentary engagement that any class of working men are subject to'—was a major source of grievance amongst the miners.
18. Quoted in K. Wilson, *Political Radicalism in the North East of England 1830-1860: Issues in Historical Sociology,* Durham University PhD Thesis, 1988, p.132.
19. E.J. Hobsbawm, 'Methodism and the Threat of Revolution in Britain', *History Today,* February 1957, p.118.
20. *Report of the Commissioner into the State of the Population in the Mining Districts,* 1846.
21. F. Hearn, *Domination, Legitimation and Resistance: The incorporation of the nineteenth-century English working class,* Greenwood, 1980, p.205.
22. Ibid., p.205.
23. M. Weber, *Economy and Society,* Guenther Ross (ed.), Bedminster, Totowa, New Jersey, 1968, p.465.
24. Quoted in K. Wilson, *Political Radicalism in the North East of England,* 1988, op.cit., p.120.

25. W. Mitchell, *The Question Answered: What Do the Pitmen Want?* Bishopwearmouth, 1844, quoted in K. Wilson, ibid., p.147.
26. W. Gammage, *History of the Chartists 1837-1854,* Merlin Books, London, 1969.
27. E.J. Hobsbawm, *Labouring Men: Studies in the History of Labour,* Weidenfeld & Nicolson, London, 1964, p.30.
28. K. Wilson, *Political Radicalism in the North East of England,* op.cit. Wilson provides a list of venues for Chartist meetings on the coalfield and this includes Cockfield, Ferryhill, Merrington, Evenwood, Toft Hill, Hetton, South Hetton, Easington Lane, Thornley, Moorsley, Broomside, Haswell, Middle, East and West Rainton, Collier Row, Lumley, Shiney Row, Quarrington Hill, Pittington, Barnard Castle, West and Bishop Auckland, Shildon, Seaham, Hartlepool, Aycliffe, Hatfield and Coxhoe. He notes that West Auckland was described as 'the stronghold of Chartism in South Durham...the colliers keep their lamp so well trimmed that aristocratic choke damp is almost powerless.' See also Dorothy Thompson, *The Chartists,* Temple Smith, London, 1984, where she points out that the miners were 'the largest occupational group amongst those transported for their part in the 1842 disturbances', p.271.
29. F. Hearn, *Domination, Legitimisation and Resistance,* 1980, op.cit., p.206.
30. R.P. Hastings, 'Chartism in South Durham and the North Riding of Yorkshire, 1838-9', *Durham County Local History Society Bulletin,* No.22, p.12.
31. Quoted in K. Wilson, *Political Radicalisation in the North East of England,* op.cit., p.156.
32. M. Weber, *Economy and Society,* op.cit., p.466.
33. Quoted in R. Page Arnot, *The Miners: A History of the Miners' Federation of Great Britain 1889-1910,* Allen and Unwin, London, 1949, pp.44-5.
34. R. Page Arnot, *The Miners,* op.cit., p.46.
35. G. H. Metcalfe, *A History of the Durham Miners' Association 1869-1915,* Durham Miners, 1947, p.13.
36. E.A. Rymer, 'The Martyrdom of the Mine or A Sixty Year Struggle for Life', 1898 facsimile reprint, *History Workshop Journal,* No.1, 1976, p.220.
37. Quoted in R. Page Arnot, *The Miners 1889-1910,* op.cit. p.42fn.
38. John Wilson, *Memories of a Labour Leader,* Caliban Books, London, 1980, p.224.
39. Ibid.
40. *Northern Star,* 27 September 1842, quoted in K. Wilson, *Political Radicalism in the North East of England,* op.cit., p.150.
41. G. Parkinson, *True Stories of Durham Pit Life,* C.H. Kelly, Third Edition, 1912, pp.13-14.
42. The parallels between this and the account offered of politics and religion in the slave south by Genovese, are interesting. See E. Genovese, *Roll Jordan Roll: the World the Slaves Made,* Vintage Books, 1972. For a criticism of this, as a piece of 'culturalist' analysis similar to E.P. Thompson's English account see Richard Johnson, 'Edward Thompson, Eugene Genovese and socialist-humanist history', *History Workshop Journal,* No.6, 1978, pp.79-100. Our interpretation differs from Genovese in a number of respects. Initially, we have no doubts that the northern Paternalists were capitalist and that the Durham Coalfield (in spite of the bond) was part of a capitalist mode of production. We accept the power of Genovese's account of a hegemonic class in the slave south. In the north of England (and perhaps too in the antebellum south) we would argue that the political culture of the labourers established an important area of antagonism in the villages. Most significant perhaps is the political freedom of the northern miners, and the ways in which this freedom was articulated through political movements in the nineteenth century. For the south of the USA and the north of England however, a similar important question remains: what kinds of political organisations did the labourers create through their activism and struggle?
43. John Wilson, *A History of the Durham Miners, 1870-1904,* J.H. Veitch and Sons, Durham 1907, p.4.
44. Ibid., p.5. For a full appreciation of Roberts see R. Challinor, *A Radical Lawyer in Victorian England,* I.B. Tauris, London, 1990.
45. For an appreciation of Cowey see, R. Page Arnot, *The Miners: 1889-1910,* op.cit., p.322 and J. Saville, *Dictionary of Labour Biography,* vol.1, Macmillan, Basingstoke, 1972.
46. G. Simmel, *The Philosophy of Money,* Routledge & Kegan Paul, London, 1987, p.300.
47. E. Rymer, 'The Martyrdom of the Mine', op.cit., p.221.

48. For a discussion of this issue see E.P. Thompson, 'On History, Sociology and Historical Relevance', *British Journal of Sociology*, vol.xxvii, no.3, 1976, and also the detailed researches of Robert Colls, especially *The Pitmen of the Northern Coalfield: Work, Culture and Protest, 1790–1850*, Manchester University Press, Manchester, 1987, ch.9.

3 A County Association

1. Table derived from data in W.A. Moyes, *The Banner Book: A Study of the Banners of the Lodges of Durham Miners' Association*, Frank Graham, Newcastle-upon-Tyne, 1974.
2. E. Allen, *The Durham Miners' Association: A Commemoration*, NUM, Durham, 1969, p.74.
3. John Wilson, *A History of the Durham Miners' Association, 1870–1904*, J.H. Veitch & Sons, Durham, 1947, p.16.
4. 'A Message Addressed to the Miners of County Durham' *DMA Circular*, February 1871.
5. John Wilson, *A History of the Durham Miners' Association*, op.cit., p.16.
6. Ibid., p.27.
7. Letter to the *Methodist Times*, quoted in K.S. Inglis, *Churches and the Working Classes in Victorian England*, Routledge & Kegan Paul, London, 1963, p.329.
8. G.H. Metcalfe, *A History of the Durham Miners' Association: 1869–1915*, Mimeo, Durham Miners' Association, 1947, p.477.
9. R. Page Arnot, *The Miners: A History of the Miners' Federation of Great Britain, 1889–1910*, Allen and Unwin, London, 1949, p.53.
10. John Wilson, *A History of the Durham Miners' Association*, op.cit., pp.37–8.
11. G.H. Metcalfe, *A History of the Durham Miners' Association*, op.cit., p.507.
12. John Wilson, *A History of the Durham Miners' Association*, op.cit., p.24.
13. Ibid., p.46.
14. Ibid., pp.83–4.
15. Ibid., p.54.
16. Ibid., p.56.
17. Ibid., pp.56–7.
18. Ibid., p.33.
19. G.H. Metcalfe, *A History of the Durham Miners' Association*, op.cit., p.70.
20. Quoted in John Wilson, *A History of the Durham Miners' Association*, op.cit., p.102.
21. Ibid., p.145.
22. Ibid.
23. Ibid., p.151.
24. Ibid.
25. Ibid., p.150.
26. Ibid., p.146.
27. Ibid., p.162.
28. Ibid., p.169.
29. Ibid., p.165.
30. R. Page Arnot, *The Miners 1889–1910*, op.cit., pp.148–9.
31. Ibid., p.85.
32. John Wilson, *A History of the Durham Miners' Association*, op.cit., p.160.
33. W.E. Patterson, *Durham Miners' Association Joint Committee: Decisions, Agreements, Practices, Rules, etc., 1875–92*, Durham, 1893.
34. Jack Lawson, *A Man's Life*, Hodder and Stoughton, London, 1932, pp.40–1.
35. Quoted in R. Page Arnot, *The Miners 1889–1910*, op.cit., p.228.
36. Ibid., p.255.
37. Ibid., p.298.
38. Ibid., p.189.
39. J. Berwick Harrod, 'Paul Knox: Pitman' *Cassell's Family Magazine*, 1877, p.20.
40. Ibid., p.11.
41. Ibid.
42. John Wilson, *A History of the Durham Miners' Association*, op.cit., pp.241–2.
43. John Wilson, *Memories of a Labour Leader*, Caliban Books, London, 1980, pp.305–6.

44. Ibid., p.309.
45. John Wilson, *A History of the Durham Miners' Association*, op.cit., p.88.
46. Ibid., p.257.
47. Ibid., p.194.
48. John Wilson, *Memories*, op.cit., pp.200–1. Chapter XXV is devoted entirely to 'conversion' and the impact of Primitive Methodism upon his life.
49. Quoted in D. Howell, *British Workers and the Independent Labour Party 1888–1906*, Manchester University Press, Manchester, 1983, pp.44–5.
50. *Sunderland Daily Echo*, 7 November 1912. Quoted in Geoff Walker, 'George Harvey: The Conflict between the Ideology of Industrial Unionism and the Practice of its Principles in the Durham Coalfield Prior to the First World War', Ruskin College, Oxford, Diploma Dissertation, 1982.
51. *Durham Chronicle*, 30 July 1909.

4 A *Labour* Aristocracy?

1. E.J. Hobsbawm, 'Lenin and the Aristocracy of Labour', *Monthly Review*, April 1970, p.47.
2. F. Engels, *The Condition of the Working Class in England*; Preface to the 1882 Edition, Oxford, 1958, p.368.
3. For a discussion of this variation and its importance see Royden Harrison (ed.), *The Independent Collier: The Coal Miner as Archetypical Proletarian Reconsidered*, Harvester, Brighton, 1978.
4. John Wilson, *Memories of a Labour Leader*, Unwin, London, 1910, p.96. These views of miners being permanently resident underground extended well into the twentieth century. See Huw Beynon, 'The end of the industrial worker?' in N. Abercrombie and A. Warde, *Social Change in Contemporary Britain*, Polity, Cambridge, 1992, pp.167–83.
5. G.D.H. Cole, *Labour in the Coal Mining Industry*, Clarendon Press, Oxford, 1923, p.1.
6. H. Clegg, *A History of British Trade Unions Since 1889, Vol.11, 1911–33*, Clarendon Press, Oxford, 1985, p.2.
7. G. Sorel, *Reflections on Violence*, Free Press, New York, 1961, p.123.
8. F. Engels, *The Condition of the Working Class in England*, op.cit., p.367.
9. S. and B. Webb, *Industrial Democracy* (Second Edition), Longmans, London, 1898, p.38.
10. Ibid.
11. Ibid., p.251.
12. B.L. Hutchins and A. Harrison, *A History of Factory Legislation*, Third Edition, reprinted Cass, London, 1966, p.81.
13. Ibid., p.82.
14. R. Page Arnot, *The Miners: Years of Struggle*, Allen and Unwin, London, 1953, p.40.
15. Ibid., p.42.
16. Ibid., p.44.
17. John Wilson, *A History of the Durham Miners' Association 1870–1904*, J.H. Veitch & Sons, Durham, 1907, p.339.
18. K. Burgess, *The Origin of British Industrial Relations, The Nineteenth Century Experience*, Croom Helm, London, 1975.
19. R.F. MacSvinney, *The Laws of Mines, Quarries and Minerals*, Third Edition, Sweet and Maxwell, London, 1907, p.668.
20. A.S.L. Carr and W. Fordham, *Recent Mining Legislation, Including the Coal Mines Act 1930*, Butterworths, London, 1931, p.62.
21. A.M. Carr-Saunders and P.A. Wilson, *The Professions*, Clarendon Press, Oxford, 1933, p.151.
22. Ibid., p.153.
23. E. Halevy, *History of the English People: Epilogue Vol.II*, Ernest Benn Ltd, London, 1934, p.438.
24. Quoted in ibid., p.440.
25. *See R. Gregory, The Miners and British Politics 1906–1914*, Oxford University Press, Oxford, 1968.

26. R. Page Arnot, *The Miners: Years of Struggle*, op.cit., p.356.
27. Ibid., p.354.
28. Ibid., p.301.
29. A.P. Orage, *National Guilds: An Inquiry into the Wage System and the Way Out*, Ernest Benn, London, 1914, p.58.
30. W. Jevons, *The Coal Question: An Inquiry Concerning the Progress of the Nation and the Probable Exhaustion of our Coal Mines*, Macmillan, London, 1865, p.38. His terminology is of interest here, it could perhaps be rephrased as 'a community apart from the rest of the class'.
31. For an account of the miners' conversion to the Labour Party see F. Bealey and H. Pelling, *Labour and Politics 1900–1906, A History of the Labour Representation Committee*, Macmillan, London, 1958, especially chapter 9, 'The Politics of Coal'.
32. R. Gregory, *The Miners and British Politics*, op.cit., p.73.
33. Ibid., p.79.
34. Jack Lawson, *A Man's Life*, Hodder and Stoughton, London, 1932, p.93.
35. R. Moore, *Pitmen, Preachers and Politics*, Cambridge University Press, Cambridge, 1974, p.186.
36. Ibid., p.177.
37. For an account of the economics of the coal industry, its industrial expansion and decline see R. Church, *The History of the British Coal Industry, volume 3, 1830–1913: Victorian Preeminence*, Oxford, Clarendon Press, 1986; B. Supple, *The History of the British Coal Industry, volume 4, 1913–1946: The Political Economy of Decline*, Oxford, Clarendon Press, 1986; Ben Fine, *The Coal Question: Political Economy and Industrial Change from the Nineteenth Century to the Present Day*, Oxford, Clarendon Press, 1990.

5 Durham Mining Villages

1. John Wilson, *Memories of a Labour Leader*, Caliban Books, London, 1980, p.84.
2. Both these songs were written by pitmen, Joe Wilson and Tommy Armstrong. For an account of popular mining songs in the north, see R. Colls, *The Collier's Rant*, Croom Helm, London, 1977 and H. Beynon, Introduction to R. Forbes (ed.), *Polisses and Candymen: The Complete Works of Tommy Armstrong*, Tommy Armstrong Trust, Durham, 1987, see also M. Vicinus, *The Industrial Muse: A Study of Nineteenth-Century British Working Class Literature*, Croom Helm, London, 1974.
3. Quoted in R. Moore, *Pitmen Preachers and Politics*, Cambridge University Press, Cambridge, 1976.
4. Ted Farbridge, 'Recollections of Stanley', Mimeo, pp.1–2.
5. Jack Lawson, *A Man's Life*, Hodder and Stoughton, London, 1938, p.28.
6. Hilda Ashby, 'Wait 'til the Banner Comes Home', in K. Armstrong and H. Beynon (eds), *Hello Are You Working? Memories of the Thirties in the North East of England*, Strong Words, Newcastle upon Tyne, 1979, p.41.
7. George Alsop, 'A Kind of Socialism', in T. Austrin, et al. (eds), *But the World Goes on the Same: Changing Times in Durham Pit Villages*, Strong Words, Newcastle upon Tyne, 1979, pp.19–20.
8. D. Beavis, *What Price Happiness? My Life from Coal Hewer to Shop Steward*, Strong Words, Newcastle upon Tyne, 1980, p.10.
9. R. Dixon, et al., *Changing Kibblesworth: A Study of a Mining Community*, Gateshead, Department of Education, n.d.
10. See G. Calhoun, 'Community: toward a variable conceptualisation for comparative research', in R.S. Neale (ed.), *History and Class*, Blackwell, Oxford, 1983, p.92; A. Cohen, 'Belonging: the experience of culture', in A. Cohen (ed.), *Belonging: Identity and Social Organisation in British Rural Cultures*, Manchester University Press, Manchester, 1982.
11. R. Holt, *Sport and the British*, The Clarendon Press, Oxford, 1989, p.63.
12. Ibid., p.186–7.
13. John Wilson, *Memories of a Labour Leader*, op.cit., pp.279–80.

14. A. Metcalfe, 'Organised Sport in the Mining Communities of South Northumberland, 1800-1889', *Victorian Studies*, 25, 4, Summer 1982, p.474.
15. Ibid, p.480.
16. D. Beavis, *What Price Happiness?*, op.cit., p.40.
17. Durham County Record Office, *Shotton Papers*, D/Sho 113.

6 Rough Cavils

1. Sir Timothy Eden, *Durham*, Vol.2., Robert Hale Ltd, 1952, pp.584-6.
2. Mark Benney, *Charity Main*, Allen and Unwin, London, 1946, E.P. Publishing edition, Wakefield, 1978, pp.39-4.
3. Ellen Wilkinson, *The Town that was Murdered*, Gollancz, London, 1939, p.18.
4. Ross Forbes (ed.) *Polisses and Candymen: The Complete Works of Tommy Armstrong*, Tommy Armstrong Trust, Durham, 1987, pp.20-1.
5. E.A. Rymer, 'The Martyrdom of the Mine, Or a 60-year Struggle for Life', facsimile edition, p.10, *History Workshop Journal*, No.1, 1976, p.10. For a radical discussion of the earlier arguments over ventilation see D. Ashbury and J. Schwartz, *Partial Progress: The Politics of Science and Technology*, Pluto Press, London, 1982, pp.10-24. For another view see: M. Flinn, *The History of the British Coal Industry, volume 2, 1700-1830: The Industrial Revolution*, Clarendon Press, Oxford, 1984.
6. *Durham Chronicle*, 19 February 1909. For a discussion of this disaster and the role of John Wilson and the trade union in the inquiry that followed see D. Little, 'Let Sleeping Dogs Lie', Northern College, Diploma Dissertation, 1984.
7. An horrific accident took place at the Elemore Colliery on 5 August 1857. At that time, men entered the mine by placing their feet in loops at the end of the haulage chain, two miners, Henry Hunter and George Lishman, having finished their shift, placed their feet in the loop of the chain, then grasped the chain with their hands. After being drawn halfway up the shaft, a loop in the descending chain somehow got itself over the head of Hunter, whose head was torn completely from his body before he could give any signal. The headless body arrived at the surface, the feet still in the loop and the hands still grasping the chain.
8. Frank Hodges, *Nationalisation of the Mines*, London, 1920, p.48.
9. The names of these people are remembered and recorded. In Murton and other lodges they were reprinted in booklets produced by the trade unions. See Murton Mining Federation Board, *Murton Pit and People, 1838-1984*, Murton, 1984.
10. Ned Cohen, *Of Mining Life and Its Ways*, Durham Miners Association, n.d., pp.26-7.
11. Dave Larimer, Easington Past and Present Archive.
12. Fenwick Whitfield, 'And of Course I've Got Some Dust', in K. Armstrong and H. Beynon (eds), *Hello Are You Working? Memories of the Thirties in the North East of England*, Strong Words, Newcastle upon Tyne, 1977, pp.60-1.
13. Dave Larimer, Easington Past and Present Archive, op.cit.
14. Maurice Ridley, 'Making a Contribution' in T. Austrin, et al. (eds), *But The World Goes on the Same: Changing Times in Durham Pit Villages*, Strong Words, Newcastle upon Tyne, 1979, p.62.
15. William Bell, *The Road to Jericho*, Iron Press, 1980, p.40.
16. Ibid., pp.33-43.
17. Dave Ayre, 'Instinctive Socialism' in T. Austrin, et al. (eds), *But the World Goes on the Same*, op.cit., pp.7-8.
18. George Alsop, 'A Kind of Socialism' in ibid., p.24.
19. George Bestford, 'When You're Starving It's Pretty Tough', in K. Armstrong and H. Beynon (eds), *Hello Are You Working?*, op.cit., p.77.
20. Dick Beavis, 'Never Again', in ibid., pp.17-18.
21. Henry Ashby, 'Send Your Sons Into the Mines', in ibid., p.35.
22. George Alsop, 'A Kind of Socialism', op.cit., p.25.
23. George Parkinson, *True Stories of Durham Pit Life*, C.H. Kelly, 3rd Edition, 1912, pp.13-14.
24. E.A. Rymer, 'The Martyrdom of the Mine', op.cit., p.3.
25. William Bell, *The Road to Jericho*, op.cit., p.37.

26. George Parkinson, *True Stories*, op.cit., p.15. See also J.G. Glenwright, *Bright Shines the Morning*, Martini Publications, London, 1949, p.25.
27. George Bestford, 'When You're Starving its Pretty Tough', op.cit., p.80.
28. R. W. Sturgess, *The Great Age of Industry in the North East 1700–1920*, Durham County Local History Society, Durham, n.d., p.24.
29. E.A. Rymer, 'The Martyrdom of the Mine', op.cit., p.5.
30. W. Paynter, *My Generation*, Allen and Unwin, London, 1972, p.21. Paynter makes clear in his account that in South Wales, 'boys went straight to the coal face when they started work in the pits. They worked with colliers and in this way they were themselves trained as colliers'. In South Wales haulage and coal getting were separated as different lines of progression for coal miners. See M. Holbrook-Jones, 'Work Industrialisation and Politics: A Study of the Work Experience of Spinners, Coal miners and Engineering workers, 1850–1914', PhD Thesis, University of Durham, 1979 and M. Daunton, 'Down the Pit: Work in the Great Northern and South Wales Coalfields 1870–1914', *Economic History Review*, 1981.
31. *National Association of Colliery Managers*, Vol.1, 1989, p.225.
32. *The Royal Commission on Accidents in the Mines*, 1881, Cuthbert Berkley Evidence, 22 June 1880.
33. R. Boulton, *Textbook on Coal Mining*, private publication, London, 1907, p.76.
34. For a discussion of these methods of coal mining see R.A.S. Redmayne, *Modern Practice in Mining, Volume 3, Method of Working Coal*, Longmans, London, 1914 and G.L. Kerr, *Practical Coalmining: A Manual for Managers*, Charles Griffin and Co., 1921.
35. Fairbridge Deposit, Durham County Record Office, DR0 D/MR/1,2.
36. Ibid.
37. M. Holbrook-Jones, 'Work, Industrialisation and Politics', op.cit., pp.229.
38. Fairbridge Deposit, Durham County Record Office, DRO D/MR/1,2.
39. Durham Coal Owners Association, *Annual Report*, 1914.
40. David Douglass, *Pit Life in Co. Durham*, Ruskin History Workshop, Pamphlet No.6, 1972, p.10.

7 A Labour of Love

1. G. Parkinson, *True Stories of Durham Pit Life*, C.H. Kelly, Newcastle upon Tyne, 3rd edition, 1912, p.14.
2. J.W. Scott and L.A. Tilley, 'Women's Work and the Family in Nineteenth Century Europe' in A.H. Amsden (ed.), *The Economics of Women and Work*, Penguin, Harmondsworth, 1980, pp.98–9.
3. Mrs Taylor, Easington Past and Present Archive.
4. Hilda Ashby, 'Wait 'til the Banner Comes Home', in K. Armstrong and H. Beynon (eds), *Hello Are You Working? Memoirs of the Thirties in the North East of England*, Strong Words, Newcastle upon Tyne, 1979, pp.42–3.
5. Ibid., p.16. There is some evidence that this process of mutual aid operated in other aspects of life. A number of women have suggested to us that 'these old women were very wise', and that in the case of illegitimate birth, for example, the home of the child (with its maternal or paternal grandparents) was influenced by an assessment of the family's earning power. 'If the father was one of a family of boys say, and the girl had just sisters then the baby would be brought up by the father's mother as hers.' This fits into a society where babies were given away or children taken in, as a consequence of circumstances. For example, in his autobiography, Ned Cohen mentions, almost in passing, that they gave their first child to his mother. N. Cohen, *Mining Life and All its Ways*, Durham City Library, Mimeo.
6. Mrs Stephenson, interview, Easington Past and Present Archive.
7. Mrs Harrison, interview, Easington Past and Present Archive.
8. Hilda Ashby, 'Wait 'til the Banner Comes Home', in K. Armstrong and H. Beynon (eds), *Hello Are You Working?*, op.cit., p.43.
9. Mrs Stephenson, Easington Past and Present Archive.
10. Mrs Harrison, Easington Past and Present Archive.
11. See J.W. Scott and L.A. Tilly, 'Women's Work and the Family in Nineteenth Century

Europe' in Alice H. Amsden, *The Economics of Women and Work*, Penguin Books, Harmondsworth, 1980, pp.91-124.
12. See e.g., L. Davidoff, 'Mastered For Life: Servant and Life in Victorian and Edwardian England', *Journal of Social History*, no.7, 1974, pp.402-28.
13. Dorothy Marshall, *The English Domestic Servant in History*, Historical Association, London, 1949, pp.27-8.
14. Mrs A. Short, Ferryhill, interview with Robin Humphreys.
15. Mrs Nixon, Easington Past and Present Archive.
16. Edie Bestford, 'My Father and Brothers are Miners' in K. Armstrong and H. Beynon (eds), *Hello Are You Working?*, op.cit., p.85.
17. Mrs Harrison, Easington Past and Present Archive.
18. Mrs Nixon, Easington Past and Present Archive.
19. Edie Bestford, 'My Father and Brothers are Miners', op.cit, p.86.
20. Margaret Powell, *Below Stairs*, Peter Davies, London, 1968, p.64.
21. Hilda Ashby, 'Wait 'til the Banner Comes Home', op.cit., p.43.
22. Mrs A. Short, interview with Robin Humphreys.
23. George Hitchin, *Pit Yacker*, Charles Birchall & Sons, London, 1962, pp.20-1.
24. Sidney Webb, *The Story of the Durham Miners 1662-1921*, The Fabian Society, London, 1921, pp.71-2.
25. Mr Porter, Easington Past and Present Archive.
26. Mrs Turner, Easington Past and Present Archive.
27. George Alsop 'A Kind of Socialism', in T. Austrin, et al. (eds), *But The World Goes on the Same: Changing Times in Durham Pit Villages*, Strong Words, Newcastle upon Tyne, 1979, pp.20-1.
28. Ibid.
29. D. Beavis, 'Never Again', in K. Armstrong and H. Beynon (eds), *Hello Are You Working?*, op cit., p.18.
30. W. McCabe, *Occupation and social change in the Durham coal field*, Durham University Certificate in Industrial Relations dissertation, 1982, pp.9-10.
31. Hilda Ashby, 'Wait 'til the Banner Comes Home', op.cit., p.41.
32. Mrs Taylor, Easington Past and Present Archive.
33. Maurice Ridley, 'Making a Contribution', in T. Austrin, et al. (eds), *But the World Goes on the Same*, op.cit., p.61.
34. Mrs Young, Easington Past and Present Archive.
35. Mr Felton, Easington Past and Present Archive.
36. Mrs Cairnes, Easington Past and Present Archive.
37. Mrs Turner, Easington Past and Present Archive.
38. George Hitchen, *Pit Yacker*, op.cit., pp.21-2.
39. D. Beavis, 'Never Again' in K. Armstrong and H. Beynon (eds), *Hello Are You Working?*, op.cit., p.19. In his subsequent autobiography, *What Price Happiness? My Life from Coal Hewer to Shop Steward*, Strong Words, Newcastle upon Tyne, 1980, his opening chapter is entitled, 'Canny Old Soul My Ma' and is devoted to a detailed account of domestic work.
40. William Bell, *The Road to Jericho*, Iron Press, North Shields, Tyne and Wear, 1980, p.17.
41. M.I. Balfour and J.C. Drury, *Motherhood in the Special Areas of Durham and Tyneside*, Council of Action, London, 1935.
42. See Dora Russell, *The Tamarisk Tree*, Elek Books, London, 1975. For a full discussion of the issue of birth control in Durham see Pat McIntyre, *The Response to the 1984-85 Miners' Strike in Durham County: Women, The Labour Party and Community*, PhD Thesis, University of Durham, 1992.
43. J.B. Priestley, *English Journey*, Heineman, London, 1934, p.334.
44. Ibid., p.335.
45. Catherine Cookson, *Our Kate, An Autobiography*, Corgi Books, London, 1974, p.26.
46. Sid Chaplin, 'Durham Mining Villages', University of Durham, Department of Sociology and Social Policy, *Working Paper*, 1, 1975, p.12.
47. Maurice Ridley, 'Making a Contribution', in T. Austrin, et al. (eds) *But the World Goes on the Same*, op.cit., pp.61-2.
48. Vera Alsop, 'The Woman's Part' in ibid., p.71.
49. Mrs Robinson, interview with Robin Humphreys.

50. Fenwick Whitfield, 'And of Course I've Got some Dust', in K. Armstrong and H. Beynon (eds), *Hello Are You Working?*, op.cit., p.57.
51. Mr and Mrs Allen, Easington Past and Present Archive.
52. Vera Alsop, op.cit., p.74.
53. J.G. Glenwright, *Bright Shines the Morning*, Martini Publications, London, 1949, pp.72–4.
54. Mr Felton, Easington Past and Present Archive.
55. George Alsop 'A Kind of Socialism' in T. Austrin, et al. (eds), *But the World Goes on the Same*, op.cit., p.21.
56. Mrs Short, interview with Robin Humphreys.
57. Mrs Turnbull, Easington Past and Present Archive.
58. Catherine Cookson, *Our Kate: An Autobiography*, op.cit., p.17.
59. Mrs Short, op.cit.
60. Vera Alsop, op.cit., p.71.
61. Mrs Nixon, Easington Past and Present Archive.

8 Community and Association

1. R. Dixon et al., *Changing Kibblesworth: The Study of a Mining Community*, Gateshead Department of Education, n.d., p.52.
2. Interview with Robin Humphreys. See also the discussion of privacy in Sid Chaplin, *Durham Mining Villages*, University of Durham, Department of Sociology and Social Policy, Working Paper No.1, 1972.
3. Boldon Lodge DMA, *Minutes*, 10 September 1919.
4. Lord Joicey, quoted in John Oxberry, *The Birth of the Movement: A Tribute to the Memory of Joseph Hopper*, Durham Aged Miner-Workers' Homes, Gateshead, 1924.
5. Durham Aged Miner-Workers' Homes, *Circular*, Shincliffe Colliery, 25 September 1906.
6. R. Dixon, et al., *Changing Kibblesworth*, op.cit., p.17.
7. Ibid., p.52.
8. Beatrice Webb, 'The Relationship between Co-operation and Trade Unionism', in S. and B. Webb, *Problems of Modern Industry*, Longmans, Green and Co., London, 1902, p.192.
9. S. Webb, *History of the Durham Miners*, Labour Publishing Co., 1924, p.24.
10. Jack Lawson, *A Man's Life*, Hodder and Stoughton, London, 1932, p.34.
11. Ibid., p.35.
12. J. Hall, *A History of Craghead*, private publication, Stanley, 1985, p.17.
13. Ibid., p.18.
14. *The History of Crook Co-operative Society*, Pelaw, 1931.
15. J.W. White and R. Simpson, *Co-operation in West Stanley and District 1876–1926*, Pelaw, 1926.
16. Ibid., p.23.
17. Linda McCullogh Thew, *The Pit Village and the Store: The Portrait of Mining Past*, Pluto Press/Co-operative Union, London, 1985, p.81.
18. Ibid., pp.70–1.
19. Ibid.
20. J. W. White and R. Simpson, *Co-operation in West Stanley and District*, op.cit, p.8.
21. Ibid., pp.109–12.
22. Quoted in T. Elkins, *So They Brewed Their Own Beer*, The Northern Clubs' Federation Brewery Limited, Newcastle upon Tyne, 1970, p.9.
23. Ibid., p.2.
24. Ibid., p.6.
25. Quoted in W. Williamson, *Class, Culture and Community: A Biographical Study of Social Change in Mining*, Routledge & Kegan Paul, London, 1982, p.109.
26. Maurice Ridley, 'Making a Contribution' in T. Austrin, et al. (eds), *But the World Goes on the Same: Changing Times in Durham Pit Villages*, Strong Words, Newcastle upon Tyne, 1979, p.61.
27. T. Elkins, *So They Brewed Their Own Beer*, op.cit., p.50.
28. *The Durham County Advertiser*, 15 May 1923.

29. Ibid.
30. Ibid., 12 June 1923.
31. Hilda Ashby, 'Wait 'til the Banner Comes Home' in K. Armstrong and H. Beynon (eds), *Hello Are You Working? Memories of the Thirties in the North East of England*, Strong Words, Newcastle upon Tyne, 1979, p.44.
32. For a discussion of the political ideology of the Club Movement see R.N. Price, 'The Working Men's Club Movement and Victorian Social Reform Ideology', in *Victorian Studies*, December 1971, pp.117–47.
33. For a discussion of this, produced with the approval of the coal owners, see P. Gee, *The Other Side of the Miner's Life: A Sketch of Welfare Work in the Mining Industry*, New Court, Lincoln's Inn, 1936.
34. Durham County Record Office, *Londonderry Papers*.
35. Ibid.

9 Ceremony and Society: The Gala

1. John Wilson, *A History of the Durham Miners' Association*, 1870–1904, J.H. Veitch & Sons, Durham, 1907, p.31.
2. *Sunderland Times*, 20 July 1871.
3. *Durham Chronicle*, 18 July 1872.
4. *Durham County Advertiser*, 20 July 1873.
5. Hilda Ashby 'Wait 'til the Banner Comes Home' in K. Armstrong and H. Beynon (eds), *Hello Are You Working? Memories of the Thirties in the North East of England*, Strong Words, Newcastle upon Tyne, 1979, p.43.
6. Jack Lawson, *A Man's Life*, Hodder and Stoughton, London, 1932.
7. Jack Lawson, *Peter Lee*, Hodder and Stoughton, London, 1936, p.239.
8. G.H. Metcalfe, *A History of the Durham Miners' Association 1869–1915*, Mimeo, Durham Miners Association, 1947, p.478.
9. Edie Bestford 'My Father and Brothers are Miners', in K. Armstrong and H. Beynon (eds), *Hello Are You Working?*, op.cit., p.87.
10. Jack Lawson, *A Man's Life*, op.cit., p.107.
11. H. Ashby, 'Wait 'til the Banner Comes Home', op.cit., pp.43–4.
12. K. Tenfelde 'Mining festivals in the nineteenth century', *Journal of Contemporary History*, vol.13, 1977, p.382.
13. Ibid.
14. R. Fynes, *History of Northumberland and Durham Miners*, reprinted 1923, Thos. Summerbell, Sunderland, p.56.
15. Ibid., p.56.
16. W.A. Moyes, *The Banner Book: A Study of the Banners and Lodges of the Durham Miners' Association*, Frank Graham, Newcastle-upon-Tyne, 1974, p.26.
17. M. Ostrogorski, *Democracy and the Organisation of Political Parties*, vol.1, Macmillan, London, 1902, p.375.
18. Ibid., p.397.
19. John Wilson, Durham Miners' *Monthly Circular*, No.199, July 1912.
20. E. Allen, *The Durham Miners' Association: A Commemoration*, DMA, 1969.
21. DMA Circular, June 1897.
22. DMA General Secretary's *Annual Report*, Durham, 1952.
23. Ibid., 1953.
24. T. Farbridge, *Recollections of Stanley*, Stanley, Mimeo, n.d.
25. Ibid.
26. M. Ridley, 'Making a contribution', in T. Austrin, et al. (eds), *But the World Goes on the Same: Changing Times in Durham Pit Villages*, Strong Words, Newcastle upon Tyne, 1979.
27. For a discussion see W.A. Moyes, *The Banner Book*, op.cit., and D. Douglass, *Pit Life in Co. Durham*, Ruskin History Workshop Pamphlet, 5, 1972.
28. *Durham Chronicle*, 26 July 1924.
29. *Durham County Advertiser*, 25 July 1924.

10 Riot, Rebellion and Strike

1. *Sunderland Times*, 4 June 1872.
2. Ibid., 22 June 1872.
3. Ibid., 25 June 1872.
4. Ibid.
5. John Wilson, *Memories of a Labour Leader*, Caliban Books, London, 1980, p.233.
6. Ibid., p.237.
7. *Northern Daily Mail*, 27 January 1910.
8. Ibid., 31 January 1910.
9. Ibid.
10. Mrs Turnbull, Easington Past and Present Archive.
11. *Northern Daily Mail*, 28 January 1910.
12. Ibid.
13. D. Smith, 'Tonypandy 1910: Definitions of Community', *Past and Present*, 87 (1980), p.162.
14. R. Page Arnot, *The Miners: Years of Struggle A History of the Miners' Federation of Great Britain from 1910 Onwards*, Lawrence and Wishart, London, 1953, p.108.
15. See, for example, F.D. Longe, 'The Coal Strike and the Minimum Wage', *Economic Journal*, Vol.IV, 1894, p.27.
16. R. Page Arnot, *The Miners: Years of Struggle*, op.cit., p.101–8.
17. See, for example, S. Olivier, 'The Miners' Battle and After', *Contemporary Review*, 64, p.754.
18. D.H. Robertson, 'A Narrative of the Coal Strike', *Economic Journal*, Vol.XXII, 1912, p.376.
19. A.E. Suffern, *Conciliation and Arbitration in the Coal Industry of America*, Houghton Mifflin Co., New York, 1915.
20. G. Askwith, *Industrial Problems and Disputes*, John Murray, London, 1920, p.209.
21. D. Sells, *The British Wage Boards: A Study in Industrial Democracy*, Institute of Economics, Washington, DC, 1939, p.22.
22. Jack Lawson, *Peter Lee*, Hodder and Stoughton, London, 1936, pp.232–3.
23. Ibid.
24. Ibid., pp.234–5.
25. G. Askwith, *Industrial Problems and Disputes*, op.cit., p.210.
26. W. Brace, 'The Mining Industry of Great Britain', *Contemporary Review*, 101, 1912, p.463.
27. Ibid.
28. Ibid., p.464.
29. Ibid.
30. Ibid.
31. Quoted in Paul Davies, 'The Making of A.J. Cook', *Llafur*, vol.2, no.3, 1978, pp.43–63.
32. Ibid.
33. Quoted in W.R. Garside, *The Durham Miners, 1919–1960*, Allen and Unwin, London, 1971, p.213.
34. County Ministry of Health Report, July 1926, DRO, p.121, quoted in P. McIntyre, 'The Influence of the Miners' Struggle on Local Politics: Durham 1924–27', Mimeo, January 1983.
35. Quoted in Les Turnbull, *Chopwell's Story*, Gateshead Library, n.d.
36. George Alsop, 'A Kind of Socialism', in T. Austrin et al. (eds), *But The World Goes on the Same: Changing Times in Durham Pit Villages*, op.cit., p.22.
37. Ibid., p.22.
38. Quoted in Les Turnbull, *Chopwell's Story*, Gateshead Library, n.d.
39. George Alsop, 'A Kind of Socialism' in T. Austrin et al. (eds), *But the World Goes on the Same*, op.cit., p.23.
40. Hilda Ashby 'Wait 'til the Banner Comes Home' in K. Armstrong and H. Beynon (eds), *Hello Are you Working? Memories of the Thirties in the North East of England*, Strong Words, Newcastle upon Tyne, 1979.
41. Interview with Connie Pickard.

11 The Checkweighmen's Party

1. Jack Lawson, *A Man's Life*, Hodder and Stoughton, London, 1932, p.119.
2. Ibid., p.137.
3. R. Miliband, *Parliamentary Socialism: A Study of the Politics of Labour*, George Allen and Unwin, London, 1962, p.29.
4. R. McKibbin, *The Evolution of the Labour Party 1910–1924*, Oxford University Press, Oxford, 1974, p.224.
5. R. MacKenzie, *British Political Parties* (2nd edition), Heinemann, London, 1963, p.476.
6. Ibid., p.476.
7. Source, R. Gregory, *The Miners and British Politics 1906–1914*, Oxford University Press, Oxford, 1968.
8. R. MacKenzie, *British Political Parties*, p.481.
9. G.D.H. Cole, *A History of the Labour Party from 1914*, Routledge and Kegan Paul, London, 1948, p.85.
10. For details of these elections see the comprehensive account by W.R. Garside, *The Durham Miners 1919–1960*, Allen and Unwin, London, 1971, pp.319–33.
11. DMA Circular, DRO/D/SHO/129.
12. S. Aster, *Anthony Eden*, Weidenfeld & Nicolson, London, 1976, p.10.
13. W.R. Garside, *The Durham Miners 1919–1960*, op.cit., p.336.
14. DMA Circular, 22 March 1922, DRO/D/SHO/129.
15. Durham County Federation of Labour Parties, *Circular No. 19*, 1925, DRO/D/SHO/129.
16. Jack Lawson, *A Man's Life*, op.cit., p.112.
17. Ibid., p.114.
18. See W.R. Garside, *The Durham Miners*, op.cit., p.343.
19. See Maureen Calcott, 'Labour Women in the North East of England', in *Bulletin of the North East Group for the Study of Labour History*, No.17.
20. Letter from Mrs Simm to Mrs Middleton, 6 June 1908, quoted in Pat McIntyre *The Response to the 1984–85 Miners' Strike in Durham County: Women, the Labour Party and Community*, PhD Thesis, University of Durham, 1992, p.72.
21. See Margaret Gibb, 'The Labour Party in the North East Between the Wars', in *Bulletin of the N.E. Group for the Study of Labour History*, no.18.
22. In Pat McIntyre's view it was clear that 'Durham women had [not] achieved equality with men in the Labour Party in terms of political representation at local authority level. And certainly no working class woman was ever encouraged by DWAC to seek election to Parliament', *The Response to the 1984–85 Miners' Strike*, op.cit., p.75.
23. Details from *Durham County Advertiser*, 14 March 1919, *Evening Chronicle*, 7 March 1919, *Sunderland Daily Echo*, 9 April 1919.
24. Details from *Durham Chronicle*, 7 April 1922, *Northern Echo*, 4 April 1922, *Durham County Advertiser*, 3 March 1922.
25. *Durham County Advertiser*, 14 March 1919.
26. Ibid., 11 April 1919.
27. R.F. Wearmouth, *The Social and Political Influences of Methodism in the Twentieth Century*, Epworth Press, London, 1957, pp.226–9.
28. Durham County Record Office, DRO/D/SHO/129.
29. Ibid.
30. John Wilson, *Memoirs of a Labour Leader*, Caliban Books, London, 1988, p.21.

12 Local Leaders

1. See R. Gregory, *The Miners and British Politics 1906–1914*, Oxford University Press, Oxford, 1968 and W.R. Garside, *The Durham Miners 1919–1960*, Allen and Unwin, London, 1971.
2. Jack Lawson, *A Man's Life*, Hodder and Stoughton, London, 1932, p.117.
3. Ibid., p.20.
4. Ibid., p.65.

5. Ibid., p.66.
6. Ibid., pp.67–8.
7. Ibid., p.67.
8. Ibid., p.71.
9. Ibid., p.106.
10. Ibid., p.78.
11. Ibid., p.76.
12. Ibid., p.65.
13. Ibid., pp.67–8.
14. Ibid., p.67.
15. Ibid., p.78.
16. Ibid., p.81.
17. Ibid., p.85.
18. Interview with Sir William Lawther, 20 September 1970, Northumberland County Record Office, NRO T/bii.
19. Jack Lawson, *Peter Lee*, Hodder & Stoughton, London, 1936, p.42.
20. Ibid., p.40.
21. Ibid., p.43.
22. Ibid., p.67.
23. Ibid., p.62.
24. Ibid., p.106.
25. Ibid., p.124.
26. Ibid., p.122.
27. Ibid., p.126.
28. 'The Golden Reign of Peter Lee', *Sunderland Echo*, 21 May 1968.
29. Ibid.
30. Ibid. Initially Lee had difficulties in accepting the post because of the financial losses it might create. The Wheatley Hill Lodge pushed him to accept and guaranteed his financial support in the short term. In the meantime a motion was passed for a sum to be provided to cover the expenses and loss of income incurred by the Chairman. It was passed without any vote against by the opposition.
31. Peter Lee, 'Labour Ideals', Durham County Record Office, *Shotton Collection.*
32. Peter Lee, 'Who Are Our Friends? Reasons Why All Workers Should Vote Labour', Durham County Record Office, *Shotton Collection.*
33. *Durham Chronicle*, 5 January 1923.
34. Ibid., 21 September 1920.
35. Ibid., 17 February 1921.
36. *Peter Lee, 'Open Letter'*, Durham County Record Office, Shotton Collection.
37. *Sunderland Daily Echo*, 14 May 1925
38. Jack Lawson, *A Man's Life*, op.cit., p.130.
39. Jack Lawson, *Peter Lee*, op.cit., p.195.
40. *Durham County Advertiser*, 20 January 1922.
41. Jack Lawson, *Peter Lee*, op.cit., p.197.
42. R. Currie, *Methodism Divided: A Study in the Sociology of Ecumenicalism*, Faber and Faber, London, 1968, p.31.
43. Jack Lawson, *Peter Lee*, op.cit., pp.312–3.
44. John Wilson, *A History of the Durham Miners' Association 1870–1904*, J.H. Veitch & Sons, Durham, 1907, p.348.
45. Ibid., p.354.
46. Ibid., p.344.
47. Jack Lawson, *Peter Lee*, op.cit., p.295.
48. *Durham Chronicle*, 6 January 1923.
49. *Evening Chronicle*, 1 April 1925.
50. Ned Cohen, *Mining Life and All its Ways*, Durham, Mimeo, p.29.
51. See e.g. E. P. Thompson, 'Time, Work—Discipline and Industrial Capitalism', *Past and Present*, 38, 1967, pp.56–97.
52. R. Robertson, 'The Salvation Army: The Persistence of Sectarianism', in B. Wilson, *Patterns of Sectarianism*, London, 1967, pp.93–4.
53. E.J. Hobsbawm, *Primitive Rebels: Studies in Archaic Forms of Social Movement in the*

Nineteenth and Twentieth Centuries, Manchester University Press, 1959, Chapter 8, 'The Labour Sects'.
54. W. Stark, *The Sociology of Religion: A Study of Christendom*, Vol.2, Routledge and Kegan Paul, London, 1967, p.57.
55. Ibid., p.137.
56. *Durham Chronicle*, 3 April 1920.
57. Ibid.
58. Jack Lawson, *Peter Lee*, op.cit., p.41.

13 Seats Safe for Fabians

1. Beatrice Webb, *Our Partnership*, Longmans, London, 1948, p.145.
2. Quoted in H. Pelling (ed.), *The Challenge of Socialism*, Macmillan, London, 1969, p.132.
3. E. Halevy, *History of the English People*, Epilogue, Vol.2, Ernest Benn Ltd., London, 1934, p.262.
4. H. Trace, *The Book of the Labour Party*, Vol.3, Labour Party, London, n.d., p.151.
5. M. Cole, *Makers of the Labour Movement*, Longmans, Green and Co., London, 1948, p.266.
6. B. Webb, *Diaries 1924–1932*, M. Cole (ed.), Longmans, Green and Co., London 1956, p.191.
7. Quoted in H. Dalton, *Call Back Yesterday: Memoirs 1887–1931*, F. Meuller, London, 1953, p.189.
8. For a detailed assessment of Henderson see R. McKibbin, 'Why is there no Marxism in Great Britain', *English Historical Review*, Vol.199, No.391, 1984; R. McKibbin, 'Arthur Henderson as Labour Leader', *International Review of Social History*, Col.23, 1978, pp.79–101; F.M. Leventhal, *Arthur Henderson*, Manchester University Press, 1989.
9. Emanuel Shinwell, *The Labour Story*, Macdonald, London, 1963, p.78.
10. Quoted in R. McKibbin, 'Arthur Henderson as Labour Leader', op.cit., p.91.
11. Beatrice Webb, *Our Partnership*, op.cit., p.4.
12. B.L. Blakely, *The Colonial Office*, University of North Carolina Press, Chapel Hill, 1972, p.203.
13. E. Halevy, *History of the English People*, op.cit., p.261.
14. Quoted in N. and J. MacKenzie, *The Fabians*, Weidenfeld & Nicolson, London, 1977, p.290.
15. B. Russell, *Portraits from Memory*, Allen and Unwin, London, 1956, p.82.
16. J. Lawson, 'The Discovery of Sidney Webb', in M. Cole (ed.), *The Webbs and Their Work*, Harvester, Brighton, 1974, p.197.
17. Ibid., p.198.
18. See Sidney and Beatrice Webb, *The History of Trade Unionism*, Longman, London, 1894; also Sidney and Beatrice Webb, *Industrial Democracy*, Longman, London 1898.
19. G.D.H. Cole, *Labour in the Coal Mining Industry*, Oxford University Press, London, 1923, p.77.
20. J. Lawson, 'The Discovery of Sidney Webb', op.cit., p.190.
21. E. Shinwell, *The Labour Story*, op.cit., p.107.
22. S. Webb (ed.), *How to Pay for the War: Being Ideas Offered to the Chancellor of the Exchequer by the Fabian Research Department*, Fabian Society, London, 1916, p.vii.
23. Ibid., p.117.
24. Ibid.
25. Ibid., p.137.
26. Ibid., p.144.
27. Ibid., p.145.
28. *Sunderland Daily Echo*, 30 October 1919.
29. *Sunderland Daily Echo*, 5 January 1920.
30. *Sunderland Daily Echo*, 5 March 1920.
31. *Sunderland Daily Echo*, 21 September 1919. The case of Webb is one of the rare occasions when an individual with support from local lodges ousted the candidate preferred by the County Association. The possibility of this being repeated was closed in

1937 through a change in the rules . . . Under a new rule, lodges would be called upon only to ratify a list of candidates agreed by the DMA. Garside, the official historian of the DMA notes:

> Lodges were allocated votes according to the number of their members paying into the local political fund and were entitled to select a candidate for their division from the Official Association's list.

Once this process was complete, the lodges were obliged to accept the result (even if their candidate lost) and 'honour bound to support the nominee at the Divisional Labour Party selection conference'. Furthermore, to incorporate the divisional parties firmly into the structure, the DMA guaranteed to 'offer the selected candidates all necessary financial and moral support'. It was an offer that could hardly have been refused. This rule revision made complete the control by the union machine over the formal political apparatus. See W.R. Garside, *The Durham Miners, 1919–1960*, Allen and Unwin, 1971, p.348.

32. *Northern Daily Mail*, 18 June 1920.
33. Sidney Webb, *The Story of the Durham Miners 1662–1921*, The Fabian Society, London, 1921.
34. *Northern Daily Mail*, 18 June 1920.
35. *Newcastle Daily Journal*, 6 November 1922.
36. *Sunderland Daily Echo*, 15 November 1922.
37. Ibid., 7 November 1922.
38. Quoted in N. MacKenzie (ed.), *The Letters of Sidney and Beatrice Webb*, Vol.3, Cambridge University Press, Cambridge, 1978, p.137.
39. Quoted in R. MacKenzie, *British Political Parties*, (2nd Edition), Heinemann, London, 1964, p.253.
40. R. Miliband, *Parliamentary Socialism: A Study of the Politics of Labour*, Allen and Unwin, London, 1961, p.1.
41. S. and B. Webb, *A Constitution for the Socialist Commonwealth of Great Britain*, Longmans, London, 1920, p.86.
42. B. Webb, in N. and J. MacKenzie (eds), *The Diaries of Beatrice Webb, Vol.3, 1905–1924: The Power to Alter Things*, Virago, London, p.385.
43. Ibid., p.386.
44. Quoted in I. Britain, *Fabianism and Culture: A Study in British Socialism and the Arts, c.1884–1918*, Cambridge University Press, Cambridge, 1982, p.242.
45. S. and B. Webb, *The Decay of Capitalist Civilisation*, Longmans, London, 1923, p.37.
46. In N. and J. MacKenzie (eds), *The Diaries of Beatrice Webb, vol.3*, op.cit., p.408.
47. Ibid., p.412.
48. N. MacKenzie (ed.), *The Letters of Sidney and Beatrice Webb*, op.cit., p.159.
49. Ibid., p.263.
50. B. Webb, *Diaries 1924–1932*, M. Cole (ed.), London, 1956, p.125.
51. Quoted in P. Clarke, *Liberals and Social Democrats*, Cambridge University Press, Cambridge, 1978, p.237.
52. See S. Webb, 'What Happened in 1931. A Record', *Political Quarterly*, vol.III, January 1932. In this account Webb provides his own personal reading of the experience of what he termed the 'Mediocrities' of the first two Labour Governments.
53. See L. MacNeil-Weir, *The Tragedy of Ramsay MacDonald*, Secker and Warburg, London, 1938, p.519.
54. N. MacKenzie (ed.), *The Letters of Sidney and Beatrice Webb*, op.cit., p.304.
55. Ibid.
56. L. MacNeil-Weir, *The Tragedy of Ramsay MacDonald*, op.cit., p.521.
57. Quoted in D. Marquand, *Ramsay MacDonald*, Jonathan Cape, London, 1977.
58. L. MacNeil-Weir, *The Tragedy of Ramsay MacDonald*, op.cit., p.521.
59. B. Webb, *Diaries, 1924–1932*, op.cit., pp.210, 269, 292.
60. H. Trace, *The Book of the Labour Party*, vol.3, The Labour Party, London, p.269.
61. J.C.C. Davidson, *Memoirs of a Conservative, 1910–1937*, Weidenfeld & Nicolson, London, 1969, p.8.
62. Quoted in B. Pimlott, *Hugh Dalton*, Jonathan Cape, London, 1985, p.112.
63. Ibid., p.134.

64. For a detailed account of the Peckham events see B. Pimlott, *Hugh Dalton,* op.cit.
65. Ibid.
66. Ibid., p.173.
67. H. Dalton, *Call Back Yesterday,* op.cit., p.206.
68. Ibid., p.211.
69. H. Dalton, Foreword to M. Cole, *Makers of the Labour Movement,* London, 1948.
70. B. Pimlott, *Hugh Dalton,* op.cit., p.176.
71. Ibid., p.176.
72. Ibid., p.177.
73. Ibid., p.181.
74. Ibid., p.176.
75. 'The Aims of the Constituency Labour Parties Movement: A Statement by the National Committee of Constituency Labour Parties', n.d., probably 1937, in Shotton Collection, Durham County Record Office, DRO/D/SHO/120.
76. H. Dalton, *Call Back Yesterday,* op.cit., p.205.

14 A Tory Seat

1. M. Cowling, *Conservative Essays,* Cassell, London, 1978, p.21.
2. Ibid.
3. C. Headlam, *Diaries,* 29 September 1922, Durham County Record Office, DRO/D/HE.15.
4. Ibid., 5 February 1919, DRO/D/HE.15.
5. Ibid., 17 February 1922, DRO/D/HE.18.
6. C. Headlam, *History of The Guards Division in the Great War 1915–1918,* British Army Publications, London, 1924, p.ix.
7. K. Middlemas, *The Pursuit of Pleasure: High Society in the 1900s,* Gordon and Cremonesi, London, 1977, p.2.
8. C. Headlam, *Diaries,* op.cit., 25 September 1919, DCRO/D/HE.15.
9. J. Galsworthy, *To Let,* William Heinemann, 1922, p.121.
10. C. Headlam, *Diaries,* op.cit., 11 August 1919, DCRO/D/HE.15.
11. Ibid., 10 February 1919, DRO/D/HE.15.
12. J. Galsworthy, *To Let,* op.cit., p.182.
13. C. Headlam, *Diaries,* op.cit., 11 December 1923, DRO/D/HE.19.
14. Ibid., 12 November 1922, DRO/D/HE.18.
15. Ibid., 12 February 1924, DRO/D/HE.20.
16. Ibid., 9 January 1924, DRO/D/HE.20.
17. Ibid., 17 January 1924, DRO/D/HE.20.
18. Ibid., 27 September 1919, DRO/D/HE.15.
19. Ibid., 19 February 1919, DRO/D/HE.15.
20. Ibid., 15 July 1919.
21. Ibid., 15 February 1919.
22. Ibid.
23. Ibid., 14 March 1919.
24. Ibid., 11 April 1919.
25. Ibid., 29 September 1919, DRO/D/HE.15.
26. Ibid., 8 June 1924, DRO/D/HE.20.
27. Ibid., 12 August 1924, DRO/D/HE.20
28. Ibid., 3 August 1924, DRO/D/HE.20.
29. Ibid., 24 August 1924, DRO/D/HE.20.
30. Ibid., 16 September 1924, DRO/D/HE.20
31. A further illustration of this sapping of the confidence of the coal owners' role can be seen in the evidence given to the 1919 Royal Commission on the coal industry by the Duke of Northumberland. For example:

    Qu: As a coal owner what service do you perform to the community?
    Ans: As the owner of coal I do not think I perform any service to the community, not as the owner of coal.

32. Ibid., 14 November 1924, DRO/D/HE.20.
33. Ibid., 18 January 1925, DRO/D/HE.21.
34. Ibid., 21 January 1925, DRO/D/HE.21.
35. Ibid., 21 April 1926, DRO/D/HE.21.
36. J.C.C. Davidson, *Memoirs of a Conservative*, Weidenfeld & Nicolson, London, 1969, p.405.
37. For details of the two organisations see *The Durham City Yearbook*, Durham, 1924.
38. Papers of the Durham Municipal and County Federation, Durham County Record Office, DRO/D/MCF.175.
39. Ibid.
40. Ibid.
41. Minutes of the Management Committee Meeting of the Durham Moderate Party, 17 December 1943, Durham County Record Office, DRO/D/MCF.175.
42. Ibid.
43. C. Headlam, *Diaries*, op.cit., 28 July 1925, DRO/D/HE.21.
44. Ibid., 31 July 1925, DRO/D/HE.21.
45. Ibid., 3 August 1925, DRO/D/HE.21.
46. Ibid., 11 July 1925, DRO/D/HE.21.
47. See A. Mason, *The General Strike in the North East*, Hull University Press, Hull, 1970. See also A. Mason, 'The Local Press and the General Strike: An Example from the North East', *Durham University Journal*, June 1969.
48. C. Headlam, *Diaries*, op.cit., 24 May 1926, DRO/D/HE.22.
49. Ibid., 17 July, 1926, DRO/D/HE.22.
50. Ibid., 17 November 1926, DRO/D/HE.22.
51. Ibid., 12 December 1926, DRO/D/HE.22.
52. Ibid., 31 May 1929, DRO/D/HE.25.
53. Letter, Lady Londonderry to J.C.C. Davidson in Davidson, *Memoirs of a Conservative*, op.cit., p.131.
54. C. Headlam, *Diaries*, op.cit., 19 December 1929, DRO/D/HE.25.
55. Ibid., 16 December 1930, DRO/D/HE.26.

15 The Beginning of the End

1. Fenwick Whitfield, 'And of course I've got some dust' in K. Armstrong and H. Beynon (eds), *Hello Are You Working? Memories of the Thirties in the North East of England*, Strong Words, Newcastle upon Tyne, 1977, pp.61–2.
2. *Langley Park Colliery 1875–1975*, Centenary Brochure, Langley Park, 1975.
3. George Bestford in K. Armstrong and H. Beynon (eds), *Hello Are You Working?*, op.cit.
4. Les Turnbull, *Chopwell's Story*, Gateshead Department of Education, Gateshead, n.d.
5. Ibid.
6. Ibid.
7. *Changing Kibblesworth*, Gateshead Department of Education.
8. Hilda Ashby, 'Wait 'til the Banner Comes Home!' in K. Armstrong and H. Beynon (eds), *Hello Are You Working?*, op.cit., p.44.
9. Henry Ashby, 'Send your Sons into the Mines' in ibid., pp.34–5.
10. Dick Beavis, *What Price Happiness? My Life From Coal Hewer to Shop Steward*, Strong Words, Newcastle upon Tyne, 1980, pp.23–4.
11. Quoted in R.J. Waller, *The Dukeries Transformed*, Clarendon Press, Oxford, 1983, pp.106–7.
12. Ibid., p.74.
13. See W.R. Garside, *The Durham Miners 1919–1960*, Allen and Unwin, 1971, pp.232–3 and A.R. Griffin and C.P. Griffin, 'The Non-Political Trade Union Movement' in A. Briggs and J. Saville (eds), *Essays in Labour History*, Croom Helm, London, 1977.
14. C. Headlam, *Diaries*, 27 September 1933, DRO/D/HE.29.
15. Ibid., 6 April 1931, DRO/D/HE.29.
16. Ibid.
17. Jack and Andy Lawther: 'Lessons of the Class Struggle', The Northern Film and Television Archive, Gateshead, n.d.

18. Ben Pimlott (ed.), *The Political Diaries of Hugh Dalton*, Jonathan Cape, London, 1986, p.96.
19. Ibid., p.157.
20. See W.R. Garside, *The Durham Miners 1919–1960*, op.cit., p.341.
21. Ibid., p.342.
22. Margaret Gibb, 'The Labour Party in the North East Between the Wars', in *Bulletin of the N.E. Group for the Study of Labour History*, vol.18, p.12.
23. D. Beavis, *What Price Happiness?*, op.cit., p.41.
24. Margaret Gibb, 'The Labour Party in the North East', op.cit., p.13.
25. Ben Pimlott (ed.), *The Political Diaries of Hugh Dalton*, op.cit., p.150.
26. Edie Bestford, 'My Father and Brothers are Miners' in K. Armstrong and H. Beynon (eds), *Hello Are You Working?*, op.cit., p.87.
27. C. Headlam, Diaries, 26 March 1928, DRO/D/HE.24.
28. Ibid., 15 January 1929, DRO/D/HE.25.
29. Ibid., 6 January 1929, DRO/D/HE.25.
30. Ibid., 28 March 1930, DRO/D/HE.26.
31. Quoted in Gareth Williams 'Compulsory Sterilisation of the Miners', *Llafur*, vol.3, no.3, 1982, pp.67–73.
32. George Bestford, 'When You're Starving It's Pretty Tough' in K. Armstrong and H. Beynon (eds), *Hello Are You Working?*, op.cit., pp.35–6.
33. Henry Ashby, 'Send Your Sons into the Mines' in ibid., pp.78–9.
34. Hilda Ashby. 'Wait 'til the Banner Comes Home' in ibid., pp.42.
35. George Bestford in *Hello Are You Working?*, op.cit., p.81.
36. *Durham County News*, 20 October 1932.
37. The Pilgrim's Trust, *Men Without Work*, Cambridge Unity Press, Cambridge, 1938, p.138.
38. George Hitchin, *Pit Yacker*, Charles Birchall & Sons Ltd., London, 1962, pp.45–6.
39. The Pilgrim's Trust, *Men Without Work*, op.cit., p.74–5.
40. Ibid., p.81.
41. C. Headlam, *Diaries*, 11 October 1932, DRO/D/He.28.
42. Ibid., 12 October 1932, DRO/D/He.28.
43. George Short, 'The General Strike and Class Struggle in the North East, 1925–1928', *Marxism Today*, October 1970, p.308.
44. Jim Ancrum, 'The WIR in the Dawdon Lockout', *Labour Monthly*, vol.11, no.9, September 1929, p.556.
45. *Durham County Advertiser*, 19 August 1921.
46. See David Howell, 'Ramsay MacDonald and the Miners', Mimeo, 1992.
47. *Durham County Advertiser*, 22 July 1921.
48. Speaking at the Annual Dinner of the NE Coast Institution of Secretaries and reported in the *Northern Daily Mail*, 12 February 1910.
49. A. Gramsci, *Selections From the Prison Notebooks*, Lawrence and Wishart, London, 1971, p.24.
50. Dick Beavis, *What Price Happiness?*, op.cit., p.24. In Durham in 1922 11.9% of coal was cut with the help of machines; in 1938 the proportion had risen to 42%. Nationally the rise was from 15.3% to 59.4%. In 1938, coalfields like Fife (89.9%), Lancashire (83.9%), North Staffordshire (92.2%), Northumberland (91.2%), Derbyshire (88%), Nottingham (70.1%) far exceeded Durham in the proportion of mechanised coal cut. See Ben Fine, *The Coal Question*, Routledge, 1992, pp.83–102 and B. Supple *The History of the British Coal Industry Vol 4 1913–1946, The Political Economy of Decline*, Clarendon Press, Oxford, 1987.
51. Dick Beavis, *What Price Happiness?*, op.cit., p.25.
52. Fenwick Whitfield, 'And of Course I've Got Some Dust', in K. Armstrong and H. Beynon (eds), *Hello Are You Working?*, op.cit., p.62.
53. Dick Beavis, *What Price Happiness?*, op.cit., p.26.
54. Fenwick Whitfield, 'And of Course I've Got Some Dust', op.cit., p.62.
55. Dick Beavis, *What Price Happiness?*, op.cit., p.39.
56. Ibid., p.26.
57. George Bestford, 'When You're Starving its Pretty Tough', in K. Armstrong and H. Beynon (eds), *Hello Are You Working?*, op.cit., pp.80–1.
58. See W.R. Garside, *The Durham Miners 1919–1960*, op.cit., for a comprehensive

discussion of this view.
59 Quoted in R. Page Arnot, *The Miners: Crisis and War*, Allen and Unwin, London, 1961, p.125.
60. Quoted in Garside, *The Durham Miners*, op.cit.
61. Ibid., p.252.
62. Ibid., p.279.
63. H. Swaffer, 'G.L. Moved to Tears by Loyalty of 100,000 miners', *Daily Herald*, 29 July 1935.
64. Quoted in the *Daily Herald*, 29 July 1935.
65. Interview with Sir William Lawther, 20 September 1970, Northumberland County Record Office, NCRO T/bii.
66. Ned Cohen, *Mining Life and All its Ways*, Mimeo, Durham, n.d., p.31.
67. Boldon DMA *Lodge Minute Book*, 1932.
68. Interview with Sir William Lawther, 20 September 1970, NCRO T/bii.

Conclusion

1. M. Weber, *Economy and Society*, University of California Press, Berkeley,
2. B. Moore, *Injustice*, Macmillan, Basingstoke, 1978, p.361.
3. J. Wilson, *Memories of a Labour Leader*, Caliban Books, London, 1980, pp.268-9.
4. R. Moore, *Pitmen, Preachers and Politics*, Cambridge University Press, Cambridge, 1974, p.200.
5. C.J. Calhoun, 'Community—Toward a Variable Conceptualisation for Comparative Research', *Social History*, Vol.5, No.1, 1980, p.109. See also his 'Class Place and Industrial Revolution' in N. Thrift and P. Williams (eds), *Class and Space*, Routledge & Kegan Paul, London, 1985.
6. See E.P. Thompson, 'On History, Sociology and Historical Relevance', *British Journal of Sociology*, vol.XXVIII, No.3, 1976, pp.398-9.
7. J.B. Elshtain, *Public Man and Private Woman*, Princeton University Press, Princeton, 1981, p.291.
8. P. Anderson, 'Origins of the Present Crisis', *New Left Review*, No.23, 1964, p.33.
9. T. Parsons, *The Social System*, Free Press, New York, 1951, p.187.

Name Index

Subject Index